Excel® 2007 Charts

John Walkenbach

BICENTENNIAL
1807
WILEY
2007
BICENTENNIAL

Wiley Publishing, Inc.

Excel® 2007 Charts

Published by
Wiley Publishing, Inc.
111 River Street
Hoboken, NJ 07030-5774
www.wiley.com

About the Author

John Walkenbach is a leading authority on spreadsheet software and principal of J-Walk and Associates Inc., a small Tucson-based consulting firm that specializes in spreadsheet application development. John is the author of about 50 spreadsheet books and has written more than 300 articles and reviews for a variety of publications, including *PC World, InfoWorld, PC Magazine, Windows,* and *PC/Computing.* He also maintains a popular Web site (The Spreadsheet Page, www.j-walk.com/ss) and is the developer of the Power Utility Pak, an award-winning add-in for Microsoft Excel. John graduated from the University of Missouri and earned a master's and Ph.D. degree from the University of Montana.

Acknowledgments

I've written many Excel books, but this one was probably the most challenging. I learned quite a bit during this project, and it furthered my belief that Excel is a never-ending source of surprises, even for us old-timers. Excel's charting feature is like an iceberg: There is much more to it than appears on the surface.

Special thanks are due to Jon Peltier, one of the planet's leading Excel chart experts and Microsoft MVP. I was able to convince Jon to be the technical editor for this book, and his contributions are sprinkled liberally throughout the pages. As in the past, it was a pleasure working with Paul Levesque, my project editor. I'm also grateful to Greg Croy, acquisitions editor at Wiley, for giving me the go-ahead to write this book.

The Excel community tends to be very open with its ideas, and this is especially apparent in the area of charting. I owe a special debt to many people who provided the inspiration for several of the examples in this book. Thanks to Stephen Bullen, Debra Dalgleish, Charley Kyd, Tushar Mehta, and Andy Pope, all of whom are Microsoft Excel MVPs and charting pros. I'm also grateful to Debbie Gewand, who amazed me with her Excel clip art. Thanks also to Nick Hodge, an Excel MVP who really likes to see his name in my books.

Many folks throughout the world have sent me charting examples. Although there wasn't room for most of them, many of the general ideas were incorporated into my examples. I send a special thanks to the following: Fernando Cinquegrani, Gilbert Dubourjale (GeeDee), Thierry Fahmy, Serge Garneau, Steve Kearley, Gary Klass, Bill Koran, Linda Mabree, Ken Mahrer, Joan Maslin, Sanjay S. Mundkur, Michael O'Callaghan, and Tony Sleigh.

Finally, I'd like to acknowledge the work of Edward R. Tufte. His books should be required reading for anyone who takes chart-making seriously.

Acquisitions, Editorial, and Media Development

Senior Project Editor: Paul Levesque

Executive Editor: Greg Croy

Copy Editor: John Edwards

Technical Editor: Jon Peltier

Editorial Manager: Leah Cameron

Media Project Supervisor: Laura Moss-Hollister

Media Development Specialist: Angela Denny

Media Development Associate Producer: Richard Graves

Editorial Assistant: Amanda Foxworth

Composition Services

Project Coordinator: Kristie Rees

Layout and Graphics: Stacie Brooks, Joyce Haughey, Jennifer Mayberry, Barbara Moore

Proofreaders: ConText Editorial Services, Inc., David Faust

Indexer: Anne Leach

Publishing and Editorial for Technology Dummies

Richard Swadley, Vice President and Executive Group Publisher

Andy Cummings, Vice President and Publisher

Mary Bednarek, Executive Acquisitions Director

Mary C. Corder, Editorial Director

Publishing for Consumer Dummies

Diane Graves Steele, Vice President and Publisher

Joyce Pepple, Acquisitions Director

Composition Services

Gerry Fahey, Vice President of Production Services

Debbie Stailey, Director of Composition Services

Contents at a Glance

WITHDRAWN

Contents

Part II: Mastering Charts

Introduction

Welcome to *Excel 2007 Charts*. This book is intended for spreadsheet users who want to get the most out of Excel's charting and graphics features. I approached this project with one goal in mind: to write the ultimate Excel charting book that would appeal to users of all levels.

As you probably know, most bookstores offer dozens of Excel books. The vast majority of these books are general-purpose user guides that explain how to use the features available in Excel (often by simply rewording the text in the help files). Most of these books include a chapter or two that cover charts and graphics. None, however, provides the level of detail that you'll find in this book.

I've used Excel for almost 15 years, and I've been creating charts for more than 30 years. Back in the precomputer days, I often spent hours creating a publication-quality chart by hand, using rulers, graph paper, and rub-off lettering. Today, creating such a chart with Excel would require only a few minutes — and would probably look much better.

Many Excel users tend to overlook the powerful charting features available. For many, creating anything but the simplest chart often seems like a daunting task. This book starts with the basics and covers every aspect of charting, including macros. If I've done my job, working through this book will give you some new insights and perhaps a greater appreciation for Excel.

What You Should Know

This is *not* a book for beginning Excel users. If you have absolutely no experience with Excel, this may not be the best book for you. To get the most out of this book, you should have some background using Excel. Specifically, I assume that you know how to:

- Create workbooks, enter data, insert sheets, save files, and perform other basic tasks.

- Navigate through a workbook.

- Use the new Excel 2007 Ribbon interface.

- Work with dialog boxes.

- Create basic formulas.

- Use common Windows features, such as file-management and copy-and-paste techniques.

Later chapters cover VBA programming, and the main focus there is on creating and controlling charts using VBA. These chapters assume a basic knowledge of VBA, and those who have some experience with VBA will benefit most from these programming chapters. They'll be able to customize the examples and make them even more powerful. These chapters may inspire nonprogrammers to spend some time understanding VBA.

NOTE

Most of the material in this book is also relevant to those who need to create charts in Microsoft Word 2007 or Microsoft PowerPoint 2007. Choose Insert ⇨ Chart from the Ribbon, and you'll have yourself the beginnings of a chart. The chart uses dummy data in an Excel workbook that's opened for you automatically. Replace the dummy data with real data, and then format the chart to your liking. The Chart Tools context menu in Word and PowerPoint is identical to the one in Excel.

What You Should Have

To use this book, you need to have a copy of Microsoft Excel 2007 for Windows. No exceptions. Excel 2007 is so different from previous versions that this book doesn't even make an attempt at backward compatibility. If you use a previous version of Excel, locate a copy of the initial edition of this book (*Excel Charts,* published in 2003 by Wiley).

To use the examples on the companion CD-ROM, you'll need a CD-ROM drive. The examples on the CD-ROM are discussed further in Appendix A, "What's on the CD-ROM?"

Hardware requirements? The faster the better. And, of course, the more memory in your system, the happier you'll be. I strongly recommend using a high-resolution video mode: at least 1024 x 768 and preferably higher. When working with charts, it's very convenient to be able to see lots of information without scrolling. My normal setup is a dual-monitor system, with two 1600 x 1200 displays.

Conventions Used in This Book

Take a minute to skim the following sections and discover some of the typographic conventions used throughout this book.

Ribbon Commands

Excel 2007 features a brand new "menuless" user interface. In place of a menu system, Excel uses a context-sensitive Ribbon system. The words along the top (such as Home, Insert, Page Layout, and so on) are known as *tabs*. Click a tab, and the Ribbon displays the commands for the selected tab. Each command has a name that is (usually) displayed next to or below the icon. The commands are arranged in groups, and the group name appears at the bottom of the Ribbon.

The convention I use is to indicate the tab name, followed by the group name, followed by the command name. So, the command used to toggle word wrap within a cell is indicated as follows:

```
Home⇨Alignment⇨Wrap Text
```

When a chart is selected, Excel displays additional "contextual" tabs. So, for example, to add a title to the selected chart, I indicate the command as follows:

```
Chart Tools⇨Layout⇨Labels⇨Chart Title⇨Above Chart
```

Formula Listings

Formulas usually appear on a separate line in `monospace font`. For example, I may list the following formula:

```
=VLOOKUP(StockNumber,PriceList,2,False)
```

VBA Code Listings

This book also contains examples of VBA code. Each listing appears in a `monospace font`; each line of code occupies a separate line. To make the code easier to read, I typically use one or more spaces to create indentations. Indentation is optional, but it does help to delineate statements that go together.

If a line of code doesn't fit on a single line in this book, I use the standard VBA line continuation sequence: a space followed by an underscore character. This indicates that the line of code extends to the next line. For example, the following two lines comprise a single VBA statement:

```
If ActiveChart Is Nothing Then _
    MsgBox "Please select a chart or activate a chart sheet."
```

You can enter this code either exactly as shown on two lines, or on a single line without the trailing underscore character.

Key Names

Names of keys on the keyboard appear in normal type — for example, Alt, Home, PgDn, and Ctrl. When you should press two keys simultaneously, the keys are connected by a plus sign: "Press Ctrl+G to display the Go To dialog box."

Functions, Procedures, and Named Ranges

Excel's worksheet functions appear in all uppercase characters, like so: "Use the SUM function to add the values in column A."

Unless you're dealing with text inside quotation marks, Excel is not sensitive to case. In other words, both of the following formulas produce the same result:

```
=SUM(A1:A50)
=sum(a1:a50)
```

Excel, however, will convert the characters in the second formula to uppercase.

In Part III, the VBA chapters, terms such as names of objects, properties, and methods that appear in code listings show up in `monospace` type in regular paragraphs as well: "In this case, `Application.ActiveChart` is an object, and `HasTitle` is a property of the object." Macro and procedure names appear in normal type: "Execute the UpdateChart procedure." I often use mixed uppercase and lowercase letters to make these names easier to read. Named ranges appear in italic: "Select the *WeeklySales* range."

Mouse Conventions

The mouse terminology in this book is all standard fare: pointing, clicking, right-clicking, dragging, and so on. You know the drill.

What the Icons Mean

Throughout the book, icons appear next to some text to call your attention to points that are particularly important.

NOTE

I use Note icons to tell you that something is important — perhaps a concept that may help you master the task at hand or something fundamental for understanding subsequent material.

TIP

Tip icons indicate a more efficient way of doing something, or a technique that may not be obvious. These will often impress your officemates.

ON THE CD-ROM

These icons indicate that an example file is on the companion CD-ROM. (See Appendix A for more details about the CD-ROM.)

 ## CROSS-REFERENCE

I use the Cross-Reference icon to refer you to other chapters that have more to say on a particular topic.

 ## WARNING

I use Warning icons when the operation that I'm describing can cause problems if you're not careful.

How This Book Is Organized

I had many ways to organize this material, but I settled on a scheme that divides the book into three main parts.

Part I: Chart Basics

This part is introductory in nature and consists of Chapters 1 through 6. Chapter 1 presents an overview of Excel's charting features. Chapter 2 presents some terminology and introduces the types of charts Excel supports. In Chapter 3, I discuss various ways to work with chart data series. Chart formatting and customizations are covered in Chapter 4. Chapter 5 discusses chart analytical features, such as trendlines and error bars. The part concludes with Chapter 6, a discussion of other types of graphics supported by Excel.

Part II: Mastering Charts

Part II consists of seven chapters that cover intermediate to advanced material. Chapter 7 covers interactive charts — charts that can be modified easily by an end user. Chapter 8 contains a wide variety of common and not-so-common charts, including ways to generate quite a few "nonstandard" charts. Chapter 9 discusses several ways to display data directly in cells, including small "sparkline" charts. Chapter 10 covers mathematical and statistical charting techniques. In Chapter 11, I cover pivot charts (charts generated from a pivot table). Chapter 12 offers suggestions to help you avoid common mistakes and make your charts more visually appealing. The final chapter in this part is Chapter 13, which is devoted to nonserious charting applications, yet contains lots of useful information.

Part III: Using VBA with Charts

The three chapters in Part III deal with VBA. Chapter 14 presents an overview of VBA as well as some basic VBA charting examples, and Chapter 15 shows more advanced examples. Chapter 16 discusses Excel's color system for VBA programmers.

Appendixes

This book includes two appendixes. Appendix A describes all the files on the companion CD-ROM. Appendix B lists additional charting-related resources on the Internet.

How to Use This Book

You can use this book any way you please. If you choose to read it from cover to cover while lounging on a sunny beach in Kauai, that's fine with me. More likely, you'll want to keep it within arm's reach while you toil away in your dimly lit cubicle.

Owing to the nature of the subject matter, the chapter order is often immaterial. Most readers will probably skip around, picking up useful tidbits here and there. If you're faced with a challenging task, you may want to check the index first to see whether the book specifically addresses your problem.

About the Power Utility Pak Offer

At the back of the book, you'll find a coupon that you can redeem for a discounted copy of my award-winning Power Utility Pak — a collection of useful Excel utilities plus many new worksheet functions. I developed this package using VBA exclusively.

You can also use this coupon to purchase the complete VBA source code for a nominal fee. Studying the code is an excellent way to pick up some useful programming techniques.

You can take the product for a test drive by installing the trial version from the companion CD-ROM.

Reach Out

I'm always interested in getting feedback on my books. The best way to provide this feedback is via e-mail. Send your comments and suggestions to:

`john@j-walk.com`

Unfortunately, I'm not able to reply to specific questions. Posting your question to one of the Excel newsgroups is, by far, the best way to get such assistance. For more information about newsgroups, see Appendix B, "Other Charting Resources."

Also, when you're out surfing the Web, don't overlook my Web site ("The Spreadsheet Page"):

`http://www.j-walk.com/ss/`

Now, without further ado, it's time to turn the page and expand your charting horizons.

Part 1

Chart Basics

Chapter 1

Introducing Excel Charts

In This Chapter

◆ What is a chart?

◆ How Excel handles charts

◆ Embedded charts versus chart sheets

◆ The parts of a chart

◆ The basic steps for creating a chart

◆ Working with charts

When most people think of a spreadsheet product such as Excel, they think of crunching rows and columns of numbers. But, as you probably know already, Excel is no slouch when it comes to presenting data visually, in the form of a chart. This chapter presents an introductory overview of Excel's charting ability, and contains enough information for a typical user to start creating and customizing charts.

What Is a Chart?

I'll start with the basics. A *chart* is a visual representation of numeric values. Charts (also known as graphs) have been an integral part of spreadsheets since the early days of Lotus 1-2-3. Charts generated by early spreadsheet products were extremely crude by today's standards. But, over the years, quality and flexibility have improved significantly. You'll find that Excel provides you with the tools to create a wide variety of highly customizable charts.

9

NOTE

In the first edition of this book, I offered an apology for the relatively poor visual quality of Excel charts. I'm pleased to be able to retract that apology for the Excel 2007 edition. The charting feature in Excel 2007 has come a long way, and Excel is now capable of producing charts with much better visual appeal.

Displaying data in a well-conceived chart can make your numbers more understandable. Because a chart presents a picture, charts are particularly useful for summarizing a series of numbers and their interrelationships. Making a chart can often help you spot trends and patterns that might otherwise go unnoticed.

Figure 1-1 shows a worksheet that contains a simple column chart that depicts a company's sales volume by month. Viewing the chart makes it very apparent that sales were off in the summer months (June through August), but they increased steadily during the final four months of the year. You could, of course, arrive at this same conclusion simply by studying the numbers. But viewing the chart makes the point much more quickly.

Figure 1-1: A simple column chart depicts the sales volume for each month.

A column chart is just one of many different types of charts that you can create with Excel. By the way, creating this chart was simple: I selected the data in A1:B13, and then I pressed Alt+F1.

 ON THE CD

All the charts pictured in this chapter are available in a workbook on the companion CD-ROM. The file is named `introductory examples.xlsx`.

How Excel Handles Charts

Before you can create a chart, you must have some numbers — sometimes known as data. The data, of course, is stored in the cells in a worksheet. Normally, the data that is used by a chart resides in a single worksheet, but that's not a strict requirement. As you'll see, a chart can use data that's stored in any number of worksheets, and the worksheets can even be in different workbooks.

A chart is essentially an "object" that Excel creates upon request. This object consists of one or more *data series,* displayed graphically. The appearance of the data series depends on the selected *chart type.* For example, if you create a line chart that uses two data series, the chart contains two lines, and each line represents one data series. The data for each series is stored in a separate row or column. Each point on the line is determined by the value in a single cell, and is represented by a marker. You can distinguish the lines by their thickness, line style, color, or data markers.

Figure 1-2 shows a line chart that plots two data series across a 6-year period. The series are identified by using different data markers (squares versus circles), shown in the *legend* at the bottom of the chart. The lines also use different colors, which is not apparent in the grayscale figure.

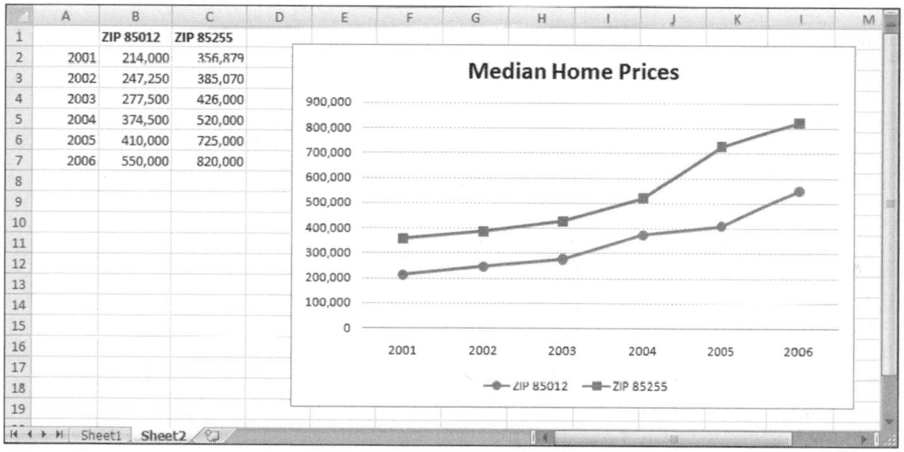

Figure 1-2: This line chart displays two data series.

A key point to keep in mind is that charts are dynamic. In other words, a chart series is linked to the data in your worksheet. If the data changes, the chart is updated automatically to reflect those changes.

After you've created a chart, you can always change its type, change the formatting, add new data series to it, or change an existing data series so that it uses data in a different range.

Charts can reside in either of two locations in a workbook:

- In a worksheet (an embedded chart)
- On a separate chart sheet

Embedded Charts

An *embedded chart* basically floats on top of a worksheet, on the worksheet's drawing layer. The charts shown previously in this chapter are both embedded charts.

As with other drawing objects (such as a text box or a shape), you can move an embedded chart, resize it, change its proportions, adjust its borders, and perform other operations. Using embedded charts enables you to view the chart next to the data that it uses. Or, you can place several embedded charts together so that they print on a single page.

When you create an Excel 2007 chart, it's always an embedded chart. The exception to this rule is when you select a range of data and press F11 to create a default chart. Such a chart is created on a chart sheet.

To make any changes to the actual chart in an embedded chart object, you must click it to *activate* the chart. When a chart is activated, Excel displays the three Chart Tools context tabs shown in Figure 1-3: Chart Tools⇨Design, Chart Tools⇨Layout, and Chart Tools⇨Format.

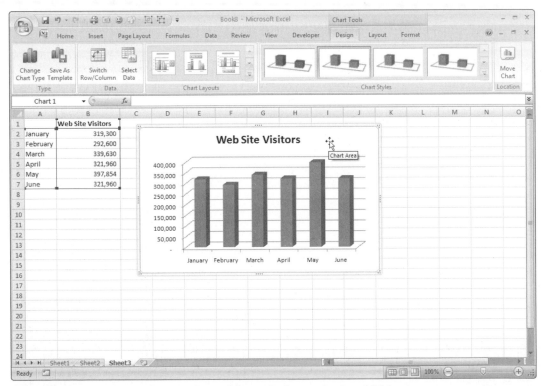

Figure 1-3: Activating a chart displays additional tabs on the Excel Ribbon.

Chart Sheets

You can move an embedded chart to its own chart sheet, so you can view it by clicking a sheet tab. When you move a chart to a chart sheet, the chart occupies the entire sheet. If you plan to print a chart on a page by itself, using a chart sheet is often your better choice. If you have many charts to create, you may want to put each one on a separate chart sheet to avoid cluttering your worksheet. This technique also makes locating a particular chart easier because you can change the names of the chart sheets' tabs to provide a description of the chart that it contains.

Figure 1-4 shows a chart on a chart sheet. When a chart sheet is activated, Excel displays the Chart Tools context tabs, as described in the previous section.

NOTE

Previous versions of Excel have a Size with Window option for charts on a chart sheet. When this setting is enabled, the chart adjusts itself when you resize the workbook window (it always fits perfectly In the window). This feature is not available in Excel 2007.

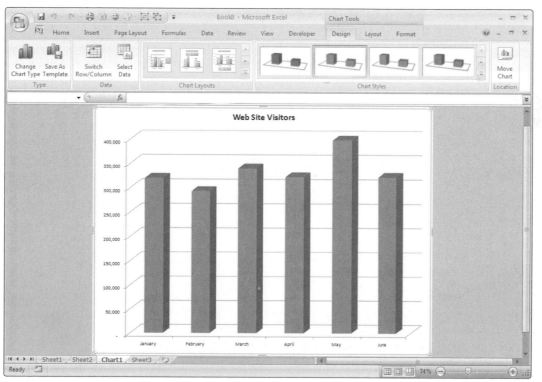

Figure 1-4: A chart on a chart sheet

What's new in Excel 2007?

In Microsoft Office 2007, the charting feature has undergone some major changes. If you've used the charting feature in a previous version of Excel, this sidebar provides a summary of what's new and what's changed.

The Office 2007 charting engine is compatible with other Office 2007 apps such as Word and PowerPoint. In most (but not all) cases, charts created in a previous version can render without a problem in Office 2007. Excel 2007 offers the following charting changes:

- **A chart is a shape:** In Office 2007, an embedded chart's container is a shape object. Although you can't change the type of shape, you can format the shape using most of the new shape-formatting options.

- **Built-in chart layouts:** Each chart type has a number of different predefined layouts that you can apply with a single mouse click.

- **Built-in chart styles:** Each chart type has a number of different predefined styles that you can apply with a single mouse click.

- **More colors:** The old 56-color limitation has been lifted, and a chart can now use any number of colors. And the default color choices are much more pleasing to the eye than the gaudy colors in previous versions.

- **Enhanced formatting:** Office 2007 provides many significant enhancements in formatting chart elements, including quite a few interesting graphic effects.

- **Chart Wizard:** In previous versions, most users invoked the Chart Wizard to assist with creating a chart. The Chart Wizard is no longer available.

- **Size with Window:** In previous versions, charts located on a chart sheet had a Size with Window command that would automatically resize the chart when the window size was changed. This feature has been removed.

- **Create a series by dragging:** You can no longer create a new chart series by selecting cells and dragging the selection into a chart. However, you can accomplish the same effect by copying and pasting.

- **Direct manipulation of data points:** In the past, you could select a data point in a chart and move it — which also changed the underlying data. This rarely used action no longer works.

- **Keyboard shortcut:** Office 2007 supports a new shortcut key combination (Alt+F1) to create an embedded chart (of the default type) from the current range selection. Pressing F11 still creates a chart sheet from the current range selection.

- **Rotating 3-D charts:** In previous versions, you could use your mouse to directly manipulate the view of a 3-D chart. In Office 2007, changing the view requires the use of a dialog box.

- **Pattern fills:** Pattern fills (such as diagonal lines) for chart elements are no longer supported. However, if you open an older file that uses pattern fills, the patterns will continue to display in Office 2007.

- **Double-clicking to format:** In the past, double-clicking a chart element (for example, an axis) displayed a formatting dialog box appropriate for that element. Double-clicking no longer displays a formatting dialog box. However, Office 2007 features a stay-on-top formatting dialog box that lets you modify the selected chart element.

- **Adding text to a chart:** In previous versions, you could add arbitrary text to a chart by selecting the chart and then typing the text (Excel created a text box automatically). That action no longer works in Office 2007. You need to explicitly insert a text box.

- **PivotCharts retain their formatting:** In previous versions, custom formatting applied to a PivotChart was lost when the underlying PivotTable was refreshed. This annoying bug has been fixed in Office 2007.

- **Log scale enhancements:** If you use a logarithmic scale for a chart's value axis, you are no longer limited to base-10 numbers. In addition, the minimum and maximum scale values for a log chart are no longer constrained to powers of 10.

- **Chart templates:** Chart templates are much easier to create and apply in Office 2007. However, they still suffer from some limitations.

- **No built-in custom chart types:** Previous versions of Excel included several built-in custom chart types (including several combination charts). These custom chart types are no longer available.

- **Charts and dialog sheets:** In Excel 2007, you can no longer add a chart to a dialog sheet. (Dialog sheets are fairly obsolete, anyway.)

- **Document themes:** Office 2007 supports document themes. A theme can be applied to a document to change its overall look by using different fonts, colors, and graphic effects. Applying a document theme changes the appearance of the charts.

- **Object model changes:** If you're a VBA programmer, you'll also discover some new twists in the charting object model.

Noticeably absent from this list are any new chart types. Unfortunately, Microsoft hasn't added any new chart types in Office 2007. Maybe in the next release . . .

Parts of a Chart

A chart is made up of many different elements, and all of these elements are optional. Yes, you can create a chart that contains no chart elements — an empty chart. It's not very useful, but Excel allows it.

Refer to the chart in Figure 1-5 as you read the following description of the chart's elements.

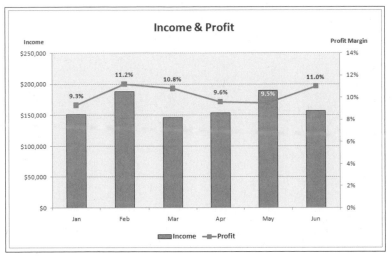

Figure 1-5: Parts of a chart

This particular chart is a "combination" chart that displays two *data series:* Income and Profit Margin. Income is plotted as vertical columns, and the Profit Margin is plotted as a line with square markers. Each bar (or marker on the line) represents a single *data point* (the value in a cell).

The chart has a horizontal axis, known as the *category axis.* This axis represents the category for each data point (January, February, and so on). This axis doesn't have a label because the category units are obvious.

Notice that this chart has two vertical axes. These are known as *value axes,* and each one has a different scale. The axis on the left is for the column series (Income), and the axis on the right is for the line series (Profit Margin).

The value axes also display scale values. The axis on the left displays scale values from 0 to 250,000, in major unit increments of 50,000. The value axis on the right uses a different scale: 0 percent to 14 percent, in increments of 2 percent. For a value axis, you can control the minimum and maximum values, as well as the increment value.

A chart with two value axes is appropriate because the two data series vary dramatically in scale. If the Profit Margin data was plotted using the left axis, the line would not even be visible.

If a chart has more than one data series, you'll usually need a way to identify the data series or data points. A *legend,* for example, is often used to identify the various series in a chart. In this example, the legend appears at the bottom of the chart. Some charts also display *data labels* to identify specific data points. The example chart displays data labels for the Profit Margin series, but not for the Income series. In addition, most charts (including the example chart) contain a *chart title* and additional labels to identify the axes or categories.

The example chart also contains horizontal *gridlines* (which correspond to the values on the left axis). Gridlines are basically extensions of the value axis scale, which makes it easier for the viewer to determine the magnitude of the data points.

In addition, all charts have a *chart area* (the entire background area of the chart) and a *plot area* (the part that shows the actual chart, including the plotted data, the axes, and the axis labels).

Charts can have additional parts or fewer parts, depending on the chart type. For example, a pie chart (see Figure 1-6) has "slices" and no axes. A 3-D chart may have *walls* and a *floor* (see Figure 1-7).

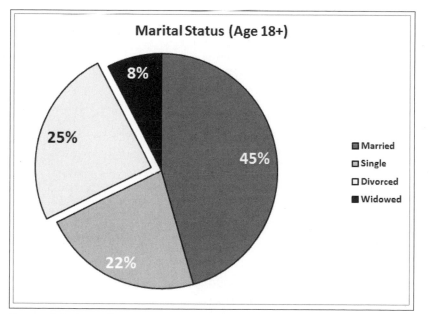

Figure 1-6: A pie chart

Several other types of items can be added to a chart. For example, you can add a *trend line* or display *error bars.*

CROSS-REFERENCE

Refer to Chapters 4 and 5 for additional information about the elements available for various chart types.

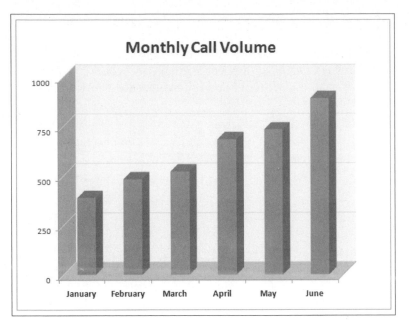

Figure 1-7: A 3-D column chart

Chart limitations

The following table lists the limitations of Excel charts.

Item	Limitation
Charts in a worksheet	Limited by available memory
Worksheets referred to by a chart	255
Data series in a chart	255
Data points in a data series	32,000
Data points in a data series (3-D charts)	4,000
Total data points in a chart	256,000

Most users never find these limitations to be a problem. However, one item that frequently *does* cause problems is the limit on the length of the SERIES formula. Each argument is limited to 255 characters, and in some situations, that's simply not enough characters. Refer to Chapter 3 for more information about SERIES formulas.

Basic Steps for Creating a Chart

The previous version of Excel featured a Chart Wizard that guided the user through the steps required in creating a chart. The Chart Wizard is not available in Excel 2007, but creating basic charts is still relatively simple. The following sections discuss how to create and customize a basic chart in Excel 2007.

Creating the Chart

Follow these steps to create a chart in Excel 2007:

1. Select the data to be used in the chart.

Make sure that you select the column headers, if the data has them. Figure 1-8 shows some data that's appropriate for a chart. Another option is to select a single cell within a range of data. Excel will then use the entire data range for the chart.

2. Click the Insert tab, and then click a Chart icon in the Charts group.

The icon expands into a gallery list that shows subtypes (see Figure 1-9).

3. Click the Chart subtype, and Excel creates the chart of the specified type.

Figure 1-10 shows a column chart created from the data.

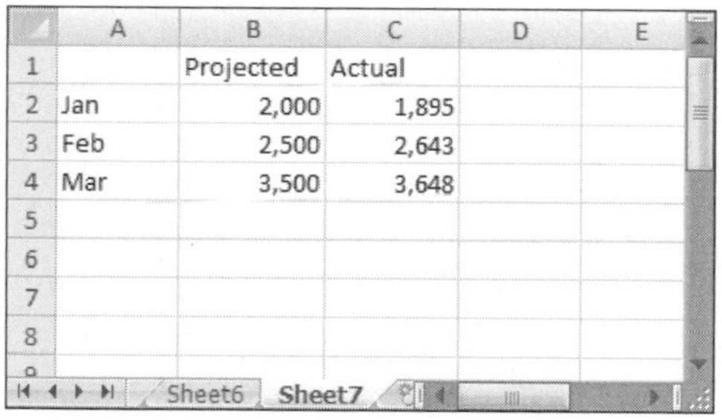

	A	B	C	D	E
1		Projected	Actual		
2	Jan	2,000	1,895		
3	Feb	2,500	2,643		
4	Mar	3,500	3,648		
5					
6					
7					
8					

Sheet6   Sheet7

Figure 1-8: This data would make a good chart.

TIP

To quickly create a default chart, select the data and press Alt+F1 to create an embedded chart, or press F11 to create a chart on a chart sheet. You can also use these keystrokes to duplicate a chart. If you select an embedded chart or chart sheet and press F11, a new default chart sheet is created using the selected chart's data. If you select an embedded chart and press Alt+F1, a new blank chart is created. Alt+F1 has no apparent effect on a chart sheet.

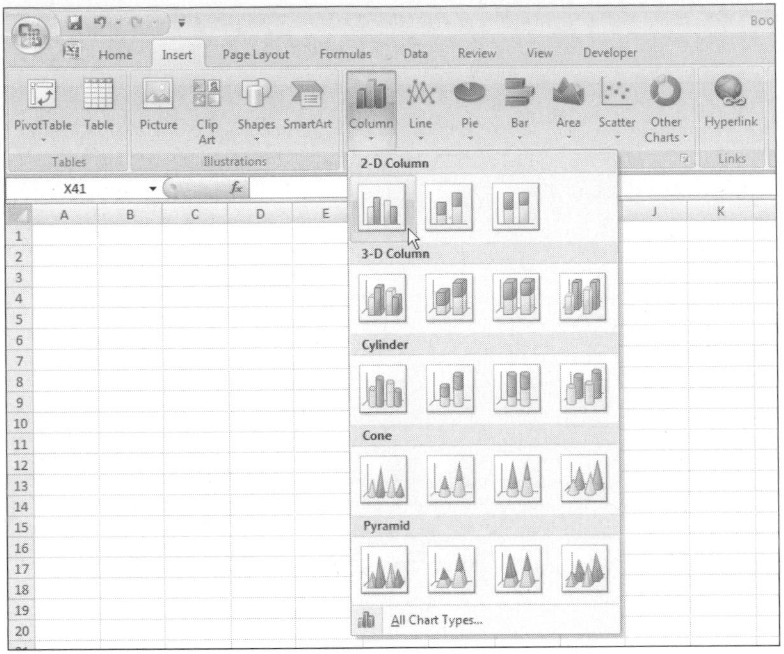

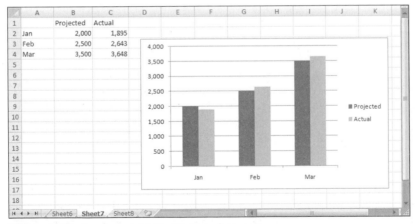

Figure 1-9: The icons in the Insert⇨Charts group expand to show a gallery of chart subtypes.

Figure 1-10: A column chart with two data series

Switching the Row and Column Orientation

When Excel creates a chart, it uses a set of rules to determine whether the data is arranged in columns or in rows. Most of the time Excel guesses correctly, but if it creates the chart using the wrong orientation, you can quickly change it by choosing

Chart Tools⇨Design⇨Data⇨Switch Row/Column. This command is a toggle, so if changing the data orientation doesn't improve the chart, just choose the command again (or click the Undo button).

The orientation of the data has a drastic effect on the look (and, perhaps, understandability) of your chart. Figure 1-11 shows the column chart after changing the orientation. Notice that the chart now has three data series, one for each month. If the goal is to compare actual with projected for each month, this version of the chart is much more difficult to interpret because the relevant columns are not adjacent.

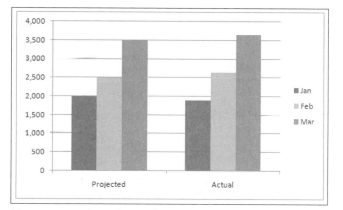

Figure 1-11: The column chart, after swapping the row/column orientation

Changing the Chart Type

After you've created a chart, you can easily change the chart type. Although a column chart may work well for a particular data set, there's no harm in checking out some other chart types. You can choose Chart Tools⇨Design⇨Type⇨Change Chart Type to display the Change Chart Type dialog box and experiment with other chart types. Figure 1-12 shows the Change Chart Type dialog box.

NOTE

If your chart uses more than one data series, make sure that a chart element other than a data series is selected when you choose the Chart Tools⇨Design⇨Type⇨Change Chart Type command. If a series is selected, the command only changes the chart type of the selected series. Selecting a single series before you issue the Change Chart Type command is the basis of creating combination charts (see Chapter 2 for more information about combination charts).

In the Change Chart Type dialog box, the main categories are listed on the left, and the subtypes are shown as icons. Select an icon and click the OK button, and Excel displays the chart using the new chart type. If you don't like the result, click the Undo button.

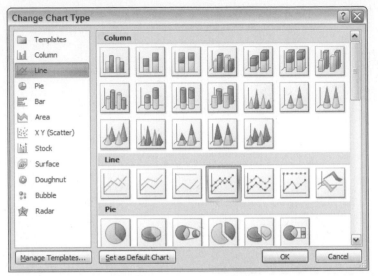

Figure 1-12: The Change Chart Type dialog box

TIP

If the chart is an embedded chart, you can also change a chart's type by using the icons in the Insert⇨Charts group. In fact, this method is more efficient because it doesn't involve a dialog box.

Applying a Chart Layout

Each chart type has a number of prebuilt layouts that you can apply with a single mouse click. A layout contains additional chart elements, such as a title, data labels, axes, and so on. This step is optional, but one of the prebuilt designs might be just what you're looking for. Even if the layout isn't exactly what you want, it may be close enough that you need to make only a few adjustments.

To apply a layout, select the chart and use the Chart Tools⇨Design⇨Chart Layouts gallery. Figure 1-13 shows how a column chart would look using various layouts.

Applying a Chart Style

The Chart Tools⇨Design⇨Chart Styles gallery contains quite a few styles that you can apply to your chart. The styles consist of various color choices and some special effects. Again, this step is optional.

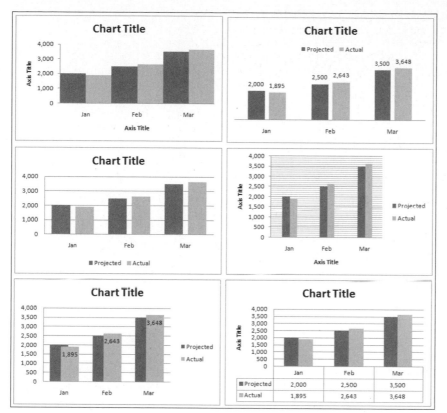

Figure 1-13: One-click design variations of a column chart

Part I

> **TIP**
>
> The styles displayed in the gallery depend on the workbook's theme. When you choose Page Layout⇨Themes to apply a different theme, you'll see a new selection of chart styles designed for the selected theme.

Adding and Deleting Chart Elements

In some cases, applying a chart layout (as described previously) gives you a chart with all the elements you need. Most of the time, however, you'll need to add or remove some chart elements and fine-tune the layout. You do this using the controls on the Chart Tools⇨ Layout tab.

For example, to give a chart a title, choose Chart Tools⇨Layout ⇨Labels⇨Chart Title. The control displays some options that determine where the title is placed. Excel inserts a title with the text Chart Title. Click the text and replace it with your actual chart title.

How to master Excel charting

I've had the pleasure of meeting some of the world's leading Excel chart experts. These people come from a variety of disciplines, but they all have two attributes in common: They are creative, and they are not afraid to experiment.

Yes, dear reader, the key to mastering Excel charting is to think outside the box (as they say) and experiment. Just because Excel doesn't support a particular type of chart doesn't mean that you can't create such a chart. This book provides plenty of chart examples that might seem to be impossible to a typical Excel user. Yet, with a bit of ingenuity (and a few tricks), Excel can do some amazing things.

So don't be afraid to experiment and try some wacky things. The more you play around with Excel, the more you discover. And most of the good stuff isn't in the Help system.

Figure 1-14 shows our column chart after adding a title and specifying that the legend should appear at the bottom of the chart (using Chart Tools⇨Layout⇨Legend⇨Show Legend at Bottom).

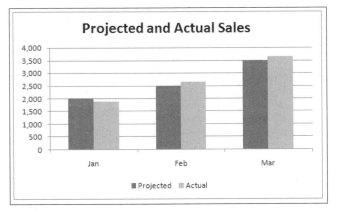

Figure 1-14: Our column chart after adding a title and moving the legend

Formatting Chart Elements

Every element in a chart can be formatted and customized in many ways. Many users are content with charts that are created using the steps described earlier in this chapter. But because you're reading this book, you probably want to find out how to customize charts for maximum impact.

Excel provides two ways to format and customize individual chart elements. Both of the following methods require that you select the chart element first:

- Use the Ribbon controls on the Chart Tools⇨Format tab.
- Press Ctrl+1 to display the Format dialog box that's specific to the selected chart element.

NOTE

The Ribbon controls allow only a small subset of the formatting options. For maximum control, use the Format dialog box.

For example, assume that you'd like to change the color of the columns for one of the series in the chart. Click any column in the series (which selects the entire series). Then, choose Chart Tools⇨Format⇨Shape Styles⇨Shape Fill and choose a color from the displayed list. To change the properties of the outline around the columns, use the Chart Tools⇨Format⇨Shape Styles⇨Shape Outline control. To change the effects used in the columns (for example, add a shadow), use the Chart Tools⇨Format⇨Shape Styles⇨Shape Effects control.

Alternatively, you can select a column in the chart, press Ctrl+1, and use the Format Data Series dialog box shown in Figure 1-15. Note that this is a tabbed dialog box. Click a tab along the left side to view additional controls. It's also a stay-on-top dialog box, so you can click another element in the chart. In other words, you don't have to close the dialog box to see the changes you specify.

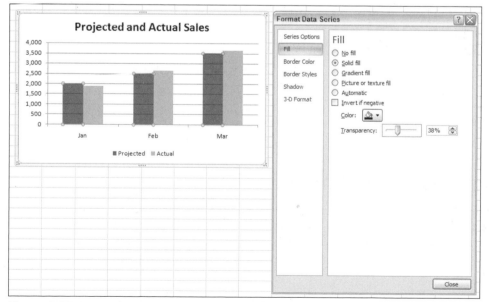

Figure 1-15: Using the Format Data Series dialog box

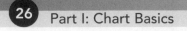

Working with Charts

The following sections cover these common chart modifications:

- Moving and resizing a chart
- Converting an embedded chart to a chart on a chart sheet
- Copying a chart
- Deleting a chart
- Adding chart elements
- Moving and deleting chart elements
- Formatting chart elements
- Copying a chart's formatting
- Renaming a chart
- Printing charts

NOTE

Before you can modify a chart, you must activate it. To activate an embedded chart, click it. Doing so activates the chart and also selects the element that you click. To activate a chart on a chart sheet, just click its sheet tab.

Moving and Resizing a Chart

If your chart is an embedded chart, you can freely move and resize it with your mouse. Click the chart's border and then drag the border to move the chart. Drag any of the eight "handles" to resize the chart. The handles consist of three dots that appear on the chart's corners and edges when you click the chart's border. When the mouse pointer turns into a double arrow, click and drag to resize the chart.

When a chart is selected, you can use the Chart Tools⇨Format⇨Size controls to adjust the height and width of the chart. Use the spinners, or type the dimensions directly into the Height and Width controls. Oddly, Excel does not provide similar controls to specify the top and left positions of the chart.

To move an embedded chart, just click its border at any location except one of the eight resizing handles. Then drag the chart to its new location. You also can use standard cut and paste techniques to move an embedded chart. Select the chart and choose Home⇨ Clipboard⇨Cut (or press Ctrl+X). Then activate a cell near the desired location and choose

Home⇨Clipboard⇨Paste (or press Ctrl+V). The new location can be in a different work-sheet or even in a different workbook. If you paste the chart to a different workbook, it will be linked to the data in the original workbook. Another way to move a chart to a different location is to choose Chart Tools ⇨Design⇨Location⇨Move Chart. This command displays the Move Chart dialog box, which lets you specify a new sheet for the chart (either a chart sheet or a worksheet).

Converting an Embedded Chart to a Chart Sheet

When you create a chart using the icons in the Insert⇨Charts group, the result is always an embedded chart. If you'd prefer that your chart be located on a chart sheet, you can easily move it.

To convert an embedded chart to a chart on a chart sheet, select the chart and choose Chart Tools⇨Design⇨Location⇨Move Chart to display the Move Chart dialog box shown in Figure 1-16. Select the New Sheet option and (optionally) provide a different name for the chart sheet.

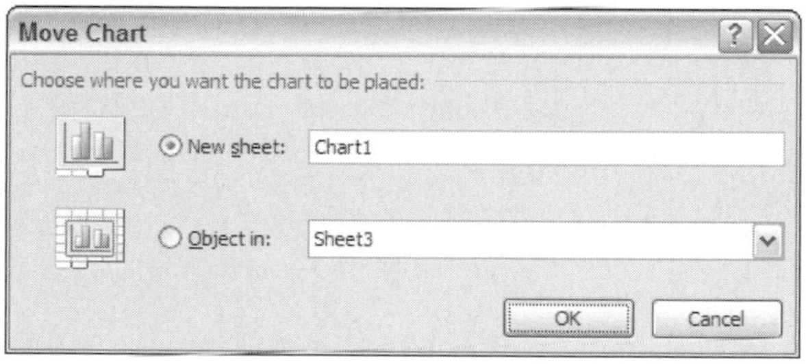

Figure 1-16: Use the Move Chart dialog box to move an embedded chart to a chart sheet (or vice versa).

To convert a chart on a chart sheet to an embedded chart, activate the chart sheet and then choose Chart⇨Tools⇨Design⇨Location⇨Move Chart to display the Move Chart dialog box. Select the Object In option and specify the sheet by using the drop-down control.

Copying a Chart

To make an exact copy of a chart, select the chart (an embedded chart or a chart sheet) and choose Home⇨Clipboard⇨Copy (or press Ctrl+C). Then activate a cell near the desired location and choose Home⇨Clipboard⇨Paste (or press Ctrl+V). The new location can be in a different worksheet or even in a different workbook. If you paste the chart to a different workbook, it will be linked to the data in the original workbook.

Another way to copy a chart is to press Ctrl while dragging an embedded chart (or while dragging a chart sheet's tab).

Deleting a Chart

To delete an embedded chart, press Ctrl and click the chart (this selects the chart as an object). Then press Delete. When the Shift key is pressed, you can select multiple charts and then delete them all with a single press of the Delete key.

To delete a chart sheet, right-click its sheet tab and choose Delete from the shortcut menu. To delete multiple chart sheets, select them by pressing Ctrl while you click the sheet tabs.

Adding Chart Elements

To add new elements to a chart (such as a title, legend, data labels, or gridlines), use the controls in the Chart Tools⇨Layout group. These controls are arranged into logical groups, and they all display a drop-down list of options.

Moving and Deleting Chart Elements

Some of the elements within a chart can be moved. The movable chart elements include the plot area, titles, the legend, and data labels. To move a chart element, simply click it to select it. Then drag its border. The easiest way to delete a chart element is to select it and then press Delete. You can also use the controls in the Chart Tools⇨Layout group to turn off the display of a particular chart element. For example, to delete data labels, choose Chart Tools⇨Layout⇨Labels⇨Data Labels⇨None.

Note that deleting a chart element by using the controls in the Chart Tools⇨Layout group deletes the element (it doesn't just hide it). For example, assume that you add a chart title and apply formatting to it. Then you use the Chart Tools⇨Layout⇨Labels⇨Chart Title⇨ None command to hide the title. If you later decide that you want the title, the previously formatted title is gone and you need to re-apply the formatting.

A few chart elements consist of multiple objects. For example, the data labels element consists of one label for each data point. To move or delete one data label, click once to select the entire element and then click a second time to select the specific data label. You can then move or delete the single data label.

Formatting Chart Elements

Many users are content to stick with the predefined chart layouts and chart styles. For more precise customizations, Excel allows you to work with individual chart elements and apply additional formatting. You can use the Ribbon commands for some modifications, but the easiest way to format chart elements is to right-click the element and choose Format from the shortcut menu. The exact command depends on the element you select. For example, if you right-click the chart's title, the shortcut menu command is Format Chart Title. Alternatively, you can press Ctrl+1 to display the Format dialog box for the selected element.

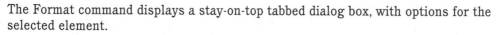

The Format command displays a stay-on-top tabbed dialog box, with options for the selected element.

Figure 1-17 shows the Format Axis dialog box, which I displayed by right-clicking the vertical axis and selecting Format Axis from the shortcut menu.

Format Axis	? ☒

Axis Options	**Axis Options**
Number	Minimum: ◉ Auto ○ Fixed `0.0`
Fill	Maximum: ◉ Auto ○ Fixed `4000.0`
Line Color	Major unit: ◉ Auto ○ Fixed `500.0`
Line Style	Minor unit: ◉ Auto ○ Fixed `100.0`
Shadow	☐ Values in reverse order
3-D Format	☐ Logarithmic scale Base: `10`
Alignment	Display units: None ⌄
	☐ Show display units label on chart
	Major tick mark type: Outside ⌄
	Minor tick mark type: None ⌄
	Axis labels: Next to Axis ⌄
	Horizontal axis crosses:
	◉ Automatic
	○ Axis value: `0.0`
	○ Maximum axis value
	[Close]

Figure 1-17: Each chart element has a formatting dialog box. This one is used to format a chart axis.

TIP

If you've applied formatting to a chart element and decide that it wasn't such a good idea, you can revert to the original formatting for the particular chart style. Right-click the chart element and choose Reset to Match Style from the shortcut menu. To reset the entire chart, select the chart area when you issue the command.

NOTE

In previous versions of Excel, double-clicking a chart element displayed its Format dialog box. That mouse action does not work in Excel 2007.

Copying a Chart's Formatting

If you create a nicely formatted chart, and realize that you need to create several more charts that have the same formatting, you have these three choices:

- Make a copy of the original chart, and then change the data used in the copied chart. One way to change the data used in a chart is to choose the Chart Tools⇨Design⇨ Data⇨Select Data command and make the changes in the Select Data Source dialog box.

- Create the other charts, but don't apply any formatting. Then, activate the original chart and press Ctrl+C. Select one of the other charts, and choose Home⇨Clipboard⇨Paste⇨ Paste Special. In the Paste Special dialog box, click the Formats option, and then click the OK button. Repeat for each additional chart.

- Create a chart template, and then use the template as the basis for the new charts. Or, you can apply the new template to existing charts. See Chapter 2 for more information about chart templates.

Renaming a Chart

When you activate an embedded chart, its name appears in the Name box (located to the left of the formula bar). It seems logical that you can use the Name box to change the name of a chart — but you can't.

To change the name of an embedded chart, use the Chart Tools⇨Layout⇨Properties⇨Chart Name box. Just type the new name and press Enter.

Why rename a chart? If a worksheet has many charts, you may prefer to activate a particular chart by name. Just type the chart's name in the Name box and press Enter. It's much easier to remember a chart named `Monthly Sales` as opposed to a chart named `Chart 9`.

Printing Charts

Printing embedded charts is nothing special; you print them the same way that you print a worksheet. As long as you include the embedded chart in the range that you want to print, Excel prints the chart as it appears on-screen. When printing a sheet that contains embedded charts, it's a good idea to preview first (or use Page Layout View) to ensure that your charts do not span multiple pages. If you created the chart on a chart sheet, Excel always prints the chart on a page by itself.

TIP

If you select an embedded chart and choose Office⇨Print, Excel prints the chart on a page by itself (as if it were a chart sheet) and does not print the worksheet.

If you don't want a particular embedded chart to appear on your printout, select the chart, choose Chart Tools⇨Format, and then click the dialog box launcher in the Size group (it's the small icon to the right of the word *Size*) to display the Size and Properties dialog box. In the Size and Properties dialog box, click the Properties tab and deselect the Print Object check box (see Figure 1-18).

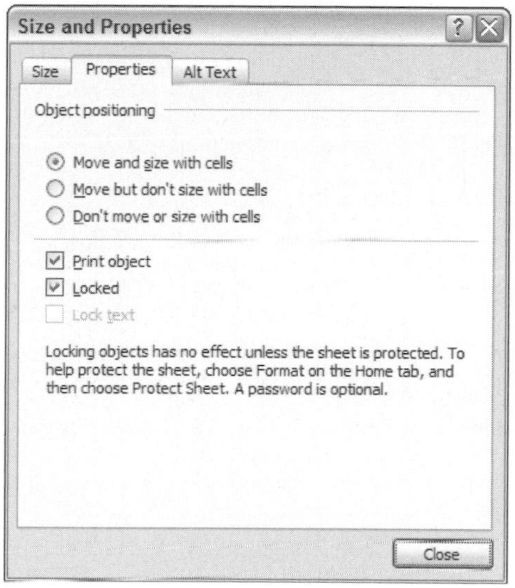

Part I

Size and Properties [?][X]

| Size | Properties | Alt Text |

Object positioning

◉ Move and size with cells
○ Move but don't size with cells
○ Don't move or size with cells

☑ Print object
☑ Locked
☐ Lock text

Locking objects has no effect unless the sheet is protected. To help protect the sheet, choose Format on the Home tab, and then choose Protect Sheet. A password is optional.

[Close]

Figure 1-18: Specifying that a chart should not be printed with the worksheet

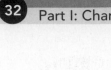

Chapter 2

Understanding Chart Types

In This Chapter

- ◆ Types of charts Excel can generate
- ◆ Examples of each chart type
- ◆ Creating and using chart templates

You're probably familiar with many types of charts: bar charts, line charts, pie charts, and so on. Excel supports all the basic chart types and even some esoteric chart types, such as radar charts and doughnut charts. This chapter presents examples of each of these chart types, along with information that may help you determine which type of chart can best depict your data.

Conveying a Message with a Chart

People who create charts usually do so to make a point or to communicate a specific message. Often, the message is explicitly stated in the chart's title or in a text box within the chart. The chart itself provides visual support for the message.

Choosing the correct chart type is often a key factor in making the message compelling. Therefore, it's often well worth your time to experiment with various chart types to determine which one is most effective.

In almost every case, the underlying message in a chart is some type of *comparison*. Examples of some general types of comparisons include the following:

- **Compare items:** For example, a chart may compare sales volume in each of a company's sales regions.

- **Compare data over time:** For example, a chart may display sales amounts by month, to indicate a trend over time.

- **Make relative comparisons:** An example is a common pie chart that depicts relative values in terms of pie slices.

- **Compare data relationships:** A scatter chart is ideal for this. For example, you might create a chart to show the relationship between monthly marketing expenditures and sales.

- **Compare frequency:** A common histogram, for example, can be used to display the number (or percentage) of students who had a test score within several ranges of scores.

- **Identify "outliers" or unusual situations:** If you have thousands of data points, creating a chart may help identify data that is not representative.

Choosing a Chart Type

A common question among Excel users is, "How do I know which chart type to use for my data?" Unfortunately, there is no cut-and-dried answer to this question. Perhaps the best answer is a vague one: *Use the chart type that gets your message across in the simplest way.*

Figure 2-1 shows the same set of data plotted using six different chart types. Although all six charts represent the same information (monthly visitors to a Web site), they look quite different from one another.

 ON THE CD

This workbook, named six chart types.xlsx, is available on the companion CD-ROM.

The column chart (upper left) is probably the best choice for this particular set of data because it clearly shows the information for each month in discrete units. The bar chart (upper right) is similar to a column chart, but the axes are swapped. Most people are more accustomed to seeing time-based information extend from left to right rather than from top to bottom.

The line chart (middle left) may not be the best choice because it seems to imply that the data is continuous — that points exist in between the 12 actual data points. This same argument could be made against using an area chart (middle right).

The pie chart (lower left) is simply too confusing and does nothing to convey the time-based nature of the data. Pie charts are most appropriate for a data series in which you want to emphasize proportions among a relatively small number of data points. If you have too many data points, a pie chart can be impossible to interpret.

The radar chart (lower right) is clearly inappropriate for this data. People are not accustomed to viewing time-based information in a circular direction!

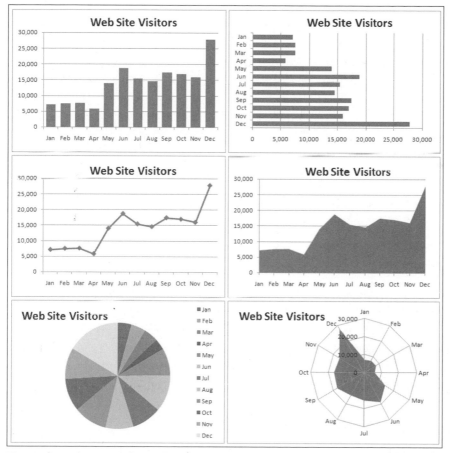

Figure 2-1: The same data, plotted using six chart types.

Fortunately, changing a chart's type is a very easy procedure, so you can experiment with various chart types until you find the one that represents your data accurately and clearly — and as simply as possible. To change a chart's type, select the chart and choose Chart Tools⇨Design⇨Change Chart Type. Then select the chart type from the Change Chart Type dialog box (see Figure 2-2).

NOTE

If your chart has more than one data series, make sure that something other than a chart series is selected when you issue the Chart Tools⇨Design⇨Change Chart Type command. If a series is selected, only the type for that series will be changed. In other words, you'll end up with a combination chart — a chart that incorporates two or more different chart types. I describe combination charts later in this chapter.

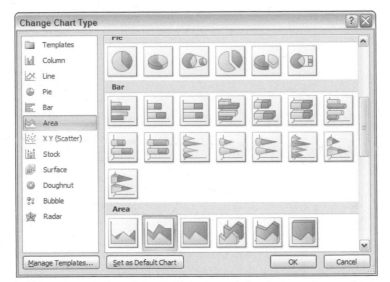

Figure 2-2: Use the Change Chart Type dialog box to change the type of a chart.

The remainder of this chapter contains lots of information about Excel's various chart types. The examples and discussion may give you a better handle on determining the most appropriate chart type for your data.

Excel's Chart Types

After you've selected the data for a chart, the next step is to click the icon in the Insert⇨ Charts group for the chart type. The icon then expands so that you can select the subtype. For example, if you choose Insert⇨Charts⇨Pie, the control expands to display the six pie chart subtypes, as shown in Figure 2-3.

If you click the All Chart Types link, you get a dialog box that lists all charts and their subtypes.

Note that you create the less frequently used chart types by choosing the Insert⇨Charts⇨ Other Charts command. The charts available from this control are stock charts, surface charts, doughnut charts, bubble charts, and radar charts.

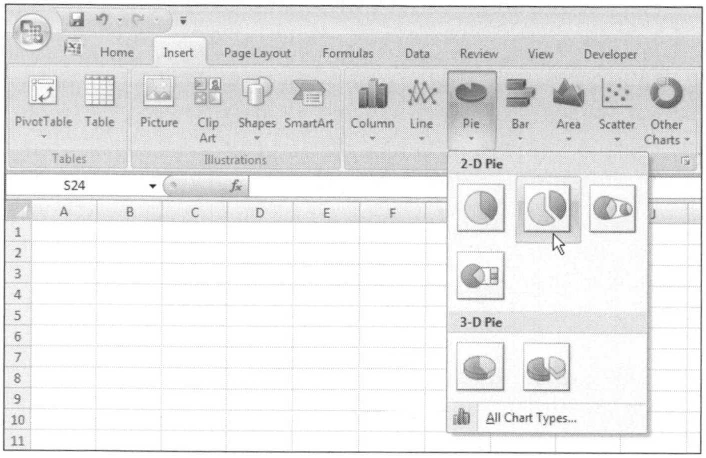

Figure 2-3: Each Chart Type icon expands to show the subtypes.

Column Charts

Column charts are one of the most common chart types. A column chart displays each data point as a vertical column, the height of which corresponds to the value. The value scale is displayed on the vertical axis, which is usually on the left side of the chart. You can specify any number of data series, and the corresponding data points from each series can be stacked on top of each other. Typically, each data series is depicted in a different color or pattern.

Column charts are often used to compare discrete items, and they can depict the differences between items in a series or items across multiple series.

Table 2-1 lists and describes Excel's 19 column chart subtypes.

TABLE 2-1   COLUMN CHART SUBTYPES

Chart Type	Description
Clustered column	Standard column chart.
Stacked column	Column chart with data series stacked.
100% stacked column	Column chart with data series stacked and expressed as percentages.
3-D clustered column	Column chart with a perspective look.
Stacked column in 3-D	Column chart with a perspective look. Data series are stacked.

continued

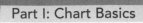

TABLE 2-1   COLUMN CHART SUBTYPES *(continued)*

Chart Type	Description
100% stacked column in 3-D	Column chart with a perspective look. Data series are stacked and expressed as percentages.
3-D column	Column chart with multiple series arranged along a third axis.
Clustered cylinder	Like a 3-D clustered column chart, but the columns are cylindrical.
Stacked cylinder	Like a stacked column in 3-D chart, but the columns are cylindrical.
100% stacked cylinder	Like a 100% stacked column in 3-D chart, but the columns are cylindrical.
3-D cylinder	Like a 3-D column chart, but the columns are cylindrical.
Clustered cone	Like a 3-D clustered column chart, but the columns are conical.
Stacked cone	Like a stacked column in 3-D chart, but the columns are conical.
100% stacked cone	Like a 100% stacked column in 3-D chart, but the columns are conical.
3-D cone	Like a 3-D column chart, but the columns are conical.
Clustered pyramid	Like a 3-D clustered column chart, but the columns are pyramidal.
Stacked pyramid	Like a stacked column in 3-D chart, but the columns are pyramidal.
100% stacked pyramid	Like a 100% stacked column in 3-D chart, but the columns are pyramidal.
3-D pyramid	Like a 3-D column chart, but the columns are pyramidal.

Figure 2-4 shows an example of a clustered column chart that depicts annual sales for two products. From this chart, it is clear that Sprocket sales have always exceeded Widget sales. In addition, Widget sales have been declining over the years, whereas Sprocket sales are increasing.

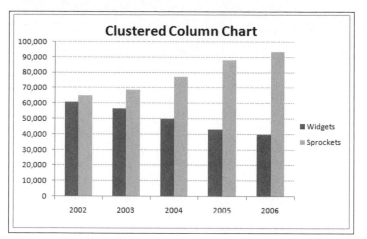

Figure 2-4: This clustered column chart compares sales for two products.

 ON THE CD

The chart examples in this section are available on the companion CD-ROM. The work-book is named column charts.xlsx.

The same data, in the form of a stacked column chart, is shown in Figure 2-5. This chart has the added advantage of depicting the combined sales over time (note the scale of the vertical axis). It shows that total sales have remained relatively steady over the years, but the relative proportions of the two products have changed.

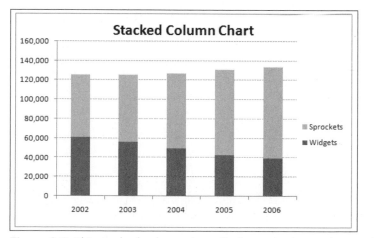

Figure 2-5: This stacked column chart displays sales by product and depicts the total sales.

Figure 2-6 shows the same sales data plotted as a 100% stacked column chart. This chart type shows the relative contribution of each product by year. Notice that the value axis displays percentage values, not sales amounts. This chart provides no information about the actual sales volumes. This type of chart is often a good alternative to using several pie charts. Instead of using a pie to show the relative sales volume in each year, the chart uses a column for each year.

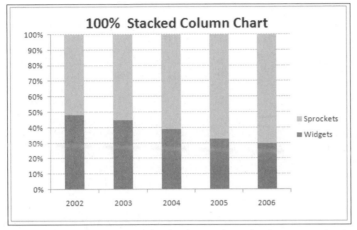

Figure 2-6: This 100% stacked column chart displays annual sales as a percentage.

3-D or not 3-D? That is the question

Some of Excel's charts are referred to as *3-D charts*. This terminology can be somewhat confusing, because some of these so-called 3-D charts aren't technically 3-D charts. Rather, they are 2-D charts with a perspective look to them; that is, they appear to have some depth. The accompanying figure shows two "3-D" charts.

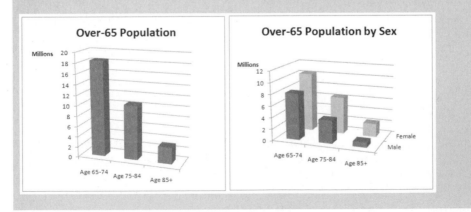

The chart on the left is a 3-D clustered column chart. However, it's not a true 3-D chart. It's just a 2-D chart that uses perspective to add depth to the columns. The chart on the right (a 3-D column chart) is a true 3-D chart because the data series extend into the third (depth) dimension.

A true 3-D chart has three axes: a value axis (the height dimension), a category axis (the width dimension), and a series axis (the depth dimension). The series axis is always a category axis — it cannot depict scaled numerical values.

When a 3-D chart is active (whether it's a true 3-D chart or not), you can change the chart's perspective and viewpoint by using the Chart Tools⇨Layout⇨Background⇨3-D Rotation command. This command displays the 3-D Rotation tab of the Format Chart Area dialog box, as shown here. You'll find that you have a great deal of control. You can distort the chart so much that it becomes virtually useless.

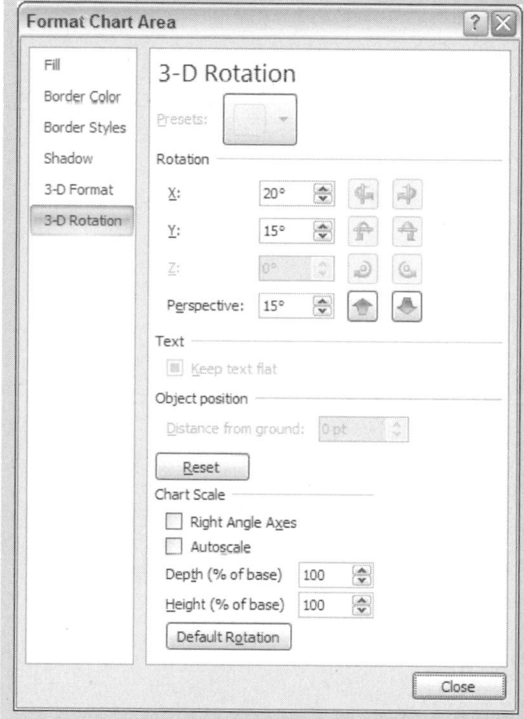

The data is plotted using a 3-D column chart in Figure 2-7. Many people use this type of chart because it has more visual pizzazz. Although it may be more appealing visually, this type of chart often makes it difficult to make precise comparisons because of the distorted perspective view. Generally speaking, a 3-D column chart is best used when the goal is to show general trends rather than precise comparisons.

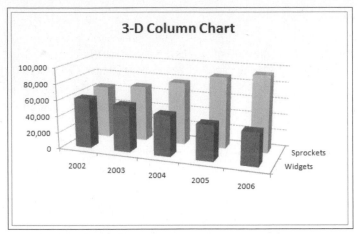

Figure 2-7: A 3-D column chart.

The final column chart variation is shown in Figure 2-8. This is a stacked cone chart. This chart subtype (as well as the cylinder and pyramid variations) is usually more difficult to interpret, compared to a standard column chart. This particular chart can be a bit misleading because the Sprockets series may be viewed as being less important because of the reduced volume at the top of the cones. In addition, note the perspective distortion. Although the combined sales for the products exceed 120,000 for all years, that fact is not apparent in this 3-D chart.

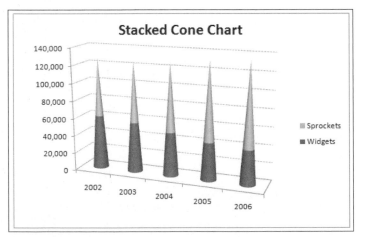

Figure 2-8: A stacked cone chart.

Bar Charts

A *bar chart* is essentially a column chart that has been rotated 90 degrees clockwise. One distinct advantage to using a bar chart is that the category labels may be easier to read. Figure 2-9 shows a bar chart that displays a value for each of ten survey items. The category labels are lengthy, and it would be difficult to display them legibly using a column chart.

ON THE CD

The chart examples in this section are available on the companion CD-ROM. The workbook is named `bar charts.xlsx`.

Table 2-2 lists Excel's 15 bar chart subtypes.

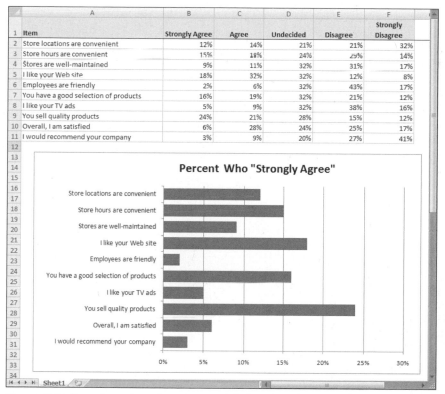

Figure 2-9: If you have lengthy category labels, a bar chart may be a good choice.

Part I

TABLE 2-2 BAR CHART SUBTYPES

Chart Type	Description
Clustered bar	Standard bar chart.
Stacked bar	Bar chart with data series stacked.
100% stacked bar	Bar chart with data series stacked and expressed as percentages.
Clustered bar in 3-D	Standard bar chart with a perspective look.
Stacked bar in 3-D	Bar chart with a perspective look. Excel stacks data series.
100% stacked bar in 3-D	Bar chart with a perspective look. Excel stacks data series and expresses them as percentages.
Clustered horizontal cylinder	Like a clustered bar chart, but the bars are cylindrical.
Stacked horizontal cylinder	Like a stacked bar chart, but the bars are cylindrical.
100% stacked horizontal cylinder	Like a 100% stacked bar chart, but the bars are cylindrical.
Clustered horizontal cone	Like a clustered bar chart, but the bars are conical.
Stacked horizontal cone	Like a stacked bar chart, but the bars are conical.
100% stacked horizontal cone	Like a 100% stacked bar chart, but the bars are conical.
Clustered horizontal pyramid	Like a clustered bar chart, but the bars are pyramidal.
Stacked horizontal pyramid	Like a stacked bar chart, but the bars are pyramidal.
100% stacked horizontal pyramid	Like a 100% stacked bar chart, but the bars are pyramidal.

NOTE
Unlike a column chart, there is no subtype that displays multiple series along a third axis (that is, there is no 3-D Bar Chart subtype).

As with a column chart, you can include any number of data series in a bar chart. In addition, the bars can be "stacked" from left to right. Figure 2-10 shows a 100% stacked bar chart. This chart summarizes the percentage of survey respondents who replied to each option.

Line Charts

Line charts are often used to plot continuous data and are useful for identifying trends over time. For example, plotting daily sales as a line chart may help you to identify sales fluctuations over time. Normally, the category axis for a line chart displays equal intervals.

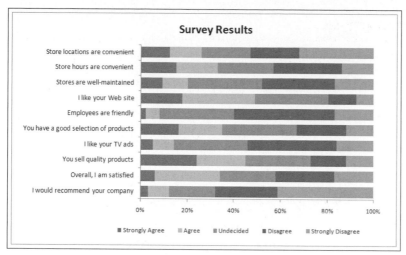

Figure 2-10: A 100% stacked bar chart.

ON THE CD

The chart examples in this section are available on the companion CD-ROM. The workbook is named `line charts.xlsx`.

Table 2-3 lists Excel's seven line chart subtypes.

TABLE 2-3   LINE CHART SUBTYPES

Chart Type	Description
Line	Standard line chart
Stacked line	Line chart with stacked data series
100% stacked line	Line chart with stacked data series expressed as percentages
Line with markers	Line chart with data markers
Stacked line with markers	Line chart with stacked data series and data markers
100% stacked line with markers	Line chart with stacked data series and line markers, expressed as percentages
3-D line	Chart that displays "ribbon-like" lines, using a third axis

See Figure 2-11 for an example of a line chart that depicts daily sales (200 data points). Although the data varies quite a bit on a daily basis, the chart clearly depicts an upward trend.

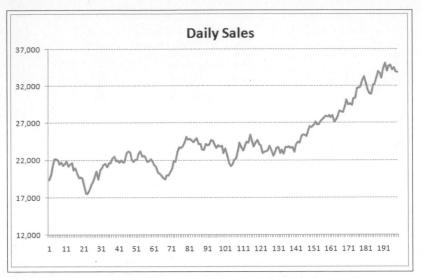

Figure 2-11: A line chart often can help you spot trends in your data.

A line chart can use any number of data series, and you distinguish the lines by using different colors, line styles, or markers. Figure 2-12 shows a line chart that uses three series, each with 48 data points. Each line is displayed in a different color and with a different marker. The series are identified by the legend.

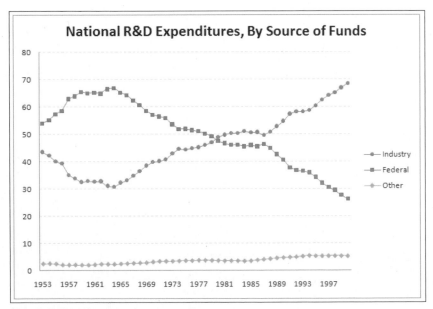

Figure 2-12: This line chart uses three series.

Figure 2-13 shows a 3-D line chart that depicts population growth for three states. Most would agree that a 3-D line chart is definitely *not* a good chart type for this data. For example, the 3-D perspective makes it virtually impossible to determine the relative growths of Washington and Oregon. In fact, the chart may present an optical illusion that makes it impossible to discern the order of the line series across the depth axis. Using a standard line chart, as in Figure 2-14, is a better choice.

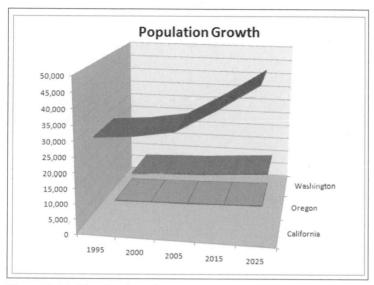

Figure 2-13: This 3-D line chart is not a good choice for this data.

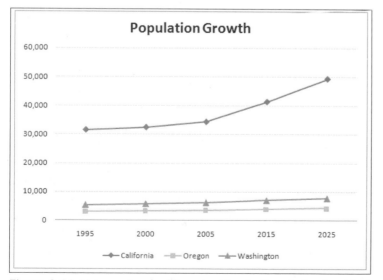

Figure 2-14: Using a standard line chart is a better choice for this data.

Pie Charts

A *pie chart* is useful when you want to show relative proportions or contributions to a whole. A pie chart can use only one data series. Pie charts are most effective with a small number of data points. Generally, a pie chart should use no more than five or six data points (or slices). A pie chart with too many data points can be very difficult to interpret.

NOTE

The values used in a pie chart must all be positive numbers. If you create a pie chart that uses one or more negative values, those values will be converted to positive values — which is probably not what you intended!

You can "explode" one or more slices of a pie chart for emphasis (see Figure 2-15). Activate the chart and click any pie slice to select the entire pie. Then click the slice that you want to explode and drag it away from the center.

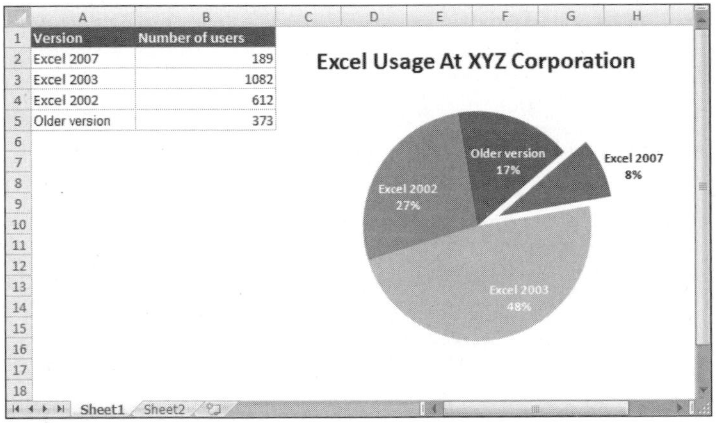

Figure 2-15: A pie chart with one slice exploded.

ON THE CD

The chart examples in this section are available on the companion CD-ROM. The workbook is named `pie charts.xlsx`.

Table 2-4 lists Excel's six pie chart subtypes.

TABLE 2-4   **PIE CHART SUBTYPES**

Chart Type	Description
Pie	Standard pie chart
Pie in 3-D	Pie chart with perspective look
Pie of pie	Pie chart with one slice broken into another pie
Exploded pie	Pie chart with one or more slices exploded
Exploded pie in 3-D	Pie chart with perspective look, with one or more slices exploded
Bar of pie	Pie chart with one slice broken into a column

Figure 2-16 shows an example of a pie in 3-D chart. You have complete control over how the chart is rotated and how much the slices are separated.

 WARNING

3-D pie charts are particularly prone to perspective distortion. This chart type can be very difficult to interpret.

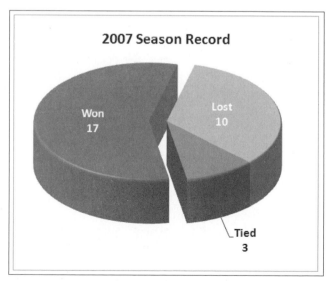

Figure 2-16: A pie chart in 3-D.

The pie of pie and bar of pie chart types enable you to display a secondary chart that provides more detail for one of the pie slices. Refer to Figure 2-17 for an example. The pie chart shows the breakdown of four expense categories: Rent, Supplies, Utilities, and Salary. The secondary bar chart provides an additional regional breakdown of the Salary category.

The pie chart.xlsx file on the companion CD-ROM includes an alternate presentation of this data, using a stack column chart.

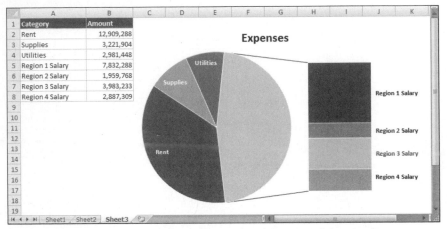

Figure 2-17: A bar of pie chart that shows detail for one of the pie slices.

Scatter Charts

Another common chart type is a *scatter chart* (also known as an XY chart). A scatter chart differs from most other chart types in that both axes display values. (A scatter chart has no category axis.)

This type of chart often is used to show the relationship between two variables. Figure 2-18 shows an example of a scatter chart that plots the relationship between sales calls made during a month (horizontal axis) and actual sales for the month (vertical axis). The chart shows that these two variables are positively related: Months in which more calls were made typically had higher sales volumes.

ON THE CD

The chart examples in this section are available on the companion CD-ROM. The workbook is named scatter charts.xlsx.

NOTE

Although these data points correspond to time, it's important to understand that the chart does not convey any time-related information. In other words, the data points are plotted based only on their two values. The Year and Month columns are not used.

CROSS-REFERENCE

Adding a trend line to this chart would assist in conveying the fact that the variables are positively correlated. See Chapter 5 for details on trend lines.

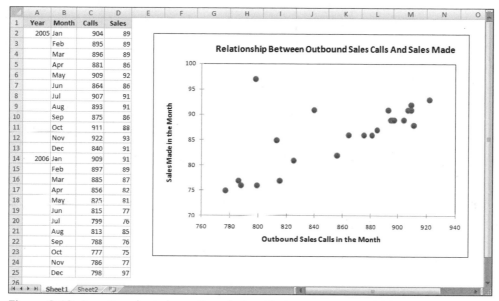

Figure 2-18: A scatter chart shows the relationship between two variables.

Table 2-5 lists Excel's five scatter chart subtypes.

TABLE 2-5   SCATTER CHART SUBTYPES

Chart Type	Description
Scatter with only markers	A scatter chart with data markers and no lines
Scatter with smoothed lines and markers	A scatter chart with data markers and smoothed lines
Scatter with smoothed lines	A scatter chart with smoothed lines and no data markers
Scatter with straight lines and markers	A scatter chart with lines and data markers
Scatter with lines	A scatter chart with lines and no data markers

Figure 2-19 shows another example of a scatter chart, this one using the straight lines and markers subtype. As you can see, the data points, when connected, draw a right triangle.

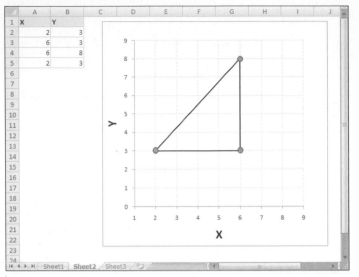

Figure 2-19: The data points in this scatter chart define a right triangle.

Another scatter chart example is shown in Figure 2-20. This chart displays 200 x-y data points, using straight lines and no markers. This is also an example of a minimalist chart. All the chart elements (except the data series) are removed.

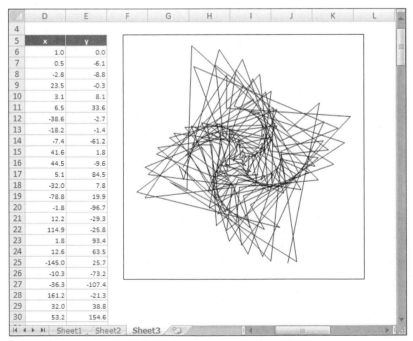

Figure 2-20: 200 data points displayed in a scatter chart.

Area Charts

Think of an *area chart* as a line chart in which the area below the line has been colored in. Table 2-6 lists Excel's six area chart subtypes.

TABLE 2-6   **AREA CHART SUBTYPES**

Chart Type	Description
Area	Standard area chart
Stacked area	Area chart; data series stacked
100% stacked area	Area chart; data series stacked and expressed as percentages
3-D area	A true 3-D area chart with a third axis
Stacked area in 3-D	Area chart with a perspective look; data series stacked
100% stacked area in 3-D	Area chart with a perspective look; data series stacked and expressed as percentages

Figure 2-21 shows an example of a stacked area chart. Stacking the data series enables you to see clearly the total sales for each quarter, plus the contribution by each series.

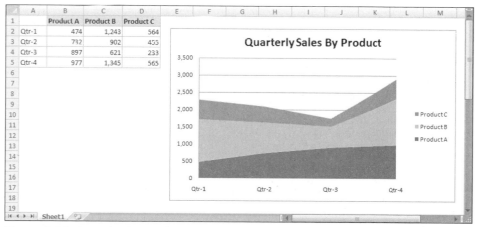

Figure 2-21: A stacked area chart.

 ON THE CD

The chart examples in this section are available on the companion CD-ROM. The workbook is named `area charts.xlsx`.

Figure 2-22 shows the same data, plotted as a 3-D area chart. Although this chart has lots of visual appeal, it has a serious weakness: The data toward the back is often obscured. In this example, the first three quarters for Product C are not even visible.

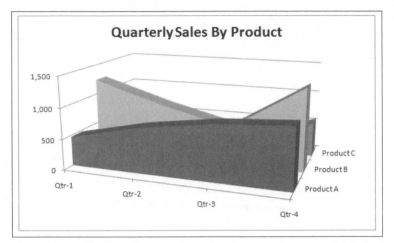

Figure 2-22: The first three quarters for Product C are not visible in this 3-D area chart.

CROSS-REFERENCE

Problems with data visibility in 3-D area charts can sometimes be solved by rotating or changing the elevation of the 3-D chart to provide a different view. In some cases, plotting the series in reverse order reveals the obscured data. For the most control, you can manually change the plot order of the series. These procedures are described in Chapter 4.

Doughnut Charts

A *doughnut chart* is similar to a pie chart, with two exceptions: It has a hole in the middle, and it can display more than one series of data. Figure 2-23 shows an example of a doughnut chart with two series (1st Half Sales and 2nd Half Sales). The legend identifies the data points. The arrows and series descriptions were added manually. Oddly, a doughnut chart does not provide a direct way to identify the series.

ON THE CD

The chart examples in this section are available on the companion CD-ROM. The workbook is named doughnut charts.xlsx.

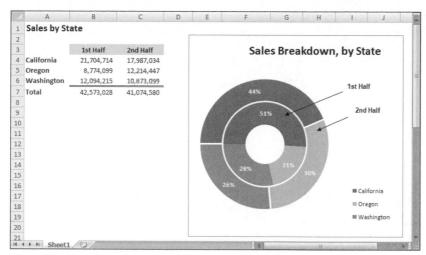

Figure 2-23: A doughnut chart with two data series.

Notice that Excel displays the data series as concentric rings. As you can see, a doughnut chart with more than one series can be very difficult to interpret. For example, the relatively larger sizes of the slices toward the outer part of the doughnut can be deceiving. Consequently, doughnut charts should be used sparingly. In many cases, a stacked or clustered column chart for such comparisons expresses your meaning better than does a doughnut chart. Figure 2-24 shows the same data, displayed in a stacked column chart.

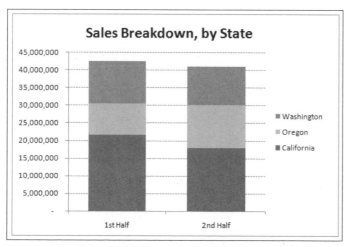

Figure 2-24: Using a stacked column chart as a doughnut chart replacement.

Perhaps the best use for a doughnut chart is to plot a single series as a visual alternative to a pie chart. Figure 2-25 shows a single-series doughnut chart, with one slice exploded. I also added a bevel to the doughnut for some additional visual appeal (or "clutter," depending on your perspective).

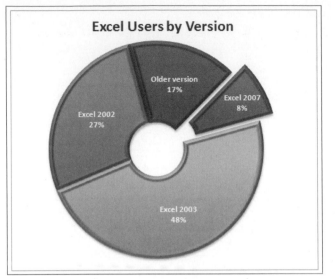

Figure 2-25: A doughnut chart with one data series.

Table 2-7 lists Excel's two doughnut chart subtypes.

TABLE 2-7 DOUGHNUT CHART SUBTYPES

Chart Type	Subtype
Doughnut	Standard doughnut chart
Exploded doughnut	Doughnut chart with all slices exploded

Radar Charts

You may not be familiar with radar charts. A *radar chart* has a separate axis for each category, and the axes extend outward from the center of the chart. The value of each data point is plotted on the corresponding axis.

Figure 2-26 shows an example of a radar chart. This chart plots two data series across 12 categories (months) and shows the seasonal demand for snow skis versus water skis. Note that the water ski series partially obscures the snow ski series — which I solved by making the water ski series semitransparent.

ON THE CD

The chart examples in this section are available on the companion CD-ROM. The workbook is named `radar charts.xlsx`.

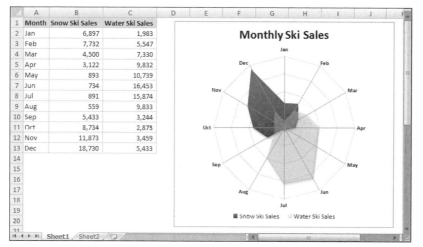

Figure 2-26: A radar chart with 12 categories and 2 series.

It's probably a safe bet that the vast majority of people would have no idea how to interpret the ski sales chart. Figure 2-27 shows a much better alternative for the data: a stacked column chart.

Figure 2-27: A stacked column chart is a better choice for the ski sales data.

Figure 2-28 shows another radar chart, with three categories. This chart depicts the red, green, and blue components for a color using the RGB color system. In the RGB color system, each color is represented by a value (between 0 and 255) for red, green, and blue.

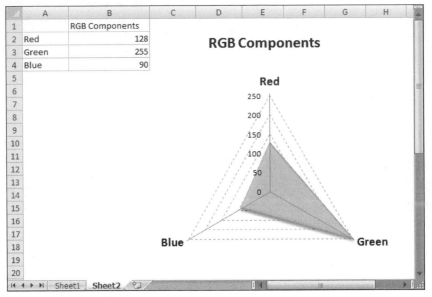

Figure 2-28: A radar chart with three categories.

Table 2-8 lists Excel's three radar chart subtypes.

TABLE 2-8   RADAR CHART SUBTYPES

Chart Type	Subtype
Radar	Standard radar chart (lines only)
Radar with data markers	Radar chart with lines and data markers
Filled radar	Radar chart with lines colored in

Surface Charts

A *surface chart* displays two or more data series as a three-dimensional surface. As Figure 2-29 shows, these charts can be quite interesting.

Unlike other charts, Excel uses color to distinguish values, not to distinguish the data series. The number of colors used is determined by the major unit scale setting for the value axis. Each color corresponds to one major unit.

 ON THE CD

The chart examples in this section are available on the companion CD-ROM. The workbook is named `surface charts.xlsx`.

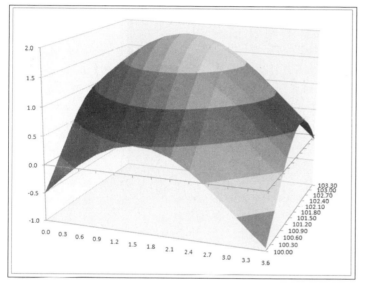

Figure 2-29: A surface chart.

Table 2-9 lists Excel's four 3-D surface chart subtypes.

TABLE 2-9 SURFACE CHART SUBTYPES

Chart Type	Description
3-D surface	Standard 3-D surface chart
Wireframe 3-D surface	3-D surface chart with no colors
Contour	3-D surface chart as viewed from above
Wireframe contour	3-D surface chart as viewed from above; no color

NOTE

You should understand that a surface chart does not plot 3-D data points. The series axis for a surface chart, as with all other 3-D charts, is a *category axis* — not a value axis. In other words, if you have data that is represented by *x*, *y*, and *z* coordinates, it cannot be plotted accurately on a surface chart unless the *x* and *y* values are equally spaced.

Figure 2-30 shows the contour subtype, using the same data as in the previous figure. As you can see, it's as if you're looking directly down on the surface chart.

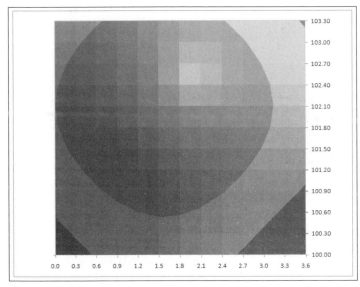

Figure 2-30: A contour chart.

Bubble Charts

Think of a *bubble chart* as a scatter chart that can display an additional data series, which is represented by the size of the bubbles. As with a scatter chart, both axes are value axes — there is no category axis.

Figure 2-31 shows an example of a bubble chart that depicts the results of a weight-loss program. The horizontal value axis represents the original weight, the vertical value axis shows the length of time in the program, and the size of the bubbles represents the amount of weight lost.

NOTE

Displaying quantitative information as bubble size can be confusing because most people cannot accurately judge the relative areas of the bubbles. Excel provides a bubble size option in the Series Options tab of the Format Data Series dialog box. You can choose to have values correspond to either the *area* of the bubbles (default) or to the width of the bubbles.

ON THE CD

The chart examples in this section are available on the companion CD-ROM. The workbook is named `bubble charts.xlsx`.

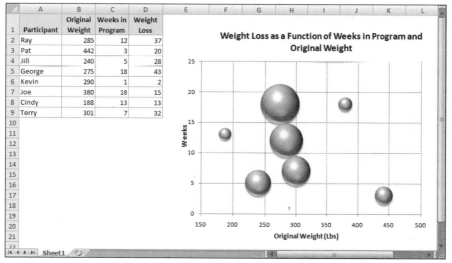

Figure 2-31: A bubble chart.

Table 2-10 lists Excel's two bubble chart subtypes.

TABLE 2-10   BUBBLE CHART SUBTYPES

Chart Type	Subtype
Bubble chart	Standard bubble chart
Bubble with a 3-D effect	Bubble chart with 3-D bubbles

Stock Charts

Stock charts are most useful for displaying stock market information. These charts require three to five data series, depending on the subtype.

Table 2-11 lists Excel's four stock chart subtypes.

TABLE 2-11   STOCK CHART SUBTYPES

Chart Type	Subtype
High-low-close	Displays the stock's high, low, and closing prices. Requires three data series.
Open-high-low-close	Displays the stock's opening, high, low, and closing prices. Requires four data series.
Volume-high-low-close	Displays the stock's volume and high, low, and closing prices. Requires four data series.
Volume-open-high-low-close	Displays the stock's volume and open, high, low, and closing prices. Requires five data series.

Figure 2-32 shows an example of each of the four stock chart types. The two charts on the bottom display the trade volume and use two value axes. The daily volume, represented by columns, uses the axis on the left. The "up bars," sometimes referred to as candlesticks, depict the difference between the opening and closing price. A black up bar indicates that the closing price was lower than the opening price. These charts can be difficult to interpret because Excel does not display symbols in the legend for all series.

 ON THE CD

The chart examples in this section are available on the companion CD-ROM. The workbook is named `stock charts.xlsx`.

A stock market chart can display any number of data points. Figure 2-33, for example, shows three years of data for a company. This chart plots all four variables: volume, high, low, and close. With this many data points, individual days are not discernible, but trends are easy to identify.

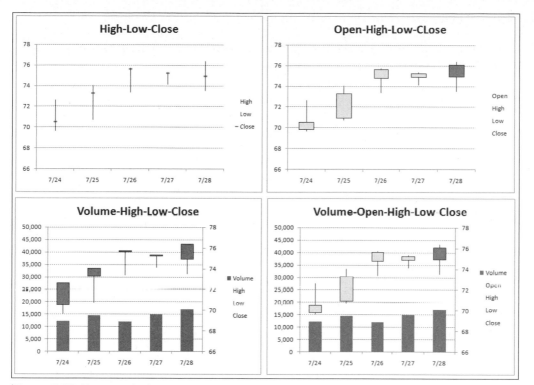

Figure 2-32: Four stock charts.

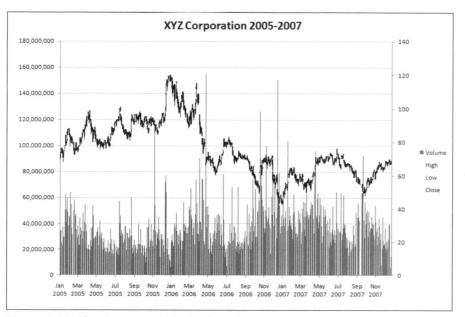

Figure 2-33: Three years (747 days) of stock market data

Keep in mind that stock charts are not limited to financial data, and this chart type can be used for a variety of other purposes. Figure 2-34 shows an example of daily temperature data displayed in a stock chart. For each day, the chart shows the high temperature, the low temperature, and the average temperature.

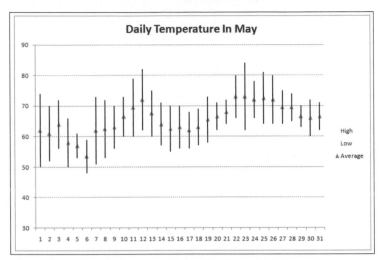

Figure 2-34: Stock charts aren't just for financial information.

Creating Combination Charts

A *combination chart* combines two different chart types, such as a column chart and a line chart. In such a case, each series is assigned its own chart type.

Excel 2007 doesn't offer a direct way to create a combination chart. In other words, you won't find "Combination Chart" in any of the drop-down controls in the Insert⇨Charts group. However, creating a combination chart is easy. Just follow these steps:

1. Create a standard chart (for example, a column chart) that uses all the data series.
2. Click one of the series to select it.
3. Choose Chart Tools⇨Design⇨Type⇨Change Chart Type to display the Change Chart Type dialog box.
4. Select a chart type for the selected series, and click the OK button.

The chart of the selected series is changed to the type you specified.

Keep in mind that the Change Chart Type dialog box behaves differently, depending on the type of chart element that's selected when you issue the command. If a series is selected, the new chart type applies only to that series. If anything other than a series is selected, the chart type applies to all series in the chart.

Figure 2-35 shows a combination chart that contains two series. One series (Sales) is depicted as columns; the other series (Goal) is depicted as a line. This chart makes it very easy to see sales performance relative to each monthly goal.

Figure 2-35: A combination chart.

 ON THE CD

The chart examples in this section are available on the companion CD-ROM. The workbook is named `combination charts.xlsx`.

In some cases, you might want to use a different vertical axis for the different chart series. Figure 2-36 shows a combination chart that displays a line chart for the average monthly temperature values and an area chart for the monthly precipitation. Because these two data series vary so widely in scale, the second vertical axis (for the precipitation) is necessary. If both series were plotted on the same axes, the precipitation series would not even be visible.

When you start experimenting with combination charts, you'll quickly discover that all *3-D charts, stock charts,* and *bubble charts* are off-limits for combination charts. You'll also find that some combinations are of limited value. For example, it's unlikely that anyone would need to create a chart that combines a radar chart and a line chart.

The combination chart shown in Figure 2-37 is an extreme example. It combines five chart types: area, column, line, pie, and scatter. This is for demonstration purposes only and is certainly *not* an example of an effective chart!

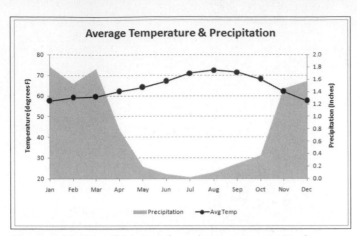

Figure 2-36: A combination chart that uses two vertical axes.

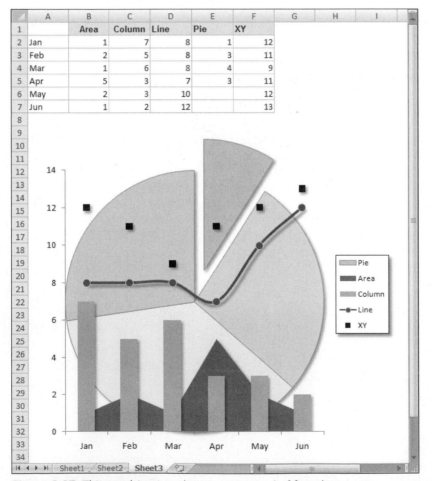

Figure 2-37: This combination chart is comprised of five chart types.

NOTE

A combination chart uses a single plot area. Therefore, you can't create, say, a combination chart that displays three pie charts.

CROSS-REFERENCE

As you see in Chapters 8 and 9, combination charts are the basis for many charting tricks that enable you to create seemingly impossible charts.

Creating and Using Chart Templates

If you find that you frequently make the same types of modifications to your charts, you might be able to save some time and energy by creating a chart template. Or, if you create lots of combination charts, you can create a combination chart template and avoid making the manual adjustments required for a combination chart.

To create a chart template, follow these steps:

1. Create a chart to serve as the basis for your template.

   The data you use for this chart is not critical, but for best results, it should be typical of the data that you'll eventually be plotting with your custom chart type.

2. Apply any formatting and customizations that you like.

   This step determines the appearance of the charts created from the template.

3. Activate the chart and choose Chart Tools⇨Design⇨Type⇨Save as Template.

   Excel displays its Save Chart Template dialog box.

4. Provide a name for the template, and click the Save button.

NOTE

In Windows XP, chart templates, by default, are stored in the following directory:

```
C:\Documents and Settings\<user name>\Application
Data\Microsoft\Templates\Charts
```

Follow these steps to create a chart based on a template:

1. Select the data to be used in the chart.

2. Choose Insert⇨Charts⇨Other Charts⇨All Chart Types.

   Excel displays its Insert Chart dialog box.

3. On the left side of the Insert Chart dialog box, select Templates.

Excel displays an icon for each custom template that has been created.

4. Select the icon that represents the template you want to use, and click the OK button.

Excel creates the chart based on the template you selected.

You can also apply a template to an existing chart. Select the chart and choose Chart Tools⇨ Design⇨Change Chart Type.

NOTE

For some reason, charts created from a template do not respond to changes in the document template. For example, if you apply a different document template, the colors in template-based charts will not change.

Chapter 3

Working with Chart Series

In This Chapter

◆ Adding and removing series from a chart

◆ Finding various ways to change the data used in a chart

◆ Using noncontiguous ranges for a chart

◆ Charting data from different worksheets or workbooks

◆ Dealing with missing data

◆ Controlling a data series by hiding data

◆ Unlinking a chart from its data

◆ Using secondary axes

Every chart consists of at least one series, and the data used in that series is (normally) stored in a worksheet. This chapter provides an in-depth discussion of data series for charts and presents lots of tips to help you select and modify the data used in your charts.

Specifying the Data for Your Chart

When you create a chart, you almost always start by selecting the worksheet data to be plotted. Normally, you select the numeric data as well as the category labels and series names, if they exist.

When creating a chart, a key consideration is the orientation of your data: by rows or by columns. In other words, is the data for each series in a single row or in a single column?

Excel attempts to guess the data orientation by applying a simple rule: If the data rows outnumber the data columns, each series is assumed to occupy a column. If the number of data columns is greater than or equal to the number of data rows, each series is assumed to occupy a row. In other words, Excel always defaults to a chart that has more categories than series.

After you create the chart, it's a simple matter to override Excel's orientation guess. Just activate the chart and choose Chart Tools⇨Design⇨Data⇨Switch Row/Column.

Your choice of orientation determines how many series the chart has, and it affects the appearance and (possibly) the legibility of your chart. Figure 3-1 shows two charts that use the same data. The chart on the left displays three series, arranged in columns. The chart on the right shows four series, arranged in rows.

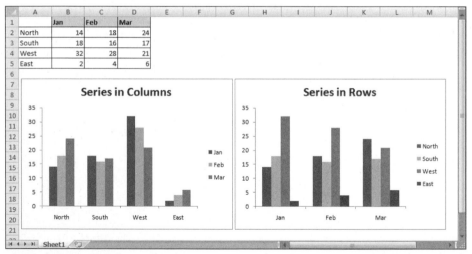

Figure 3-1: Your choice of data orientation (by row or by column) determines the number of series in the chart.

NOTE

Excel allows you to create an empty chart — a chart with no data. For example, select an empty cell and choose Insert⇨Charts⇨Pie, and you get a blank chart. To add data to the chart, choose Chart Tools⇨Design⇨Data⇨Select Data.

Dealing with numeric category labels

It's not uncommon to have category labels that consist of numbers. For example, you may create a chart that shows sales by year, and the years are numeric values. If your category labels include a heading, Excel will (incorrectly) interpret the category labels as a data series. The following figure shows an example.

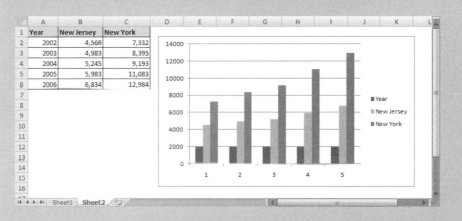

You can, of course, choose Chart Tools⇨Design⇨Data⇨Select Data and use the Select Source Data dialog box to fix the chart. But a more efficient solution is to make a simple change before you create the chart: Remove the header text above the category labels! The following figure shows the chart that was created when the heading was removed from the category label column.

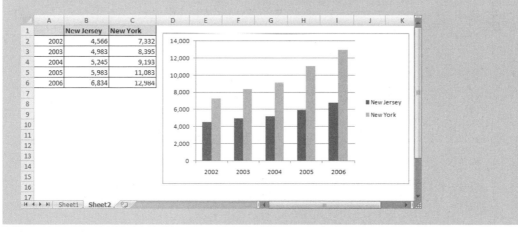

In many situations, you may find it necessary to modify the ranges used by a chart. Specifically, you may want to do the following:

- Add a new series to the chart
- Delete a series from the chart

- Extend the range used by a series (show more data)
- Contract the range used by a series (show less data)
- Add or modify the series names

All these topics are covered in the following sections.

 NOTE

Chart types vary in the number of series that they can use. All charts are limited to a maximum of 255 series. Other charts require a minimum number of series. For example, a high-low-close stock chart requires three series. A pie chart can use only one series.

Adding a New Series to a Chart

Excel provides four ways to add a new series to an existing chart:

- Copy the range, and then paste the data into the chart.
- Use the Select Source Data dialog box.
- Select the chart and extend the blue highlighting rectangle to include the new series.
- Activate the chart, click in the formula bar, and type a SERIES formula manually.

These techniques are described in the sections that follow.

 NEW

In previous versions of Excel, you can select a range of data and drag it into the chart to create a new series. This action does not work in Excel 2007.

 NOTE

Attempting to add a new series to a pie chart has no apparent effect, because a pie chart can have only one series. The series, however, is added to the chart but is not displayed. If you select a different chart type for the chart, the added series is then visible.

Adding a New Series by Copying a Range

One way to add a new series to a chart is to perform a standard copy/paste operation. Follow these steps:

1. Select the range that contains the data to be added.

2. Choose Home⇨Clipboard⇨Copy (or press Ctrl+C).

3. Click the chart to activate it.

4. Choose Home⇨Clipboard⇨Paste (or press Ctrl+V).

For more control when adding data to a chart, choose Home⇨Clipboard⇨Paste⇨Paste Special in Step 4. This command displays the Paste Special dialog box. Figure 3-2 shows a new series (using data in column D) being added to a line chart.

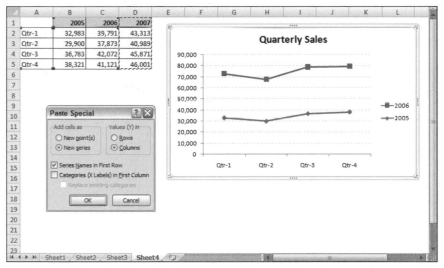

Figure 3-2: Using the Paste Special dialog box to add a series to a chart.

Following are some pointers to keep in mind when you add a new series using the Paste Special dialog box:

- Make sure that the New Series option is selected.

- Excel will guess at the data orientation, but you should verify that the Rows or Columns option is guessed correctly.

- If the range you copied included a cell with the series name, ensure that the Series Names in First Row/Column option is selected.

- If the first column of your range selection included category labels, make sure that the Categories (X Labels) in First Column/Row check box is selected.

- If you want to replace the existing category labels, select the Replace Existing Categories check box.

Adding a New Series by Extending the Range Highlight

If the data for the new series is contiguous with the existing chart's data, you can drag the blue range highlight to add a new series.

Start by selecting any chart element *except* a series. Excel highlights the range with a blue outline. Drag a corner of the blue outline to include the new data, and Excel creates a new series in the chart.

NOTE

This technique works only if the chart uses a contiguous range of data. If the ranges used by the chart series are not contiguous, Excel does not display the blue range highlight.

Adding a New Series Using the Select Source Data Dialog Box

The Select Source Data dialog box provides another way to add a new series to a chart, as follows:

1. Click the chart to activate it.

2. Choose Chart Tools⇨Design⇨Data⇨Select Data to display the Select Source Data dialog box.

3. Click the Add button to display the Edit Series dialog box.

4. Use the range selector controls to specify the cell for the Series Name (optional) and Series Values. (See Figure 3-3.)

5. Click the OK button to close the Edit Series dialog box and return to the Select Source Data dialog box.

6. Click the OK button to close the Select Source Data dialog box, or click the Add button to add another series to the chart.

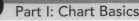

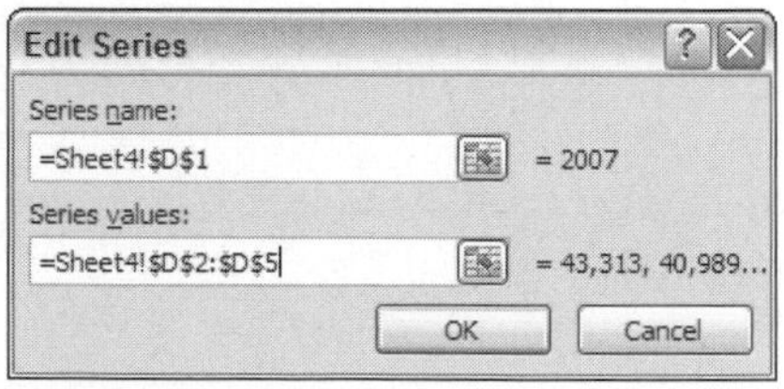

Figure 3-3: Using the Edit Series dialog box to add a series to a chart.

NOTE

The configuration of the Edit Series dialog box varies, depending on the chart type. For example, if the chart is a scatter chart, the Edit Series dialog box displays range selectors for the Series Name, the Series X Values, and the Series Y Values. If the chart is a bubble chart, the dialog box displays an additional range selector for the Series Bubble Size.

Adding a New Series by Typing a New SERIES Formula

Excel provides yet another way to add a new series: Type a new SERIES formula. Follow these steps:

1. Click the chart to activate it.

2. Click the formula bar.

3. Type the new SERIES formula and press Enter.

Figure 3-4 shows a new SERIES formula in the formula bar. When the user presses Enter, this SERIES formula will add the data in column D to the chart.

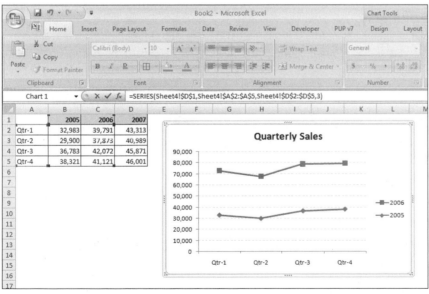

Figure 3-4: Entering a new SERIES formula for a chart creates a new series.

This method is certainly not the most efficient way to add a new series to a chart. It requires that you understand how the SERIES formula works, and (as you might expect) it can be rather error-prone. Note, however, that you don't need to type the SERIES formula from scratch. You can copy an existing SERIES formula, paste it into the formula bar, and then edit the SERIES formula to create a new series.

CROSS-REFERENCE

For more information about the SERIES formula, see the "SERIES formula syntax" sidebar, later in this chapter.

Deleting a Chart Series

The easiest way to delete a series from a chart is to use the keyboard: Select the series and press Delete.

NOTE

Deleting the only series in a chart does not delete the chart. Rather, it gives you an empty chart. If you'd like to delete this empty chart, just press Delete a second time.

You can also use the Select Source Data dialog box to delete a series. Choose Chart Tools➪ Design➪Data➪Select Data to display this dialog box. Then select the series from the list and click the Remove button.

NEW

In previous versions of Excel, you could delete a series via the chart's legend: Select the legend, click the legend text, and press Delete. This technique does not work in Excel 2007. It deletes the legend entry, but not the associated series.

Modifying the Data Range for a Chart Series

After you've created a chart, you may want to modify the data ranges used by the chart. For example, you may need to expand the range to include new data. Or, you might need to substitute an entirely different range. Excel offers a number of ways to perform these operations:

- Drag the range highlights
- Use the Select Source Data dialog box
- Edit the SERIES formula

Each of these techniques is described in the sections that follow.

CROSS-REFERENCE

Chapter 7 discusses a number of techniques that enable you to set up a "dynamic" range such that the chart adjusts automatically when you add new data.

Using Range Highlighting to Change Series Data

When you select a series in a chart, Excel highlights the worksheet ranges used in that series. This range highlighting consists of a colored outline around each range used by the series. Figure 3-5 shows an example in which the chart series (Region 1) is selected. Excel highlights the following ranges:

- C2 (the series name)
- B3:B8 (the category labels)
- C3:C8 (the values)

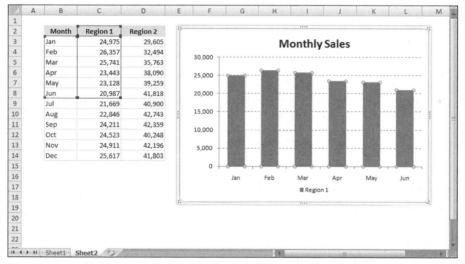

Figure 3-5: Selecting a chart series highlights the data used by the series.

Note that these cell addresses for these ranges also appear in the SERIES formula for the selected series. Each of the highlighted ranges contains a small "handle" at each corner. You can perform two operations with the highlighted data:

- **Expand or contract the data range:** Click one of the handles and drag it to expand the outlined range (specify more data) or contract the data range (specify less data). When you move your cursor over a handle, the mouse pointer changes to a double arrow.

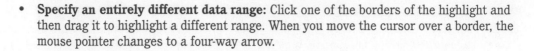

- **Specify an entirely different data range:** Click one of the borders of the highlight and then drag it to highlight a different range. When you move the cursor over a border, the mouse pointer changes to a four-way arrow.

Figure 3-6 shows the chart after the data range has been changed. In this case, the highlight around cell C2 was dragged to cell D2, and the highlight around C3:C8 was dragged to D3:D8 and then expanded to include D3:D14. Notice that the range for the category labels (B3:B8) has not been modified. To finish the job, that range needs to be expanded to B3:B14.

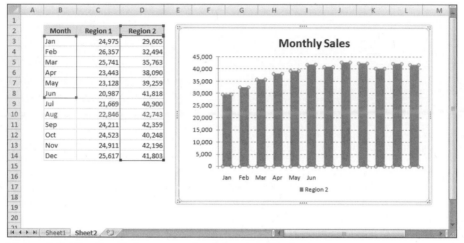

Figure 3-6: The chart's data range has been modified.

Modifying chart source data by using the range highlights is probably the simplest method. Note, however, that this technique works only with embedded charts (not with chart sheets). In addition, it does not work when the chart's data is in a worksheet other than the sheet that contains the embedded chart.

NOTE

A surface chart is a special case. You cannot select an individual series in a surface chart. But when you select the plot area of a surface chart, Excel highlights all the data used in the chart. You can then use the range highlighting to change the ranges used in the chart.

Using the Select Data Source Dialog Box to Change Series Data

Another method of modifying a series data range is to use the Select Data Source dialog box. Select your chart and then choose Chart Tools⇔Design⇔Data⇔Select Data. Figure 3-7 shows the Select Data Source dialog box.

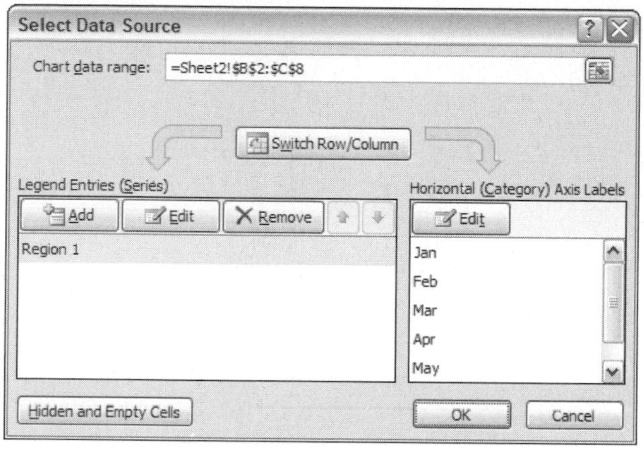

Figure 3-7: The Select Data Source dialog box.

Notice that the Select Data Source dialog box has three parts:

- The top part of the dialog box shows the entire data range used by the chart. You can change this range by selecting new data.

- The lower-left part displays a list of each series. Select a series and click the Edit button to display the Edit Series dialog box to change the data used by a single series. (See Figure 3-8.)

- The lower-right part displays the category axis labels. Click the Edit button to display the Axis Labels dialog box to change the range used as the axis labels.

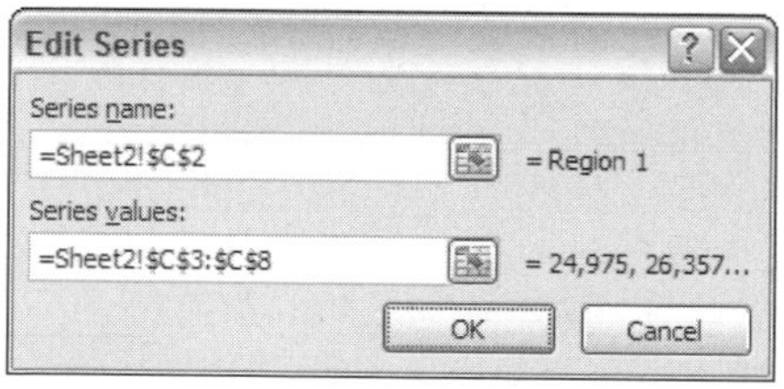

Figure 3-8: The Edit Series dialog box is one way to change the data used by a series.

NOTE

The Edit Series dialog box can vary somewhat, depending on the chart type. The Edit Series dialog box for a bubble chart, for example, has four range selector controls: Series Name, Series X Values, Series Y Values, and Series Bubble Size.

Editing the SERIES Formula to Change Series Data

Every chart series has its own SERIES formula. When you select a data series in a particular chart, its SERIES formula appears in the formula bar. In Figure 3-9, for example, you can see one of two SERIES formulas in the formula bar for a chart that displays two data series.

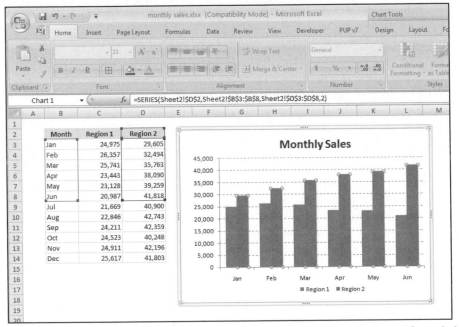

Figure 3-9: The SERIES formula for the selected data series appears in the formula bar.

Although a SERIES formula is displayed in the formula bar, it is not a "real" formula. In other words, you can't put this formula into a cell, and you can't use worksheet functions within the SERIES formula. You can, however, edit the arguments in the SERIES formula to change the ranges used by the series. To edit the SERIES formula, just click in the formula bar and use standard editing techniques. Refer to the nearby sidebar, "SERIES formula syntax," to find out about the various arguments for a SERIES formula.

NOTE

When you modify a series data range using either of the techniques discussed previously in this section, the SERIES formula is also modified. In fact, those techniques are simply easy ways of editing the SERIES formula.

Following is an example of a SERIES formula:

```
=SERIES(Sheet2!$D$2,Sheet2!$B$3:$B$8,Sheet2!$D$3:$D$8,2)
```

SERIES formula syntax

A SERIES formula has the following syntax:

```
=SERIES(series_name, category_labels, values, order, sizes)
```

The arguments you can use in the SERIES formula include the following:

- *series_name*: (Optional) A reference to the cell that contains the series name used in the legend. If the chart has only one series, the name argument is used as the title. This argument can also consist of text, in quotation marks. If omitted, Excel creates a default series name (for example, Series 1).

- *category_labels*: (Optional) A reference to the range that contains the labels for the category axis. If omitted, Excel uses consecutive integers beginning with 1. For scatter charts, this argument specifies the *x* values. A noncontiguous range reference is also valid. (The ranges' addresses are separated by a comma and enclosed in parentheses.) The argument may also consist of an array of comma-separated values (or text in quotation marks) enclosed in braces.

- *values*: (Required) A reference to the range that contains the values for the series. For scatter charts, this argument specifies the *y* values. A noncontiguous range reference is also valid. (The ranges' addresses are separated by a comma and enclosed in parentheses.) The argument may also consist of an array of comma-separated values enclosed in braces.

- *order*: (Required) An integer that specifies the plotting order of the series. This argument is relevant only if the chart has more than one series. Using a reference to a cell is not allowed.

- *sizes*: (Only for bubble charts) A reference to the range that contains the values for the size of the bubbles in a bubble chart. A noncontiguous range reference is also valid. (The ranges' addresses are separated by a comma and enclosed in parentheses.) The argument may also consist of an array of values enclosed in braces.

This SERIES formula does the following:

- Specifies that cell D2 (on Sheet2) contains the series name

- Specifies that the category labels are in B3:B8 on Sheet2

- Specifies that the data values are in D3:D8, also on Sheet2

- Specifies that the series will be plotted second on the chart (the final argument is 2)

Notice that range references in a SERIES formula always include the worksheet name, and the range references are always absolute references. An absolute reference, as you may know, uses a dollar sign before the row and column part of the reference. If you edit a SERIES formula and remove the sheet name or make the cell references relative, Excel will override these changes.

Understanding Series Names

Every chart series has a name, which is displayed in the chart's legend. If you don't explicitly provide a name for a series, it will have a default name, such as Series1, Series2, and so on.

The easiest way to name a series is to do so when you create the chart. Typically, a series name is contained in a cell adjacent to the series data. For example, if your data is arranged in columns, the column headers usually contain the series names. If you select the series names along with the chart data, those names will be applied automatically.

Figure 3-10 shows a chart with three series. The series names, which are stored in B3:D3, are Main, N. County, and Westside. The SERIES formula for the first data series is as follows:

```
=SERIES(Sheet1!$B$3,Sheet1!$A$4:$A$8,Sheet1!$B$4:$B$8,1)
```

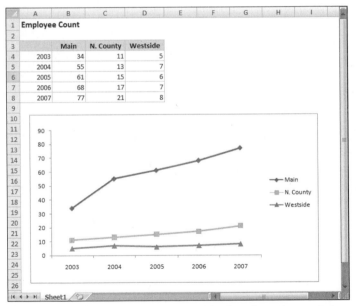

Figure 3-10: The series names are picked up from the worksheet.

Note that the first argument for this SERIES formula is a reference to the cell that contains the series name.

Changing a Series Name

The series name is the text that appears in a chart's legend. In some cases, you may prefer the chart to display a name other than the text that's in the worksheet. It's a simple matter to change the name of a series. Follow these steps:

1. Activate the chart.

2. Choose Chart Tools⇨Design⇨Data⇨Select Data to display the Select Data Source dialog box.

3. In the Select Data Source dialog box, select the series that you want to modify, and click the Edit button to display the Edit Series dialog box.

4. Type the new name in the Series Name box.

Normally, the Series Name box contains a cell reference. But you can override this and enter any text.

NOTE
If you go back to a series that you've already renamed, you'll find that Excel has converted your text into a formula — an equal sign, followed by the text you entered (the new series name), in quotation marks.

Figure 3-11 shows the previous chart, after changing the series names. The first argument in each of the SERIES formulas no longer displays a cell reference. It now contains the literal text. For example, the SERIES formula for the first series is as follows:

```
=SERIES("Branch 1",Sheet1!$A$4:$A$8,Sheet1!$B$4:$B$8,1)
```

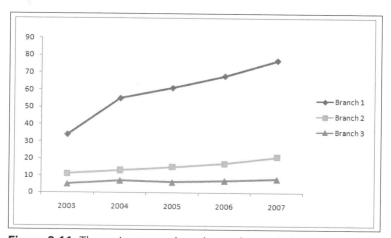

Figure 3-11: The series names have been changed; the new names are shown in the legend.

If you need to change the name of a series, you may find it easier to edit the SERIES formula directly.

Deleting a Series Name

To delete a series name, use the Edit Series dialog box as described previously. Highlight the range reference (or text) in the Series Name box and press Delete.

Alternatively, you can edit the SERIES formula and remove the first argument. Here's an example of a SERIES formula for a series with no specified name (it will use the default name):

```
=SERIES(,Sheet2!$A$2:$A$6,Sheet2!$B$2:$B$6,1)
```

 NOTE

When you remove the first argument in a SERIES formula, make sure that you do not delete the comma that follows the first argument. The comma is required as a place-holder to indicate the missing argument.

To create a series with no name, use a set of empty quotation marks for the first argument in the SERIES formula. A series with no name still appears in the chart's legend, but no text is displayed.

Adjusting the Series Plot Order

Every chart series has a plot order parameter. A chart's legend usually displays the series names in the order in which they are plotted. I say usually, because you do find exceptions. For example, consider a combination chart that displays a column series and a line series. Changing the series order does not change the order in which the series are listed in the legend.

To change the plot order of a chart's data series, use the Select Data Source dialog box. In the lower-left list, the series are listed in the order in which they are plotted. Select a series, and then use the up- or down-arrow buttons to adjust its position in the list — which also changes the plot order of the series.

Alternatively, you can edit the SERIES formulas — specifically, the fourth parameter in the SERIES formulas. See the "SERIES formula syntax" sidebar, earlier in this chapter, for more information about SERIES formulas.

For some charts, the plot order is not important. For others, however, you may want to change the order in which the series are plotted. Figure 3-12 shows a stacked column chart generated from the data in A1:E1. Notice that the columns are stacked, beginning with the first data series (Region 1) on the bottom. You might prefer to stack the columns in the order in which the data appears. To do so, you need to change the plot order.

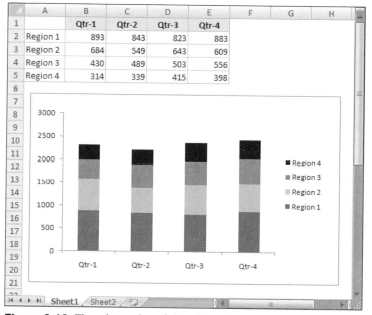

Figure 3-12: The plot order of this chart does not correspond to the order of the data.

After changing the plot order of the series, the chart now appears as in Figure 3-13.

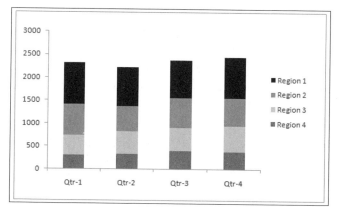

Figure 3-13: After changing the plot order, the stacked columns correspond to the order of the data.

Figure 3-14 shows another example. This chart displays three data series in a 3-D column chart. The columns for the Laptops and PDAs series are obscured by the columns for the Desktops series. One solution is to edit the plot order parameter of the SERIES formulas, as described previously. But in this case, you can use a more direct solution. Follow these steps:

1. Select the depth axis (which contains the series names), and press Ctrl+1 to display the Format Axis dialog box.

2. Click the Axis Options tab in the Format Axis dialog box.

3. Select the Series in Reverse Order check box.

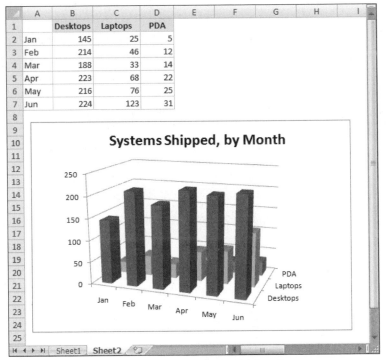

Figure 3-14: Some of the data points are obscured.

The result, shown in Figure 3-15, is a much more legible chart. Note that the option to plot the series in reverse order does not actually change the plot order for the SERIES formulas. The SERIES formulas remain the same, but Excel displays them in reverse order on the series axis. Consequently, if the chart has a legend, the order of the entries in the legend remains the same.

NOTE

Perhaps a better solution to hidden columns in a 3-D chart is to use a different chart type that doesn't suffer from this problem.

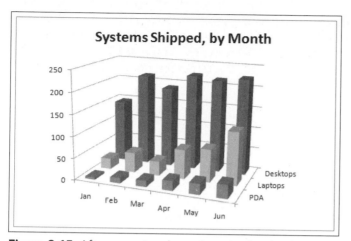

Figure 3-15: After reversing the series axis, the chart is more legible.

Charting a Noncontiguous Range

Most of the time, a chart series consists of a contiguous range of cells. But Excel does allow you to plot data that is not in a contiguous range. Figure 3-16 shows an example of a noncontiguous series. This chart displays monthly data for the first and fourth quarter. The data in this single series is contained in rows 2:4 and 11:13. Notice that the category labels display Jan, Feb, Mar, Oct, Nov, and Dec.

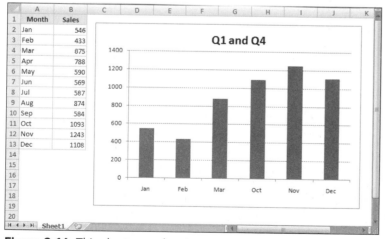

Figure 3-16: This chart uses data in a noncontiguous range.

The SERIES formula for this series is as follows:

```
=SERIES(,(Sheet1!$A$2:$A$4,Sheet1!$A$11:$A$13),(Sheet1!$B$2:$B$4,Sheet1!$B$11:$B$13),1)
```

The first argument is omitted, so Excel uses the default series name. The second argument specifies six cells in column A as the category labels. The third argument specifies six corresponding cells in column B as the data values. Note that the range arguments for the noncontiguous ranges are displayed in parentheses, and each subrange is separated by a comma.

NOTE

When a series uses a noncontiguous range of cells, Excel does not display the range highlights when the series is selected. Therefore, the only way to modify the series is to use the Select Data Source dialog box or to edit the SERIES formula manually.

Using Series on Different Sheets

Typically, data to be used on a chart resides on a single sheet. Excel, however, does allow a chart to use data from any number of worksheets, and the worksheets need not even be in the same workbook.

NOTE

Although a chart series can refer to data in other worksheets, the data for each series must reside on a single sheet.

Normally, you select all the data for a chart before you create the chart. But if your chart uses data from different worksheets, you need to create the chart using data from a single sheet and then either edit the existing series or add new series after the chart is made (see the section "Adding a New Series to a Chart," earlier in this chapter).

Figure 3-17 shows a chart that uses data from two other worksheets.

The SERIES formulas for this chart are as follows:

```
=SERIES(Region1!$A$2,Region1!$B$1:$G$1,Region1!$B$2:$G$2,1)
=SERIES(Region2!$A$2,,Region2!$B$2:$G$2,2)
```

TIP

Another way to handle data in different worksheets is to create a summary range in a single worksheet. This summary range consists of simple formulas that refer to the data in other sheets. Then, you can create a chart from the summary range.

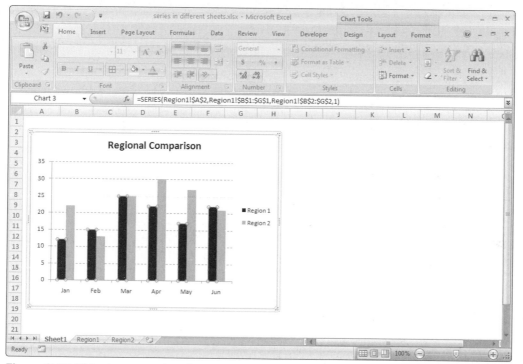

Figure 3-17: This chart uses data from two worksheets.

Handling Missing Data

Sometimes, data that you use in a chart may lack one or more data points. Excel offers the following ways to handle the missing data:

- Ignore the missing data. Plotted data series will have a gap.

- Treat the missing data as zero values.

- Interpolate the missing data (for line and scatter charts only).

For some reason, Excel makes these options rather difficult to locate. The Ribbon doesn't contain these options, and you don't specify these options in the Format Data Series dialog box. Rather, you must follow these steps:

1. Select your chart.

2. Choose Chart Tools⇨Design⇨Data⇨Select Data to display the Select Data Source dialog box.

3. In the Select Data Source dialog box, click the Hidden and Empty Cells button. Excel displays the dialog box shown in Figure 3-18.

4. Choose the appropriate option, and click the OK button.

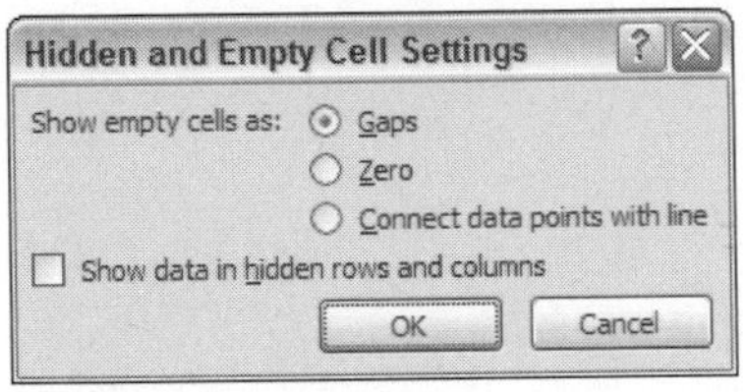

Figure 3-18: Use the Hidden and Empty Cell Settings dialog box to specify how to handle missing data.

The setting that you choose applies only to the active chart and applies to all series in the chart. In other words, you can't specify a different missing data option for different series in the same chart.

NOTE

These settings are applicable only for line charts, scatter charts, and radar charts. For all other chart types, missing data is simply not plotted.

Figure 3-19 shows three charts that depict the three missing data options. The chart shows temperature readings at one-hour intervals, and four data points are missing. The "correct" missing data option depends on the message that you want to convey. In the top chart, the missing data is obvious because of the gaps in the line. In the middle chart, the missing data is shown as zero — which is clearly misleading. In the bottom chart, the missing data is interpolated. Because of the time-based and relatively "smooth" nature of the data, interpolating the missing data may be an appropriate choice.

TIP

For line charts, you can force Excel to interpolate missing values by placing =NA() in the empty cells. Those cell values will be interpolated, regardless of the missing data option that is in effect for the chart. For other charts, =NA() is interpreted as zero.

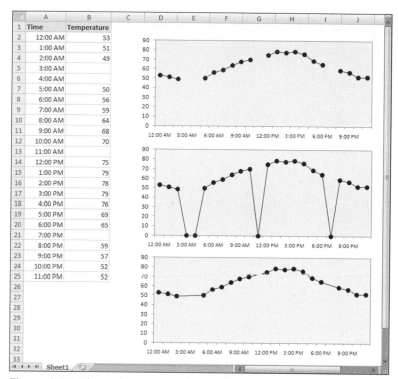

	A	B
1	Time	Temperature
2	12:00 AM	53
3	1:00 AM	51
4	2:00 AM	49
5	3:00 AM	
6	4:00 AM	
7	5:00 AM	50
8	6:00 AM	56
9	7:00 AM	59
10	8:00 AM	64
11	9:00 AM	68
12	10:00 AM	70
13	11:00 AM	
14	12:00 PM	75
15	1:00 PM	79
16	2:00 PM	78
17	3:00 PM	79
18	4:00 PM	76
19	5:00 PM	69
20	6:00 PM	65
21	7:00 PM	
22	8:00 PM	59
23	9:00 PM	57
24	10:00 PM	52
25	11:00 PM	52

Figure 3-19: These three charts depict the three ways to present missing data in a chart.

Controlling a Data Series by Hiding Data

Usually, Excel doesn't plot data that is in a hidden row or column. You can sometimes use this to your advantage, because it's an easy way to control what data appears in the chart.

Figure 3-20 shows a scatter chart that uses data stored in a table (created by choosing Insert⇨Tables⇨Table). Figure 3-21 shows the same chart after I applied a filter to the table. The filter hides all rows except those in which the x value is greater than or equal to 300.

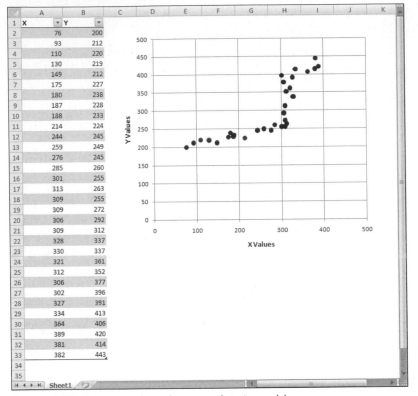

Figure 3-20: A scatter chart that uses data in a table.

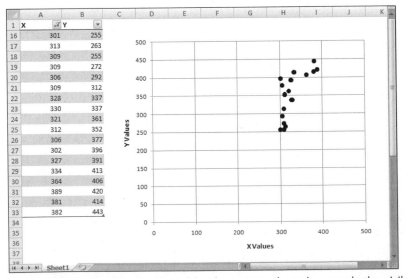

Figure 3-21: After filtering the table, the scatter chart shows only the visible rows.

> **Use range names in a SERIES formula? Not anymore**
>
> In previous versions of Excel, you could substitute a range name for a range address in a SERIES formula. Unfortunately, this handy technique no longer works reliably in Excel 2007. However, if you open an older workbook that uses a range name in a SERIES formula, the chart displays fine — but you can't edit the SERIES formula.
>
> Maybe this is a just a problem with the initial release of Excel 2007; it might be fixed in a subsequent service pack.

In some cases, when you're working with outlines or filtered tables (both of which use hidden rows), you may not like the idea that hidden data is removed from your chart. To override this, activate the chart and choose Chart Tools➪Design➪Data➪Select Data to display the Select Data Source dialog box. Click the Hidden and Empty Cells button, and select the Show Data in Hidden Rows and Columns check box.

NOTE

The Show Data in Hidden Rows and Columns setting applies only to the active chart. It is not a global setting that would be applied to all charts.

Unlinking a Chart Series from Its Data Range

Normally, an Excel chart uses data stored in a range. Change the data in the range, and the chart updates automatically. In some cases, you may want to "unlink" the chart from its data ranges and produce a *static chart* — a chart that never changes. For example, if you plot data generated by various what-if scenarios, you may want to save a chart that represents some baseline so that you can compare it with other scenarios. You can create such a chart in the following ways:

- Convert the chart to a picture
- Convert the range references to arrays

Converting a Chart to a Picture

To convert a chart to a static picture, follow these steps:

1. Create the chart as usual and make any necessary modifications.
2. Click the chart to activate it.

3. Choose Home⇨Clipboard⇨Copy (or press Ctrl+C).

4. Click any cell to deselect the chart.

5. Choose Home⇨Clipboard⇨Paste⇨Paste as Picture.

The result is a picture of the original chart. This picture can be edited as a picture, but not as a chart. In other words, you can no longer modify properties such as chart type, data labels, and so on.

Although a chart converted to a picture cannot be edited as a chart, it can be edited as a picture. When you select such a picture, you see Excel's Picture Tools⇨Format tab. Figure 3-22 shows a few examples of built-in formatting options applied to a picture of a chart.

Converting Range Reference to Arrays

The other way to unlink a chart from its data is to convert the SERIES formula range references to arrays. Figure 3-23 shows an example of a pie chart that does not use data stored in a worksheet. Rather, the chart's data is stored directly in the SERIES formula, which is as follows:

```
=SERIES(,{"Work","Sleep","Drive","Eat","Other"},{9,7,2,1,5},1)
```

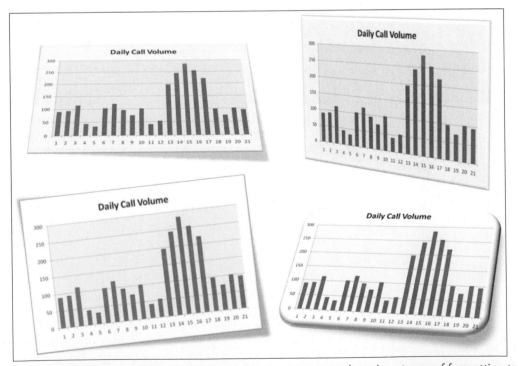

Figure 3-22: After converting a chart to a picture, you can apply various types of formatting to the picture.

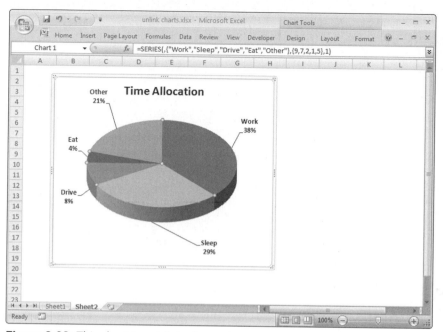

Figure 3-23: This chart is not linked to a data range.

The first argument, the series name, is omitted. The second argument consists of an array of five text strings. Notice that each array element appears in quotation marks and is separated by a comma. The array is enclosed in braces. The chart's data is stored as another array (the third argument).

This chart was originally created by using data stored in a range. Then, the SERIES formula was "delinked" from the range and the original data was deleted. The result is a chart that does not rely on data stored in a range.

Follow these steps to convert the range references in a SERIES formula to arrays:

1. Create the chart as usual.

2. Click the chart series.

   The SERIES formula appears in the formula bar.

3. Click the formula bar.

4. Press F9.

5. Press Enter, and the range references are converted to arrays.

Repeat this procedure for each series in the chart. This method of unlinking a chart series (as opposed to creating a picture) enables you to continue to edit the chart. Note that you can also convert just a single argument to an array. Highlight the argument in the SERIES formula and press F9.

NOTE

Excel imposes a 1,024-character limit to the length of a SERIES formula, so this technique does not work if a chart series contains a large number of values or category labels.

Working with Multiple Axes

A chart can use zero, two, three, or four axes, and any or all of them can be hidden if desired.

Pie charts and doughnut charts have no axes. Common chart types, such as a standard column or line chart, use a single category axis and a single value axis. If your chart has at least two series — and it's not a 3-D chart — you can create a secondary value axis. Each series is associated with either the primary or the secondary value axis. Why use two value axes? Two value axes are most often used when the data being plotted in a series varies drastically in scale from the data in another series.

CREATING A SECONDARY VALUE AXIS

Figure 3-24 shows a line chart with two data series: Income and Profit Margin. Compared to the Income values, the Profit Margin numbers (represented by squares) are so small that they barely show up on the chart. This is a good candidate for a secondary value axis.

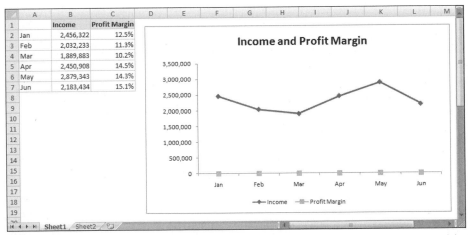

Figure 3-24: The values in the Profit Margin series are so small that they aren't visible in the chart.

To add a secondary value axis, follow these steps:

1. Select the Profit Margin series on the chart.
2. Press Ctrl+1 to display the Format Data Series dialog box.
3. In the Format Data Series dialog box, click the Series Options tab.
4. Choose the Secondary Axis option.

A new value axis is added to the right side of the chart, and the Profit Margin series uses that value axis. Figure 3-25 shows the dual-axis chart. I added axis titles (by choosing Chart Tools⇨Layout⇨Labels⇨Axis Titles) so that the reader can tell which axis applies to which data series.

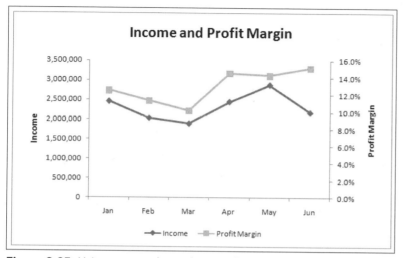

Figure 3-25: Using a secondary value axis for the Profit Margin series.

CREATING A CHART WITH FOUR AXES

Very few situations warrant a chart with four axes. The problem, of course, is that using four axes almost always causes the chart to be difficult to understand. An exception is scatter charts. Figure 3-26 shows a scatter chart that has two series, and the series vary quite a bit in magnitude on both dimensions. If the objective is to compare the shape of the lines, this chart does not do a very good job because most of the chart consists of white space. Using four axes might solve the problem.

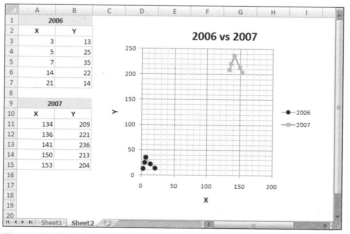

Figure 3-26: The two series vary in magnitude.

Follow these steps to add two new value axes for this scatter chart:

1. Select the 2007 series.

2. Press Ctrl+1 to display the Format Data Series dialog box.

3. In the Format Data Series dialog box, click the Series Options tab.

4. Choose the Secondary Axis option.

   At this point, each of the series has its own y-value axis (one on the left; one on the right), but they share a common x-value axis.

5. Choose Chart Tools⇨Layout⇨Axes⇨Secondary Horizontal Axis⇨Show Default Axis.

   Note that this Ribbon command is available only if you've assigned a series to the secondary axis.

Figure 3-27 shows the result. The 2006 series uses the left and bottom axes, and the 2007 series uses the right and top axes (I added axis titles to clarify this). The scales for each axis can be adjusted separately.

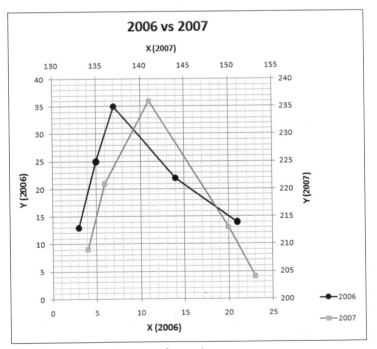

Figure 3-27: This chart uses four value axes.

Chapter 4

Formatting and Customizing Charts

In This Chapter

◆ Getting an overview of chart formatting

◆ Formatting fill and borders

◆ Formatting chart background elements

◆ Working with chart titles

◆ Working with legends, data labels, gridlines, and data tables

◆ Understanding chart axes

◆ Formatting 3-D charts

Excel usually does an adequate job of transforming a range of numbers into a chart. Often, the basic chart that Excel creates is good enough. If not, many users are content to apply a different prebuilt layout (using Chart Tools⇨Design⇨Chart Layouts) or switch to a different prebuilt style (using Chart Tools⇨Design⇨Chart Styles).

If you create a chart for your own use, spending a lot of time on formatting and customizing the chart may not be worth the effort. But if you want to create the most effective chart possible, or if you need to create a chart for presentation purposes, you will want to take advantage of the additional customization techniques available in Excel.

This chapter discusses the ins and outs of formatting and customizing your charts. It's easy to become overwhelmed with all the chart customization options. However, the more you work with charts, the easier it becomes. Even advanced users tend to experiment a great deal with chart customization, and they rely heavily on trial and error — a technique that I strongly recommend.

Chart Formatting Overview

Customizing a chart involves changing the appearance of its elements, as well as possibly adding new elements to it or removing elements from it. These changes can be purely cosmetic (such as changing colors or modifying line widths) or quite substantial (such as changing the axis scales or rotating a 3-D chart).

Before you can customize a chart, you must activate it:

- To activate an *embedded chart*, click anywhere within the chart.

- To deactivate an embedded chart, just click anywhere in the worksheet (or, press Esc once or twice).

- To activate a chart on a *chart sheet*, click its sheet tab.

TIP

If you press Ctrl while you activate an embedded chart, the chart is selected as an object. In fact, you can select multiple charts using this technique. When a group of charts is selected, you can move and resize them all at once. In addition, the tools in the Drawing Tools⇨Format⇨Arrange group are available. For example, you can align the selected charts vertically or horizontally.

Selecting Chart Elements

Modifying a chart is similar to everything else you do in Excel: First you make a selection (in this case, select a chart element); then you issue a command to do something with the selection.

You can select only one chart element at a time. For example, if you want to change the font for two axis labels, you must work on each label separately. The exceptions to the single-selection rule are elements that consist of multiple parts, such as gridlines. Selecting one gridline selects them all.

Excel provides three ways to select a particular chart element:

- Use the mouse
- Use the keyboard
- Use the Chart Elements control

These selection methods are described in the following sections.

SELECTING WITH THE MOUSE

To select a chart element with your mouse, just click the element.

TIP

To ensure that you've selected the chart element that you intended to select, check the name that's displayed in the Chart Elements control. The Chart Elements control is available in two Ribbon groups: Chart Tools⇨Layout⇨Current Selection, and Chart Tools⇨Format⇨Current Selection. The Chart Elements control displays the name of the selected chart element, and you can also use this control to select a particular element. See the section "Selecting with the Chart Elements Control," later in this chapter.

When you move the cursor over a selected chart, a small "chart tip" displays the name of the chart element under the mouse pointer. When the mouse pointer is over a data point, the chart tip also displays the series, category, and value of the data point. If you find these chart tips annoying, you can turn them off. Select Office⇨Excel Options, and click the Advanced tab in the Excel Options dialog box. In the Display section, you'll find two check boxes: Show Chart Element Names on Hover, and Show Data Point Values on Hover.

Some chart elements (such as a chart series, a legend, and data labels) consist of multiple items. For example, a chart series is made up of individual data points. To select a single data point, you need to click twice: First click the series to select it; then click the specific element within the series (for example, a column or a line chart marker). Selecting an individual element enables you to apply formatting only to a particular data point in a series. This might be useful if you'd like one marker in a line chart to stand out from the others.

NOTE

If you find that some chart elements are difficult to select with the mouse, you're not alone. If you rely on the mouse for selecting a chart element, it may take several clicks before the desired element is actually selected. And in some cases, selecting a particular element with the mouse is impossible. Unfortunately, this problem has gotten worse in Excel 2007. Fortunately, Excel provides other ways to select a chart element, and it's worth your while to be familiar with them.

SELECTING WITH THE KEYBOARD

When a chart is active, you can use the up- and down-arrow keys on your keyboard to cycle among the chart's elements. Again, keep your eye on the Chart Elements control to verify which element is selected.

When a chart series is selected, use the left- and right-arrow keys to select an individual data point within the series. Similarly, when a set of data labels is selected, you can select a specific data label by using the left- or right-arrow key. And when a legend is selected, you can select individual elements within the legend by using the left- or right-arrow keys.

Chart element selection weirdness

As you gain experience working with Excel 2007 charts, you may notice some odd things when you try to select chart elements. For example, if you add a text box to a chart, you may find that it "disappears" before you can add text to it. It may take several attempts to click the text box before it is activated. Unfortunately, you can't use the Chart Elements control to select the text box. But you can use the arrow keys method — but only the down-arrow key. If you cycle through the chart elements using the up-arrow key, text boxes are ignored!

Other times, you may discover that the arrow keys don't work at all. Even though a chart is activated, pressing the up- and down-arrow keys selects worksheet cells rather than chart elements.

If the Format dialog box is displayed, things get even quirkier. Sometimes, the arrow keys select the different tabs in the Format dialog box. Other times, they work normally. And, I've discovered that sometimes you can't use the Delete key to delete a chart element (or a chart) when the Format dialog box is displayed.

Hopefully, this quirky behavior will be fixed in a future service release.

SELECTING WITH THE CHART ELEMENTS CONTROL

As I noted earlier, the Chart Elements control displays the name of the selected chart element. This control contains a drop-down list of all chart elements (except shapes and text boxes), so you can also use it to select a particular chart element.

TIP

Although the Chart Elements control is available in two Ribbon groups (Chart Tools⇨ Layout⇨Current Selection, and Chart Tools⇨Format⇨Current Selection), you may find that you also need to use it when the Chart Tools⇨Design tab is displayed. You may prefer to put this control on your Quick Access toolbar so that it's always visible. Just right-click the drop-down arrow on the right side of the Chart Elements control and choose Add to Quick Access Toolbar from the shortcut menu.

The Chart Elements control is a drop-down list that lets you select a particular chart element from the active chart (see Figure 4-1). This control lists only the top-level elements in the chart. To select an individual data point within a series, for example, you need to select the series and then use one of the other techniques to select the desired data point.

NOTE

When a single data point is selected, the Chart Elements control *will* display the name of the selected element, even though it's not actually available for selection in the drop-down list.

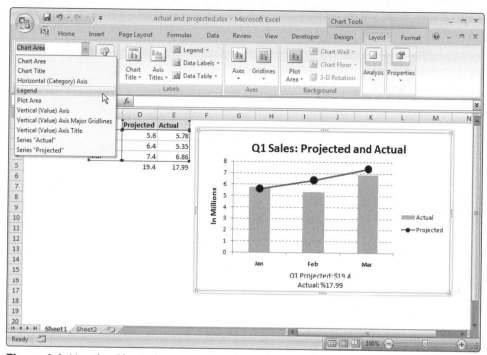

Figure 4-1: Use the Chart Elements control to select an element on a chart.

Common Chart Elements

Table 4-1 contains a list of the various chart elements that you may encounter. Note that the actual chart elements that are present in a particular chart depend on the chart type and on the customizations that you've performed on the chart.

TABLE 4-1   CHART ELEMENTS

Part	Description
Category Axis	The axis that represents the chart's categories.
Category Axis Title	The title for the category axis.
Chart Area	The chart's background.
Chart Title	The chart's title.
Data Label	A data label for a point in a series. The name is preceded by the series and the point. Example: Series 1 Point 1 Data Label.

continued

TABLE 4-1   **CHART ELEMENTS** *(continued)*

Part	Description
Data Labels	Data labels for a series. The name is preceded by the series. Example: Series 1 Data Labels.
Data Table	The chart's data table.
Display Units Label	The units label for an axis.
Up/Down Bars	Vertical bars in a line chart or stock market chart.
Drop Lines	Lines that extend from each data point downward to the axis (line and area charts only).
Error Bars	Error bars for a series. The name is preceded by the series. Example: Series 1 Error Bars.
Floor	The floor of a 3-D chart.
Gridlines	A chart can have major and minor gridlines for each axis. The element is named using the axis and the type of gridlines. Example: Vertical Axis Major Gridlines.
High-Low Lines	Vertical lines in a line chart or stock market chart.
Legend	The chart's legend.
Legend Entry	One of the text entries inside a legend.
Plot Area	The chart's plot area — the actual chart, without the legend.
Point	A point in a data series. The name is preceded by the series name. Example: Series 1 Point 2.
Secondary Category Axis	The second axis that represents the chart's categories.
Secondary Category Axis Title	The title for the secondary category axis.
Secondary Value Axis	The second axis that represents the chart's values.
Secondary Value Axis Title	The title for the secondary value axis.
Series	A data series.
Series Axis	The axis that represents the chart's series (3-D charts only).
Series Lines	A line that connects a series in a stacked column or stacked bar chart.
Trendline	A trendline for a data series.
Trendline Equation	The equation for a trendline.

Part	Description
Value Axis	The axis that represents the chart's values. There also may be a Secondary Value Axis.
Value Axis Title	The title for the value axis.
Walls	The walls of a 3-D chart only (except 3-D pie charts).

User Interface Choices for Formatting

When a chart element is selected, you have some choices as to which user interface method you can use to format the element:

- The Ribbon
- The Mini toolbar
- The Format dialog box

FORMATTING BY USING THE RIBBON

The controls in the Chart Tools⇨Format tab are used to change the appearance of the selected chart element. For example, if you would like to change the color of a series in a column chart, one approach is to use one of the predefined styles in the Chart⇨Tools⇨ Format⇨Shape Styles group.

For a bit more control, follow these steps:

1. Click the series to select it.
2. Choose Chart Tools⇨Format⇨Shape Styles⇨Shape Fill, and select a color.
3. Choose Chart Tools⇨Format⇨Shape Styles⇨Shape Outline, and select a color for the outline of the columns. You can also modify the outline width and the type of dashes (if any).
4. Choose Chart Tools⇨Format⇨Shape Styles⇨Shape Effects, and add one or more effects to the series.

Note that you can modify the Shape Fill, Shape Outline, and Shape Effects for almost every element in a chart.

Here's one way to change the formatting of a chart's title so that the text is white on a black background:

1. Click the chart title to select it.

2. Choose Chart Tools⇨Format⇨Shape Styles⇨Shape Fill, and select black.

3. Choose Chart Tools⇨Format⇨WordArt Styles⇨Text Fill, and select white.

Notice that some of the controls in the Home⇨Font and Home⇨Alignment groups are also available when a chart element is selected. An alternate way of changing a chart's title to white on black is as follows:

1. Click the chart title to select it.

2. Choose Insert⇨Font⇨Fill Color, and select black.

3. Choose Insert⇨Font⇨Font Color, and select white.

 NOTE

It's important to understand that the Ribbon commands do not contain all possible formatting options for chart elements. In fact, the Ribbon controls contain only a small subset of the chart formatting commands. For optimal control, you need to use the Format dialog box (discussed later in this chapter).

FORMATTING BY USING THE MINI TOOLBAR

When you right-click a chart element that contains text, Excel displays its shortcut menu, with the Mini toolbar on top. Figure 4-2 shows the Mini toolbar that appears when you right-click a chart title. Use the Mini toolbar to make formatting changes to the text (including the fill and border). Note that the Mini toolbar also works if you've selected only some of the characters in the chart element. In such a case, the text formatting applies only to the selected characters.

 NOTE

A few of the common keystroke combinations also work when a chart element that contains text is selected — specifically: Ctrl+B (bold), Ctrl+I (italic), and Ctrl+U (underline).

FORMATTING BY USING THE FORMAT DIALOG BOX

For complete control over text element formatting, use the Format dialog box. Each chart element has a unique Format dialog box, and the dialog box has several tabs.

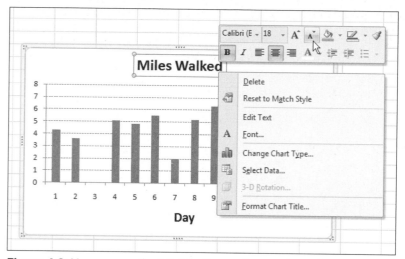

Figure 4-2: You can use the Mini toolbar to format chart elements that contain text.

You can access the Format dialog box by using either of the following methods:

- Select the chart element and press Ctrl+1.

- Right-click the chart element and choose Format *xxxx* from the shortcut menu (where *xxxx* is the chart element's name).

In addition, some of the Ribbon controls contain a menu item that, when clicked, opens the Format dialog box and displays a specific tab. For example, when you choose Chart Tools➪ Format➪Shape Outline➪Weight, the menu displays the More Lines option. Click this option and Excel displays the Format dialog box with the Border Styles tab selected. This tab enables you to specify formatting that's not available on the Ribbon.

Figure 4-3 shows an example of a Format dialog box. Specifically, the figure shows the Legend Options tab of the Format Legend dialog box. As I noted, each chart element has a different Format dialog box.

NOTE

The Format dialog box is a stay-on-top dialog box. In other words, you can keep this dialog box open while you're working on a chart. It's not necessary to close the dialog box to see the changes on the chart. In some cases, however, you need to activate a different control in the dialog box to see the changes you've specified. Usually, pressing Tab will move to the next control in the dialog box and force Excel to update the chart.

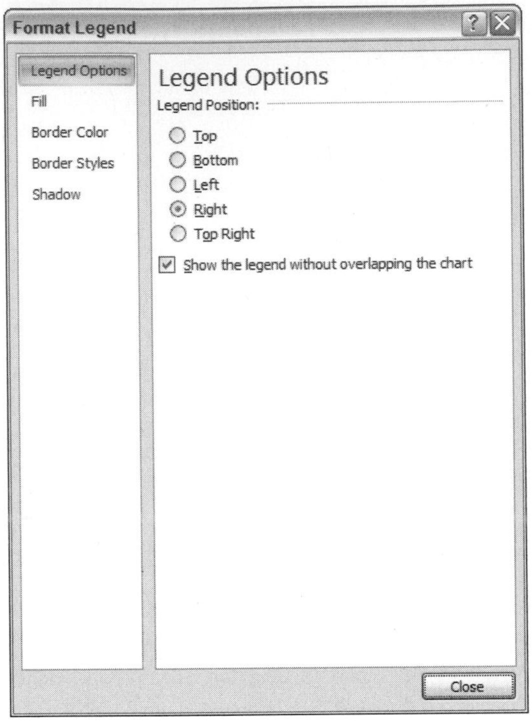

Figure 4-3: Each chart element has its own Format dialog box. This dialog box controls formatting for the chart's legend.

Adjusting Fills and Borders: General Procedures

Many of the Format dialog boxes for chart elements include a tab named Fill as well as other tabs that deal with border formatting. These tabs are used to change the interior and border of the selected element.

About the Fill Tab

Figure 4-4 shows the Fill tab in the Format Chart Area dialog box when the Solid Fill option is selected. The controls on this tab change, depending on which option is selected.

Although the Fill tabs of the various Format dialog boxes are similar, they are not identical. Depending on the chart element, the dialog box may have additional options that are relevant for the selected item. For example, the Fill tab of the Format Data Series dialog box includes a check box that can vary the colors for each data point.

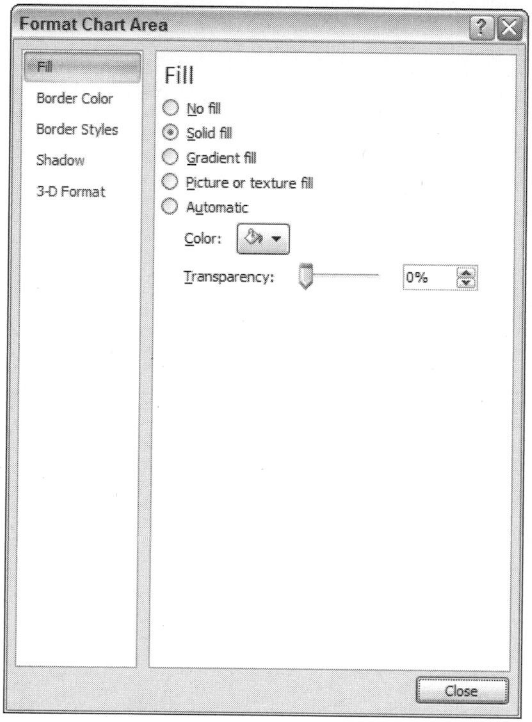

Figure 4-4: The Fill tab of the Format Chart Area dialog box.

Not all chart elements can be filled. For example, the Format Major Gridlines dialog box does not have a Fill tab because filling a line makes no sense. You can, however, change the gridline formatting by using the tabs that *are* displayed.

The main Fill tab options are as follows:

- **No Fill:** Makes the chart element transparent.

- **Solid Fill:** Displays a color selector so that you can choose a single color. You can also set the transparency for the color.

- **Gradient Fill:** Displays several additional controls that allow you to select a prebuilt gradient or construct your own gradient. A gradient consists of from two to ten colors that are blended together in various ways. You have literally millions of possibilities. See the nearby "Specifying gradients" sidebar for more information.

- **Picture or Texture Fill:** Enables you to select from 24 built-in textures, choose an image file, or use clip art for the fill. You can control how the picture is displayed: stretched, stacked, or stacked and scaled. This feature can often be useful in applying special effects to data series. See the section "Formatting Chart Series," later in this chapter.

- **Automatic:** Sets the fill to the default color.

Figure 4-5 shows a rather ugly chart with various types of fill formatting applied. The column data series has clip art, in the form of stacked monkeys. The plot area uses a texture, and the chart area uses a gradient fill.

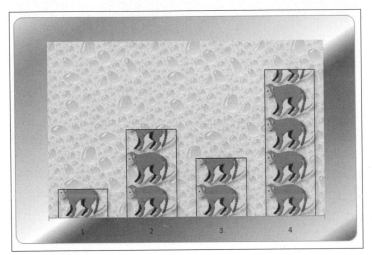

Figure 4-5: Using too many fill types is a quick way to create a very ugly chart.

Formatting Borders

A *border* is the line around an object. Excel offers four general choices for formatting a border:

- **No Line:** The chart element has no line.
- **Solid Line:** The chart element has a solid line. You can specify the color, the transparency, and a variety of other settings.
- **Gradient Line:** The chart element has a line that consists of a color gradient.
- **Automatic:** The default setting. Excel decides the border settings automatically.

Figure 4-6 shows the Border Styles tab of the Format Chart Area dialog box. If you explore this dialog box, you'll soon discover that a border can have a huge number of variations. Keep in mind that all settings are not available for all chart elements. For example, the Arrow Settings are disabled when a chart element that can't display an arrow is selected.

Specifying gradients

The Fill tab in many of the Format dialog boxes lets you specify a gradient fill for the chart element. Excel includes 24 preset color gradients, and each of these can be changed by setting the type (*linear, radial, rectangular,* or *path*). For a linear or radial gradient, you can also specify a direction, and for a linear fill you can specify the direction more precisely in terms of an angle (0 to 360 degrees). These combinations work out to tens of thousands of different prebuilt gradients.

But the fun is only beginning. You can create your own gradients by defining up to ten "stops" in the dialog box. A stop is a color, a transparency setting, and a position (expressed as a percent) within the gradient.

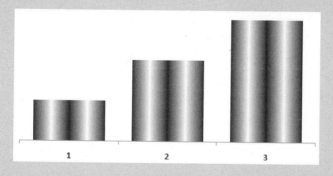

The accompanying figure shows a custom gradient applied to a column series. This linear gradient has five stops, is displayed at a 0-degree angle, and uses these settings:

- Stop 1: Stop position 0%, color black
- Stop 2: Stop position 25%, color white
- Stop 3: Stop position 50%, color black
- Stop 4: Stop position 75%, color white
- Stop 5: Stop position 100%, color black

The best way to find out about gradients is to experiment. You can spend quite a bit of time creating a custom gradient. But, unfortunately, you can't save a custom gradient.

Figure 4-7 shows a simple line chart with some extreme border formatting applied — for demonstration purposes only. The data series has thick lines and arrows, the plot area has a line with dashes, the horizontal axis has a thick line with a round cap type, and the chart area has a compound line with rounded corners.

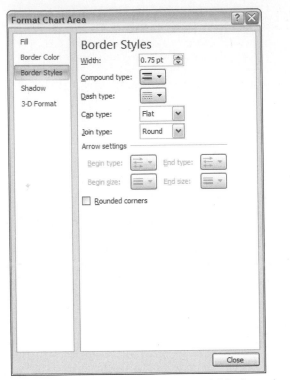

Figure 4-6: Some of the settings available for a chart element border.

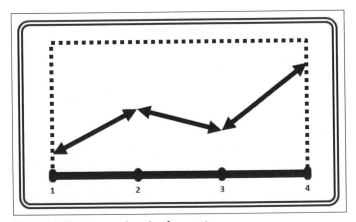

Figure 4-7: Extreme border formatting.

Formatting Chart Background Elements

Every chart has two key components that play a role in the chart's overall appearance:

- **The chart area:** The background area of the chart object
- **The plot area:** The area (within the chart area) that contains the actual chart

The default colors of the chart area and the plot area depend on which chart style you choose from the Chart Tools⇨Design⇨Chart Styles gallery.

Working with the Chart Area

The chart area is an object that contains all other elements on the chart. You can think of it as a chart's master background. The chart area is always the same size as the chart object (the chart's container).

 NOTE

If you delete the chart area, you delete the entire chart. If the chart is on a chart sheet, you can't delete the chart area — which is actually the basis for a useful trick that enables you to place multiple charts on a chart sheet. See Chapter 8 for an example.

When the chart area is selected, you can adjust the font for all the chart elements. In other words, if you want to make all text in a chart 12 point, select the chart area and then apply the font formatting.

In some cases, you may want to make the chart area transparent so that the underlying worksheet shows through. Figure 4-8 shows a column chart with a transparent chart area. You can accomplish this by setting the chart area's fill to No Fill, or set it to a Solid Fill and make it 100% transparent.

When a chart is on a chart sheet, you can resize the chart by dragging a corner of the chart area. After you've made the chart area smaller, you can drag it to a different location on the chart sheet.

Working with the Plot Area

The plot area is the part of the chart that contains the actual chart. The plot area contains all chart elements except the chart title and the legend.

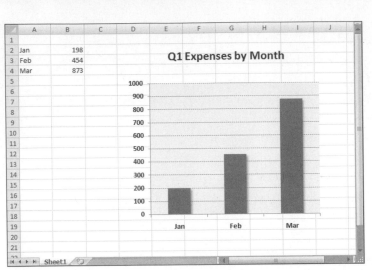

Figure 4-8: The chart area for this chart is transparent. The plot area, however, contains a fill color.

Although the plot area consists of elements such as axes and axis labels, when you change the fill of the plot area, these "outside" elements are not affected — except for a 3-D chart. Figure 4-9 shows a 2-D column chart and a 3-D column chart. Both charts have their plot area shaded and enclosed in a heavy dashed border. Notice that the plot area for the 3-D chart includes the axis labels. Typically, a 3-D chart has a transparent plot area, and color fills are used for the walls and floor elements.

TIP

If you set the Fill option to No Fill, the plot area will be transparent. Therefore, the color and patterns applied to the chart area will show through. You can also set the plot area to a solid color and adjust the Transparency setting so that the chart area shows through partially.

You can insert an image into the plot area. To do so, use the Fill tab of the Format Plot Area dialog box, and choose the Picture or Texture Fill option. The image can come from a file, the clipboard, or clip art. Figure 4-10 shows a column chart that uses a graphic in the plot area.

To reposition the plot area within the chart area, select the plot area and then drag a border to move it. To change the size of the plot area, drag one of the corner "handles." If you like, you can expand the plot area so that it fills the entire chart area.

You'll find that different chart types vary in how they respond to changes in the plot area dimensions. For example, you cannot change the relative dimensions of the plot area of a pie chart or a radar chart (it's always square). But with other chart types, you can change the aspect ratio of the plot area by changing either the height or the width.

Also, be aware that the size of the plot area can be changed automatically when you adjust other elements of your chart. For example, if you add a legend or title to a chart, the size of the plot area may be reduced to accommodate the legend.

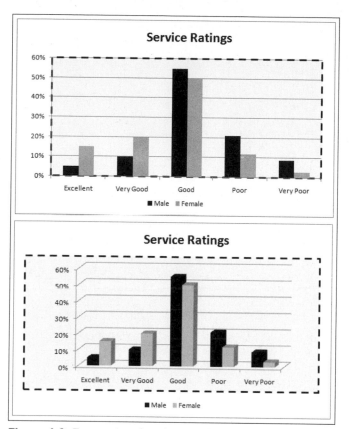

Figure 4-9: Formatting the plot area for a 3-D chart includes the axes and axis labels.

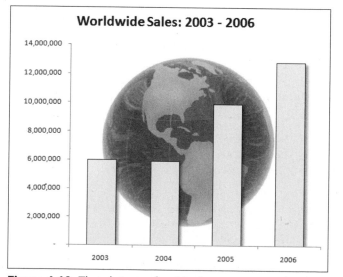

Figure 4-10: The plot area for this chart uses a graphic image.

Copying chart formatting

You created a killer chart and spent hours customizing it. Now you need to create another one just like it. What are your options? You have several choices:

- **Copy the formatting.** Create a standard chart with the default formatting. Then select your original chart and press Ctrl+C. Click your new chart and choose Home⇨Clipboard⇨Paste⇨Paste Special. In the Paste Special dialog box, select Formats.

- **Copy the chart; change the data sources.** Select the original chart and press Ctrl+C. Then, activate any cell and press Ctrl+V. This creates an exact copy of your chart. Then, drag the range highlights to the new ranges. Or, you can choose Chart Tools⇨Design⇨Data⇨Select Data to display the Select Data Source dialog box.

- **Create a chart template.** Select your chart and then choose Chart Tools⇨Design⇨Type⇨Save as Template. In the Save Chart Template dialog box, provide a descriptive filename. When you create your next chart, choose Insert⇨Charts⇨Other Charts⇨All Chart Types, and select the Templates tab. Then, specify the template you created.

TIP

Changing the size and position of the plot area can have a dramatic effect on the overall look of your chart. When you're fine-tuning a chart, you'll probably want to experiment with various sizes and positions for the plot area.

Formatting Chart Series

Making a few simple formatting changes to a chart series can make a huge difference in the readability of your chart. When you create a chart, Excel uses its default colors and marker styles for the series. In many cases, you'll want to modify these colors or marker styles for clarity (basic formatting). In other cases, you may want to make some drastic changes for impact.

You can apply formatting to the entire series or to a single data point within the series — for example, make one column a different color to draw attention to it.

ON THE CD

The examples in this section are available on the companion CD-ROM. The file name is `series.xlsx`.

Basic Series Formatting

Basic series formatting is very straightforward: Just select the data series on your chart and use the tools in the Chart Tools➪Format➪Shape Styles group to make changes. For more control, press Ctrl+1 and use the Format Data Series dialog box.

Using Pictures and Graphics for Series Formatting

You can add a picture to several chart elements, including data markers on line charts and series fills for column, bar, area, bubble, and filled radar charts. Figure 4-11 shows a column chart that uses a clip art image of a car. The picture was added using the Fill tab of the Format Data Series dialog box. I selected the Picture or Texture Fill option, and then clicked the Clip Art button to select the image. In addition, I scaled the image so that each car represents 20 units.

Figure 4-11: This column chart uses a clip art image.

Part I

Figure 4-12 shows another example. The data markers in this line chart display a shape that was inserted in the worksheet and then copied to the clipboard. I selected the line series and pressed Ctrl+V to paste the shape.

You can also use the Marker Fill tab of the Format Data Series dialog box to specify Picture or Texture Fill. However, the result is very different. If you use the Clipboard button to paste the copied shape, the pasted image will fill the existing marker (not replace it). You'll probably need to increase the marker size and hide the marker borders.

Figure 4-12: The data markers use a shape that was copied to the clipboard.

CROSS-REFERENCE

Data series elements are not the only type of chart element that can have a picture or graphic displayed. You can also apply a picture to the chart area, the plot area, the legend, and even text elements. For 3-D charts, you can apply a picture to the walls or floor. Refer to Chapter 6 for more information about combining graphics with charts.

Additional Series Options

Chart series offer a number of additional options. These options are located in the Series Options tab of the Format Data Series dialog box. The set of options varies, depending on the chart type of the series. In most cases, the options are self-explanatory. But, if you are unsure about a particular series option, try it! If the result isn't satisfactory, change the setting to its original value or choose Undo.

About those fancy effects

Excel 2007 includes several new formatting options, which are known as *effects*. Access these effects by choosing Chart Tools➪Format➪Shape Styles➪Shape Effects. Note that not all effects work with all chart elements.

Following is a general description of the effect types:

- **Shadow:** Adds a highly customizable shadow to the selected chart element. Choose from a number of prebuilt shadows, or create your own using the Shadow tab of the Format dialog box. Shadows, when used tastefully, can improve the appearance of a chart by adding depth.

- **Reflection:** Adds one of six prebuilt reflections. As far as I can tell, this effect is not available for any native chart element. However, you can apply a reflection to shapes or text boxes that you add to a chart.

- **Glow:** Adds a color glow around the element. I have yet to see a chart that is improved by adding a glow to any element.

- **Soft Edges:** Makes the edges of the element softer. Extreme settings make the element appear to be out of focus, smaller, or even disappear.

- **Bevel:** Adds a 3-D bevel look to the element. This effect is highly customizable, and you can use it to create a frame for your chart (see the accompanying figure).

- **3-D Rotation:** This effect does not work with any chart elements.

Perhaps the best advice regarding these effects is to use them sparingly with charts. Generally, a chart's formatting shouldn't draw attention away from the point you're trying to make with the chart.

Figure 4-13, for example, shows the series options available for a doughnut chart. This particular chart type has three series options, which affect the appearance of the series.

Figure 4-13: The Series Options tab of the Format Data Series dialog box lists additional options.

Figure 4-14 shows an example of modifying series settings. The chart on the left uses the default settings (Series Overlap of 0% and Gap Width of 150%). The chart on the right uses a Series Overlap of 50% and a Gap Width of 28%.

Figure 4-14: A column chart, before and after adjusting the Series Overlap and Gap Width settings.

Working with Chart Titles

A chart can have as many as five different titles:

- Chart title
- Category axis title
- Value axis title
- Secondary category axis title
- Secondary value axis title

The number of titles depends on the chart type. For example, a pie chart supports only a chart title because it has no axes. Figure 4-15 shows a chart that contains four titles: the chart title, the horizontal category axis title, the vertical value axis title, and the secondary vertical axis title.

 ON THE CD

The examples in this section are available on the companion CD-ROM. The file name is `titles.xlsx`.

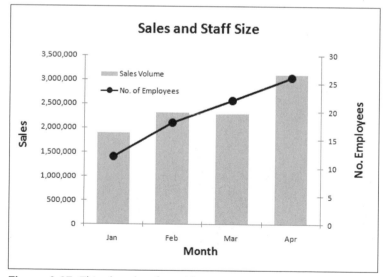

Figure 4-15: This chart has four titles.

Part I

Adding Titles to a Chart

To add a chart title to a chart, activate the chart and use the Chart Tools⇨Layout⇨ Labels⇨Chart Title control. This control drops down to display placement options.

To add axis titles to a chart, activate the chart and use the Chart Tools⇨Layout⇨Labels⇨ Axis Titles control. This control drops down to display placement options. Keep in mind that the options include only those that are appropriate for the chart. For example, if the chart doesn't have a secondary value axis, you don't have an option to add a title to the nonexistent axis.

NOTE

Contrary to what you might expect, you cannot resize a chart title. When you select a title, it displays the characteristic border and handles — but the handles cannot be dragged to change the size of the object. The only way to change the size is to change the size of the font used in the title. For more control over a chart's title, you can use a text box instead of an official title.

Changing Title Text

When you add a title to a chart, Excel inserts generic text to help you identify the title. To edit the text used in a chart title, click the title once to select it; then click a second time inside the text area. If the title has a vertical orientation, things get a bit tricky, because you need to use the up- and down-arrow keys rather than the left- and right-arrow keys.

TIP

For lengthy titles, Excel handles the line breaks automatically. To force a line break in the title, press Enter. To add a line break within existing title text, press Ctrl+Shift+Enter.

Formatting Title Text

Unfortunately, Excel does not provide a "one-stop" place to change all aspects of a chart title. The Format Chart Title dialog box provides options for changing the fill, border, shadows, 3-D format, and alignment. If you want to change anything related to the font, you need to use the Ribbon (or, right-click and use the Mini toolbar). Yet another option is to right-click the chart element and choose Font from the shortcut menu. This displays the Font dialog box, with options that aren't available elsewhere. For example, the Font dialog box lets you control the character spacing of the text.

Most of the font changes you make will use the tools in the Home⇨Font group. You may be tempted to use the controls in the Chart Tools⇨Format⇨WordArt Styles group, but these controls are primarily for special effects.

TIP

You can easily modify the formatting for individual characters within a title. Select the title, highlight the characters that you want to modify, and apply the formatting. The formatting changes you make will affect only the selected characters. Figure 4-16 shows an example of a two-line chart title that uses different sizes and styles of text.

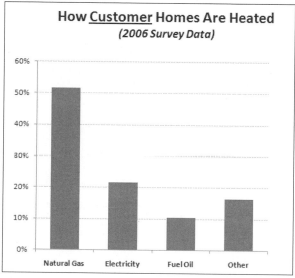

Figure 4-16: Formatting has been applied to individual characters in the chart's title.

Linking Title Text to a Cell

When you create a chart, you might like to have some of the chart's text elements linked to cells. That way, when you change the text in the cell, the corresponding chart element updates. And, of course, you can even link chart text elements to cells that contain a formula. For example, you might link the chart title to a cell that contains a formula that returns the current date.

You can create a link to a cell for the chart title, a vertical axis title, or a horizontal axis title. Follow these steps:

1. Select the chart element that will contain the cell link. Make sure that the text element itself is selected (don't select text within the element).
2. Click the formula bar.
3. Type an equal sign (=).
4. Click the cell that will be linked to the chart element.

Adding free-floating text to a chart

Text in a chart is not limited to titles. In fact, you can add free-floating text anywhere you want by inserting a text box into the chart. To do so, follow these steps:

1. Select the chart.

2. Choose Chart Tools⇨Layout⇨Insert⇨Text Box.

3. Click and drag within the chart to create the text box.

4. Start typing the text.

You can click and drag the text box to change its size or location. And when the text box is selected, you can access the formatting tools using the controls on the Drawing Tools⇨Format tab.

The accompanying figure shows a chart with a text box that contains quite a bit of formatted text. The chart's plot area was reduced in size to accommodate the text box.

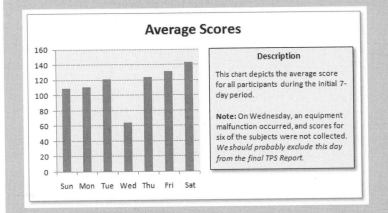

If you would like to link the text box to a cell, follow these steps:

1. Select the text box.

2. Click the formula bar.

3. Type an equal sign (=).

4. Click the cell that will be linked to the chart element.

After you create the link, the text box will always display the contents of the cell it's linked to.

Some people prefer to use a text box in place of a chart's title because a text box provides a lot more control over formatting. When a text box is selected, its Format Shape dialog box provides several additional options, compared to the Format Chart Title dialog box.

Figure 4-17 shows a chart that has links for the following elements: chart title, the vertical axis title, the horizontal axis title, and a text box.

Figure 4-17: The titles in this chart are linked to cells.

Working with a Chart's Legend

A chart legend identifies the series in the chart and consists of text and keys. A *key* is a small graphic image that corresponds to the appearance of the corresponding chart series. The order of the items within a legend varies, depending on the chart type.

NOTE

If you've added a trendline to your chart, the trendline also appears in the legend. For more information about trendlines, refer to Chapter 5.

Legends are appropriate for charts that have at least two series. But even then, all charts do not require a legend. You may prefer to identify relevant data using other methods, such as a data label, a text box, or a shape with text. Figure 4-18 shows a chart in which the data series are identified by using text in shapes, which were added to the chart using Insert⇨Illustrations⇨Shapes.

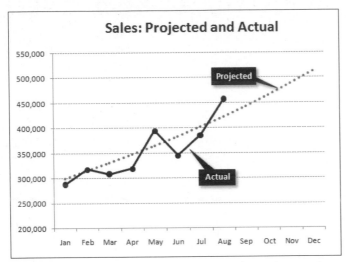

Figure 4-18: This chart uses shapes as an alternative to a legend.

 CROSS-REFERENCE
Refer to Chapter 6 for more information about using shapes with charts.

Adding or Removing a Legend

To add a legend to your chart, choose Chart Tools⇨Layout⇨Labels⇨Legend. This drop-down control contains several options for the legend placement. After you've added a legend, you can drag it to move it anywhere you like.

The quickest way to remove a legend is to select it and press Delete.

Moving or Resizing a Legend

To move a legend, click it and drag it to the desired location. Or, you can use one of the options in the Chart Tools⇨Layout⇨Labels⇨Legend control.

If you move a legend from its default position, you may want to change the size of the plot area to fill in the gap left by the legend. Just select the plot area and drag a border to make it the desired size.

To change the size of a legend, select it and drag any of its corners. Excel will adjust the legend automatically and may display it in multiple columns.

Formatting a Legend

You can select an individual legend entry within a legend and format it separately. For example, you may want to make the text bold to draw attention to a particular data series. To select an element in the legend, first select the legend and then click the desired entry.

You can't change the formatting of individual characters in a legend entry. For example, if you'd like the legend to display a superscript or subscript character, you're out of luck.

When a single legend entry is selected, you can use the Format Legend Entry dialog box to format the entry. When a legend entry is selected and you apply any type of formatting except text formatting, the formatting affects the legend key and the corresponding series. In other words, the appearance of the legend key will *always* correspond to the data series.

NOTE

You can't use the Chart Elements drop-down list to select a legend entry. You must either click the item or select the legend itself, and then press the right-arrow key until the desired element is selected.

Changing the Legend Text

The legend text corresponds to the names of the series on the chart. If you didn't include series names when you originally selected the cells to create the chart, Excel displays a default series name (Series 1, Series 2, and so on) in the legend.

To add series names, choose Chart Tools⇨Design⇨Select Data to display the Select Data Source dialog box. Select the series name and click the Edit button. In the Edit Series dialog box, type the series name or enter a cell reference that contains the series name. Repeat for each series that needs naming. Alternatively, you can edit the SERIES formula, as described in Chapter 3.

Deleting a Legend Entry

For some charts, you may prefer that one or more of the data series not appear in the legend. To delete a legend entry, just select it and press Delete. The legend entry will be deleted, but the data series will remain intact.

If you've deleted one or more legend entries, you can restore the legend to its original state by deleting the entire legend and then adding it back.

Working with Chart Axes

As you know, charts vary in the number of axes that they use. Pie and doughnut charts have no axes. All 2-D charts have at least two axes, and they can have three (if you use a secondary value or category axis) or four (if you use a secondary category axis and a secondary value axis). Three-dimensional charts have three axes — the "depth" axis is known as the series axis.

CROSS-REFERENCE

Refer to Chapter 8 for a variety of chart examples that use additional axes.

Excel provides you with a great deal of control over the look of chart axes. To modify any aspect of an axis, access its Format Axis dialog box. The dialog box varies, depending on which type of axis is selected.

ON THE CD

The examples in the section are available on the companion CD-ROM. The file name is `axes.xlsx`.

All aspects of axis formatting are covered in the sections that follow.

Value Axis versus Category Axis

Before getting into the details of formatting, it's important to understand the difference between a category axis and a value axis. A category axis displays arbitrary text, whereas a value axis displays numerical intervals. Figure 4-19 shows a simple column chart with two series. The horizontal category axis displays labels that represent the categories. The vertical value axis, on the other hand, is a numerical scale.

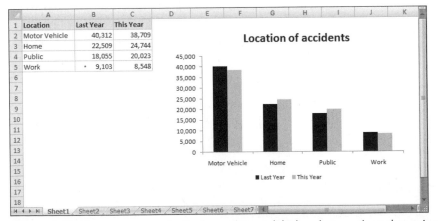

Figure 4-19: The category axis displays arbitrary labels, whereas the value axis displays a numerical scale.

In this example, the category labels happen to be text. Alternatively, the categories *could* be numbers. Figure 4-20 shows the same chart after replacing the category labels with numbers. Even though the chart becomes fairly meaningless, it should be clear that the category axis does not display a true numeric scale. The numbers displayed are completely arbitrary, and the chart itself was not affected by changing these labels.

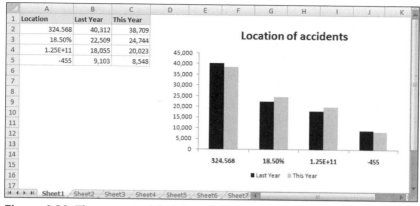

Figure 4-20: The category labels have been replaced with numbers — but the numbers do not function as numbers.

Two of Excel's chart types are different from the other chart types in one important respect. Scatter charts and bubble charts use *two* value axes. For these chart types, both axes represent numeric scales.

Figure 4-21 shows two charts (a scatter chart and a line chart) that use the same data. The data shows world population estimates for various years. Note that the interval between the years in column A is not consistent.

The scatter chart, which uses two value axes, plots the years as numeric values. The line chart, on the other hand, uses a (non-numeric) category axis, and it assumes that the categories (the years) are equally spaced. This, of course, is not a valid assumption, and the line chart presents a very inaccurate picture of the population growth: It appears to be linear, but it's definitely not.

 CROSS-REFERENCE

For more information about time-based axes, refer to the section "Using Time-Scale Axes," later in this chapter.

Value Axis Scales

The numerical range of a value axis represents the axis's scale. By default, Excel automatically scales each value axis. It determines the minimum and maximum scale values for the axis, based on the numeric range of the data. Excel also automatically calculates a major unit and a minor unit for each axis scale. These settings determine how many intervals (or tick marks) are displayed on the axis and determine how many gridlines are displayed. In addition, the value at which the axis crosses the category axis is also calculated automatically.

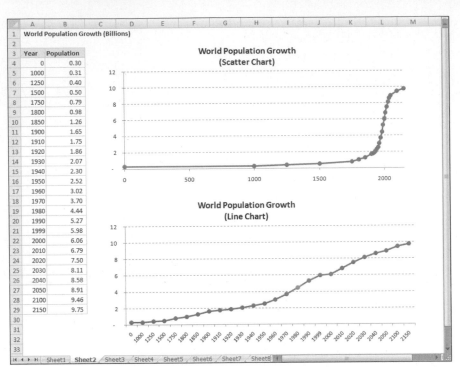

Figure 4-21: These charts plot the same data but present very different pictures.

You can, of course, override this automatic behavior and specify your own minimum, maximum, major unit, minor unit, and cross-over for any value axis. You set these specifications on the Axis Options tab of the Format Axis dialog box (see Figure 4-22).

NOTE

A category axis does not have a scale because it simply displays arbitrary category names. For a category axis, the Axis Options tab of the Format Axis dialog box displays a number of other options that determine the appearance and layout of the axis.

On the Axis Options tab, the four sets of option buttons at the top determine the scale of the axis (its minimum, maximum, and intervals). By default, Excel determines these values based on the numerical range of the data, and the default setting is Auto. You can override Excel's choice and set any or all of them to Fixed and then enter your own values.

Adjusting the scale of a value axis can dramatically affect the chart's appearance. Manipulating the scale, in some cases, can present a false picture of the data. Figure 4-23 shows two line charts that depict the same data. The top chart uses Excel's default axis scale values, which extend from 8,200 to 9,200. In the bottom chart, the Minimum scale value was set to 0, and the Maximum scale value was set to 10,000. A casual viewer might draw two very different conclusions from these charts. The top chart makes the differences in the data seem more prominent. The lower chart gives the impression that not much change has occurred over time.

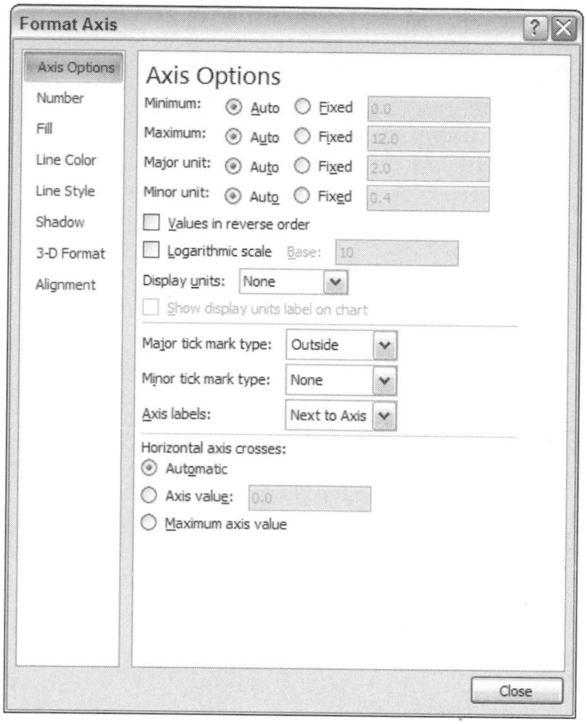

Figure 4-22: The Axis Options tab of the Format Axis dialog box.

The actual scale that you use depends on the situation. There are no hard-and-fast rules regarding setting scale values, except that you shouldn't misrepresent data by manipulating the chart to prove a point that doesn't exist. In addition, most agree that the value axis of a bar or column chart should always start at zero (and even Excel follows that rule).

If you're preparing several charts that use similarly scaled data, keeping the scales constant across all charts facilitates comparisons across charts. The charts in Figure 4-24 show the distribution of responses for two survey questions. For the top chart, the value axis scale ranges from 0% to 50%. For the bottom chart, the value axis scale extends from 0% to 35%. Because the same scale was not used on the value axes, however, comparing the responses across survey items is difficult.

Another option in the Format Axis dialog box is Values in Reverse Order. The top chart in Figure 4-25 uses default axis settings. The bottom chart uses the Values in Reverse Order option, which reverses the scale's direction. Notice that the category axis is at the top. If you would prefer that it remain at the bottom of the chart, select the Maximum Axis Value option for the Horizontal Axis Crosses setting.

If the values to be plotted cover a very large range, you may want to use a logarithmic scale for the value axis. A log scale is most often used for scientific applications. Figure 4-26 shows two charts. The top chart uses a standard scale, and the bottom chart uses a logarithmic scale. Note that the base is 10, so each scale value in the chart is 10 times greater than the one below it. Increasing the base unit to 100 would result in a scale in which each tick mark value is 100 times greater than the one below.

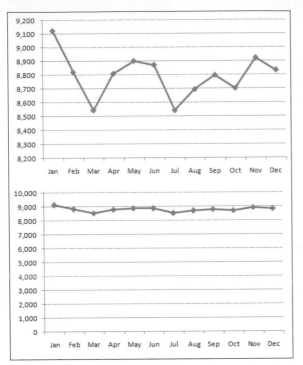

Figure 4-23: These two charts show the same data, but they use different value axis scales.

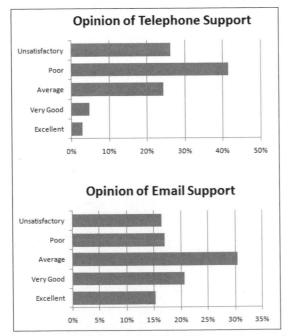

Figure 4-24: These charts use different scales on the value axis, making a comparison between the two difficult.

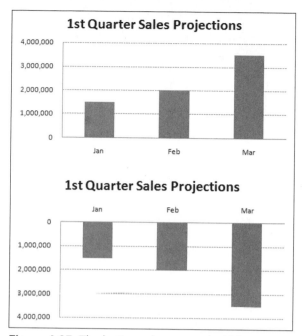

Figure 4-25: The bottom chart uses the Values in Reverse Order option.

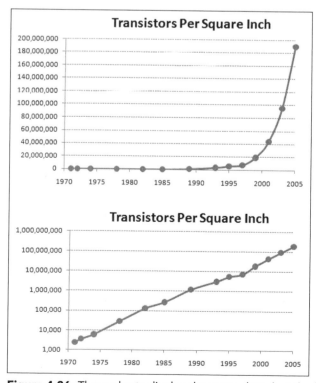

Figure 4-26: These charts display the same data, but the lower chart uses a logarithmic scale.

NOTE

A log scale works only for positive values. A new feature in Excel 2007 enables you to specify a base value between 2 and 1,000.

If your chart uses very large numbers, you may want to change the Display Units settings. Figure 4-27 shows a chart that uses very large numbers. The lower chart uses the Display Units as Millions setting, with the option to Show Display Units Label on Chart. Excel inserted the label "Millions," which I edited to display as "Million of Miles."

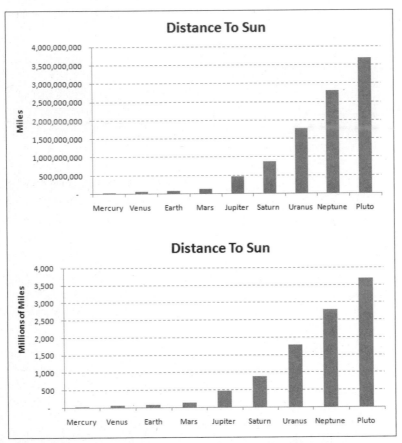

Figure 4-27: The lower chart uses display units of millions.

TIP

Another way to change the number display is to use a custom number format for the axis values. For example, to display the values in millions, click the Number tab of the Format Axis dialog box, select the Custom category, and then enter this format code:

```
#,##0,,
```

An axis also has tick marks — the short lines that depict the scale units and are perpendicular to the axis. In the Axis Options dialog box, you can select the type of tick mark for the major units and the minor units. The options are as follows:

- **None:** No tick marks
- **Inside:** Tick marks on the inside of the axis only
- **Outside:** Tick marks on the outside of the axis only
- **Cross:** Tick marks on both sides of the axis

How Excel calculates automatic axis scales

When you create a chart, Excel analyzes the data and then sets the axis scaling. Did you ever wonder how Excel calculates the minimum and maximum scale values? Part of the answer can be found at Microsoft's Product Support Services web site.

It turns out that Excel uses a relatively complex algorithm. The calculation varies, depending on the sign of the minimum and maximum values (both positive, both negative or zero, or one negative and the other positive). The calculations depend on the following:

- The Major Unit specified on the Axis Options tab of the Format Axis dialog box
- The minimum value (MIN)
- The maximum value (MAX)

When the values to be plotted are all positive numbers, the automatic maximum scale value for the value axis is the first major unit that is greater than or equal to the value returned by this expression:

```
MAX + 0.05 * (MAX - MIN)
```

Otherwise, the automatic maximum for the value axis is the first major unit greater than or equal to the maximum value. But if the difference between the maximum and minimum values is greater than 16.667 percent of the value of the maximum value, the automatic minimum for the value axis is zero.

If the difference between the maximum and minimum values is less than 16.667 percent of the maximum value, the automatic minimum for the value axis is the first major unit that is less than or equal to the value returned by this expression:

```
MIN - [(MAX - MIN) / 2]
```

But wait! If the chart is a scatter chart or a bubble chart, the automatic minimum for the value axis is the first major unit that is less than or equal to the minimum value. Microsoft has not revealed how the major unit value is calculated.

Got all that? If not, don't worry. If you don't like the way Excel scales a chart axis, it's a simple matter to override it.

You can also control the position of the tick mark labels. The options are as follows:

- **None:** No labels.

- **Low:** For a horizontal axis, labels appear at the bottom of the plot area; for a vertical axis, labels appear to the left of the plot area.

- **High:** For a horizontal axis, labels appear at the top of the plot area; for a vertical axis, labels appear to the right of the plot area.

- **Next to axis:** Labels appear next to the axis (the default setting).

 NOTE
Major tick marks are the axis tick marks that normally have labels next to them. Minor tick marks are between the major tick marks.

When you combine these settings with the Axis Crosses At option, you have a great deal of flexibility, as shown in Figure 4-28. These charts all display the same data, but the axes are formatted differently.

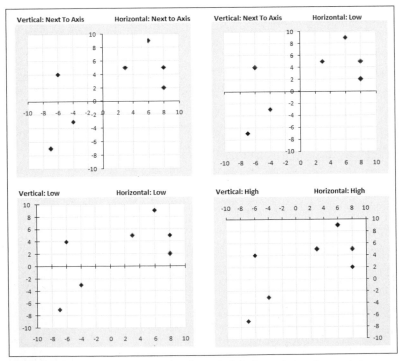

Figure 4-28: Various ways to display axis labels and crossing points.

Using Time-Scale Axes

When you create a chart, Excel attempts to determine whether your category axis contains date or time values. If so, it creates a time-series chart. Figure 4-29 shows a simple example. Column A contains dates, and column B contains the values plotted on the column chart. The data consists of values for only 10 dates, yet Excel created the chart with 31 intervals on the category axis. It recognized that the category axis values were dates, and created an equal-interval scale.

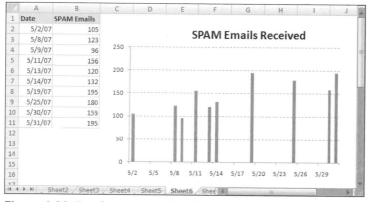

Figure 4-29: Excel recognizes the dates and creates a time-based category axis.

If you would like to override Excel's decision to use a time-based category axis, you need to access the Axes Options tab of the Format Axis dialog box. There, you'll discover that the default category axis option is Automatically Select Based on Data. Change this option to Text Axis, and the chart will resemble Figure 4-30. On this chart, the dates are treated as arbitrary text labels.

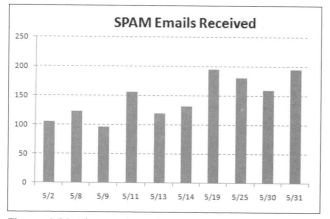

Figure 4-30: The previous chart, using a standard category axis.

NOTE
A time-scale axis option is available only for the category axis (not the value axis).

When a category axis uses dates, the Axis Options tab of the Format Axis dialog box lets you specify the Base Unit, the Major Unit, and the Minor Unit — each in terms of days, months, or years (see Figure 4-31).

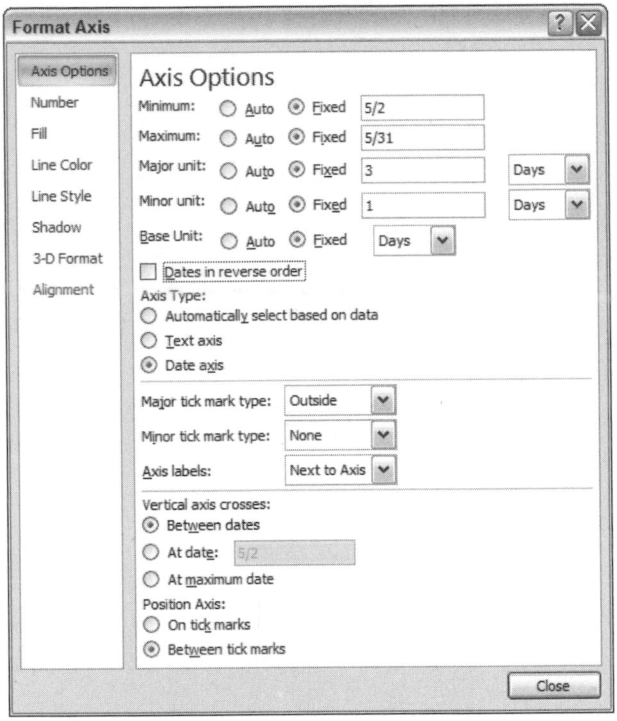

Figure 4-31: When a category axis uses dates, the Format Axis dialog box displays additional options.

If you need a time-scale axis for smaller units (such as hours), you need to use a scatter chart. That's because a date-scale axis treats all values as integers. Therefore, every time value is plotted as midnight of that day. Figure 4-32 shows a scatter chart that plots scheduled versus actual arrival times for flights. Note that both of the value axes display times, in one-hour increments.

Unfortunately, Excel does not allow you to specify time values on the Axis Options tab of the Format Axis dialog box. If you want to override the default minimum, maximum, or major unit values, you must manually convert the time value to a decimal value. In previous versions of Excel, you could simply enter a time value, and Excel would perform the conversion.

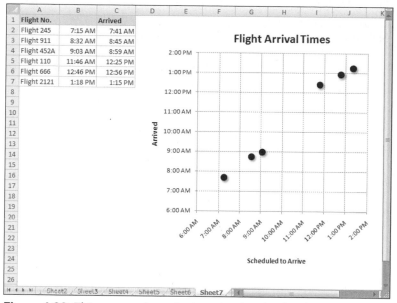

Figure 4-32: This scatter chart displays times on both value axes.

For this chart, I entered the following scale values:

- Minimum axis scale value: .25 (6:00 am)

- Maximum axis scale value: .58333 (2:00 pm)

- Major unit: .041666 (1:00:00)

To convert a time value to a decimal number, enter the time value into a cell. Then apply General number formatting to the cell. Time values are expressed as a percentage of a 24-hour day. For example, 12:00 noon is 0.50.

Creating a Multiline Category Axis

Most of the time, the labels on a category axis consist of data from a single column or row. You can, however, create multiline category labels, as shown in Figure 4-33. This chart uses the text in columns A:C for the category axis labels.

When this chart was created, range A1:E10 was selected. Excel determined automatically that the first three columns would be used for the category axis labels.

NOTE

This type of data layout is common when you work with PivotTables, and PivotCharts often use multiline category axes. Refer to Chapter 9 for more information about PivotTables and PivotCharts.

Part I

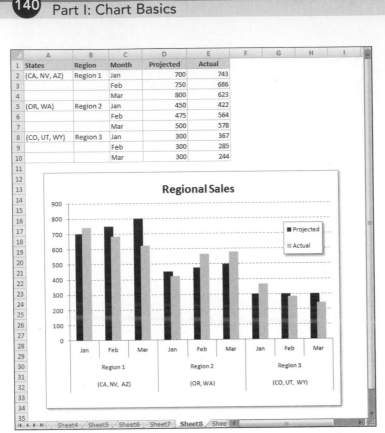

Figure 4-33: The category axis contains labels from three columns.

Adding and Removing Axes

To change the visibility of an axis from the chart, use the Chart Tools⇨Layout⇨Axes⇨Axes command. This drop-down control also contains a number of display options for the axis — the same options that are available in the Format Axis dialog box.

A more direct way to remove an axis is to select it and then press Delete.

Figure 4-34 shows three charts with no axes displayed. Using data labels makes the value axis superfluous, and it is assumed that the reader understands what the horizontal axis represents.

Axis Number Formats

A value axis, by default, displays its values using the same number format that's used by the chart's data. You can provide a different number format, if you like, by using the Number tab of the Format Axis dialog box. Changing the number format for a category axis that displays text will have no effect.

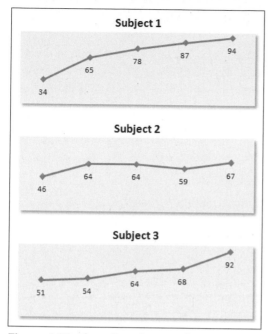

Figure 4-34: Three line charts with no axes.

TIP

Don't forget about custom number formats. Figure 4-35 shows a chart that uses the following custom number format for the value axis:

General " mph"

This number format causes the text *mph* to be appended to each value.

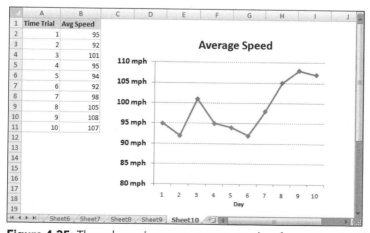

Figure 4-35: The value axis uses a custom number format to provide units for the values.

Working with Gridlines

Gridlines can help the viewer determine the values represented by the series on the chart. Gridlines are optional, and you have quite a bit of control over the appearance of gridlines. Gridlines simply extend the tick marks on the axes. The tick marks are determined by the major unit and minor unit specified for the axis.

 NOTE

Gridlines are applicable to all chart types except pie charts and doughnut charts.

Some charts look better with gridlines; others appear more cluttered. It's up to you to decide whether gridlines can enhance your chart. Sometimes, horizontal gridlines alone are enough, although scatter charts often benefit from both horizontal and vertical gridlines. In many cases, gridlines will be less overpowering if you make them dashed lines, with a gray color.

Adding or Removing Gridlines

To add or remove gridlines, use the Chart Tools⇨Layout⇨Axes⇨Gridlines command. Each axis has two sets of gridlines: major and minor. Major units are the ones that display a label. Minor units are those in between the labels. If you're working with a chart that has a secondary category axis, a secondary value axis, or a series axis (for a 3-D chart), the dialog box has additional options for three sets of gridlines.

A more direct way to remove a set of gridlines is to select the gridlines and press Delete.

 NOTE

If a chart uses a secondary axis, you can specify either or both secondary axes to display gridlines. As you might expect, displaying two sets of gridlines in the same direction can be confusing and result in additional clutter.

To modify the properties of a set of gridlines, select one gridline in the set (which selects all in the set) and access the Format Gridlines dialog box. Or, use the controls in the Chart Tools⇨Format⇨Shape Styles group.

Figure 4-36 shows a scatter chart with major and minor gridlines displayed for both axes. The major gridlines are thicker and darker than the minor gridlines.

 NOTE

You can't apply different formatting to individual gridlines within a set of gridlines. All gridlines in a set are always formatted identically.

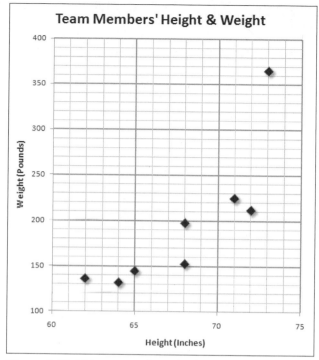

Figure 4-36: This scatter chart displays gridlines for both axes.

Working with Data Labels

For some charts, you may wish to identify the individual data points in a series by displaying data labels.

Adding or Removing Data Labels

Some of the layouts in the Chart Tools⇨Design⇨Chart Layouts gallery include data labels. To add data labels to a chart, select the chart and choose Chart Tools⇨Layout⇨Labels⇨Data Labels. This control is a drop-down list, which displays placement options.

NOTE

If a chart series is selected, the Chart Tools⇨Layout⇨Labels⇨Data Labels command adds data labels only to the selected series. If a single point is selected, this command adds a data label only to the selected point. If a chart element other than a series (or single point) is selected, the command adds data labels to all series in the chart.

To remove data labels from a particular series, select the data labels and press Delete. To remove a single data label, select the individual label and press Delete. To remove the data labels from all series in a chart, select an element other than data labels and choose Chart Tools⇨Layout⇨Labels⇨Data Labels⇨None.

ON THE CD

The examples in this section are available on the companion CD-ROM. The file name is `data labels.xlsx`.

Editing Data Labels

After adding data labels to a series, you can apply formatting to the labels by using the Format Data Labels dialog box. Just select the data labels for a series (or, select an individual data label) and press Ctrl+1. You specify the contents of the data labels by using the Label Options tab of the Format Data Labels dialog box. Figure 4-37 shows this dialog box for a pie chart.

NOTE

Excel lets you either format all data labels at once or format just one data label. When you click a data label *once*, the labels for the entire series are selected. If you click a second time (on a single label), only that data label is selected.

The types of information that can be displayed in data labels are as follows:

- The series name
- The category name
- The numeric value
- The value as a percentage of the sum of the values in the series (for pie charts and doughnut charts only)
- The bubble size (for bubble charts only)

Other options are as follows. Keep in mind that not all options are available for all chart types.

- **Show Leader Lines:** If selected, Excel displays a line that connects the data label with the chart series data point.
- **Label Position:** Specifies the location of the data labels, relative to each data point.
- **Include Legend Key in Label:** If selected, each data label displays its legend key image next to it.
- **Separator:** If you specify multiple contents for the data labels, this control enables you to specify the character that separates the elements (a comma, a semicolon, a period, a space, or a line break).

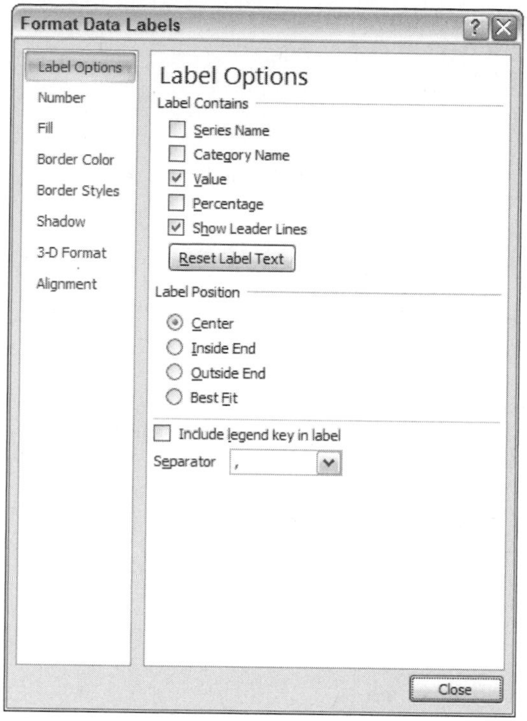

Part I

Format Data Labels

Label Options

Label Options

Number

Fill

Border Color

Border Styles

Shadow

3-D Format

Alignment

Label Contains

☐ Series Name
☐ Category Name
☑ Value
☐ Percentage
☑ Show Leader Lines

Reset Label Text

Label Position

◉ Center
○ Inside End
○ Outside End
○ Best Fit

☐ Include legend key in label

Separator , ▼

Close

Figure 4-37: Options for displaying data labels.

The Format Data Labels dialog box also lets you specify a variety of other formatting options.

The column chart in Figure 4-38 contains data labels that display category names and their values. These labels are positioned to appear on the Outside End. I specified the New Line separator option, so the value appears on a separate line. By including the category name in the data labels, I was able to delete the redundant text in the horizontal category axis.

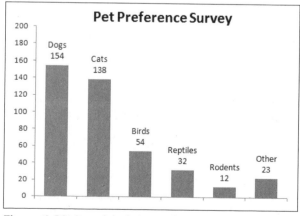

Figure 4-38: Data labels in a column chart.

> **NOTE**
>
> The data labels display the values for each data point. For this particular chart, it would be preferable to display the value as a percentage of the total. Unfortunately, the Percent option is available only for a pie or doughnut chart. The alternative is to calculate the percentages using formulas and then plot the percentage data rather than the actual value data.

Figure 4-39 shows a line chart in which the data labels substitute for the series markers. In this chart, the markers were set to None, and the data labels were positioned using the Center option. I formatted the data label fill and added a shadow. I also deleted the category axis (which originally showed month names), because that information is available in the data labels.

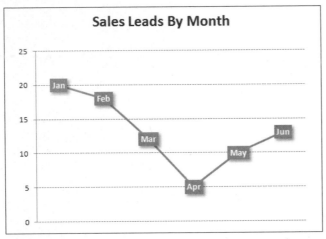

Figure 4-39: Using data labels in place of series markers.

To override a particular data label with other text, select the label and enter the new text. To select an individual data label, click once to select all the data labels; then click the specific data label to select it.

To link a selected data label to a cell, follow these steps:

1. Click in the formula bar.

2. Type an equal sign (=).

3. Click the cell that contains the text.

4. Press Enter.

After adding data labels, you'll often find that the data labels aren't positioned optimally. For example, one or more of the labels may be obscured by another data point or a gridline. If you select an individual label, you can drag the label to a better location.

A data label trick

One way to get around Excel's data label limitation is to use a custom number format for each of your x values. The trick is to use a number format that consists only of text. The cell will still be treated as a number, but only the text will be displayed. Also, the formatted value is what appears in the chart data label!

The accompanying figure shows a chart that uses the data in columns C and D. Column C contains actual values, but the cells are formatted to display as text. Each value uses a different custom number format. For example, the value in cell C27 uses this custom number format: "Abigail." The x values are duplicated in column B but formatted as numbers. The data labels in the chart use the X Value option, and the custom formats (not the actual values) are displayed. These custom labels also display along the x axis, so you'll need to change the number formatting for the axis (as I did in the figure).

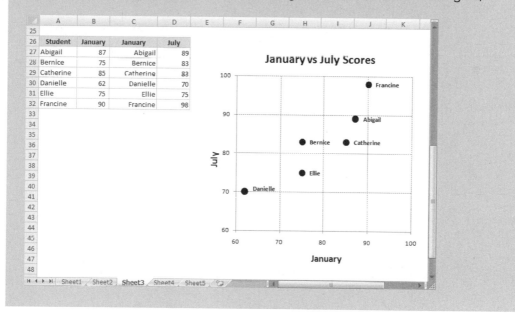

Problems and Limitations with Data Labels

As you work with data labels, you will probably discover that Excel's Data Labels feature leaves a bit to be desired. For example, it would be nice to be able to specify a range of text to be used for the data labels. This would be particularly useful in scatter charts in which you want to identify each data point with a particular text item. Figure 4-40 shows a scatter chart. If you would like to apply data labels to identify the student for each data point, you're out of luck.

Despite what must amount to thousands of requests, Microsoft still has not added this feature to Excel! You need to add data labels and then manually edit each label.

ON THE CD

My Power Utility Pak add-in includes a utility that makes it easy to add data labels to a chart by specifying an arbitrary range of labels for a series (see Figure 4-41). The companion CD-ROM includes a trial version of this add-in.

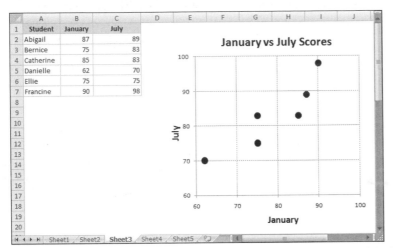

Figure 4-40: Excel provides no direct way to add descriptive data labels to the data points.

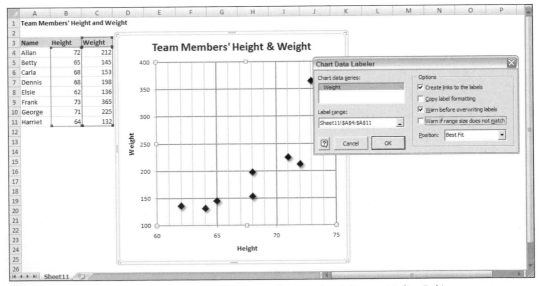

Figure 4-41: The Chart Data Labeler utility (part of the author's Power Utility Pak) overcomes a limitation in Excel.

As you work with data labels, you'll find that this feature works best for series that contain a relatively small number of data points. The chart in Figure 4-42, for example, contains 24 data points. You can't display all the data labels on this chart and keep the chart legible.

One option is to delete some of the individual data labels. For example, you might want to delete all the data labels except those at the high and low points of the series. Deleting only certain data labels is, however, a manual process. To delete an individual data label, select it and press Delete. Using gridlines provides another way to let the reader discern the values for the data points. Yet another alternative is to use a data table, which is described in the next section.

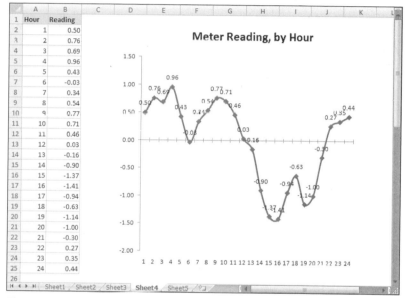

Figure 4-42: Data labels don't work well for this chart.

Working with a Chart Data Table

In some cases, you might want to display a data table for a chart. A data table displays the chart's data in tabular form, directly in the chart's chart area. Figure 4-43 shows a chart that includes a data table.

 ON THE CD

The examples in this section are available on the companion CD-ROM. The file name is `data table.xlsx`.

NOTE

Data tables can be used with only a few chart types. You cannot use a data table with scatter charts, pie charts, doughnut charts, radar charts, bubble charts, and surface charts.

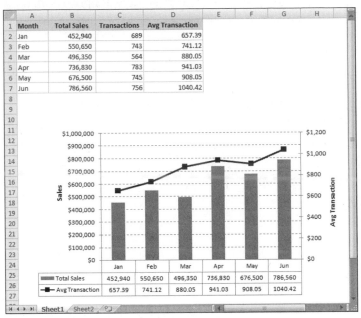

Figure 4-43: This chart includes a data table.

Adding and Removing a Data Table

To add a data table to a chart, select the chart and choose Chart Tools⇨Layout⇨Labels⇨ Data Table⇨Show Data Table.

To remove a data table from a chart, select the chart and choose Chart Tools⇨Layout⇨ Labels⇨Data Table⇨None. Or, select the data table element in the chart and press Delete.

Problems and Limitations with Data Tables

One problem with data tables, as I mentioned previously, is that this feature is available for only a few chart types. Formatting options for a data table are relatively limited. Data table formatting changes are made in the Format Data Table dialog box.

The Fill tab is a bit misleading because it does not actually allow you to change the fill color for the data table. Rather, you are limited to formatting the background of the text and numbers in the data table.

Unfortunately, you cannot apply different font formatting to individual cells or rows within the data table. You also can't change the number formatting. The numbers displayed in a data table always use the same number formatting as the source data.

When you add a data table to a chart, the data table essentially replaces the axis labels on the horizontal axis. The first row of the data table contains these labels, so losing them isn't a major problem. However, you will not be able to apply separate formatting to the axis labels — they will have the same formatting as the other parts of the data table.

NOTE

An exception to the behavior described in the preceding paragraph occurs with bar charts and charts with a time-scale category axis. For these types of charts, the data table is positioned below the chart and does not replace any axis labels.

Another potential problem with data tables occurs when they are used with embedded charts. If you resize the chart to make it smaller, the data table may not show all the data.

Using a data table is probably best suited for charts on chart sheets. If you need to show the data used in an embedded chart, you can do so using data in cells, which provides you with much more flexibility in terms of formatting.

Formatting 3-D Charts

The only marginally useful 3D charts in Excel are surface/contour charts, and they must still be used with great care to avoid distorting the message of the data.

One of the most interesting classes of Excel charts is 3-D charts. Certain situations benefit from the use of 3-D charts, because these charts let you depict changes over two different dimensions. Even a simple column chart commands more attention if you present it as a 3-D chart. Be aware, however, that the perspective of a 3-D chart can often obscure differences among data points and make the chart more difficult to understand.

NOTE

Not all charts that are labeled "3-D" are true 3-D charts. A true 3-D chart has three axes. Some of Excel's 3-D charts are simply 2-D charts with a perspective look to them.

All 3-D charts have a few additional parts that you can customize. For example, most 3-D charts have a *floor* and *walls*, and the true 3-D charts also have an additional axis (the series axis). You can select these chart elements and format them to your liking. To change the depth of a 3-D chart, use the Depth setting on the 3-D Rotation tab of the Format Plot Area dialog box. Or, you can select the floor element and use the 3-D Rotation tab of the Format Floor dialog box.

Figure 4-44 shows a 3-D column chart with three series (Apples, Oranges, and Pears). As you can see, it's virtually impossible to use the gridlines to determine an accurate value for any of the columns. For example, can you tell that the January value for Apples is 154? Even though that column appears next to the vertical axis, the numerical value for the column is not at all obvious.

ON THE CD

The examples in this section are available on the companion CD-ROM. The file name is `3-d charts.xlsx`.

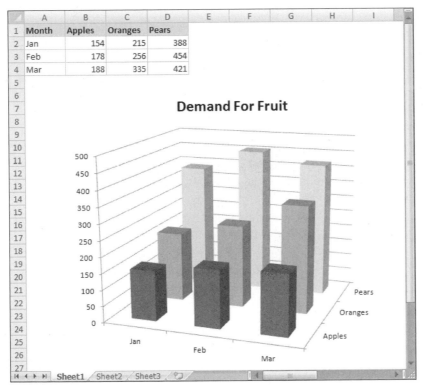

Figure 4-44: A 3-D column chart.

Rotating 3-D Charts

When you start flirting with the third dimension, you have a great deal of flexibility regarding the viewpoint for your charts. Figure 4-45 shows a 3-D column chart that has been rotated to show four different views. It should be clear that Excel allows you to rotate a 3-D chart in such a way that it becomes useless.

To rotate a 3-D chart, select the chart and choose Chart Tools⇨Layout⇨3-D Rotation. Excel displays the 3-D Rotation tab of the Format Chart Area dialog box. You can make your rotations and perspective changes by clicking the appropriate controls. Experiment with the controls, and you'll quickly understand how they affect the chart views.

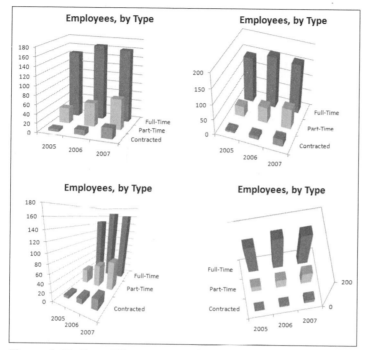

Figure 4-45: Four different views of the same chart.

NOTE

Previous versions of Excel allow you to rotate a 3-D chart by dragging the one of the corners of the wall. This technique does not work in Excel 2007.

Formatting a Surface Chart

A surface chart is different from the other chart types because you cannot select any of the series in the chart. Another difference is that the colors in the chart are based on the values.

The number of colored bands used in the chart depends on the major unit setting for the value axis. Figure 4-46 shows two surface charts. In the chart on the left, the value axis major unit is 0.05 (the default). In the chart on the right, the value axis major unit is 0.4, which covers the entire scale for the chart. Consequently, this chart displays a single color.

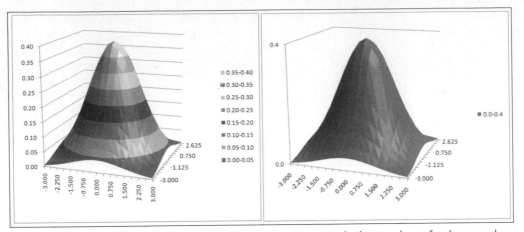

Figure 4-46: Changing the major unit for the value axis controls the number of colors used on a surface chart.

The procedure to adjust the colors used on a surface chart is rather counterintuitive. After you create the surface chart, follow these steps:

1. Make sure that the chart displays a legend.

2. Click the legend to select it, and then click the legend entry that corresponds to the color you want to change.

3. Press Ctrl+1 to display the Format Band dialog box.

4. Use the Fill tab in the Format Band dialog box to change the color and use the Border Color tab to change the line color.

   The controls on the other tabs in the Format Band dialog box have no effect on the chart.

To change the view point of a surface chart, choose Chart Tools⇨Layout⇨3-D Rotation, which displays the 3-D Rotation tab of the Format Chart Area dialog box.

Chapter 5

Working with Trendlines and Error Bars

In This Chapter

◆ Adding a trendline to a data series

◆ Forecasting and predicting with trendlines

◆ Using error bars

◆ Adding other types of series enhancements

This chapter discusses charting features that can make certain charts more informative. A trendline is an additional line added to a chart that depicts general trends in your data. In some cases, you can forecast future data with a trendline. Error bars, used primarily in scientific applications, indicate "plus or minus" information that reflects uncertainty in the data. In addition, some chart series can display other enhancements such as series lines, drop lines, high-low lines, and up/down bars. These topics are all covered in this chapter.

Working with Trendlines

The best way to become acquainted with trendlines is to see one. Figure 5-1 shows a column chart that displays monthly income for 65 time periods. A trendline has been added to the chart. Although this data fluctuates quite a bit, the trendline indicates that income, in general, has been increasing — something that might not be readily apparent without the assistance of the trendline.

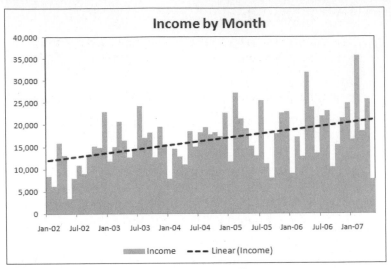

Figure 5-1: This chart displays a linear trendline.

When a trendline is added to a chart, Excel draws the line such that it minimizes the differences between each data point and the corresponding value on the trendline. In other words, the trendline is the "best fit" line for the data series.

Chart Types That Support Trendlines

You can add a trendline to any of the following data series types:

- Scatter chart
- Area chart
- Bar chart
- Column chart
- Line chart
- Stock market chart
- Bubble chart

You *cannot* add a trendline to any type of 3-D chart, stacked chart, radar chart, pie chart, or doughnut chart. If you add a trendline and then change the chart type or data series to an unsupported type, the trendline is deleted.

Data Appropriate for a Trendline

The type of data used in a chart determines whether the chart is appropriate for a trendline. Generally, charts that are suited for a trendline fall into two categories:

- Paired numeric data, as is typically plotted on a scatter chart. Both axes are value axes.

- Time-based data, often plotted on scatter charts, line charts, column charts, and area charts.

Trendlines assume that the category axis contains equal-interval values. This will always be the case with scatter charts, bubble charts, and other chart types that use a time-based category axis. For example, a line chart that displays months or weeks along its category axis is a candidate for a trendline — as long as no gaps exist in the data.

Charts that use an arbitrary category axis are not appropriate for a trendline, although Excel won't object if you add one. If the chart uses an arbitrary category axis, the trendline interprets the categories as values beginning with 1 and incrementing by 1.

Figure 5-2 shows a column chart with a trendline. Because the category axis contains non-numeric text, Excel assigned the value of 1 to Adam, 2 to Ernie, 3 to Jenny, and so on. Consequently, the trendline is completely meaningless.

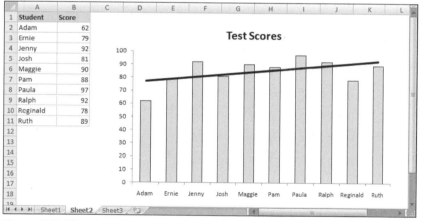

Figure 5-2: This chart is not appropriate for a trendline.

Figure 5-3 shows an example of a chart that *is* appropriate for a trendline. In this case, the chart compares individual performance on two tests using a scatter chart. Because both axes are numeric, the trendline is valid. It indicates a positive linear relationship: Students who did well on Test 1 also tended to do well on Test 2.

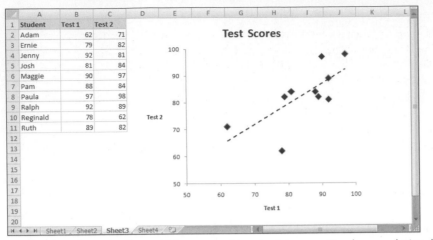

Figure 5-3: The trendline on this scatter chart depicts a positive linear relationship between two variables.

Adding a Trendline

A trendline is always associated with a particular data series. To add a trendline to a chart series, select the series and then choose Chart Tools⇨Layout⇨Analysis⇨Trendline. This command displays a drop-down list with several options:

- **None:** Removes the existing trendline from the series

- **Linear Trendline:** Adds a linear trendline for the series

- **Exponential Trendline:** Adds an exponential trendline for the series

- **Linear Forecast Trendline:** Adds a linear trendline that extends beyond the existing data

- **Two Period Moving Average:** Adds a trendline that displays a moving average

- **More Trendline Options:** Adds a linear trendline and displays the Format Trendline dialog box

These options represent those that Microsoft considers to be the most common types of trendlines. For additional trendline options, you need to use the Format Trendline dialog box.

TIP

A more efficient way to add a trendline is to right-click a data series and choose Add Trendline from the shortcut menu. This method adds a linear trendline and displays the Format Trendline dialog box. You can then use this dialog box to adjust the trendline.

NOTE

An apparent bug in the initial release of Excel 2007 causes the Chart Tools⇨Layout⇨ Analysis⇨Trendline control to be disabled when the chart is an area chart. If you need to add a trendline to an area chart, you must right-click the data series and choose Add Trendline from the shortcut menu. Hopefully, this problem will be fixed in a future update.

Figure 5-4 shows the Trendline Options tab of the Format Trendline dialog box. Use this dialog box to change an existing trendline to a different type, specify options for a trend-line, or apply formatting to the trendline. Not all the options are available for all trendline types.

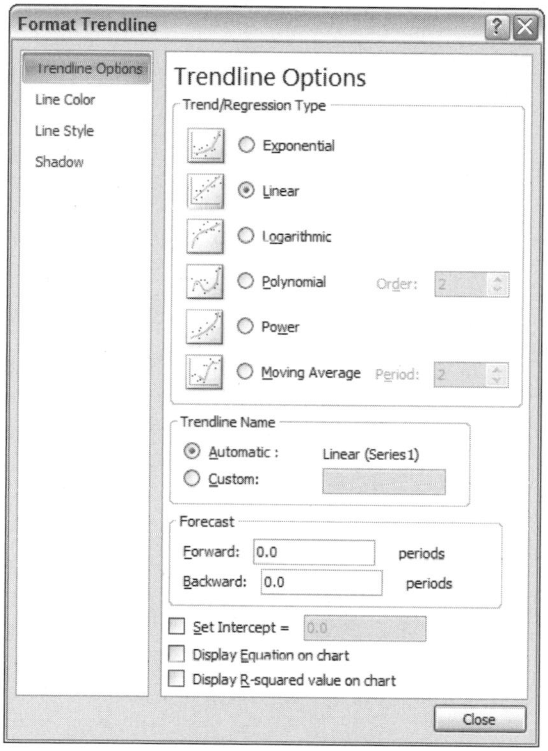

Figure 5-4: The Format Trendline dialog box offers additional trendline options that aren't available by using the Ribbon.

The trendline options are briefly described in the list that follows and are discussed in more detail later in the chapter:

- **Trend/Regression Type:** Select one of the six types of trendlines. The type of trendline that you choose depends on your data. Linear trends are the most common type, but you can describe some data more effectively with other types of trendline. The Power and Exponential trendlines are not available if the data series contains any zero or negative values.

- **Trendline Name:** If you choose Custom, you can provide a different caption for the trendline. This is the text that appears in the legend. If you do not specify a custom name, the legend text consists of the trendline type, followed by the series name in parentheses.

- **Forecast:** These options enable you to extend the trendline forward, backward, or in both directions. You specify the number of periods to forecast.

- **Set Intercept:** Enables you to specify the point on the value axis where the trendline crosses the axis.

- **Display Equation on Chart:** If selected, the regression equation for the trendline will be displayed on the chart.

- **Display R-Squared Value on Chart:** If selected, the R-squared value for the trendline will be displayed on the chart.

 NOTE

A chart can have any number of trendlines, and a single series can have more than one trendline associated with it. For example, you may want to display two different trendlines to determine which type better fits the data.

Figure 5-5 shows a chart with the monthly income data presented earlier in this chapter, along with an additional series for the corresponding monthly expenses (expressed as negative values). A trendline was added to each series. The trendlines indicate that income has been increasing. Expenses have also been increasing, but at a much slower pace than income.

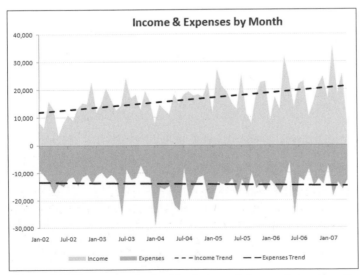

Figure 5-5: The two series in this chart each have a linear trendline.

Formatting a Trendline

When Excel inserts a trendline, it may appear to be a new data series, but it's not. Rather, a trendline is a new chart element with a name, such as Series 1 Trendline 1. And, of course, a trendline does not have a corresponding SERIES formula.

Select a trendline and press Ctrl+1 to display the Format Trendline dialog box, which enables you to change its formatting or its options (discussed in the previous section).

Formatting a Trendline Label

If you choose either of the options that display a trendline equation or the R-squared value, the trendline will be accompanied by a text item that displays the requested information. Figure 5-6 shows a trendline label in the upper-left corner of a scatter chart.

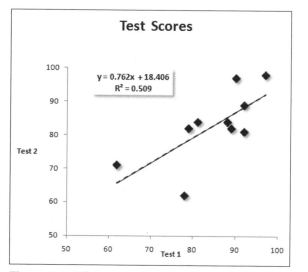

Figure 5-6: When you add a trendline, you have an option to include the equation and R-squared value.

When the data changes, the trendline label is updated automatically to display the recalculated equation. To move the trendline label, just drag it. To change the formatting, select the label and press Ctrl+1 to display the Format Trendline Label dialog box.

A common type of formatting change is to increase the number of decimal places displayed in the equation. Use the Number tab of the Format Trendline Label dialog box to adjust the number formatting. For example, you can choose Number in the Category list and then specify five decimal places.

NOTE

In previous versions of Excel, you change the number of decimal places in a trendline equation by using the Increase Decimal or Decrease Decimal buttons. Those buttons (located in the Home⇨Number group) do not work with a trendline label in Excel 2007.

You can also use Ribbon commands and the Mini toolbar to change the text formatting of a trendline label.

NOTE

Excel allows you to edit the text contained in a trendline label, but after you do so, Excel no longer updates the trendline label if the data is changed. Therefore, it will display an incorrect equation. To make the trendline equation dynamic again, delete it and then add it again by using the Trendline Options tab of the Format Trendline dialog box.

Linear Trendlines

A linear trend describes data in which two variables are related in a linear manner, or in which one variable changes steadily over time. Figure 5-7 shows a scatter chart that plots the height and weight for 15 individuals. A linear trendline has been added to the chart.

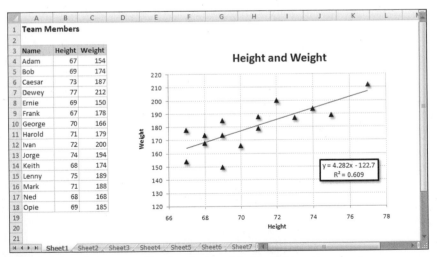

Figure 5-7: A linear trendline has been added to this scatter chart.

ON THE CD

The examples in this section are available on the companion CD-ROM. The filename is `linear trendlines.xlsx`.

The chart also uses the options to display the equation and the R-squared value for the trendline. In this example, the equation is as follows:

`y = 4.282x - 122.7`

The R-squared value is 0.609.

What do these numbers mean? You may remember from algebra classes that a straight line can be described with an equation of the form:

`y = mx + b`

The variable m represents the slope of the line and b represents the y-intercept. The slope of a line is the amount by which the y value changes for a 1-unit change in x. The y-intercept is the value at which the line crosses the y-axis.

NOTE

In the preceding example, the y-intercept is –122.7. However, the trend line *appears* to intersect the y-axis at (approximately) the 160 value. This apparent discrepancy is due to the fact that the scale value for the x-axis does not begin with 0. If you change the axis scaling and extend the trendline, you'll see that it meets the y-axis at the –122.7 value.

For each value of x (in this case, column B), you can calculate the predicted value of y (the value that falls on the trendline) by using the trendline equation. For example, Adam has a height (x) of 67 inches and a weight (y) of 154 pounds. Adam's *predicted* weight (y), using the following formula, is 164.06:

`y = (4.282 * 67) - 122.7`

In other words, 164.06 is the y value on the linear trend line when x is 67. If a new 6'0" member were recruited for the team, the best guess of his weight would be 185.46, as calculated by this formula:

`y = (4.282 * 72) - 122.7`

The R-squared value, sometimes referred to as the *coefficient of determination,* ranges in value from 0 to 1. This value indicates how closely the estimated values for the trendline correspond to the actual data — a "goodness of fit" measure of the overall reliability of the trend. A trendline is most reliable when its R-squared value is near 1 and is least reliable when it's near 0. If all the data points fell exactly on the trendline, the R-squared value would be 1.0.

TIP

A simpler way to generate the predicted *y* values for a linear trendline is to use the TREND function in a multicell array formula. Using the preceding example, select D4:D18 and enter the following array formula:

```
=TREND(C4:C18,B4:B18)
```

Enter the formula by pressing Ctrl+Shift+Enter. The range will display the predicted *y* values for the data in B4:B18.

Linear Forecasting

Thus far, the discussion has focused on making predictions for data that falls within the existing numerical range (*interpolation*). In addition, you can make estimates for data that falls outside the existing range of data. This is known as *forecasting* or *extrapolation*.

Calculating the slope, y-intercept, and R-squared values

As described in this chapter, you can use the FORECAST function to calculate the points on a linear trendline and forecast other values. Alternatively, you can calculate the slope and y-intercept for the best-fit line, and then use these values to calculate the data points.

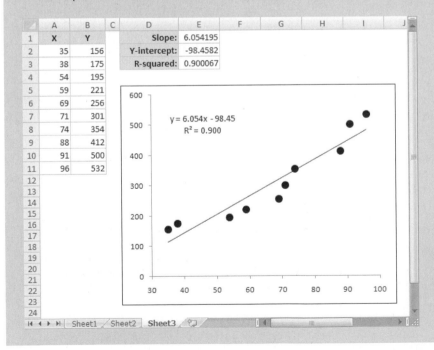

Assume that the x values are in A2:A11 and the y values are in B2:B11. To calculate the slope, you can use the SLOPE function, as follows:

```
=SLOPE(B2:B11,A2:A11)
```

Use the following formula to calculate the y-intercept:

```
=INTERCEPT(B2:B11,A2:A11)
```

When you know the values for the slope and the y-intercept, you can calculate the predicted y value for each x using a formula in this form:

$$y = mx + b$$

The accuracy of forecasted values depends on how well the linear trendline fits your actual data. The value of R-squared represents the degree of fit. R-squared values closer to 1 indicate a better fit and will yield more accurate predictions. Statistically speaking, you can interpret R-squared as the proportion of the variance in y that is attributable to the variance in x.

To calculate R-squared, you can use the RSQ function, as in this formula:

```
=RSQ(B2:B11,A2:A11)
```

Or, calculate the correlation coefficient and square it:

```
=CORREL(B2:B11,A2:A11)^2
```

Keep in mind that the value of R-squared calculated by the RSQ function or CORREL function is valid only for a linear trendline.

When your chart contains a trendline, you can instruct Excel to extend the trendline to forecast additional values of x. You do this on the Trendline Options tab of the Format Trendline dialog box. Just specify the number of periods to forecast (either forward or backward in time).

This limitation on backward forecasting also applies to a date-scale axis, which is apparently a bug. In prior versions of Excel, the backward forecasting on a time scale axis was not limited in this way.

Excel does not accept a negative forecast value. To draw a trendline for a subset of the series data, you need to plot another series that omits the points you want to exclude.

Figure 5-8 shows a line chart with monthly sales data for 21 months, along with a trendline that forecasts results for 3 subsequent months. The forecasted data is derived by simply extending the linear trendline to cover three additional periods.

 NOTE

Because the category axis displays non-numeric data, Excel uses consecutive integers in its calculations.

Figure 5-8: Using a trendline to forecast sales for three additional periods of time.

Getting the Trendline Values

The preceding example leads, of course, to the question *What are the actual forecasted sales values?* As described previously, you can use the slope and y-intercept values to calculate the predicted *y* value for a given value of *x*. It's a fairly simple exercise to create formulas to perform these calculations.

One approach is to copy the slope and y-intercept values displayed in the trendline's equation, and use these values to calculate the predicted *y* values. (This is the method used earlier in this chapter to predict a person's weight, based on his or her height.) For increased accuracy, you can calculate the slope and y-intercept and use these values to calculate the predicted values. (See the nearby sidebar, "Calculating the slope, y-intercept, and R-squared values.") The simplest approach (for linear trendlines only) is to use Excel's FORECAST function.

Figure 5-9 shows the data from the sales forecast chart. Column A contains the month names (for reference only), and column B contains consecutive month numbers. The actual sales figures are in column C. Column D contains formulas that return the predicted *y* values displayed in the trendline.

The formula in cell D2 is as follows:

```
=FORECAST(B2,$C$2:$C$25,$B$2:$B$25)
```

This formula was copied to the 24 cells below. As you can see, values for the final 3 months are forecast, based on the trend for the first 21 months.

	A	B	C	D	E
1	**Month**	**Month No.**	**Sales**	**Predicted**	
2	Jan	1	146,899	147,426	
3	Feb	2	147,456	148,386	
4	Mar	3	141,865	149,346	
5	Apr	4	153,690	150,306	
6	May	5	153,554	151,266	
7	Jun	6	151,644	152,226	
8	Jul	7	158,500	153,186	
9	Aug	8	153,780	154,147	
10	Sep	9	154,834	155,107	
11	Oct	10	151,391	156,067	
12	Nov	11	155,012	157,027	
13	Dec	12	162,688	157,987	
14	Jan	13	161,601	158,947	
15	Feb	14	161,203	159,907	
16	Mar	15	168,586	160,867	
17	Apr	16	156,097	161,827	
18	May	17	162,608	162,787	
19	Jun	18	163,089	163,747	
20	Jul	19	161,577	164,707	
21	Aug	20	167,043	165,668	
22	Sep	21	164,445	166,628	
23	Oct	22		167,588	
24	Nov	23		168,548	
25	Dec	24		169,508	
26					
27					

Sheet1 Sheet2

Figure 5-9: Column D uses the FORECAST function to calculate points on a trendline.

NOTE

The calculated values in column D, if plotted on a chart, would display a line that's identical to the linear trendline.

Nonlinear Trendlines

Although linear trendlines are most common, an Excel chart can display nonlinear trendlines of the following types:

- **Exponential:** Used when data values rise or fall at increasingly higher rates. The data cannot contain zero or negative values.

- **Logarithmic:** Used when the rate of change in the data increases or decreases quickly and then flattens out.

- **Polynomial:** Used when data fluctuates in an orderly pattern. You can specify the order of the polynomial (from 2 to 6), depending on the number of fluctuations in the data.

- **Power:** Used when the data consists of measurements that increase at a specific rate. The data cannot contain zero or negative values.

- **Moving Average:** A moving average isn't a trendline. This option, however, can be useful for smoothing out "noisy" data.

Earlier in this chapter, I noted that the equation for a straight line uses the slope and y-intercept. Nonlinear trendlines also have equations, but these equations are more complex. The following sections cover the nonlinear trendlines available in Excel, and I provide the equations for each type.

 ON THE CD

The examples in this section are available on the companion CD-ROM. The filename is `nonlinear trendlines.xlsx`.

Logarithmic Trendline

A logarithmic trendline might be appropriate for data that follows a logarithmic curve: The values increase or decrease quickly and then level out. A logarithmic trendline appears as a straight line on a chart with a linear y-axis scale and a logarithmic x-axis scale. The equation for a logarithmic trendline is as follows

```
y = [c * LN(x)] - b
```

Figure 5-10 shows a chart with a logarithmic trendline added. The formula in cell E2, which follows, calculates *c*:

```
=INDEX(LINEST(B2:B11,LN(A2:A11)),1,1)
```

The formula to calculate *b*, in cell F2, is as follows:

```
=INDEX(LINEST(B2:B11,LN(A2:A11)),1,2)
```

Column C shows the predicted *y* values for each value of *x*, using the calculated values for *b* and *c*. For example, the formula in cell C2 is as follows:

```
=($E$2*LN(A2))+$F$2
```

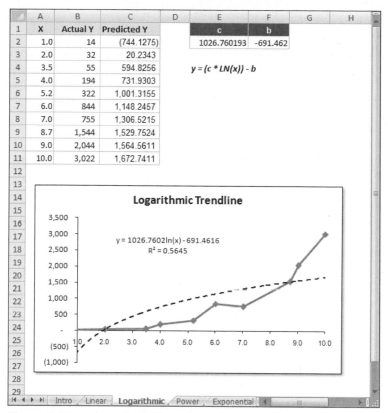

Figure 5-10: A chart displaying a logarithmic trendline.

Power Trendline

A power trendline describes data that increases (or accelerates) at a specific rate. A power trendline appears as a straight line on a chart with a logarithmic y-axis and a logarithmic x-axis scale. This trendline is limited to positive values. The equation for a power trendline looks like this:

```
y = c * x^b
```

Figure 5-11 shows a chart with a power trendline added. Cell E2 contains the following formula, which calculates b:

```
=INDEX(LINEST(LN(B2:B11),LN(A2:A11)),1,1)
```

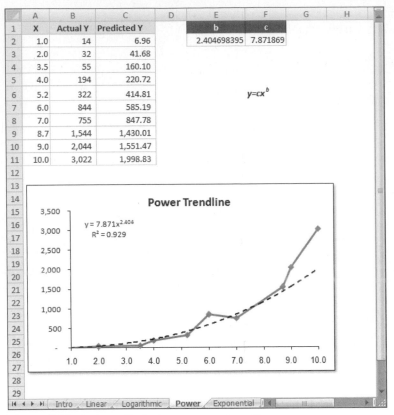

Figure 5-11: A chart displaying a power trendline.

The value for *c* is calculated in F2, using this formula:

```
=EXP(INDEX(LINEST(LN(B2:B11),LN(A2:A11)),1,2))
```

Column C shows the predicted *y* values for each value of *x*, using the calculated values for *b* and *c*. For example, the formula in cell C2 is as follows:

```
=$F$2*(A2^$E$2)
```

Exponential Trendline

An exponential trendline is used for data that rises or falls at an increasing rate. An exponential trendline appears as a straight line on a chart with a logarithmic y-axis scale and a linear x-axis scale. As with the power trendline, the exponential trendline does not work with data that contains zero or negative values. The equation for an exponential trendline looks like this:

```
y = c * EXP(b * x)
```

Figure 5-12 shows a chart with an exponential trendline added. The value for *c* is calculated in cell G2, which contains this formula:

```
=EXP(INDEX(LINEST(LN(B2:B11),A2:A11),1,2))
```

Cell F2 contains this formula, which calculates the value for *b*:

```
=INDEX(LINEST(LN(B2:B11),A2:A11),1,1)
```

Column C shows the predicted *y* values for each value of *x*, using the calculated values for *b* and *c*. For example, the formula in cell C2 is as follows:

```
=$G$2*EXP($F$2*A2)
```

Column D contains a multicell array formula that produces the same results. The array formula in range D2:D11 is:

```
=GROWTH(B2:B11,A2:A11)
```

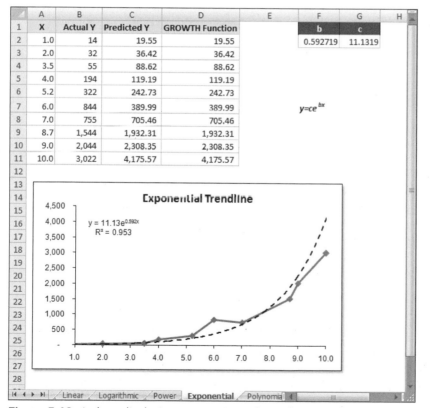

Figure 5-12: A chart displaying an exponential trendline.

Polynomial Trendline

A polynomial trendline defines a curved line and describes data that fluctuates in an orderly pattern. When you request a polynomial trendline, you also need to specify the order of the polynomial (ranging from 2 through 6). The equation for a polynomial trendline depends on the order of the polynomial.

SECOND-ORDER TRENDLINE

A second-order trendline (also known as a quadratic trendline) describes data that resembles a U or an inverted U. Following is the equation for a second-order polynomial trendline:

```
y = (c2 * x^2) + (c1 * x^1) + b
```

Notice that two c coefficients appear (one for each order).

Figure 5-13 shows a chart with a second-order polynomial trendline added. Formulas entered in E2:G2 calculate the values for each of the c coefficients and the b constant. The formulas are as follows:

```
E2:    =INDEX(LINEST(B2:B11,A2:A11^{1,2}),1,1)
F2:    =INDEX(LINEST(B2:B11,A2:A11^{1,2}),1,2)
G2:    =INDEX(LINEST(B2:B11,A2:A11^{1,2}),1,3)
```

Column C shows the predicted y values for each value of x, using the calculated values for b and the two c coefficients. For example, the formula in cell C2 is as follows:

```
=($E$2*A2^2)+($F$2*A2^1)+$G$2
```

HIGHER-ORDER POLYNOMIAL TRENDLINES

A polynomial trendline can use between two and six coefficients. Higher-order trendlines can often describe data sets that have complex or multiple curves. Figure 5-14 shows a chart with a third-order polynomial trendline. The equation for this trendline is similar to the second-order polynomial trendline equation, but with an additional coefficient:

```
y = (c3 * x^3) + (c2 * x^2) + (c1 * x^1) + b
```

Formulas in E2:H2 calculate the values for each of the c coefficients and the b constant. The formulas are as follows:

```
E2:    =INDEX(LINEST(B2:B11,A2:A11^{1,2,3}),1,1)
F2:    =INDEX(LINEST(B2:B11,A2:A11^{1,2,3}),1,2)
G2:    =INDEX(LINEST(B2:B11,A2:A11^{1,2,3}),1,3)
H2:    =INDEX(LINEST(B2:B11,A2:A11^{1,2,3}),1,4)
```

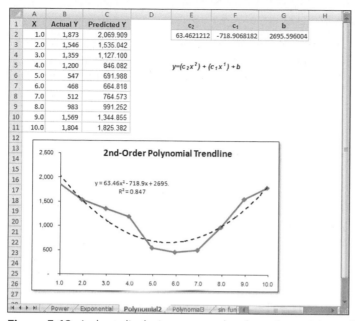

Figure 5-13: A chart displaying a second-order polynomial trendline.

NOTE

Formulas to generate the values for other orders of polynomial trendlines follow a pattern similar to the formulas listed previously. For example, a fifth-order polynomial has five coefficients and one constant. The first coefficient for a fifth-order polynomial is calculated with the following formula:

```
=INDEX(LINEST(B2:B11,A2:A11^{1,2,3,4,5}),1,1)
```

Figure 5-15 shows a sine curve (for x values of 1 through 8.25), along with a 6th-order polynomial trendline. The trendline, with an R-squared value of 1, is such a good fit that it corresponds exactly to the sine curve.

NOTE

The sine curve trendline illustrates a danger with the overuse of polynomial curve fitting. If you forecast on either side of the data, the trendline will fit horribly, and the forecast will not be accurate.

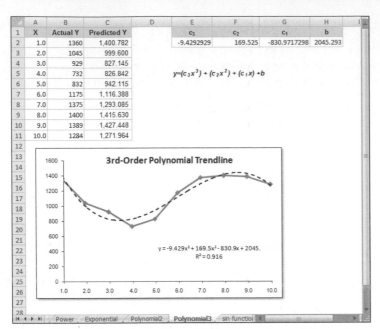

The following equation is shown in the worksheet:

$$y = (c_3 x^3) + (c_2 x^2) + (c_1 x) + b$$

The chart is titled "3rd-Order Polynomial Trendline" and displays:

$$y = -9.429x^3 + 169.5x^2 - 830.9x + 2045.$$
$$R^2 = 0.916$$

Figure 5-14: A chart displaying a third-order polynomial trendline.

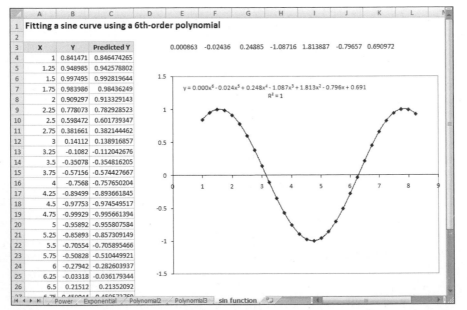

The worksheet is titled "Fitting a sine curve using a 6th-order polynomial" with the chart displaying:

$$y = 0.000x^6 - 0.024x^5 + 0.248x^4 - 1.087x^3 + 1.813x^2 - 0.796x + 0.691$$
$$R^2 = 1$$

Figure 5-15: A 6th-order polynomial trendline for a sine curve corresponds with the data so precisely that the trendline and the data overlap.

Displaying a Moving Average

One of the trendline type options is Moving Average. But as I noted earlier, a moving average is not really a trendline. A moving average displays a line that depicts the data series, averaged over a specified number of data points.

Adding a Moving Average Line

To add a moving average line, select the chart series and choose Chart Tools⇨Layout⇨ Analysis⇨Trendline⇨More Trendline Options. Excel adds a linear trendline and displays the Trendline Options tab of the Format Trendline dialog box. Choose the Moving Average option and specify the number of periods to average.

If you like, choose the Custom option and enter a name for the moving average line. This is the text that will be displayed in the chart's legend.

A moving average is useful for smoothing out noisy data; it may also help to uncover trends that may otherwise be difficult to spot. Figure 5-16 shows a line chart with 50 data points, along with a moving average line with a period of 7. (It displays the average of every seven data points.) As you can see, the moving average line is much smoother and clearly depicts the general upward trend in the data.

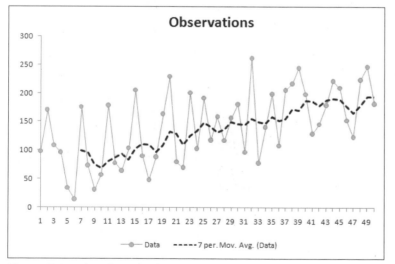

Figure 5-16: This chart displays a moving average.

On the CD

The examples in this section are available on the companion CD-ROM. The filename is `moving average.xlsx`.

Notice that the moving average line does not begin with the first data point. In this case, the line begins at the seventh data point because the period is 7. The beginning of the line is the average of the first seven data points. The second point is the average of data points 2 through 8, the third point is the average of data points 3 through 9, and so on. Generally, using a larger period results in a smoother line — but the line gets shorter as the period increases.

Creating Your Own Moving Average Data Series

You can, of course, create formulas to calculate a moving average for a data series, and then plot the moving average as a separate chart series. For example, assume that your data is in the range A1:A50. To create a moving average with a period of 7, enter this formula into cell B7:

```
=AVERAGE(A1:A7)
```

Then, copy the formula down the column, ending with cell B50. Add B1:B50 as a new data series, and the result will be identical to adding a moving average line via the Add Trendline dialog box.

This technique offers two advantages: You can add a moving average line to chart types that don't support trendlines, and you have more control over the appearance of the moving average line.

Figure 5-17, for example, shows a 3-D line chart. (This type of chart does not support trendlines.) The chart displays an additional series with a calculated moving average.

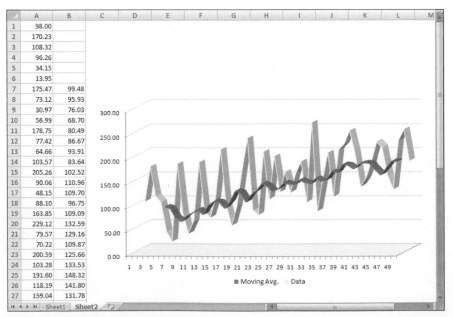

Figure 5-17: This 3-D line chart uses a data series in place of a moving average line.

Part I

Using Error Bars in a Chart Series

A chart series can include error bars to convey additional information about the data. For example, you might use error bars to indicate the amount of error or uncertainty associated with each data point.

Figure 5-18 shows a line chart with error bars above and below each data point, to indicate an error range for each data point. In this case, the error bars are based on percentage: the value plus or minus 10 %.

 ON THE CD

The examples in this section are available on the companion CD-ROM. The filename is error bars.xlsx.

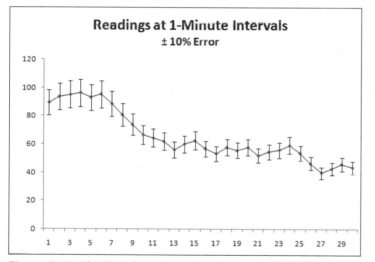

Figure 5-18: This line chart series displays error bars based on percentage.

Chart Types That Support Error Bars

Error bars are available for chart series of the following 2-D chart types:

- Area charts
- Bar charts
- Column charts
- Line charts

- Scatter charts
- Bubble charts

Because scatter charts and bubble charts each have two value axes, you can display error bars for the *x* values, the *y* values, or both.

Adding Error Bars to a Series

To add error bars, select the data series in the chart and choose Chart Tools⇨Layout⇨ Error Bars. This is a drop-down control that offers three types of error bars.

For maximum control, choose More Error Bar Options, which displays the Vertical Error Bars tab of the Format Error Bars dialog box. (See Figure 5-19.)

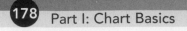

Figure 5-19: The Vertical Error Bars tab of the Format Error Bars dialog box.

 NOTE

If the chart is a scatter chart or a bubble chart, Excel adds two sets of error bars to the series (horizontal and vertical). If you don't need both sets of error bars, you can select one of the sets and press Delete to delete it.

The Format Error Bars dialog box lets you select the direction of your error bars. Vertical error bars display above each data point (Plus), below each data point (Minus), or both above and below each data point (Both). Horizontal error bars (available for scatter charts and bubble charts) offer the same options, but in the horizontal direction.

You can also choose the End Style: display the bars with a Cap or No Cap.

 NEW

Excel 2007 provides line formatting options that aren't available in previous versions. For example, you can specify an arrowhead to display at the end points of your error bars. Specify the arrow settings in the Line Style tab in the Format Error Bars dialog box. If you use arrowheads, make sure that you specify No Cap as the End Style in the Vertical (or Horizontal) Error Bars tab of the Format Error Bars dialog box.

The Error Amount options determine the length of the error bars. These options are as follows:

- **Fixed Value:** The error bars will be offset from each data point by a fixed amount that you specify. Each error bar will be the same height (or same width, for horizontal error bars).

- **Percentage:** The error bars will be offset from each data point by a percentage of the data point's value. For example, if you specify 5 % as the percentage, a data point at 100 would display error bars at values of 95 and 105. Error bars based on percentage will vary in size. Negative error bars that use a percentage of 100 will result in drop lines to the axis.

- **Standard Deviation(s):** The error bars will be centered along an invisible line that represents the average of the data series values, plus or minus the number of standard deviations specified. For this option, the error bars are fixed in size and do not vary with each data point.

- **Standard Error:** The error bars will be offset from each data point by the standard error. The standard error is the standard deviation, divided by the square root of the sample size. Each error bar will be the same height (or same width, for horizontal error bars).

- **Custom:** The error bars will be determined by the values in a range you specify. Usually, this range contains formulas that use the data values.

Figure 5-20 shows a chart that uses error bars to indicate sampling error in a poll. Note that, in this example, the error bars use the Fixed Value option, with a value of .035 to represent a sampling error of 3.5 %. In other words, the percentage of those in favor of the bond issue in October is 40%, plus or minus 3.5% (a range of 36.5% to 43.5%). Notice that the error bars do *not* use the Percentage option, which displays as a percentage of each data point.

Figure 5-21 shows a scatter chart that displays vertical error bars using the Standard Deviation option. Unlike other error bar options, error bars that use the Standard Deviation option are not displayed relative to each data value. Rather, these error bars use the entire data set. In this example, the 100 data points have a mean of 31.64 and a standard deviation of 3.08. Therefore, the error bars display the mean, plus or minus 3.08. Using error bars in this chart makes it clear that the majority of the data points fall within one standard deviation of the mean.

NOTE

Because the x values for this chart are consecutive values, the data points (and the error bars) are equally spaced in the horizontal direction. This spacing creates a useful banding effect.

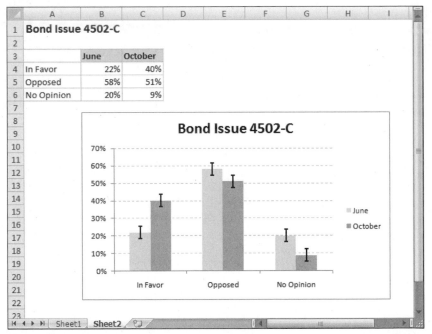

Figure 5-20: This chart uses error bars to indicate sampling error in a poll.

Figure 5-22 shows a scatter chart that uses both vertical and horizontal error bars. Both sets of error bars display the corresponding value plus or minus 12.5 %. The two sets of error bars are independent of each other and can use different options.

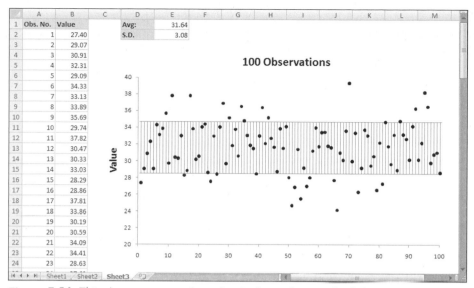

Figure 5-21: This chart uses error bars that indicate the standard deviation.

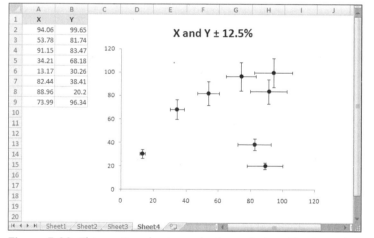

Figure 5-22: This scatter chart uses both vertical and horizontal error bars.

Using Custom Error Bars

The Custom option for error bars enables you to create error bars that aren't otherwise available. In most cases, you'll need first to create formulas that calculate the error bar values and then to specify those formula cells as the range(s) for the error bars.

The chart in Figure 5-23 shows a line chart that plots monthly sales. It uses error bars to depict the relative sales volume for the *previous* year. In this case, an error bar that appears above a data point indicates that the previous year's sales were higher in that month. When it appears below the data point, the prior year's sales were lower for that month. This chart represents an alternative to displaying an additional data series. In this case, adding another series would make the chart cluttered and perhaps less legible.

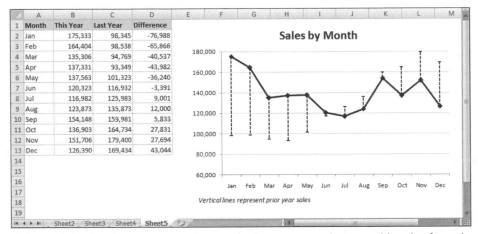

Figure 5-23: This chart uses error bars to depict corresponding monthly sales from the previous year.

Column D contains a simple formula that calculates the difference between the data in columns B and C. Following are the steps I used to create these error bars:

1. Create a line chart using the data in A1:B13.

2. Choose Chart Tools⇨Layout⇨Analysis⇨Error Bars⇨More Error Bar Options.

   Excel adds default error bars to the series and displays the Vertical Error Bars tab of the Format Error Bars dialog box.

3. In the Format Error Bars dialog box, select the Custom option in the Error Amount section and click the Specify Value button.

   Excel displays a Custom Error Bars dialog box that lets you specify the range that contains the error bar values.

4. In the Custom Error Bars dialog box, specify range D2:D13 for either the Positive Error Value range or the Negative Error Value range. Because the error bar values are positive and negative, it doesn't matter which you choose.

5. Use the Format Error Bars dialog box to apply formatting to the error bars. I used a dashed line and made the bars a bit thicker.

Because using error bars in this manner is not a standard technique, I added a text box to the chart to explain how to interpret the error bars.

Figure 5-24 shows another example of a chart that uses custom error bars. This column chart plots the average daily call volume for each of six weeks. The error bars depict the daily minimum and maximum for each week. For example, in Week-1, the average call volume was 103.71 calls per day. The maximum for the week was 173 and the minimum was 32.

The daily data appears in range B3:G9. Additional calculations were made for the data that appears in the chart. Row 13 contains the calculated average, which is the data used for the columns in the chart. Formulas in rows 14 and 15 calculate the maximums and minimums. Formulas in rows 16 and 17 calculate the data that's used for the error bars. The formulas in row 16 subtract the average from the maximum to yield the values used in the Positive Error Value range for the error bars. The formulas in row 17 subtract the minimum from the average to get the values used in the Negative Error Value range for the error bars.

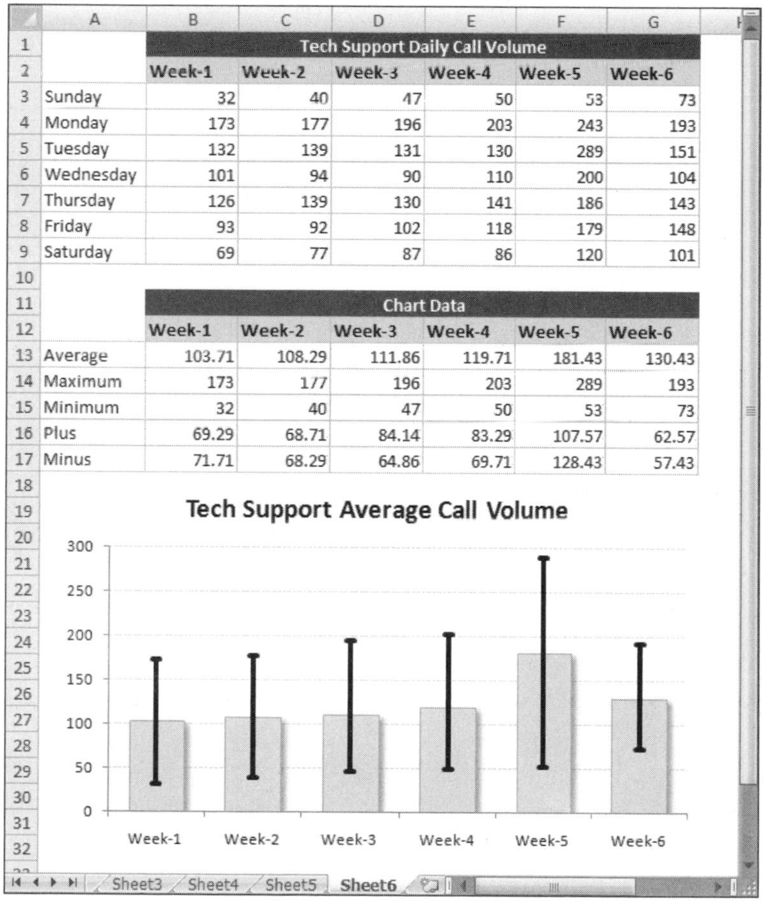

	Tech Support Daily Call Volume					
	Week-1	Week-2	Week-3	Week-4	Week-5	Week-6
Sunday	32	40	47	50	53	73
Monday	173	177	196	203	243	193
Tuesday	132	139	131	130	289	151
Wednesday	101	94	90	110	200	104
Thursday	126	139	130	141	186	143
Friday	93	92	102	118	179	148
Saturday	69	77	87	86	120	101

	Chart Data					
	Week-1	Week-2	Week-3	Week-4	Week-5	Week-6
Average	103.71	108.29	111.86	119.71	181.43	130.43
Maximum	173	177	196	203	289	193
Minimum	32	40	47	50	53	73
Plus	69.29	68.71	84.14	83.29	107.57	62.57
Minus	71.71	68.29	64.86	69.71	128.43	57.43

Figure 5-24: The columns depict the weekly average; the custom error bars show the minimum and maximum for the week.

Connecting Series Points to a Trendline with Error Bars

If you add a trendline to a chart, you can use error bars to indicate the deviations between the actual and the predicted values. Figure 5-25 shows an example.

First, create the scatter chart and add a linear trendline. (Choose Chart Tools➪Layout➪ Trendline➪Linear Trendline.) Then, create formulas to calculate the predicted *y* values (the values along the trendlines). For this example, the range C2:C11 contains the following multicell array formula (entered by pressing Ctrl+Shift+Enter):

```
=TREND(B2:B11,A2:A11)
```

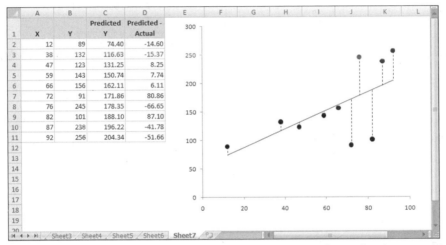

Figure 5-25: This scatter chart uses vertical error bars to indicate the deviation between the actual *y* values and the predicted *y* values on the trendline.

Next, create formulas to calculate the difference between each predicted *y* value and each actual *y* value. In this example, cell D2 contains the following formula, which was copied down to cell D11:

```
=C2-B2
```

The final step is to add vertical error bars to the chart. Follow these steps:

1. Choose Chart Tools➪Layout➪Analysis➪Error Bars➪More Error Bars Options.

   Excel adds horizontal and vertical error bars to the series and displays the Vertical Error Bars tab of the Format Error Bars dialog box.

2. In the Format Error Bars dialog box, choose the Custom option and click the Specify Values button.

   Excel displays the Custom Error Bars dialog box.

3. In the Custom Error Bars dialog box, specify D2:D11 for the Positive Error Value range and click the OK button.

4. On the Vertical Error Bars tab of the Format Error Bars dialog box, choose the No Cap option for the end style. Apply other formatting as desired.

Because it's a scatter chart, Excel also adds horizontal error bars. Just select the horizontal error bars and press Delete. You might need to use the Chart Elements control to select these error bars.

For data points in which the predicted y value is greater than the actual y value, the error bar extends upward from the data point. For data points in which the predicted y value is less than the actual y value, the error bar extends downward from the data point. The sum of these deviations will always be 0.

Error Bar Alternatives

In some cases you may prefer to "roll your own" error bars by adding one or two additional series to your chart. Figure 5-26 shows two charts. The chart on the top uses standard error bars to display one standard deviation. The chart on the bottom uses two additional series to plot lines that represent plus and minus one standard deviation.

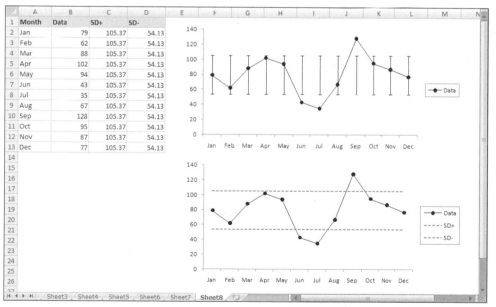

Figure 5-26: Using two additional series as a substitute for error bars.

The data for the additional ranges used in the second chart are in columns C and D. The formula in C2, which was copied to the cells below, is as follows:

```
=AVERAGE($B$2:$B$13)+STDEV($B$2:$B$13)
```

The formula in D2, also copied to the cells below, is as follows:

```
=AVERAGE($B$2:$B$13)-STDEV($B$2:$B$13)
```

The easiest way to add these two data series to the chart is to activate the chart and drag the range outline to include the new data in C1:D13. This action adds two new line series to the chart (with series names), and then you can format them as you like.

One advantage of these additional series is that you have more control over the formatting. Vertical error bars, for example, always appear as vertical lines, and the lines cannot be connected horizontally. In addition, using a series for error bars enables you to display a description in the legend. Most would agree that the bottom chart is less cluttered and more legible.

Other Series Enhancements

So far, this chapter has covered trendlines and error bars. These are two common ways to augment a chart data series. In addition, some chart series can be enhanced with the following:

- Series lines
- Drop lines
- High-low lines
- Up/down bars
- Varied colors

These features are discussed in the sections that follow.

ON THE CD

The examples in this section are available on the companion CD-ROM. The filename is `other series enhancements.xlsx`.

Series Lines

A series line is applicable for the 2-D variants of stacked bar charts and stacked column charts, as well as pie of pie charts and bar of pie charts. Figure 5-27 shows an example of a stacked column chart with the series line option enabled. As you can see, the series lines simply connect the top of each data point with the next data point in the series.

To turn series lines on or off, select the chart and choose Chart Tools⇨Layout⇨ Analysis⇨Lines.

TIP

For a single-series bar chart or column chart, the Chart Tools⇨Layout⇨Analysis⇨Lines command is disabled. If you would like to display a series line on such a chart, you need to change the chart type to a stacked column chart (which will not change the chart's appearance).

To change the appearance of a series line, select a series line and press Ctrl+1 to display the Format Series Lines dialog box. Formatting changes apply to all the series lines on the chart.

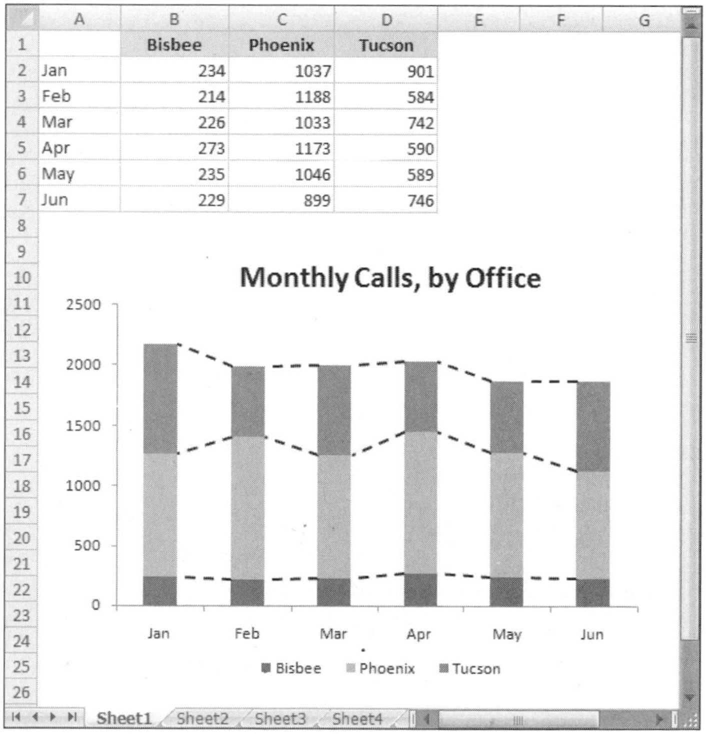

	A	B	C	D	E	F	G
1		**Bisbee**	**Phoenix**	**Tucson**			
2	Jan	234	1037	901			
3	Feb	214	1188	584			
4	Mar	226	1033	742			
5	Apr	273	1173	590			
6	May	235	1046	589			
7	Jun	229	899	746			

Monthly Calls, by Office

■ Bisbee ■ Phoenix ■ Tucson

Sheet1 Sheet2 Sheet3 Sheet4

Figure 5-27: This stacked column chart uses series lines.

Drop Lines

Line charts and area charts can display drop lines, as shown in Figure 5-28. When this option is in effect, a line drops from each data point to the category axis.

TIP

To simulate drop lines in a scatter chart, use error bars. Specify negative error bars with a percentage of 100%.

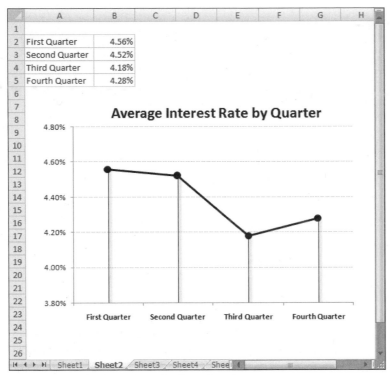

Figure 5-28: This line chart displays drop lines.

To turn drop lines on, select the chart and choose Chart Tools⇨Layout⇨Analysis⇨ Lines⇨Drop Lines. To delete drop lines, select a drop line and press Delete.

Normally, drop lines apply to all series in the chart. However, if you have a combination chart that consists of a line and an area series, you can select one of the series before you choose the Drop Lines command, and only that series will display drop lines

To apply drop lines to only one series in a multiseries chart, specify a secondary value axis for the series before you apply the drop lines. Figure 5-29 shows a line chart with two series. One of the series uses a secondary value axis, and only that series displays drop lines. For details regarding secondary axes, refer to Chapter 4.

To change the appearance of drop lines, select a drop line and press Ctrl+1 to display the Format Drop Lines dialog box.

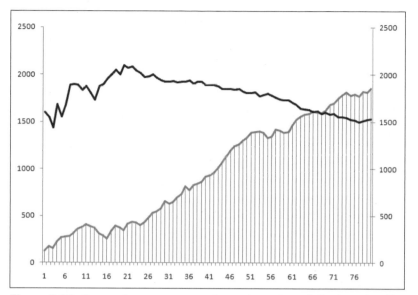

Figure 5-29: One series uses a secondary value axis and displays drop lines.

High-Low Lines

High-low lines are frequently used in stock market charts. In fact, when you create a stock market chart, high-low lines are added automatically. However, this feature can be used in any line chart that has at least two series.

The high-low lines connect the maximum data point in the category with the minimum data point in the category. Figure 5-30 shows an example that uses two data series. The high-low lines depict the difference between the sales goal and the actual sales made.

To add high-low lines to a line chart, select the chart and choose Chart Tools⇨Layout⇨ Analysis⇨Lines⇨High-Low Lines. To delete high-low lines, select a high-low line and press Delete.

To change the appearance of high-low lines, select a high-low line and press Ctrl+1 to display the Format High-Low Lines dialog box.

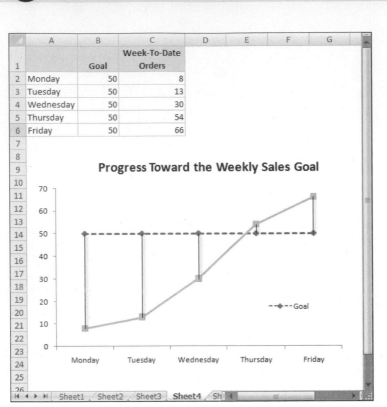

Figure 5-30: High-low lines connect the highest and lowest points within a category.

Up/Down Bars

As with high-low lines, up/down bars are commonly used in stock market charts. Up/down bars are available only with 2-D line charts that have at least two series.

In a stock market chart, up/down bars (sometimes referred to as *candlesticks*) connect the day's opening price with the closing price. If the closing price is higher than the opening price, the bar is a lighter color. Otherwise, the bar is a darker color. You can format up/down bars any way you like.

Figure 5-31 shows a line chart with up/down bars. The first series plots income and the second plots expenses. The up/down bars connect each corresponding data point and represent the net profit for the month. Note that in January, February, and April, expenses exceeded income, so the bars for those months are down bars and they display in a lighter different color.

How up/down bars work

Up/down bars rely on the plot order of the series. The up/down bars always connect the first series with the last series. If a line chart has six data series, the up/down bars will connect the first and the sixth. The only way to control which series get connected is to change the series plot order.

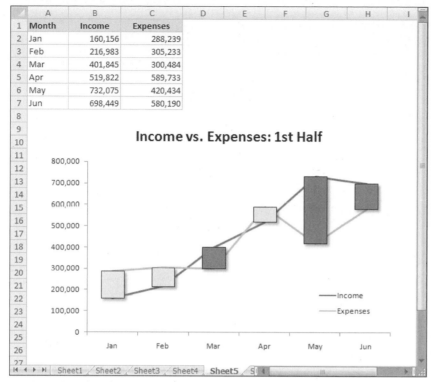

Figure 5-31: This chart uses up/down bars to depict net profit by month.

 CROSS-REFERENCE

Refer to Chapter 3 for more information about changing the plot order for data series.

To add up/down bars to a line chart, select the chart and choose Chart Tools⇨Layout⇨ Analysis⇨Up/Down Bars⇨Up/Down Bars. If the up/down bars do not connect the desired series, adjust the plot order.

To remove up/down bars, choose Chart Tools⇨Layout⇨Analysis⇨Up/Down Bars⇨None. Or, select an up/down bar and press Delete.

To change the appearance of up/down bars, select an up/down bar and press Ctrl+1 to display either the Format Up Bars or Format Down Bars dialog box. Note that the dialog box varies, depending on which type of bar is selected. In other words, you can apply different formatting to each of the two types of bars.

Another example of up/down bars is shown in Figure 5-32. This is a line chart with two series that display the normal high and low temperatures, by month. The lines are connected by up/down bars.

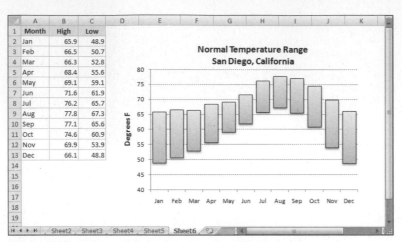

Figure 5-32: Using up/down bars to create floating columns.

Notice that the two series lines are invisible. This effect was done using the Line Color tab of the Format Data Series dialog box. I set the line color to No Line for both series. The result is a "floating column" chart that is not obscured by lines.

Chapter 6

Working with Shapes and Other Graphics

In This Chapter

◆ Inserting and customizing shapes

◆ Working with other types of graphics

◆ Introducing Office 2007 SmartArt

◆ Using shapes with charts

When it comes to visuals to enhance a presentation, Excel has a lot more up its sleeve than charts. As you probably know, you can insert a wide variety of graphic images into your worksheet to add pizzazz to an otherwise boring report. And, as you'll see, you can even combine these graphics with your charts.

This chapter describes the non–chart-related graphic tools available in Excel. These consist of shapes, SmartArt, clip art, and imported images.

Using Shapes

The Microsoft Office applications, including Excel, provide access to a variety of customizable graphic images known as *shapes*. You can add a shape to a worksheet's drawing layer or to a chart.

Access these shapes by using the Insert⇨Illustrations⇨Shapes gallery. If a chart is activated, you can also activate the Shapes gallery by choosing Chart Tools⇨Layout⇨Insert⇨Shapes.

193

The Shapes gallery is shown in Figure 6-1.

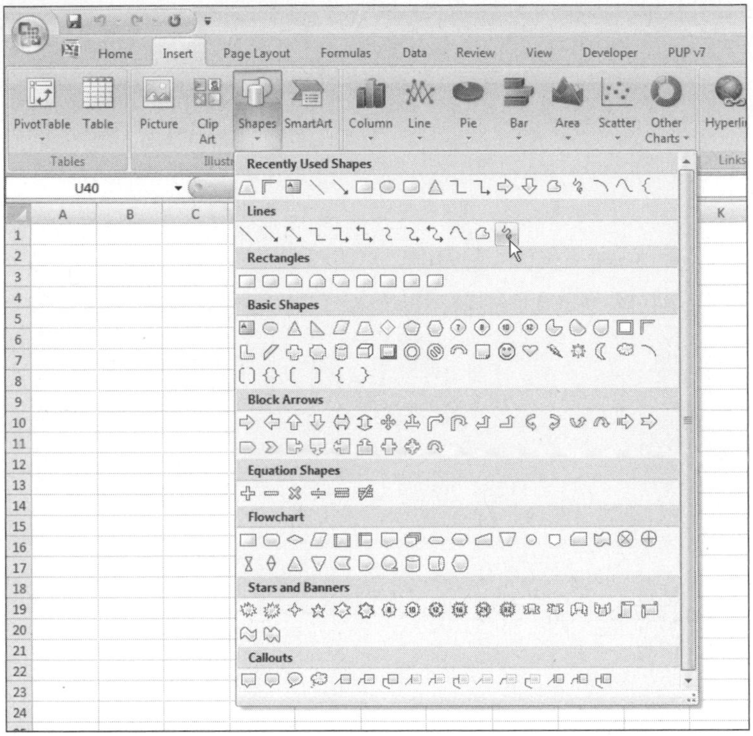

Figure 6-1: The Shapes gallery.

Drawing a shape is easy and very intuitive. The shapes in the gallery are grouped into the following categories:

- **Recently Used Shapes:** Contains the shapes that you've used recently, making it easy to find those shapes again
- **Lines:** Twelve styles of lines, including arrows and freehand drawing
- **Rectangles:** Nine styles of rectangles
- **Basic Shapes:** Forty-two basic shapes, including standard shapes such as rectangles and circles, plus nonstandard shapes such as a smiley face and a heart
- **Block Arrows:** Twenty-seven arrow shapes
- **Equation Shapes:** Six shapes that represent common characters used in equations
- **Flowchart:** Twenty-eight shapes suitable for flowchart diagrams
- **Stars and Banners:** Twenty shapes in the form of stars and banners
- **Callouts:** Sixteen callouts, suitable for annotating cells or chart elements

TIP

You can access additional shapes in the Clip Art gallery. Choose Insert⇨Illustrations⇨ Clip Art to display the Clip Art task pane. Then search for "shape".

Inserting Shapes

You can either add a shape to a worksheet's drawing layer or insert it into a chart. To insert a shape in a worksheet, start by selecting any cell. To insert a shape on a chart, start by activating the chart. Next, access the Shapes gallery, click a shape, and then drag in the worksheet (or chart) to create the shape. Or, you can just click in the worksheet (or chart), and Excel inserts the shape using its default size and proportions.

When you release the mouse button, the shape is selected, the Drawing Tools⇨Format tab is displayed, and the shape's name appears in the Name box (see Figure 6-2).

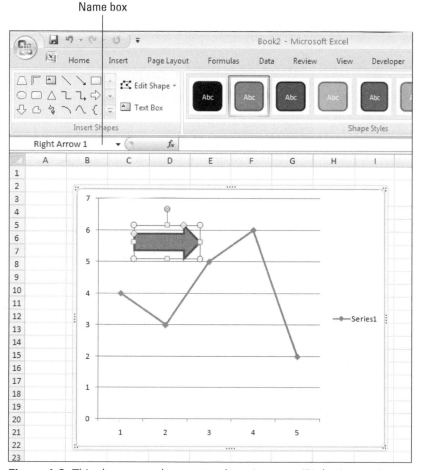

Figure 6-2: This shape was drawn on a chart. Its name (Right Arrow 1) appears in the Name box.

Part I

NOTE

If a chart is not activated when you insert the shape, you can still insert a shape on top of a chart. The shape may appear to be added to the chart, but it will actually reside on the worksheet's drawing layer. Consequently, a shape added on top of a chart will not be moved or resized with the chart.

About the drawing layer

Every worksheet has what's known as a *drawing layer.* This invisible surface can hold shapes, graphic images, embedded charts, inserted objects, and so on.

Objects placed on the drawing layer can be moved, resized, copied, and deleted — with no effect on any other elements in the worksheet. Objects on the drawing layer have properties that relate to how they are moved and sized when underlying cells are moved and sized. When you right-click a graphic object and choose Size and Properties from the shortcut menu, you get a tabbed dialog box (see the accompanying figure). Click the Properties tab to adjust how the object moves or resizes with its underlying cells. Your choices are as follows:

Size and Properties	? X

Size | **Properties** | Alt Text

Object positioning

- ⦿ Move and size with cells
- ○ Move but don't size with cells
- ○ Don't move or size with cells

- ☑ Print object
- ☑ Locked
- ☑ Lock text

Locking objects has no effect unless the sheet is protected. To help protect the sheet, choose Format on the Home tab, and then choose Protect Sheet. A password is optional.

Close

- **Move and Size with Cells:** If this option is selected, the object appears to be attached to the cells beneath it. For example, if you insert rows above the object, the object moves down. If you increase the column width, the object gets wider.

- **Move but Don't Size with Cells:** If this option is selected, the object moves if rows or columns are inserted, but it never changes its size if you change row heights or column widths.

- Don't Move or Size with Cells: This option makes the object independent of the underlying cells.

The preceding options control how an object is moved or sized with respect to the underlying cells. Excel also lets you *attach* an object to a cell. To do so, simply display the Excel Options dialog box, click the Advanced tab, and select the Cut, Copy, and Sort Inserted Objects with Their Parent Cells check box. After you do so, graphic objects on the drawing layer are attached to the underlying cells.

Chart sheets and embedded also have a drawing layer, and objects placed on the drawing layer float above the other chart elements.

Note: An embedded chart also has a Size and Properties dialog box, but Microsoft makes it difficult to access. To display the Size and Properties dialog box for an embedded chart, select the chart and click the dialog box launcher in the Chart Tools ⇨ Format ⇨ Size group. The dialog box launcher is the small icon to the right of the word Size.

A few of the shapes require a slightly different approach. For example, when adding a Freeform shape (from the Lines category), you can click repeatedly to create lines. Or, click and drag to create a nonlinear shape. Double-click to finish drawing and create the shape. The Curve shape (also in the Lines category) also requires several clicks while drawing. If you choose the Scribble shape, you must do your scribbling with the left mouse button held down.

Following are a few tips to keep in mind when creating shapes:

- Shapes are given descriptive names. For example, if you create a rectangle shape, it will be named *Rectangle n,* where *n* represents the next shape number. To change the name of a shape, select it, type a new name in the Name box, and press Enter.

- To select a shape by name, type its name in the Name box and press Enter.

- When you create a shape by dragging, hold down Shift to maintain the object's default proportions. For example, the Rectangle shape will be rendered as a perfect square and the Oval shape will make a perfect circle.

- To constrain a line or arrow object to angles that are evenly divisible by 22.5 degrees, press Shift while you draw the object.

- You can control how objects appear on-screen in the Advanced tab of the Excel Options dialog box (choose Office⇨Excel Options). This setting appears in the Display Options for This Workbook section. Normally, the All option is selected under For Objects Show. You can hide all objects by choosing Nothing (Hide Objects). Hiding objects may speed things up if your worksheet contains complex objects that take a long time to redraw.

Adding Text to a Shape

Many of the Shape objects support text. To add text to such a shape, just select the shape and start typing your text. Or, right-click and choose Edit Text from the shortcut menu. If a shape doesn't support text, its shortcut menu does not display the Edit Text command.

To change the formatting for all the text in a shape, select the Shape object. You can then use the Ribbon commands in the Home⇨Font group. Or, right-click and use the commands in the Mini toolbar. To change the formatting of specific characters within the text, select only those characters so that text formatting commands apply only to the selected characters. In addition, you can dramatically change the look of the text by using the tools in the Drawing Tools⇨Format⇨WordArt Styles group.

Additional text-related commands are available on the Text Box tab of the Format Shape dialog box (which is displayed when you press Ctrl+1). This tab lets you specify the text alignment and margins. In addition, you can click the Columns button and specify multiple columns for your text. Figure 6-3 shows a Parallelogram object with a famous speech displayed in three columns of text.

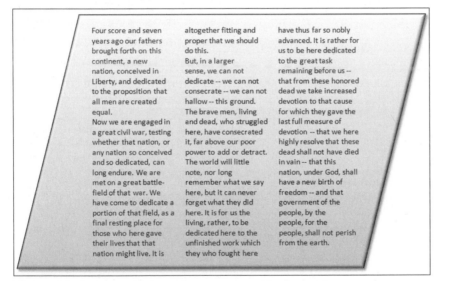

Figure 6-3: A shape with lots of text, arranged in three columns.

Note that the columns option makes the text flow in "snaking" columns. You cannot use this option to enter tabular data in separate columns.

Formatting Shapes

You have a great deal of control when it comes to formatting shapes. First, you must select the shape. If the object is filled with a color or pattern, you can click anywhere on the object to select it. If the object is not filled (formatted with "No Fill" to make it transparent), you must click the shape's border.

When you select a Shape, Excel displays its Drawing Tools⇨Format context tab, with the following groups of commands:

- **Insert Shapes:** Insert new shapes; change a shape to a different shape.

- **Shape Styles:** Change the overall style of a shape or modify the shape's fill, outline, or effects.

- **WordArt Styles:** Modify the appearance of the text within a shape.

- **Arrange:** Adjust the "stack order" of shapes, align shapes, group multiple shapes, and rotate shapes.

- **Size:** Change the size of a shape by entering its height and width.

Some of the commands that are available on the Ribbon are also available on the Shape's shortcut menu, which you access by right-clicking the shape. In addition, you can use your mouse to perform some operations directly (for example, resize or rotate a shape).

You can make quite a few formatting changes by using the controls on the Drawing Tools⇨ Format tab. In addition, you can select the shape and press Ctrl+1 to display the Format Shape dialog box. The Format Shape dialog box has several tabs, and the best way to find out about the options is to experiment.

Figure 6-4 shows a few shapes that demonstrate the variety of formatting that you can apply.

I could probably write 20 pages about formatting shapes, but it would be a waste of paper and certainly not a very efficient way to understand shape formatting. The best way, by far, to find out about formatting shapes is to experiment. Create some shapes, click some commands, and see what happens. The commands are fairly intuitive, and you can always use Undo if something unexpected happens.

Figure 6-4: A few formatted shapes.

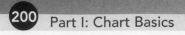

Selecting Multiple Objects

In many cases, you may want to work with several shapes at one time. Excel provides several methods that enable you to select multiple objects in a worksheet or on a chart:

- Press Ctrl while you click the objects.

- Use the Selection and Visibility task pane. To display this task pane, select any shape and choose Drawing Tools⇨Format⇨Arrange⇨Selection Pane. Press Ctrl while you click shape names in the task pane.

- Choose Home⇨Editing⇨Find & Select⇨Select Object. This command puts Excel into object selection mode. In object selection mode, the mouse pointer is an arrow. Just click and drag, and all the underlying shapes are selected. To get back to normal mode, choose the command again (or press Esc).

- To select *all* objects on the worksheet, choose Home⇨Editing⇨Find & Select⇨Go to Special to display the Go to Special dialog box. Choose the Objects option, and click the OK button. This method is particularly useful if you want to delete all objects in a worksheet. When the objects are selected, press Delete.

Grouping Objects

Excel lets you combine two or more objects into a single object. This feature is known as *grouping*. For example, if you create a design that uses four separate shapes, you can combine them into a group. Then you can manipulate this group as a single object (format it, move it, resize it, and so on).

To group two or more objects, select all the objects and then right-click. Choose Group⇨Group from the shortcut menu. Or, choose Drawing Tools⇨Format⇨Arrange⇨Group⇨Group. When objects are grouped, you can still work with an individual object in the group. Click once to select the group, and then click again to select the object.

And, of course, you can always split a group back into its parts. Right-click the grouped object and choose Group⇨Ungroup from the shortcut menu. Or, choose Drawing Tools⇨Format⇨Arrange⇨Group⇨Ungroup.

TIP
You can also group two or more embedded charts. Doing so ensures that the charts stay together and enables you to move and resize them together.

Moving Shapes

To move a shape, click it and drag. For more precise control, use the arrow keys to move the selected object one pixel at a time. Or, press the Alt key while moving or sizing a shape to make the shape's edges snap to the cell boundaries.

> **NOTE**
>
> If the selected object is a chart, the arrow keys won't move the chart by pixels. Rather, you need to select the chart as an object by pressing Ctrl while you click the chart. When a chart is selected as an object, you can use the arrow keys to position it precisely.

Copying Objects

You can use Excel's standard Copy and Paste operations to copy graphic objects in a worksheet or on a chart. Another alternative is to select one or more objects and then press Ctrl while you drag in the worksheet. Note that Ctrl+dragging also copies an embedded chart — but this operation has become somewhat unreliable in Excel 2007. It's easier to select the chart and use Ctrl+C (to copy) and Ctrl+V (to paste).

To copy an object from the worksheet's drawing layer onto a chart, select the object and press Ctrl+C. Then activate your chart and press Ctrl+V. Excel places the copied shape in the upper-left corner of the chart. You can then drag it to its desired location.

Changing the Stack Order of Objects

As you add objects to the drawing layer of a worksheet (or to a chart), you find that objects are "stacked" on top of each other in the order in which you add them. New objects are stacked on top of older objects.

In some cases, an object may be partially or completely hidden by an object higher in the stack. You can change the order in this stack. Right-click the object and select one of the following commands from the shortcut menu:

- **Bring to Front⇨Bring to Front:** Brings the object to the top of the stack
- **Bring to Front⇨Bring Forward:** Brings the object one step higher toward the top of the stack
- **Send to Back⇨Send to Back:** Sends the object to the bottom of the stack
- **Send to Back⇨Send Backward:** Sends the object one step lower toward the bottom of the stack

These commands are also located in the Drawing Tools⇨Format⇨Arrange group.

Aligning and Spacing Objects

When you have several objects in a worksheet, you may want to align and evenly space these objects. You can do it manually by dragging the objects with your mouse (which isn't very precise). Or, you can use the keyboard arrow keys to move a selected object one pixel at a time. The fastest way to align and space objects is to let Excel do it for you.

To align multiple objects, start by selecting them (press Ctrl and click the objects). Then use the tools in the Drawing Tools⇨Format⇨Arrange⇨Align drop-down control.

NOTE

Unfortunately, you can't specify which object is used as the basis for the alignment. When you're aligning objects to the left (or right), they're always aligned with the left-most (or rightmost) object that's selected. When you're aligning objects to the top (or bottom), they're always aligned with the topmost (or bottommost) object. Aligning the centers (or middles) of objects will align them along an axis halfway between the left and right (or top and bottom) extremes of the selected shapes.

You can instruct Excel to distribute three or more objects so that they're equally spaced horizontally or vertically. Use the Drawing Tools⇨Format⇨Arrange⇨Align drop-down control and select Distribute Horizontally or Distribute Vertically.

To align objects to the cell grid when you create, resize, or move them, you need to turn on the Snap to Grid option. Select an object, and then choose Drawing Tools⇨Format⇨ Arrange⇨Align⇨Snap to Grid. (This command is a toggle.) When that option is in effect, all objects that are created or resized will be aligned with the cell borders. And when you move an object, its upper-left corner will always be at a cell intersection. At least that's the way it's supposed to work. This feature is not very reliable in Excel 2007.

The Snap to Grid command also changes the Snap to Shape setting (Drawing Tools⇨Format⇨ Arrange⇨Align⇨Snap to Shape). It's not clear what effect (if any) Snap to Shape has.

Changing a Shape to a Different Shape

You can easily change a shape to a different shape. Select the shape and choose Drawing Tools⇨Format⇨Insert Shapes⇨Edit Shapes⇨Change Shape. Excel displays its Shapes gallery, and you can click a shape to replace the selected shape. Formatting that you applied to the original shape is maintained.

 NOTE

This procedure does not work with shapes from the Lines category. Shapes in this category cannot be changed to a different type.

Reshaping Shapes

Excel has many shapes to choose from, but sometimes the shape you need isn't in the gallery. In such a case, you may be able to modify one of the existing shapes using one of these techniques:

- **Rotate the shape:** When you select a shape, it displays a small green dot. Click and drag this dot to rotate the shape.

- **Group multiple shapes:** You may be able to create the shape you need by combining two or more shapes and then grouping them. (See the section "Grouping Objects," earlier in this chapter.)

- **Reconfigure the shape:** Many of the shapes display one or more small yellow diamonds when the shape is selected. You can click and drag this diamond to change the shape's outline. The exact behavior varies with the shape, so you should experiment and see what happens. Figure 6-5 shows just a few variations of a Right Arrow object. (The upper-left arrow is the default.)

- **Create a Freeform shape:** Select the Freeform shape (in the Lines category of the Shapes gallery) to create a custom shape. Click and drag to draw any shape you like.

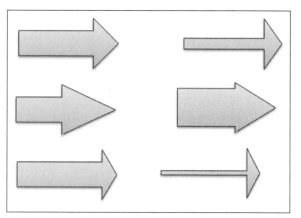

Figure 6-5: A few variations of a Right Arrow shape.

- **Convert an existing shape to a Freeform shape:** If an existing shape is close to what you want, convert it to a Freeform shape and then edit its points. Select the shape and choose Drawing Tools⇔Format⇔Insert Shapes⇔Edit Shape⇔Convert to Freeform. Then, with the shape still selected, choose Drawing Tools⇔Format⇔Insert Shapes⇔ Edit Shape⇔Edit Points. You can then drag the points to reconfigure the shape. Figure 6-6 shows the Smiley Face shape made a bit less happy.

Figure 6-6: A shape, before and after editing its points.

Changing the Shape Defaults

When you insert a shape, Excel applies a shape style named Colored Fill - Accent 1. The actual appearance depends on which document theme is in effect. If you use the default Office document theme, inserted shapes are blue with a thick dark blue border.

You can easily change the default settings for new shapes that you draw. For example, you may prefer a different fill color, a different outline style, and a particular type of shadow.

To change the default settings, create a shape and format it as you like. Then select the formatted shape, right-click, and choose Set as Default Shape from the shortcut menu.

Printing Objects

By default, objects are printed along with the worksheet. To avoid printing a shape, right-click the shape and choose Size and Properties. In the Size and Properties dialog box, select the Properties tab and deselect the Print Object check box.

Working with SmartArt

Excel's shapes are fairly impressive, but the new SmartArt feature is downright amazing. Using SmartArt, you can insert a wide variety of highly customizable diagrams into a worksheet, and you can change the overall look of the diagram with a few mouse clicks. This Office 2007 feature is probably more useful for PowerPoint users, but I think many Excel users can find some uses for SmartArt. In some cases, a SmartArt diagram may even be a viable alternative to a chart.

Inserting SmartArt

To insert SmartArt into a worksheet, choose Insert⇨Illustrations⇨SmartArt. Excel displays the dialog box shown in Figure 6-7. The diagrams are arranged in categories along the left. When you find one that looks appropriate, click it for a larger view in the panel on the right, which also provides some usage tips. Click the OK button to insert the graphic.

 NOTE
Don't be concerned about the number of elements in the SmartArt graphics. You can customize the SmartArt to display the number of elements you need.

Figure 6-8 shows a SmartArt diagram, after I customized it and added text. When you insert or select a SmartArt diagram, Excel displays its SmartArt Tools context tab, which provides many customization options.

 NOTE
SmartArt isn't quite as smart as it could be. Unfortunately, you can't link text to cells.

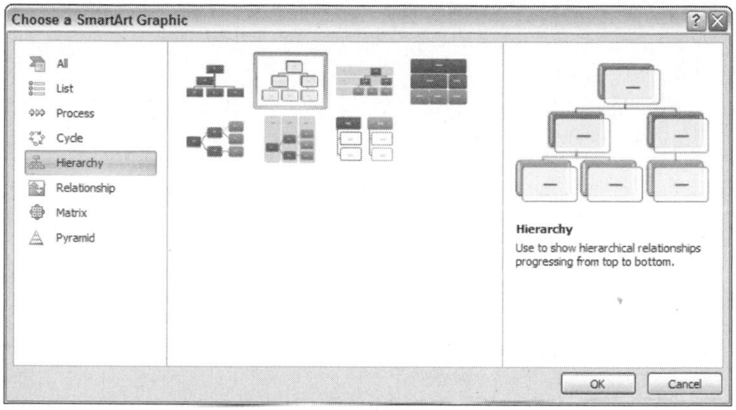

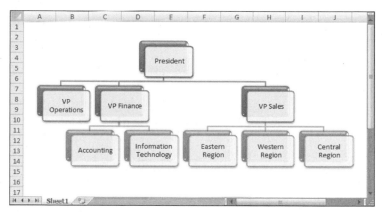

Figure 6-7: Inserting a SmartArt graphic.

Figure 6-8: This SmartArt diagram shows a simple organizational chart.

Customizing SmartArt

Figure 6-9 shows a SmartArt graphic (from the Process category) immediately after I inserted it into a worksheet. The Type Your Text Here window makes it very easy to enter text into the elements of the image. If you prefer, you can click one of the [Text] areas in the image and type the text directly.

When working with SmartArt, keep in mind that you can move, resize, or format individually any element within the graphic. Select the element and then use the tools on the SmartArt Tools⇨Format tab. Or, press Ctrl+1 and use the Format Shape dialog box.

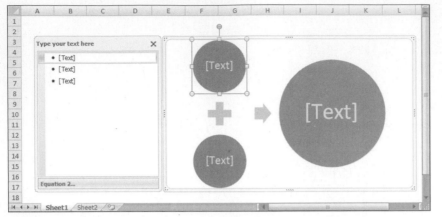

Figure 6-9: This SmartArt needs to be customized.

Figure 6-10 shows the SmartArt after I added some text.

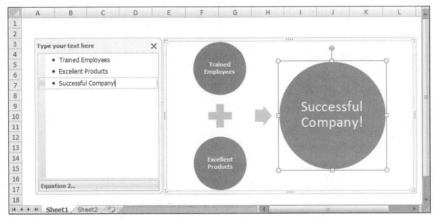

Figure 6-10: The SmartArt now has text.

This particular diagram depicts two items combining into a third item. Suppose that your boss sees this graphic and tells you that you need a third item: Advanced Technology. To add an element to the SmartArt graphic, just select an item and choose SmartArt Tools⇨ Design⇨Create Graphic⇨Add Shape. Or, you can just select an item and press Enter. Figure 6-11 shows the modified SmartArt diagram.

You may have noticed that a SmartArt diagram is actually composed of several shapes. In fact, you can select a shape in a SmartArt diagram and press Ctrl+C to copy it. Then, activate a cell and press Ctrl+V to paste a copy. However, this operation does not work in the opposite direction. You can't copy a shape and paste it into a SmartArt diagram.

NOTE

If you go overboard in customizing a SmartArt diagram, you can reset it to its original state. Right-click the diagram and choose Reset Graphic from the shortcut menu.

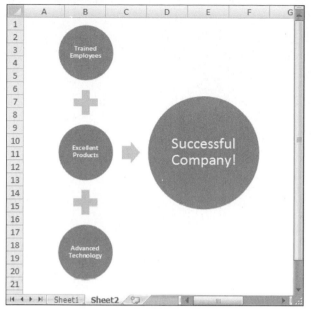

Figure 6-11: The SmartArt, after adding a new element.

Changing the Layout

You can easily change the layout of a SmartArt diagram. Select the diagram and then choose SmartArt Tools⇨Design⇨Layouts. Any text that you've entered remains intact. Figure 6-12 shows a few alternate layouts for the previous example.

Changing the Style

After you decide on a layout, you may want to consider other styles or colors available in the SmartArt Tools⇨Design⇨SmartArt Styles group. Figure 6-13 shows the diagram after choosing a different style and changing the colors.

TIP

The SmartArt styles that are available vary, depending on the document theme assigned to the workbook. To change a workbook's theme, choose Page Layout⇨Themes⇨ Themes. Switching to a different theme can have a dramatic impact on the appearance of SmartArt diagrams.

Finding Out More about SmartArt

The previous sections provided a basic introduction to SmartArt. The topic is complex enough to deserve an entire book — but the feature is also remarkably easy to use. I think most users can master SmartArt simply by experimenting with the commands.

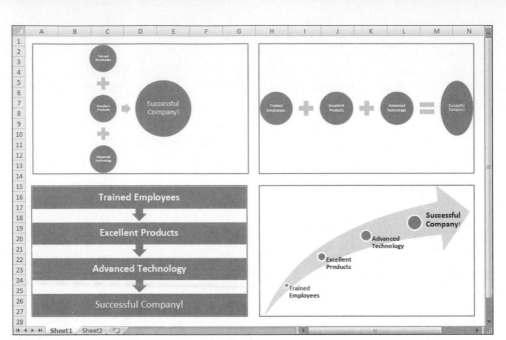

Figure 6-12: A few different layouts for the SmartArt.

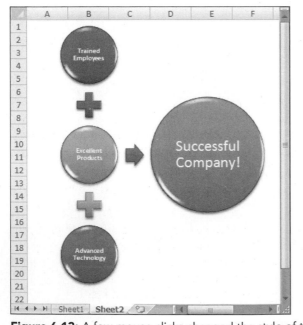

Figure 6-13: A few mouse clicks changed the style of this diagram.

Using WordArt

WordArt has been available in previous versions of Excel, but this feature has gotten a well-needed facelift in Excel 2007. You can use WordArt to create graphical effects in text. Figure 6-14 shows a few examples of WordArt.

Figure 6-14: WordArt examples.

To insert a WordArt graphic in a worksheet, choose Insert⇨Text⇨WordArt and then select a style from the gallery. Excel inserts an object with the text "Your text here." Replace that text with your own, resize it, and apply other formatting if you like.

When you select a WordArt image, Excel displays its Drawing Tools context menu. Use the controls to vary the look of your WordArt.

Note that the controls in the Drawing Tools⇨Format⇨Shape Styles group operate on the shape that contains the text, not the text itself. If you want to apply text formatting, use the control in the Drawing Tools⇨Format⇨WordArt Styles group. You can also use some of the standard formatting controls on the Home tab or the Mini toolbar. In addition, right-click the WordArt and select Format Text Effects for more formatting options.

Working with Other Graphic Types

Excel can import a variety of graphics into a worksheet. You have several choices:

- Use the Clip Art task pane to locate and insert an image.
- Import a graphic file directly.
- Copy and paste an image using the Windows Clipboard.

About Graphics Files

Graphics files come in two main categories: *bitmap* and *vector* (picture). Bitmap images are made up of discrete dots. They usually look pretty good at their original size, but often lose clarity if you increase the size. Vector-based images, on the other hand, are comprised of points and paths that are represented by mathematical equations, so they retain their crispness regardless of their size. Examples of common bitmap file formats include BMP, PNG, JPG, TIFF, and GIF. Examples of common vector file formats include CGM, WMF, EMF, and EPS.

You can find thousands of graphics files free for the taking on the Internet. Be aware, however, that some graphics files have copyright restrictions.

 WARNING
Using bitmap graphics in a worksheet can dramatically increase the size of your workbook, resulting in more memory usage and longer load and save times.

Using the Clip Art Task Pane

The Clip Art task pane is a shared program that is also accessible from other Microsoft Office applications. Besides providing an easy way to locate and insert images, the task pane lets you insert sound and video files. This tool also gives you direct access to Microsoft's Design Gallery Live on the Web.

Display the Clip Art task pane by choosing Insert⇨Illustrations⇨Clip Art. You can search for clip art by using the controls at the top of the task pane. Figure 6-15 shows the task pane, along with the thumbnail images resulting from a search for "cactus". To insert an image into the active worksheet, just double-click the thumbnail. For additional options, right-click the thumbnail image.

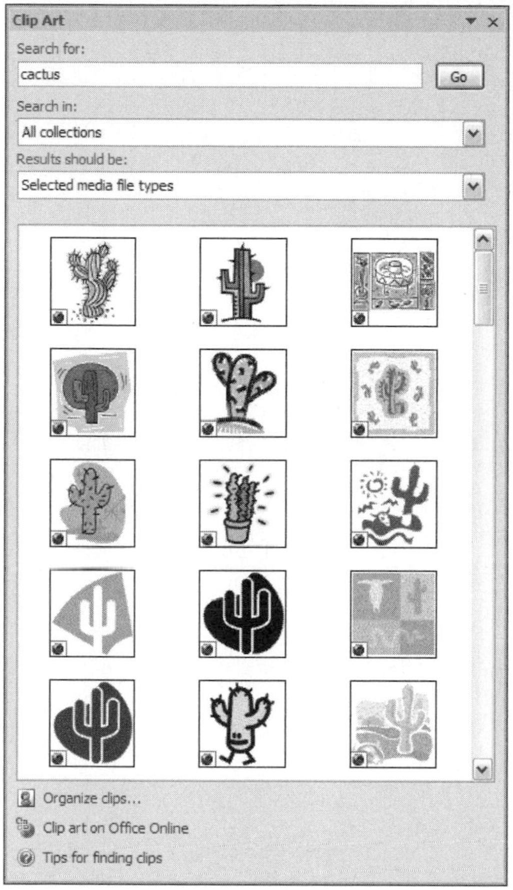

Figure 6-15: Use the Excel task pane to search for clip art and other multimedia files.

You may prefer to use the Microsoft Clip Organizer to access image files. Clip Organizer is essentially a stand-alone version of the Clip Art task pane. To display the Clip Organizer, click the Organize Clips link at the bottom of the task pane. Figure 6-16 shows the Microsoft Clip Organizer.

Want a great graphics file viewer?

Many users are content to use the graphics file-viewing capabilities built into Windows. But if you do a lot of work with graphics files, you owe it to yourself to get a *real* file-viewing program.

Many graphics viewers are available, but one of the best products in its class is IrfanView. It enables you to view just about any graphics file you can find, and it has features and options that will satisfy even hard-core graphics mavens. Best of all, it's *free*. To download a copy, visit www.irfanview.com.

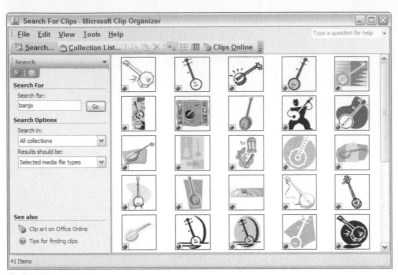

Figure 6-16: Microsoft Clip Organizer.

You can also add new files to the Clip Organizer. You may want to do so if you tend to insert a particular graphic file (such as your company logo) into your worksheets quite often.

If you can't find a suitable image, you can go online and browse through the extensive clip art at Microsoft's Clip Gallery Live Web site. Click the Clips Online button on the Clip Organizer toolbar, and your Web browser will be activated, at which point you can view the images (or listen to the sounds) and add those you want to your Clip Organizer.

Inserting Graphics Files

If the graphic image that you want to insert is available in a file, you can easily import the file into your worksheet. Choose Insert➪Illustrations➪Picture. Excel displays its Insert Picture dialog box, which enables you to browse for the file.

When you insert a picture in a worksheet, you can modify the picture in a number of ways. First, select the picture to have Excel display its Picture Tools➪Format context tab, which you can then use to adjust the color, contrast, and brightness. In addition, you can add borders, shadows, reflections, and so on — similar to the operations available for shapes.

Don't overlook the Picture Tools➪Format➪Picture Styles group. These commands can transform your image in some very interesting ways. Figure 6-17 shows various styles for a picture.

In addition to using the Ribbon, you can select a picture and press Ctrl+1 to display the Format Picture dialog box.

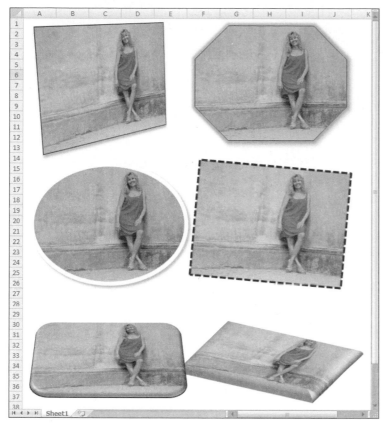

Figure 6-17: Displaying a picture in a number of different styles.

Copying Graphics by Using the Clipboard

In some cases, you may need to use a graphic image that's not stored in a separate file or is in a file that Excel can't import. For example, you may have an obscure drawing program that uses a file format that Excel doesn't support. You may be able to export the file to a supported format, but it may be easier to load the file into the drawing program and copy the image to the Clipboard (using that program's Edit⇨Copy command). Then you can activate Excel and paste the image to the drawing layer by choosing Home⇨Clipboard⇨Paste.

Suppose that you see a graphic displayed on-screen, but you can't select it — it may be part of a program's logo, for example. In this case, you can copy the entire screen to the Clipboard and then paste it into Excel. To copy all or part of the screen, use the following keyboard commands:

- **Print Screen:** Copies the entire screen to the Clipboard
- **Alt+Print Screen:** Copies the active window to the Clipboard

Most of the time, you don't want the entire screen — just a portion of it. The solution is to crop the image by using a graphics program. Or, you can crop it in Excel by choosing Picture Tools⇨Format⇨Size⇨Crop. Keep in mind, however, that cropping in Excel does not actually reduce the size of the image. The full-sized image is still stored with the workbook.

The most common graphics file formats are GIF, JPG, PNG, and BMP, but Excel supports many other formats.

Displaying a Worksheet Background Image

If you want to use a graphic image for a worksheet's background (similar to wallpaper on the Windows desktop), use the Page Layout⇨Page Setup⇨Background command and select a graphics file. The selected graphics file is tiled in the worksheet. Unfortunately, worksheet background images are for on-screen display only. These images do not appear when the worksheet is printed.

A Gallery of Graphic Examples

In the following sections, I provide you with some examples of Excel's drawing tools. Perhaps these examples will get your own creative juices flowing.

Using Shapes and Pictures with Charts

Combining shapes and other graphics with charts opens the door to some interesting visual effects. The examples in the following sections demonstrate a few possibilities. Have fun experimenting, but be careful not to overdo these effects. Whereas one or two embellishments can drive a point home, too many can obscure the chart's meaning.

ANNOTATING CHARTS

A common use for shapes is to annotate a chart. For example, you can use shapes from the Callouts category to add descriptive text that calls attention to a particular data point. This technique works for both embedded charts and charts on chart sheets. Figure 6-18 shows an example of an embedded chart that has been annotated with a text box and a shape from the Callouts category.

 ON THE CD

All the examples in this section are available on the companion CD-ROM. The filename is `annotating charts.xlsx`.

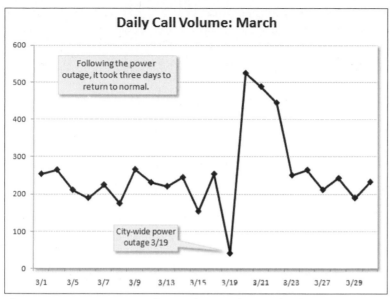

Figure 6-18: Annotating a chart with a text box and a shape.

Another example of chart annotation is shown in Figure 6-19. This pie chart is actually grouped with a rectangle shape that displays text. The text, which summarizes the chart, is aligned to the upper-right corner of the rectangle. The image also includes a small clip art logo in the lower-right corner, which is grouped with the chart and shape.

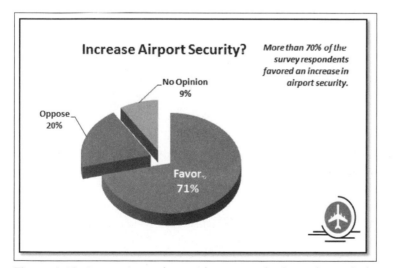

Figure 6-19: Annotating a chart with a rectangle shape that includes text.

Figure 6-20 shows another example of shapes from the Callout category. This chart displays two lines, and shapes (rather than a legend) are used to identify the lines. This technique can be useful when charts are printed in black and white. In such a case, the line colors are often difficult or impossible to ascertain.

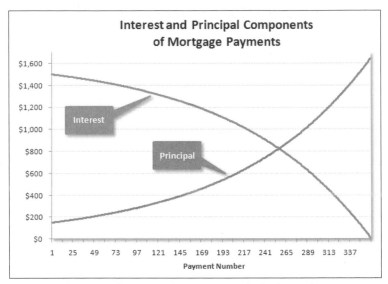

Figure 6-20: Using shapes (with text) instead of a legend.

USING AN IMAGE AS A CHART BACKGROUND

For added impact, consider placing a chart on top of a shape or other image.

Figure 6-21 shows four charts, each of which is positioned on top of a cube shape and then grouped with the shape. The four groups are arranged to form an interesting set of charts.

ON THE CD

The examples in this section are all available on the companion CD-ROM. The filename is chart backgrounds.xlsx.

Two examples of using clip art for a background for charts are shown in Figure 6-22. The images are used as a backdrop to display three pie charts. After positioning the charts on top of the clip art image, the objects were grouped together.

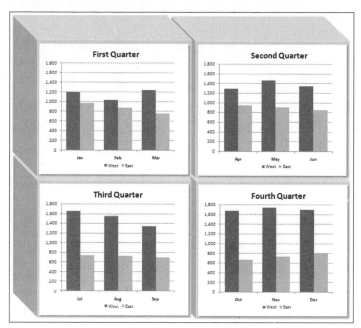

Figure 6-21: A chart placed on top of a shape.

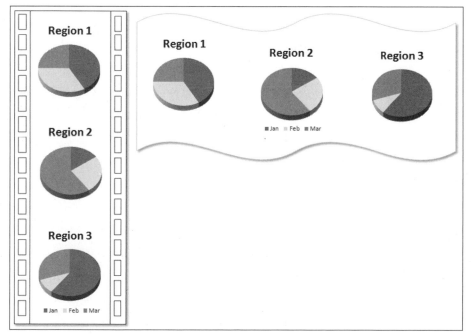

Figure 6-22: Pie charts placed on top of clip art images.

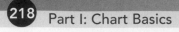

USING GRAPHICS IN A CHART SERIES

Excel offers a wide variety of chart types, but sometimes you may want something else for added impact. One of the easiest ways to make a chart more interesting is to replace the series elements (bars, columns, areas, pie slices, or line markers) with a graphic image.

To paste an image into a chart series, copy the image to the Clipboard, select the data series or single data point, and press Ctrl+V. Or, you can use the Fill tab of the Format Data Series dialog box. Select the Picture or Texture Fill option, and then click the File button (to choose an image file), the Clipboard button (to paste the image currently on the Clipboard), or the Clip Art button (to select a clip art image).

For more control over how the image appears, use the options on the Fill tab of the Format Data Series dialog box. For example, in a column chart, you may want to stack the image rather than stretch it.

The shapes provide many images to work with, and you can also use clip art and WordArt. Figure 6-23 shows a standard column chart (left), and the same chart using an arrow-shaped shape (with a shadow effect) for the columns.

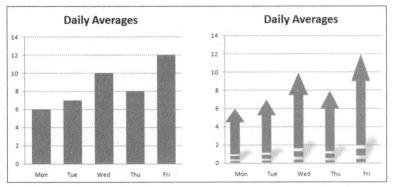

Figure 6-23: A column chart, before and after replacing the columns with a shape.

 ## ON THE CD

The examples in this section are all available on the companion CD-ROM. The filename is `images in a chart series.xlsx`.

You can also use this procedure with standard text entered into a cell. It works best with markers in a line chart. The trick is to copy the cell as a picture.

After formatting the cell to your liking, select the cell and choose Home⇨Clipboard⇨ Paste⇨As Picture⇨Copy as Picture. In the Copy Picture dialog box, select the Bitmap option. Select the line (or an individual marker on the line) and press Ctrl+V. Figure 6-24 shows an example. Each of the line markers was replaced by a graphic created from the text in column A. In this case, the horizontal category axis is superfluous, so I removed it.

CROSS-REFERENCE

For a similar effect, use data labels instead of line markers. See Chapter 4 for an example.

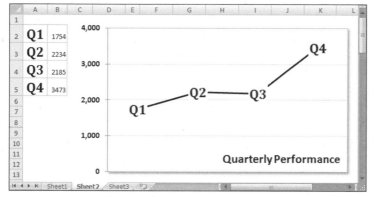

Figure 6-24: Each line marker was replaced by text in a cell, copied as a picture.

The example in Figure 6-25 uses images that are stacked and scaled, with each image representing two units. In this chart, the data series was given the name "= 2 Tons" so that the legend would provide information about the image scaling.

Figure 6-25: This chart uses an image scaled to represent two units.

TIP

Charts that use series which have been customized using an image can be saved as a template. See Chapter 2 for more information about creating chart templates.

USING A PICTURE IN A CHART'S PLOT AREA OR CHART AREA

Every chart has two background elements: the plot area and the chart area. By default, these areas display a single fill color. You can, however, insert a graphic image for visual appeal.

To add a graphic image, select either the plot area or the chart area of your chart. Display the Format dialog box for the element and click the Fill tab. Then select the Picture or Text Fill option, and click the button that corresponds to the source of the image.

Figure 6-26 shows a pie chart that uses a clip art image in its chart area.

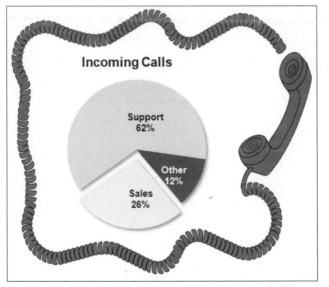

Figure 6-26: Using clip art in the chart area can add visual appeal to an otherwise dull chart.

ON THE CD

The examples in this section are all available on the companion CD-ROM. The filename is `image in plot or chart area.xlsx`.

Figure 6-27 shows a line chart that uses a clip art image in the plot area. I inserted the image in a worksheet, and then used the controls in the Picture Tools⇨Format⇨Adjust group to lighten the image and reduce the contrast. I then copied it to the Clipboard, and added it to the chart using the Fill tab in the Format Plot Area dialog box.

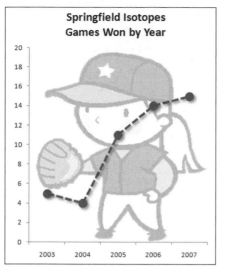

Figure 6-27: A clip art image in the plot area.

Figure 6-28 shows a few other examples of charts that use an image in their plot area or chart area.

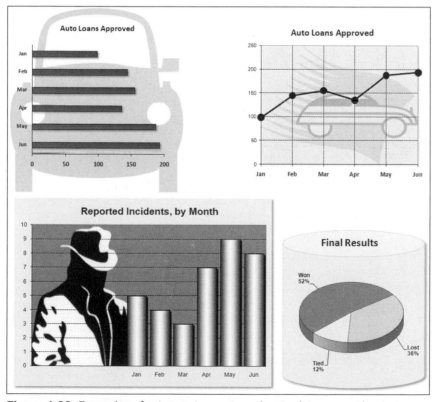

Figure 6-28: Examples of using an image in a chart's plot area or chart area.

The chart in Figure 6-29 uses a photo of a dollar bill in the plot area. This chart is actually a 100% stacked line chart. The chart consists of six series, each of which uses two identical data points.

Figure 6-29: This chart depicts the relative expenses by using a 100% stacked line chart with custom data markers.

Figure 6-30 shows the original chart, before I added the image and made a few other modifications. I deleted the data markers for each series, and made each line thick, with the same color as the chart area's color. The effect is a "broken" dollar bill that depicts the breakdown of expenses (similar to a pie chart). The descriptive labels are data labels, which I positioned manually. Also, note that the maximum scale value must be equal to the sum of the amounts — otherwise, the top slice of the dollar will be too large.

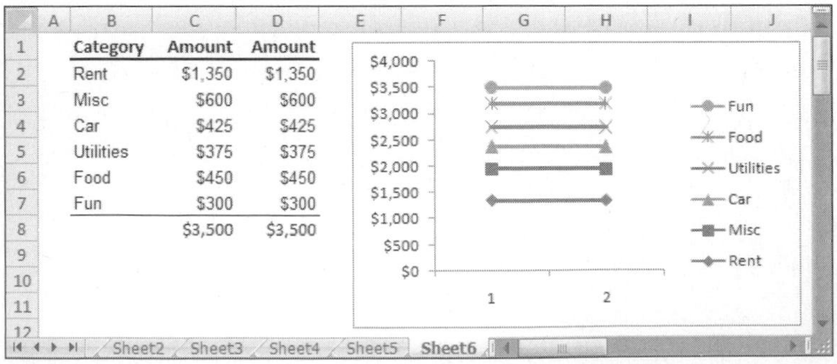

	Category	Amount	Amount
1	Category	Amount	Amount
2	Rent	$1,350	$1,350
3	Misc	$600	$600
4	Car	$425	$425
5	Utilities	$375	$375
6	Food	$450	$450
7	Fun	$300	$300
8		$3,500	$3,500

Figure 6-30: The original version of the dollar bill chart.

Exporting graphics

If you create a graphic in Excel using shapes, SmartArt, or WordArt, you may want to save the graphic as a separate file for use in another program. Unfortunately, Excel doesn't provide a direct way to export a graphic, but here's a trick you can use. Make sure that your graphic appears the way you want it and then follow these steps:

1. Save your workbook.

2. Choose Office⇨Save As to save your workbook as a Web page. In the Save As dialog box, select Web Page (*.htm; *.html) from the Save as Type drop-down list.

3. Close the workbook.

4. Use Windows Explorer to locate the HTML file you saved in Step 2. You'll notice that Excel also creates a separate companion directory for the HTML file. If you save the file as `graphics.htm`, the directory will be named `graphics_files`.

5. Open the directory, and you'll find `*.png` graphics files — one for each graphic object in your workbook. The `*.png` files have a transparent background.

Alternatively, you can copy the shape as a bitmap, paste it into a graphics program, and then save the file. To copy a shape as a bitmap, select the object, choose Home⇨Clipboard⇨Paste⇨As Picture⇨Copy as Picture, and choose the Bitmap option.

Calling Attention to a Cell

Many of the shapes — particularly those in the Callouts and the Stars and Banners categories — are useful for calling attention to a particular cell or range to make it stand out from the others. Figure 6-31 shows two examples of how you can make a cell's value stand out. One of the shapes contains text; the other has no fill, so the underlying cell contents are visible.

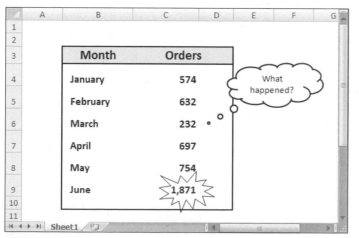

Figure 6-31: Two ways of making a particular cell stand out.

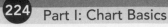

Changing the Look of Cell Comments

The following sections describe two ways to modify cell comments: changing the shape and adding an image.

CHANGING THE SHAPE OF A CELL COMMENT

If a cell contains a cell comment, you can replace the normal comment box with a shape.

Figure 6-32 shows a standard cell comment as well as a cell comment after it's been spiffed up a bit by applying a different shape.

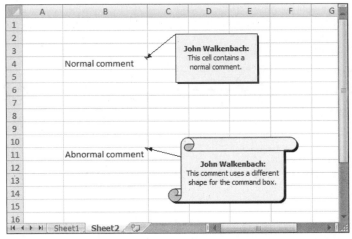

Figure 6-32: A typical cell comment and a cell comment with a different shape.

To change the shape of a cell comment, you need to add a command to your Quick Access Toolbar (QAT). Follow these steps:

1. Right-click the QAT and select Customize Quick Access Toolbar. The Customization section of the Excel Options dialog box appears.

2. In the drop-down list labeled Choose Commands From, select Drawing Tools | Format Tab.

3. In the list on the left, select Change Shape and click the Add button.

4. Click the OK button to close the Excel Options dialog box.

After performing these steps, your QAT has a new Change Shape icon.

To change the shape of a comment, make sure that it's visible (right-click the cell and select Show/Hide Comments). Then click the comment's border to select it as a shape (or, Ctrl+click the comment to select it as a shape). Click the Change Shape button on the QAT and choose a new shape for the comment.

ADDING A GRAPHIC TO A CELL COMMENT

Most users don't realize it, but a cell comment can display an image. The image must reside in a file. In other words, you can't use shapes or clip art that is copied to the Clipboard.

Follow these steps to add an image to a comment:

1. Make sure that the comment is visible (right-click the cell and select Show/Hide Comments).

2. Click the comment's border to select it as a shape (or, Ctrl+click the comment to select it as a shape).

3. Right-click the comment's border and choose Format Comment from the shortcut menu.

4. In the Format Comment dialog box, click the Colors and Lines tab.

5. Click the Color drop-down list and select Fill Effects.

6. In the Fill Effects dialog box, click the Picture tab and then click the Select Picture button to specify a graphics file.

Figure 6-33 shows a comment that contains a picture.

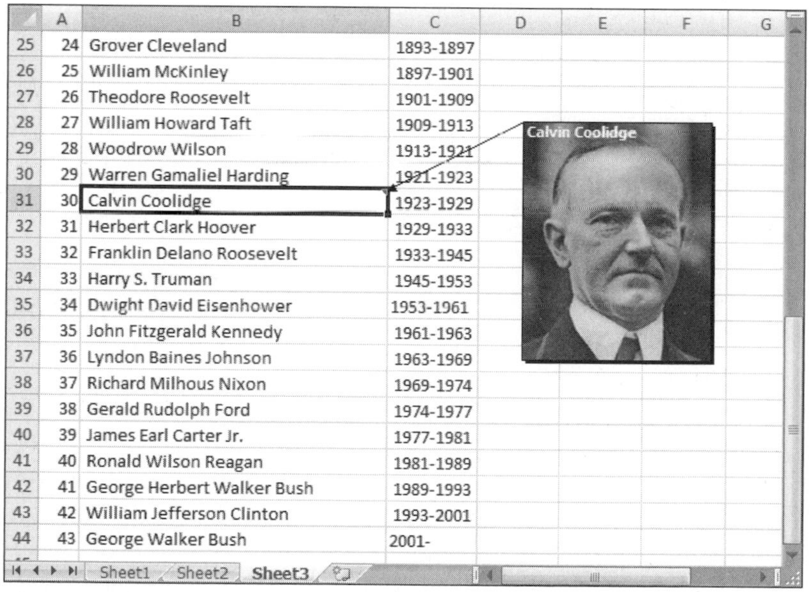

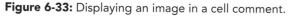

	A	B	C	D	E	F	G
25	24	Grover Cleveland	1893-1897				
26	25	William McKinley	1897-1901				
27	26	Theodore Roosevelt	1901-1909				
28	27	William Howard Taft	1909-1913				
29	28	Woodrow Wilson	1913-1921				
30	29	Warren Gamaliel Harding	1921-1923				
31	30	Calvin Coolidge	1923-1929				
32	31	Herbert Clark Hoover	1929-1933				
33	32	Franklin Delano Roosevelt	1933-1945				
34	33	Harry S. Truman	1945-1953				
35	34	Dwight David Eisenhower	1953-1961				
36	35	John Fitzgerald Kennedy	1961-1963				
37	36	Lyndon Baines Johnson	1963-1969				
38	37	Richard Milhous Nixon	1969-1974				
39	38	Gerald Rudolph Ford	1974-1977				
40	39	James Earl Carter Jr.	1977-1981				
41	40	Ronald Wilson Reagan	1981-1989				
42	41	George Herbert Walker Bush	1989-1993				
43	42	William Jefferson Clinton	1993-2001				
44	43	George Walker Bush	2001-				

Sheet1 Sheet2 **Sheet3**

Figure 6-33: Displaying an image in a cell comment.

Part I

Pasting Pictures of Cells

Excel 2007 makes it easy to convert a range of cells into a picture. The picture can either be a "dead" image (it doesn't change if the original range changes), or it can be a "live" picture (which reflects changes in the original range). The range can even contain objects such as a chart.

CREATING A STATIC IMAGE OF A RANGE

To create a snapshot of a range, start by selecting a range of cells, and then press Ctrl+C to copy the range to the Clipboard. Then choose Home⇨Clipboard⇨Paste⇨As Picture⇨ Paste as Picture. The result is a graphic image of the original range. When you select this image, Excel displays its Picture Tools context menu — which means that you can apply some additional formatting to the picture.

Figure 6-34 shows a range of cells (B2:E9), along with a picture of the range after I applied one of the built-in styles from the Picture Tools⇨Format⇨Picture Styles gallery.

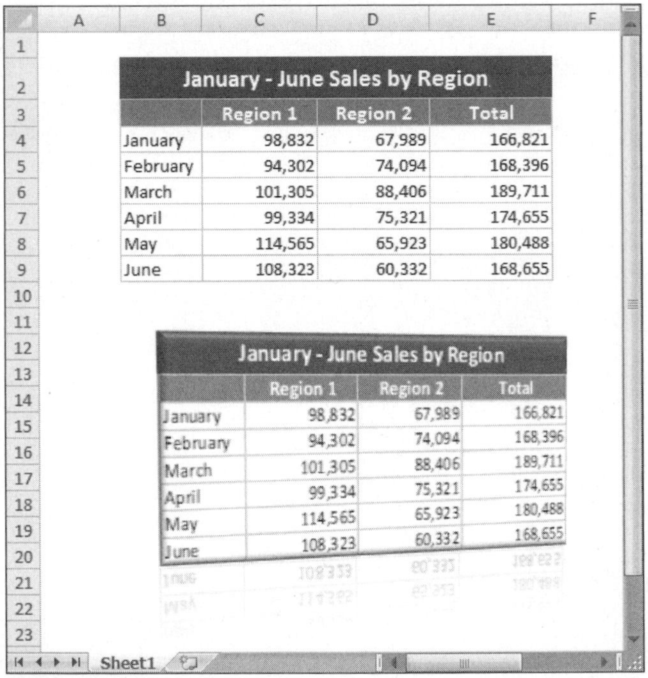

Figure 6-34: A picture of a range, after applying some picture formatting.

CREATING A LIVE IMAGE OF A RANGE

To create an image that's linked to the original range of cells, select the cells and press Ctrl+C to copy the range to the Clipboard. Then choose Home⇨Clipboard⇨Paste⇨As Picture⇨ Paste Picture Link. Excel pastes a picture of the original range, and the picture is linked — if you make changes to the original, those changes are shown in the linked picture.

Notice that when you select the linked picture, the formula bar displays the address of the original range. You can edit this range reference to change the cells that are displayed in the picture. To "unlink" the picture, just delete the formula in the formula bar.

You can also cut and paste this picture to a different worksheet, if you like. That makes it easy to refer to information on a different sheet. Unfortunately, Excel does not allow much formatting of this picture. You can change its size by dragging a corner, but none of the standard picture formatting commands is available.

Figure 6-35 shows a linked picture of a range placed on top of a shape, which has lots of interesting formatting capabilities. Placing a linked picture on top of a shape is a good way to make a particular range stand out.

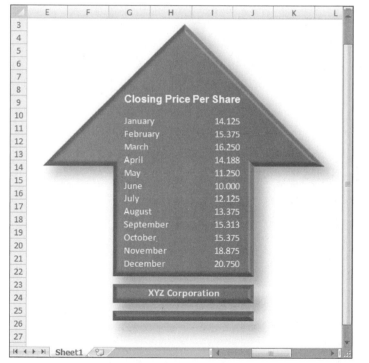

Figure 6-35: A linked picture of a range, placed on top of a shape.

Part I

If you use the linked picture feature frequently, you can save some time by adding Excel's Camera tool to your Quick Access Toolbar (QAT). Follow these steps:

1. Right-click your QAT and choose Customize Quick Access Toolbar.

2. On the Customization tab of the Excel Options dialog box, select Command Not on the Ribbon from the drop-down list on the left.

3. Select Camera from the list and click the Add button.

4. Click the OK button to close the Excel Options dialog box.

After you've added the Camera tool to your QAT, you can select a range of cells and click the Camera tool to take a picture of the range. Then click in the worksheet, and Excel places a live picture of the selected range on the worksheet's draw layer.

Part II

Mastering Charts

Chapter 7

Creating Interactive Charts

In This Chapter

◆ Introducing the concept of interactive charts

◆ Creating a self-expanding chart — a chart that updates automatically when data is added or deleted

◆ Using a scroll bar to specify the data in a series

◆ Using a drop-down list to choose a beginning point and an end point for a series

◆ Plotting the last *n* data points in a series

◆ Plotting every *n*th data point in a series

◆ Using a check box or a drop-down list to select a series to plot

The term *interactive chart,* as used in this book, refers to a chart that changes automatically, based on the worksheet environment. In a sense, all charts are interactive because chart series are linked to ranges, and the chart updates automatically when the data is changed. This is not the type of interactivity covered in this chapter.

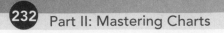

Introducing Interactive Charts

If you create spreadsheets that are used by others, you'll probably find several useful techniques in this chapter. Many of these examples have a single goal: to make it easier for users (especially novice users) to deal with a workbook that contains charts.

A few examples of interactive charts include the following:

- A chart that updates itself to use data added to the end of the series

- A chart that updates itself when data is deleted

- A chart that limits the amount of data displayed in a series (for example, only the last 12 data points)

- A chart that displays a series based on a value entered into a cell or an item chosen from a drop-down list.

This chapter provides the information you need to create several types of charts that update automatically based on information contained in the workbook. You'll also discover how to use dialog box controls (such as check boxes and drop-down lists) to make your charts interactive. None of the examples in this chapter uses macros.

 CROSS-REFERENCE

Another way to create an interactive chart is to use a pivot chart. Refer to Chapter 11 for information about creating and using pivot charts.

Hands-On: Creating a Self-Expanding Chart

One of the most common questions related to charting is, "How can I create a chart that will expand automatically when I add new data to the worksheet?"

To understand this issue, examine Figure 7-1, which shows a worksheet set up to store sales information that is updated daily. The chart displays all the data in the worksheet. When new data is entered, the chart series must be expanded to include the new data. On the other hand, if data is deleted, the chart series should also be contracted to exclude the deleted cells.

Wouldn't it be nice if the chart series would expand and contract automatically?

The good news is that the table feature in Excel 2007 is "chart-aware." If your chart data resides in a table (created by choosing Insert⇨Tables⇨Table), the chart will always display all the data in the table — even if the table is expanded. In other words, if your data is in a table, the information in this section is not relevant.

Figure 7-1: If this were a self-expanding chart, it would update automatically when new data is entered.

 NOTE

If you plan to share your workbook with someone who uses an earlier version of Excel, things get a bit complicated. Excel 2003 can handle an Excel 2007 table, and the software treats it as a list (charts that use data in an Excel 2003 list are self-expanding). But if you open the file with a version prior to Excel 2003, the chart is not self-expanding. In other words, you need to use the technique described in this section to create a self-expanding chart.

 CROSS-REFERENCE

Chapter 3 describes several ways to change the source data used in a chart series. Although none of those techniques is particularly difficult, each requires manual intervention. Creating a self-expanding chart requires a bit of extra effort, but the result is a chart that updates automatically, with no user intervention required.

One option, of course, is to specify a larger-than-required range for the data series. Figure 7-2 shows an example in which the data series includes empty cells that will eventually be filled. The result is a lopsided chart that displays lots of empty space. In the majority of situations, this solution is not satisfactory.

As an introduction to the world of interactive charts, the following sections present a hands-on, step-by-step example. You'll create a standard chart and then make the changes necessary to make the chart expand automatically when new data is added, and contract when data is deleted.

The example makes use of a simple worksheet that has dates in column A and sales amounts in column B. The assumption is that a new date and sales figure are each added daily, and the chart should display all the data.

	A	B	C	D	E	F	G	H	I	J	K	L
1	Date	Sales										
2	1-May	489										
3	2-May	603										
4	3-May	581										
5	4-May	633										
6	5-May	635										
7	6-May	621										
8	7-May	512										
9	8-May	666										
10												
11												
12												
13												
14												
15												
16												
17												

Figure 7-2: Specifying blank cells in the data range is usually not a viable solution.

Creating the Chart

The first step is to create a standard chart, using the data that currently exists. Figure 7-1, presented earlier, shows the data and a column chart created from the data.

ON THE CD

The workbook used in this example, named `daily.xlsx`, is available on the companion CD-ROM.

The chart contains a single series, and its SERIES formula is as follows:

`=SERIES(Sheet1!$B$1,Sheet1!$A$2:$A$9,Sheet1!$B$2:$B$9,1)`

This SERIES formula specifies that:

- The series name is in cell B1.
- The category labels are in A2:A9.
- The values are in B2:B9.

So far, this is just a common chart. If you add a new date and value, the chart will not display the new data. But that will soon change.

Creating Named Formulas

In this step, you create two named formulas. The names will eventually serve as arguments in the SERIES formula. In case you're not familiar with the concept of a named formula, it is explained later in this section. To create the named formulas, follow these steps:

1. Choose Formulas⇨Defined Names⇨Define Name to display the New Name dialog box.

2. In the Name field, enter **Date**. In the Refers To field, enter this formula:

   ```
   =OFFSET(Sheet1!$A$2,0,0,COUNTA(Sheet1!$A:$A)-1,1)
   ```

3. Click the OK button to create the formula named *Date*.

   Notice that the OFFSET function refers to the first category label (cell A2) and uses the COUNTA function to determine the number of labels in the column. Because column A has a heading in row 1, the formula subtracts 1 from the number.

Next, create a name for the sales data as follows:

1. Choose Formulas⇨Define Name to display the New Name dialog box.

2. Type **Sales** in the Name field. Enter this formula in the Refers To field:

   ```
   =OFFSET(Sheet1!$B$2,0,0,COUNTA(Sheet1!$B:$B)-1,1)
   ```

   In this case, the OFFSET function refers to the first data point (cell B2). Again, the COUNTA function is used to get the number of data points, and it is adjusted to account for the label in cell B1.

3. Click the Add button to create the formula named *Sales*.

After you perform these steps, the workbook contains two new names, *Date* and *Sales*.

Modifying the Series

The final step is to modify the chart so that it makes use of the two new names rather than the hard-coded range references. Follow these steps:

1. Activate the chart and choose Chart Tools⇨Design⇨Data⇨Select Data to display the Select Data Source dialog box (see Figure 7-3).

2. Click Sales in the Series list and then click the Edit button to display the Edit Series dialog box.

3. In the Series Values field, enter **Sheet1!Sales**.

4. Click the OK button to close the Edit Series dialog box and return to the Select Data Source dialog box.

5. Click the Edit button for the Horizontal (Category) Axis Labels to display the Axis Labels dialog box.

6. In the Axis Label Range field, enter **Sheet1!Date**.

7. Click the OK button to return to the Select Data Source dialog box.

8. Click the OK button to close the Select Data Source dialog box.

In Steps 3 and 6, note that the name was preceded by the worksheet name and an exclamation point. Because named formulas are, by default, workbook-level names (not sheet-level names), you should (technically) enter the *workbook* name, an exclamation point, and the name. However, Excel is very accommodating in this regard, and changes it for you. If you look at the SERIES formula (or access the Select Data Source dialog box again), you'll discover that Excel substituted the workbook's name for the sheet reference you entered:

```
=daily.xls!Sales
```

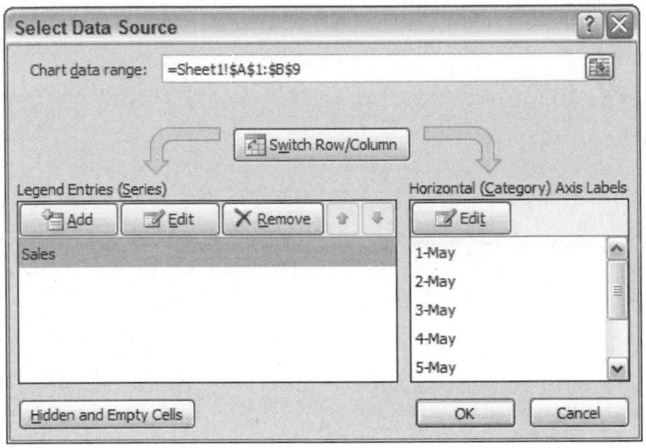

Figure 7-3: Using the Select Data Source dialog box to change the references used in a chart series.

Bottom line? When using these named formulas, you can precede the name with either the worksheet name or the workbook name. (I find it easier to use the worksheet name.) But keep in mind that if the sheet name or workbook name includes a space character, you must enclose it in single quotation marks, like this:

```
='daily sales.xls'!Sales
```

or

```
='sales data'!sales
```

For more information about names, refer to the nearby sidebar, "How Excel handles names."

TIP

An alternative to using the Select Data Source dialog box is to edit the chart's SERIES formula directly. The modified SERIES formula is the following:

```
=SERIES(Sheet1!$B$1,daily.xlsx!Date,daily.xlsx!Sales,1)
```

Part II

How Excel handles names

Excel supports two types of names: workbook-level names and worksheet-level names. The scope of a workbook-level name is the entire workbook. Normally, when you create a name for a cell or range, that name can be used in any worksheet.

You can also create sheet-level names. A sheet-level name incorporates the sheet name as part of its name. For example, Sheet1!Data is a sheet-level name. When you create this name, you can use it in formulas in Sheet1 without the sheet qualifier. For example:

```
=Data*4
```

But if you enter this formula in a different worksheet, Excel will not recognize the name unless you fully qualify it:

```
=Sheet1!Data*4
```

Sheet-level names are useful because they enable you to use the same name in different worksheets. For example, you might create sheet-level names such as Sheet1!Interest, Sheet2!Interest, and Sheet3!Interest. Each name refers to a cell on its own sheet. A formula that uses the name Interest uses the definition for its own sheet.

The named formulas used in this chapter are workbook-level names because they are not preceded by a sheet name. But when you enter a name in a field in the Select Data Source dialog box, Excel (for some reason) requires that you qualify the name with either the sheet name or the workbook name.

Testing the Self-Expanding Chart

To test the results of your efforts, enter new data in columns A and B, or delete data from the bottom of the columns. If you performed the preceding steps correctly, the chart will update automatically. If you receive an error message or the chart doesn't update itself, review the preceding steps carefully.

WARNING
If you adjust the range used by the chart by dragging the range highlights, the names (Date and Sales) will be replaced by actual cell references, and the chart will no longer be a self-updating chart.

Understanding How the Self-Expanding Chart Works

Many people use this self-expanding chart technique without fully understanding how it works. There's certainly nothing wrong with that. If you go through the hands-on exercise described previously, you should be able to adapt the procedures to your own charts. But understanding *how* it works will make it possible to go beyond the basic concept and create more powerful types of dynamic charts.

About Named Formulas

Many of the interactive chart techniques described in this chapter take advantage of a powerful feature called *named formulas.* You're probably familiar with the concept of named cells and ranges. But did you know that naming cells and ranges is really a misnomer? When you create a name for a range, you are really creating a *named formula.*

When you work with the New Name dialog box, the Refers To field contains the formula, and the Name field contains the formula's name. You'll find that the contents of the Refers To field always begin with an equal sign — a sure sign that it's a formula.

Unlike a normal formula, a named formula doesn't exist in a cell. Rather, it exists in Excel's memory and does not have a cell address. But you can access the result of a named formula by referring to its name, either in a standard formula or in a chart's SERIES formula.

After defining the two named formulas, Excel evaluates these formulas every time the worksheet is calculated. But these named formulas aren't used in any cells, so there is no visible effect of creating these named formulas — until you use them to define the chart series.

To get a better handle on named formulas, use the New Name dialog box to create the following formula, and name it **Sum12Cells**.

```
=SUM($A$1:$A$12)
```

After you've created the named formula, enter the following formula into any cell:

```
=Sum12Cells
```

This formula will return the sum of A1:A12.

About the OFFSET Function

The key to mastering self-expanding charts lies in understanding the OFFSET function. This function returns a range that is "offset" from a specified reference cell. Arguments for the OFFSET function let you specify the distance from the reference cell and the dimensions of the range (the number of rows and columns).

The OFFSET function has five arguments, as follows:

- *reference:* The first argument for the OFFSET function is essentially the "anchor" cell, used by the second and third argument.

- *rows:* This argument indicates how many rows to move from the reference address to begin the range.

- *cols:* This argument indicates how many columns to move from the reference address to begin the range.

- *height:* This argument indicates the number of rows to be included in the range.

- *width:* The final argument indicates the number of columns to be included in the range.

NOTE:

If the columns used for the data contain any other entries, COUNTA will return an incorrect value. To keep things simple, don't put any other data in the column. If the column contains additional information, you'll need to adjust the *height* argument in the COUNTA function.

Recall that the named formula Sales was defined as follows:

```
=OFFSET(Sheet1!$B$2,0,0,COUNTA(Sheet1!$B:$B)-1,1)
```

If 9 entries are in column B (in range B1:B9), the COUNTA function returns 9. This result is reduced by 1 to account for the column heading. Therefore, the named formula can be expressed as follows:

```
=OFFSET(Sheet1!$B$2,0,0,8,1)
```

This formula uses cell B2 as the anchor cell and returns a reference to the range that is as follows:

- Offset from cell B2 by 0 rows (second argument, *rows*)

- Offset from cell B2 by 0 columns (third argument, *cols*)

- Eight cells high (fourth argument, *height*)

- One cell wide (fifth argument, *width*)

In other words, the OFFSET function returns a reference to range B2:B9, and this is the range used by the chart series. When a new data point is added, the OFFSET function returns a reference to range B2:B10.

Subsequent examples in this chapter use the same basic concept but vary in the arguments supplied to the OFFSET function.

NOTE

To keep things simple, the charts in this chapter make use of a single data series. However, these techniques can be applied to charts with any number of data series. You will, however, have to make the necessary adjustments for each series.

Controlling a Series with a Scroll Bar

The example in the following sections demonstrates another type of interactivity. Figure 7-4 shows a chart that uses a Scroll Bar control to specify the number of months (from 1 to 12) to display in the chart.

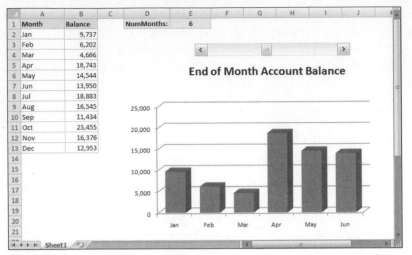

Figure 7-4: The Scroll Bar control at the top of the chart determines how many months are displayed.

ON THE CD

This workbook, named `chart with scrollbar.xlsx`, is available on the companion CD-ROM.

Creating the Chart

Refer to Figure 7-4 and use the data in columns A:B to create a chart. (The example uses a standard 3-D column chart.) Because the number of data points will vary, it's a good idea to turn off automatic scaling for the vertical axis. Set the Maximum scale value to a large enough value to accommodate all the data (25,000 in this case). Doing this keeps the value axis constant, regardless of the number of data points displayed.

Defining the Names

This example uses several names, which are described in this section.

Cell E1 contains a value that determines the number of months displayed in the chart. For convenience, this cell is named NumMonths.

In addition, the workbook has two named formulas, which are used in the chart's series. The Month formula is defined as follows:

```
=OFFSET(Sheet1!$A$2,0,0,NumMonths,1)
```

The Balance formula is defined as follows:

```
=OFFSET(Sheet1!$B$2,0,0,NumMonths,1)
```

If you understand how the named formulas worked in the previous example, you should have no problem understanding this variation. As you can see, the OFFSET functions use NumMonths for their height argument. The result is that the NumMonths cell controls how many data points are displayed in the chart.

TIP

Another approach, which is a bit simpler, is to define Balance as an offset from the Month range. Using this approach, the definition for Balance would be as follows:

```
=OFFSET(Month,0,1)
```

As in the previous example, these two named formulas are then used for the category labels and values range for the chart series. This is done by using the Select Data Source dialog box. The net effect? Change the value in cell E1, and the chart updates immediately.

Adding the Scroll Bar Control

The Scroll Bar control isn't really necessary, but it adds a touch of convenience. Moving the scroll bar with the mouse is a bit easier than changing the value in cell E1.

NOTE

Previous versions of Excel allowed you to add a control to the embedded chart itself. This was convenient because the control moves with the chart. Unfortunately, you can't add a control to an Excel 2007 embedded chart. Therefore, the Scroll Bar control must be added to the worksheet. Also, note that Excel does not allow you to group a chart with a control.

NOTE

To add a control to a worksheet, Excel must display its Developer tab. If this tab is not visible, choose Office➪Excel Options, click the Popular tab, and select the Show Developer Tab in the Ribbon check box.

The following instructions add a Scroll Bar control to the worksheet and link the control to cell E1:

1. Choose Developer➪Controls➪Insert and then click the Scroll Bar icon in the Forms section.

2. Click and drag in the worksheet to create the control. You can size and position it just as you can any other graphic object.

3. Right-click the Scroll Bar control and choose Format Control from the shortcut menu. This displays the Format Control dialog box.

5. In the Format Control dialog box, click the Control tab (see Figure 7-5).

6. Enter **1** in the Minimum Value field. In the Maximum Value field, enter **12** (the maximum number of data points for the chart).

7. Set the Incremental Change field to **1** and the Page Change field to **3**.

8. In the Cell Link field, enter **NumMonths**. This links the Scroll Bar control with cell E1 (which is named NumMonths).

9. Click the OK button to close the dialog box.

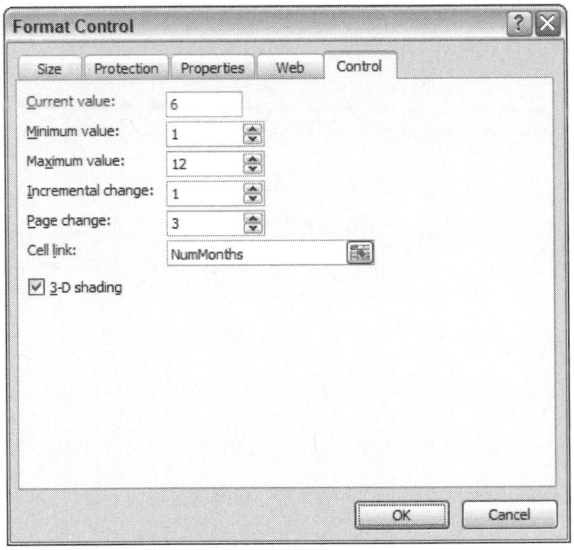

Figure 7-5: Linking a Scroll Bar control to a cell.

After performing these steps, the value in cell E1 is controlled by the scroll bar and will have a numeric range of 1–12. This value, in turn, will control the number of data points shown on the chart.

NOTE

Excel offers two general types of controls: Forms controls and ActiveX controls. Controls in the Forms category are easier to use, but they don't offer as much flexibility as ActiveX controls. For example, the Forms controls offer virtually no formatting options. To keep it simple, all the examples in this chapter use controls from the Forms category.

Specifying the Beginning and End Point for a Series

If a chart uses a lot of data, you may want to be able to limit the data that's displayed in the chart. Figure 7-6 shows an example.

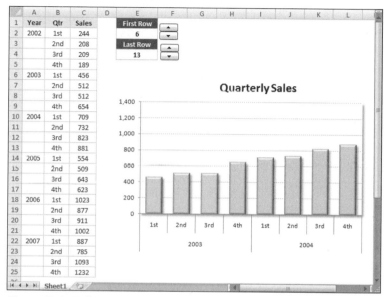

Figure 7-6: Cells E2 and E4 control the amount of data that's displayed in a chart.

Cell E2 contains a value that represents the first row to be plotted, and cell E4 contains a value that represents the last row to be plotted. The chart is displaying the data in rows 6 through 13. If cell E2 or E4 is changed, the chart adjusts accordingly. This example uses Spinner controls linked to cells E2 and E4. These controls make it easy to change the values in these cells.

ON THE CD

This workbook, named `first and last point in series.xlsx`, is available on the companion CD-ROM.

Creating the Chart

Refer to Figure 7-6 and create a chart from the data in columns A:C. The chart in this example is a standard column chart. It uses two columns (A:B) for the category axis labels, which results in having two rows of category labels in the chart.

Defining the Names

For convenience, cell E2 is named FirstRow and cell E4 is named LastRow.

In addition, the workbook has two named formulas. The Date formula is defined as follows:

```
=OFFSET(Sheet1!$A$2,FirstRow-2,0,LastRow-FirstRow+1,2)
```

Because the category labels occupy two columns, the OFFSET function uses 2 as its final argument. In other words, the function returns a range that's two columns wide.

The Sales formula is defined as follows:

```
=OFFSET(Sheet1!$C$2,FirstRow-2,0,LastRow-FirstRow+1,1)
```

As an alternative, you can define the Sales formula in terms of the Date formula:

```
=OFFSET(Date,0,2,,1)
```

After creating these named formulas, they are then specified as the category labels and values range for the chart's series, using the Select Data Source dialog box (or by editing the SERIES formula directly). For more information about using named formulas for a chart series, refer to the section "Modifying the Series," earlier in this chapter.

 WARNING

There's a serious bug in the initial release of Excel 2007. If you enter a non-numeric value in cell E2 or E4, the named formulas return error values. Excel displays the rather uninformative error message shown in Figure 7-7, and the chart series will probably disappear! To make the series reappear, correct the erroneous entry and save the workbook using a different name. Hopefully, this problem will be fixed in a subsequent update.

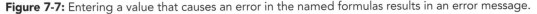

Figure 7-7: Entering a value that causes an error in the named formulas results in an error message.

Adding Spinner Controls

For additional convenience, you may wish to add Spinner controls to the worksheet to make adjusting the FirstRow and LastRow values easier. To do so, follow these steps:

1. Choose Developer⇨Controls⇨Insert, and click the Spinner icon in the Forms section.

2. Click and drag in the worksheet to create the control. You can size and position it just as you can any other graphic object.

3. Right-click the Spinner control and choose Format Control from the shortcut menu. This displays the Format Control dialog box.

4. In the Format Control dialog box, click the Control tab.

5. In the Minimum Value field, enter **2**.

6. In the Maximum Value field, enter **25** (or a number that corresponds to the row that contains the last data point for the chart).

7. In the Cell Link field, enter **FirstRow**. This links the Spinner control with cell D2.

8. Click the OK button to close the dialog box.

9. Repeat Steps 3–8 to add another Spinner control for the LastRow cell. In Step 7, specify **LastRow** as the Cell Link.

After performing these steps, you can use the linked Spinners to quickly adjust the values that control the first and last data points on the chart.

Specifying the First Point and Number of Points for a Series

The example in the following sections is similar to the previous example. Rather than enabling the user to specify the first row and last row to be plotted, this example allows the user to specify the first row (as a meaningful date) and the number of data points.

Figure 7-8 shows a worksheet that contains daily sales information. Cell D2 contains the first date to be plotted, and cell D4 contains the number of data points to appear in the chart.

This example utilizes two (optional) user interface enhancements: a drop-down list to select the start day and a Spinner control to specify the number of days. The drop-down list (not visible in the figure) is accomplished with Excel's Data Validation feature.

 ON THE CD

This workbook, named `first point and number of points.xlsx`, is available on the companion CD-ROM.

Creating the Chart

Use the data in columns A:B to create a chart. The chart in the figure is a standard line chart but this technique will work with any chart type.

Part II

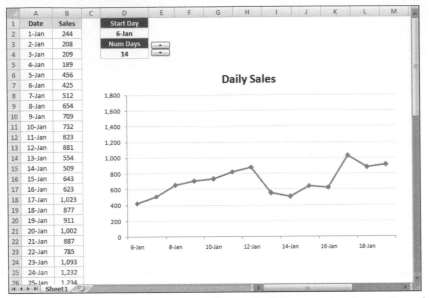

Figure 7-8: Cell D2 contains the start day, and cell D4 contains the number of days to be plotted.

Defining the Names

In this example, cell C2 is named StartDay and cell C4 is named NumDays. The workbook has two named formulas. The Date formula is defined as follows:

```
=OFFSET(Sheet1!$A$2,MATCH(StartDay,Sheet1!$A:$A,1)-2,0,NumDays,1)
```

The Sales formula is defined as follows:

```
=OFFSET(Sheet1!$A$2,MATCH(StartDay,Sheet1!$A:$A,1)-2,1,NumDays,1)
```

The second argument for the OFFSET function uses the MATCH function. The MATCH function returns the relative position of an item in a range. In this case, it returns the position of the date in column A that matches the date in the StartDay cell. This, of course, is just another way of determining the first row to include in the chart.

As in the previous example, these two named formulas are then used for the category labels and values range for the chart series. For more information about using named formulas for a chart series, refer to the section "Modifying the Series," earlier in this chapter.

Adding the User Interface Elements

The NumDays cell has a linked Spinner control to make it easier to specify the number of days to include in the chart. (See the previous section for information about adding a linked Spinner control.)

You can't use a Spinner control for the StartDay cell because it needs to display dates, and the Spinner control has a maximum value of 30,000. (The date serial number values exceed this number.) A scroll bar is an option, but a drop-down list of available dates would be perfect. Fortunately, Excel's Data Validation feature makes adding a drop-down list to a cell very easy. To do so, follow these steps:

1. Select cell D2, and make sure that it's formatted to display a date.

2. Choose Data⇨Data Tools⇨Data Validation to display the Data Validation dialog box.

3. In the Data Validation dialog box, click the Settings tab.

4. In the Allow field, choose List.

5. In the Source field, enter **=$A$2:$A$60**, which is the worksheet range that contains the dates. (See Figure 7-9.)

6. Click the OK button to close the Data Validation dialog box.

![Data Validation dialog box showing the Settings tab with Allow field set to List and Source field set to =$A$2:$A$60]

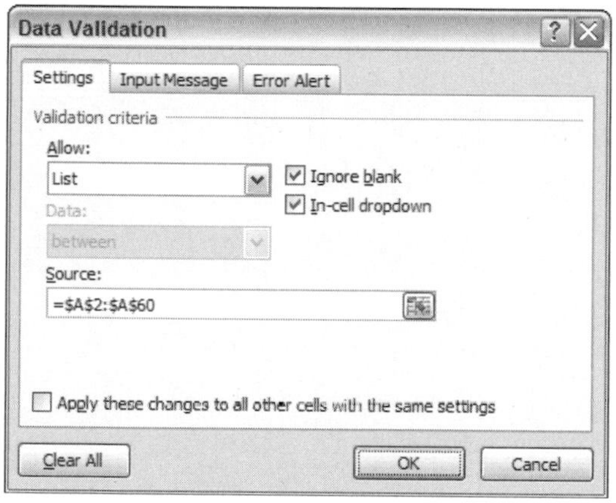

Figure 7-9: Specifying a range of dates for the drop-down data validation list.

After entering the data validation settings, you can then select a date when cell D2 is activated. The selected date will be the first date in the chart. The Spinner control determines how many total data points appear in the chart.

TIP

In Step 5 in the preceding list, you can take a different approach. Rather than enter the range address into the Source field, you can enter the following formula, which adjusts automatically if additional dates are added:

```
=OFFSET($A2,0,0,COUNTA($A:$A)-1,1)
```

Part II

Plotting the Last *n* Data Points in a Series

Another interactive chart variation is to make a chart show only the most recent *n* data points in a column. For example, you can create a chart that always displays the most recent six months of data (see Figure 7-10). In this example, cell F1 holds the number of data points to display in the chart.

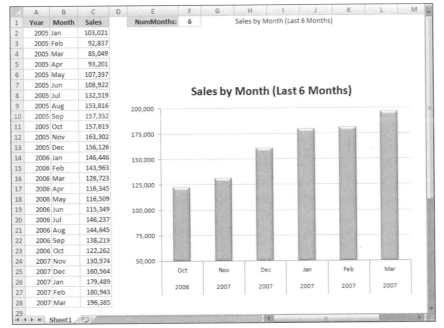

Figure 7-10: This chart displays the six most recent data points. The number plotted is controlled by the value in cell F1.

 ON THE CD

This workbook, named `plot last n data points.xlsx`, is available on the companion CD-ROM.

Creating the Chart

Create a chart using the data in columns A:C. The chart in this example is a standard column chart, but this technique will work with any chart type. The horizontal category axis uses two columns (A and B).

Defining the Names

In this example, cell F1 is named NumMonths. The workbook has two other named formulas. The Date formula is defined as follows:

```
=OFFSET(Sheet1!$A$2,COUNTA(Sheet1!$B:$B)-NumMonths-1,0,NumMonths,2)
```

The Sales formula is defined as follows:

```
=OFFSET(Sheet1!$C$2,COUNTA(Sheet1!$C:$C)-NumMonths-1,0,NumMonths,1)
```

The chart title uses a link to cell H1, which contains the following formula:

```
="Sales by Month (Last " & NumMonths &" Months)"
```

This formula uses the cell name NumMonths to ensure that the chart title always displays the number of months plotted.

After you create the names, you use these two named formulas for the category labels and values range for the chart series. For more information about using named formulas for a chart series, refer to the section "Modifying the Series," earlier in this chapter. The number of data points in the chart will then be controlled by the value in cell F1. New data added to the worksheet will be accommodated automatically.

Plotting Every *n*th Data Point in a Series

Suppose that you have a large amount of data in a column, and you want to plot only every 10th tenth data point. The following sections present two techniques that enable you to do just that. This technique is most useful for large data sets in which the data varies smoothly and continuously. In some cases, important data may be obscured if some of the data points are not displayed.

 ON THE CD

A workbook that contains the two examples in these sections is available on the companion CD-ROM. The file is named `plot every nth value.xlsx`.

Using Filtering

One way to plot every *n*th data point in a range is to use filtering in conjunction with a formula. Filtering allows you to hide rows that don't meet specified criteria. Excel, by default, doesn't plot data that resides in a hidden row. Therefore, the trick is to create formulas that return a specific value based on the data's row number and then use the results of these formulas as the basis for filtering the list.

Figure 7-11 shows a worksheet with filtering in effect (note the hidden rows). Cell F1 contains a value that represents *n*. For example, when F1 contains 5, the chart displays every 5th data point: the value in rows 2, 7, 12, and so on.

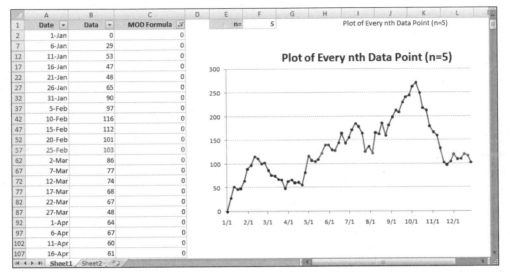

Figure 7-11: This chart plots every *n*th data point (specified in cell F1) by ignoring data in the rows hidden by filtering.

NOTE

If your data is in a table (created by choosing Insert⇨Tables⇨Table), filtering is turned on automatically for the table. If your data is not in a table, choose Data⇨Sort & Filter⇨ Filter to enable filtering. In either case, the header row displays drop-down arrows in each cell. Click an arrow to specify the filter for the column.

Column A contains 365 dates, and column B contains 365 corresponding data points. Column C contains formulas that return a value which is used to determine whether the row should be hidden. The formula in cell C2, which is copied to the cells below, is as follows:

```
=MOD(ROW()-ROW($B$2),$F$1)
```

This formula uses the MOD function to calculate the remainder when the row number minus the row number of the first row is divided by the value in F1. As a result, every *n*th cell in column C contains 0.

Use the drop-down arrow in cell C1 to display only the rows that contain a 0 in column C. This technique does not work if the Show Data in Hidden Rows and Columns option is in effect for the chart. By default, this setting is disabled. To check (or change) this setting, select the chart and choose Chart Tools⇨Design⇨Select Data. In the Select Data Source dialog box, click the Hidden and Empty Cells button to display a dialog box that lets you determine how hidden cells are plotted.

TIP

If the chart is next to the data, you'll find that the chart's height is reduced when rows are hidden. To prevent this, activate the chart and display the Size and Properties dialog box. To display this dialog box, click the dialog box launcher in the Chart Tools⇨Format⇨ Size group. (The dialog box launcher is the small icon to the right of the word Size.) In the Size and Properties dialog box, select the Properties tab and select Don't Move Or Size With Cells.

NOTE

The main problem with this technique is that it's not fully automatic. When you change the value in cell F1, you need to respecify the filter criteria for column C. The rows do not hide automatically.

Using Array Formulas

The preceding technique works well, but it would be nice to make it fully automated. Tushar Mehta, an Excel charting expert, developed a clever technique that uses named formulas. The example in this section is an adaptation of his method.

Figure 7-12 shows the same data used in the previous example. This workbook uses three named ranges: Nth (cell H1), Dates (range A2:A366), and Data (range B2:B366). The Nth cell is linked to a Spinner control.

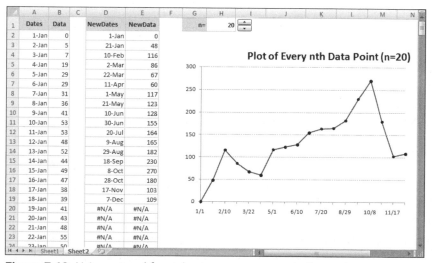

Figure 7-12: Using named formulas to return every *n*th data point.

Notice two additional columns of formulas (columns D and E). Both of these are multicell array formulas. The array formula in D2:D366 is as follows:

```
=N(OFFSET(Dates,(ROW(OFFSET($A$1,0,0,ROWS(Dates)/Nth))-1)*Nth,0))
```

This formula returns an array that consists of every nth row in the Dates range.

The array formula in E2:E366, as follows, is very similar and returns an array that consists of every nth row in the Data range:

```
=N(OFFSET(Data,(ROW(OFFSET($A$1,0,0,ROWS(Data)/Nth))-1)*Nth,0))
```

When you enter a multicell array formula, select all the cells first. Then type the formula and press Ctrl+Shift+Enter.

NOTE

These array formulas are complex, and a complete explanation is beyond the scope of this book. However, you don't have to fully understand them to use them. They can easily be adapted to other data sets. Be aware that the reference to cell $A$1 must remain intact. This cell is used to generate a series of offsets that reference cells within the original range.

Creating Named Formulas

If you create a chart from the data in columns D:E, the result would not be very satisfactory. Every nth value would be plotted, but the chart would display a lengthy series of empty (#NA) cells.

The solution is to call upon the named formulas technique to substitute for the two array formulas. These named formulas are identical to the array formulas listed in the previous section.

Define NewDates as follows:

```
=N(OFFSET(Dates,(ROW(OFFSET(Sheet2!$A$1,0,0,ROWS(Dates)/Nth))-1)*Nth,0))
```

Define NewData as follows:

```
=N(OFFSET(Data,(ROW(OFFSET(Sheet2!$A$1,0,0,ROWS(Data)/Nth))-1)*Nth,0))
```

After you create the names, you use these two named formulas for the category labels and values range for the chart series. For more information about using named formulas for a chart series, refer to the section "Modifying the Series," earlier in this chapter. The result? The arrays used by the charts consist only of the values (no #NA values).

Because the named formulas substitute for the array formulas, the formulas in columns D:E are no longer needed.

Using Check Boxes to Select Series to Plot

The example shown in Figure 7-13 displays a line chart with three series. The number of series that are actually displayed is controlled by three Check Box controls. When all three check boxes are selected, the chart displays data for Product A, Product B, and Product C. Deselect a check box, and the corresponding series disappears from the chart.

On the CD

This workbook, named `select series with checkboxes.xlsx`, is available on the companion CD-ROM.

Month	Product A	Product B	Product C
Jan	1,450	569	983
Feb	1,532	578	1,200
Mar	1,636	691	1,200
Apr	1,719	699	1,188
May	1,546	601	904
Jun	1,435	543	912
Jul	1,654	784	1,056
Aug	1,854	1,035	1,004
Sep	1,891	1,182	889
Oct	1,900	1,332	809
Nov	1,909	1,347	1,042
Dec	2,043	1,540	905

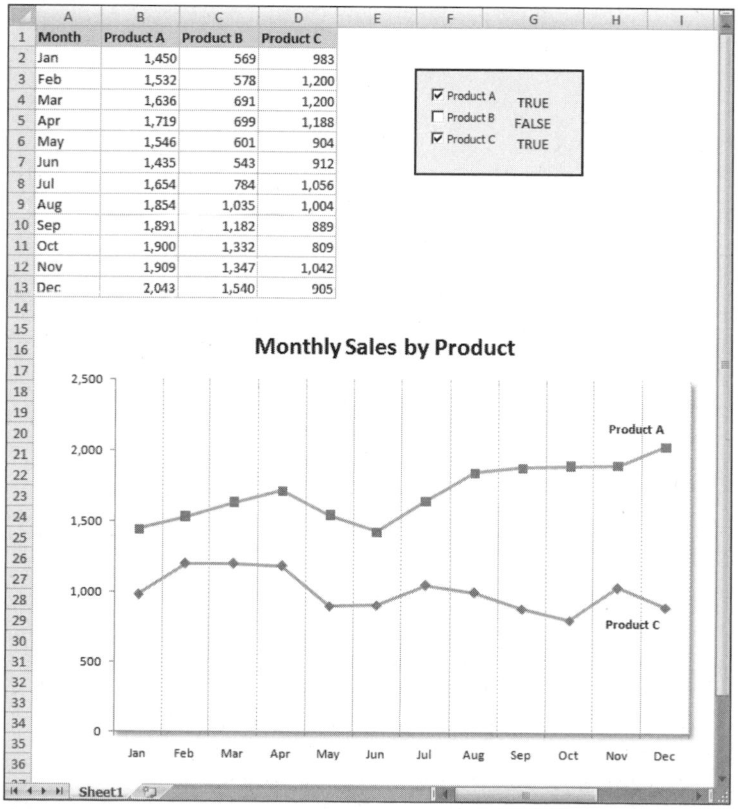

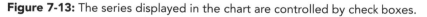

Figure 7-13: The series displayed in the chart are controlled by check boxes.

Creating the Chart

The chart in this example is a standard line chart that uses the data in A1:D13.

Adding the Check Box Controls

This section describes how to add the Check Box controls and link each of them to a cell.

NOTE

To add a control to a worksheet, Excel must display its Developer tab. If this tab is not visible, choose Office⇨Excel Options, click the Popular tab, and select the Show Developer Tab in the Ribbon check box.

To add the check boxes to the worksheet, follow these steps:

1. Choose Developer⇨Insert, and click the Check Box icon in the Forms section.

2. Click and drag in the worksheet to create the control. You can size and position it just as you can any other graphic object.

3. Right-click the Check Box control and choose Format Control from the shortcut menu. This displays the Format Control dialog box.

4. In the Format Control dialog box, click the Control tab.

5. In the Cell Link field, enter **$G$4**. This links the Check Box control with cell G4, which will display either TRUE or FALSE, depending on the state of the Check Box control.

6. Click the OK button to close the dialog box.

7. Repeat Steps 2–6 to add two more Check Box controls, linked to cells G5 and G6.

Defining the Names

This example uses quite a few names, which are listed in Table 7-1. Note that SeriesA, SeriesB, and SeriesC are named formulas. The other names all refer to cells or ranges. Also, note that range E2:E13 is empty. This is the range that will be used if a series is not selected.

TABLE 7-1   DEFINED NAMES

Name	Refers To
Month	=Sheet1!$A$2:$A$13
ProductA	=Sheet1!$B$2:$B$13

Name	Refers To
ProductB	=Sheet1!$C$2:$C$13
ProductC	=Sheet1!$D$2:$D$13
BlankRange	=Sheet1!$E$2:$E$13
ShowProductA	=Sheet1!$G$4
ShowProductB	=Sheet1!$G$5
ShowProductC	=Sheet1!$G$6
SeriesA	=IF(ShowProductA,ProductA,BlankRange)
SeriesB	=IF(ShowProductB,ProductB,BlankRange)
SeriesC	=IF(ShowProductC,ProductC,BlankRange)

Part II

The three named formulas are quite a bit different from the previous examples in the chapter. These formulas use an IF function that checks the corresponding check box value (stored in a cell in column G). If it's TRUE, the named formula returns the range reference for the corresponding product's data. If the check box is not selected, the named formula returns a reference to the blank range (E2:E13).

Modifying the Chart Series

The final step is to modify the three chart series so that they use the named formulas for the values range. The easiest way to do this is to edit the SERIES formulas. For example, the SERIES formula for Product A is as follows:

```
=SERIES(Sheet1!$B$1,Sheet1!Month,Sheet1!SeriesA,1)
```

Or, you can use the Select Data Source dialog box.

The Product B and Product C series are modified in a similar manner.

NOTE

I used data labels (one per series) in lieu of a chart legend because the legend always shows all three series — even if a series is not actually displayed on the chart.

Creating a *Very* Interactive Chart

The final example, shown in Figure 7-14, is a useful application that allows the user to choose two U.S. cities (from a list of 284 cities) and view a chart that compares the cities by month in any of the following categories: average precipitation, average temperature, percent sunshine, and average wind speed.

ON THE CD

This workbook, named `climate data chart.xlsx`, is available on the companion CD-ROM.

The interactivity is provided by using Excel's built-in features — no macros required. The cities are chosen from a drop-down list, using Excel's Data Validation feature, and the data option is selected using four Option Button controls. The pieces are all connected using a few formulas.

NOTE

This example uses some named ranges. But, unlike the previous examples in this chapter, it does not use named formulas. Rather, the chart uses data that is retrieved by using VLOOKUP formulas.

This example demonstrates that it is indeed possible to create a user-friendly, interactive application without the assistance of macros.

The following sections describe the steps I took to set up this application.

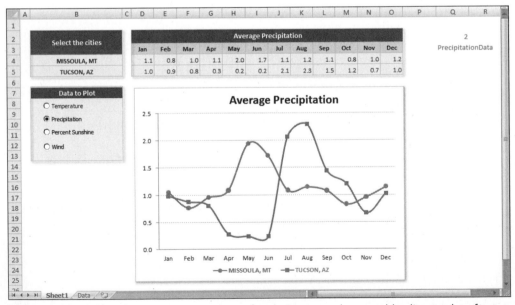

Figure 7-14: This application uses a variety of techniques to plot monthly climate data for two selected U.S. cities.

Getting the Data

I did a Web search and spent about five minutes locating the data I needed at the National Climatic Data Center. I copied the data from my browser window, pasted it into an Excel worksheet, and did a bit of cleanup work. The result was four 13-column tables of data, which I named PrecipitationData, TemperatureData, SunshineData, and WindData. To keep the interface as clean as possible, I put the data on a separate sheet (named Data).

Creating the Option Button Controls

I needed a way to allow the user to select the data to plot and decided to use Option Button controls from the Forms toolbar. Because option buttons work as a group, the four Option Button controls are all linked to the same cell (cell Q2). Cell Q2, therefore, contains a value from 1 to 4, depending on which option button is selected.

I needed a way to obtain the name of the data table based on the numeric value in cell O3. The solution was to write a formula (in cell Q3) that uses Excel's CHOOSE function:

```
=CHOOSE(Q2,"TemperatureData","PrecipitationData","SunshineData","WindData")
```

Therefore, cell Q3 (which is named DataToUse) displays the name of one of the four named data ranges.

Creating the City Lists

Next step in setting up the application: Create drop-down lists to enable the user to choose the cities to be compared on the chart. Excel's Data Validation feature makes creating a drop-down list in a cell very easy. Cell B4 contains the first city list and is named City1. Cell B5, which is named City2, contains the second city list.

To make working with the list of cities easier, I created a named range, CityList, which refers to the first column in the PrecipitationData table.

Following are the steps I used to create the drop-down lists:

1. Select cell B4.
2. Choose Data⇨Data Tools⇨Data Validation to display Excel's Data Validation dialog box.
3. Click the Settings tab in the Data Validation dialog box.
4. In the Allow field, choose List.
5. In the Source field, enter **=CityList**.
6. Click the OK button.
7. Copy cell B4 to cell B5. This duplicates the data validation settings for the second city.

Figure 7-15 shows the result.

Select the cities
MISSOULA, MT
TUCSON, AZ
TOLEDO, OH
TOPEKA, KS
TUCSON, AZ
TULSA, OK
TUPELO, MS
UNALAKLEET, AK
VALDEZ, AK
VALENTINE, NE
Wind
Jan
Feb
Mar
Apr
1.1
0.8
1.0
1.0
0.9
0.8
2.5
2.0
1.5

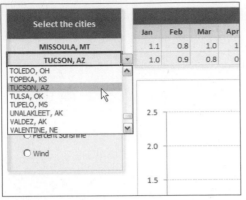

Figure 7-15: Using the data validation drop-down box to select a city.

Creating the Chart's Data Range

The key to this application is that the chart uses data in a specific range. The data in this range is retrieved from the appropriate data range using formulas that utilize the VLOOKUP function. Figure 7-16 shows the range of data that is used by the chart.

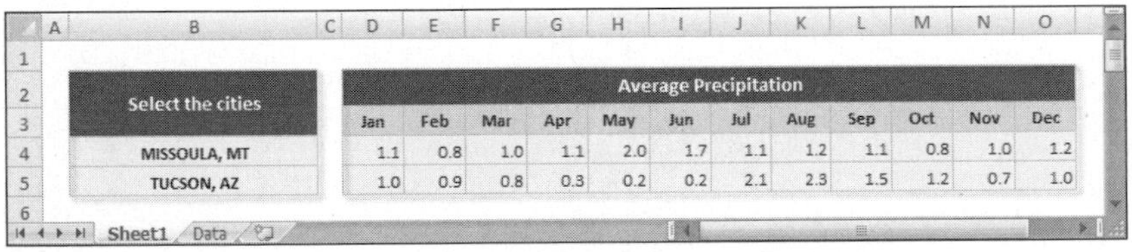

Select the cities
MISSOULA, MT
TUCSON, AZ
Average Precipitation
Jan Feb Mar Apr May Jun Jul Aug Sep Oct Nov Dec
1.1 0.8 1.0 1.1 2.0 1.7 1.1 1.2 1.1 0.8 1.0 1.2
1.0 0.9 0.8 0.3 0.2 0.2 2.1 2.3 1.5 1.2 0.7 1.0
Sheet1
Data

Figure 7-16: The chart uses the data retrieved by formulas.

The formula in cell D4, which looks up data based on the contents of City1, is as follows:

```
=VLOOKUP(City1,INDIRECT(DataToUse),COLUMN()-2,FALSE)
```

For example, assume that City1 contains Aberdeen, SD, and the Precipitation option button is selected. That option button causes the cell named DataToUse to display the text PrecipitationData. Therefore, the formula in cell D4 looks for the row in the PrecipitationData range that contains the text Aberdeen, SD. Because cell D4 is in column 4, the function retrieves the data in the column number minus 2 (that is, column 2) of the PrecipitationData range. That column contains the precipitation data for January.

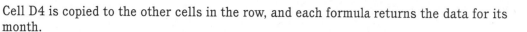

Cell D4 is copied to the other cells in the row, and each formula returns the data for its month.

The formula in cell D5 is the same, except that it is looking up data based on the contents of City2, as follows:

```
=VLOOKUP(City2,INDIRECT(DataToUse),COLUMN()-2,FALSE)
```

The label above the months (in merged cells D2:O2) is generated by a formula that refers to the DataToUse cell and constructs a descriptive title. The formula is as follows:

```
="Average " &LEFT(DataToUse,LEN(DataToUse)-4)
```

Creating the Chart

After completing the previous tasks, the final step — creating the actual chart — is a breeze. The line chart has two data series and uses the data in D4:O5, and category labels in D3:O3. The chart title is linked to cell D2. The data in rows 4 and 5 changes whenever an Option Button control is selected or a new city is selected from either of the data validation lists.

Chapter 8

Charting Techniques and Tricks

In This Chapter

◆ Adding lines and background elements to a chart

◆ Working with single-point charts that resemble a thermometer or gauge

◆ Using an XY series to simulate an axis

◆ Creating specialty charts that make use of a variety of tricks

◆ Stacking and overlaying charts

◆ Putting more than one chart on a chart sheet

This chapter might best be described as the catch-all chapter. You'll find a wide variety of useful charting examples that incorporate various tricks of the trade. These examples may give you some new ideas and stimulate your imagination.

Many of the examples in this chapter assume that you're familiar with the material presented in previous chapters. In other words, I focus on the general technique and assume that you know the basic procedures.

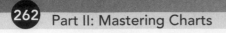

Adding Lines and Backgrounds to a Chart

The following sections present examples of charts that have been augmented in a number of ways to display various types of lines and background elements. Several of the examples involve tricks that make use of combination charts.

Adding Horizontal Reference Lines to a Chart

Many charts benefit from adding one or more reference lines. Figure 8-1 shows an area chart that depicts a product's defect rate over a 20-day period. This chart displays an additional line. Data points that appear above this line represent an unacceptable level of defects.

	A	B	C
1	Day	Defect Rate	Acceptable Level
2	1	4.2%	5.0%
3	2	4.2%	5.0%
4	3	4.4%	5.0%
5	4	5.2%	5.0%
6	5	5.6%	5.0%
7	6	5.9%	5.0%
8	7	7.5%	5.0%
9	8	7.8%	5.0%
10	9	6.8%	5.0%
11	10	5.8%	5.0%
12	11	6.1%	5.0%
13	12	5.7%	5.0%
14	13	4.0%	5.0%
15	14	2.7%	5.0%
16	15	4.0%	5.0%
17	16	2.9%	5.0%
18	17	3.3%	5.0%
19	18	2.7%	5.0%
20	19	1.7%	5.0%
21	20	1.5%	5.0%
22			

Defect Rate: Last 20 Days

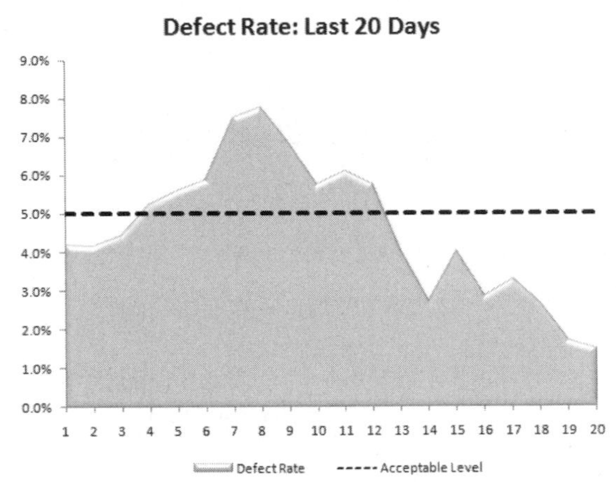

Figure 8-1: This combination chart displays a comparison line.

Adding a reference line is very simple. Just add a new series to the chart that displays as a straight horizontal line. In this case, the line uses the data in column C, which consists of a single value repeated for each data point.

This is just a simple combination chart. The chart started as a line chart, and then I converted the Defect Rate series to an area chart series. I removed the gridlines to make the line more prominent. You can, of course, add any number of reference lines to a chart. Each line requires a new data series.

ON THE CD

This workbook, named `horizontal reference line.xlsx`, is available on the companion CD-ROM.

Adding a Vertical Line to a Chart with an XY Series

The previous section describes how to display a horizontal line on a chart. Adding a *vertical* line to a chart is a bit more challenging. Figure 8-2 shows a chart that displays monthly sales. The vertical line represents the date of a merger and provides a reference point for comparing pre-merger and post-merger sales, depicted in the column series.

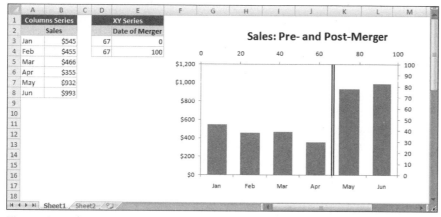

Figure 8-2: The vertical line is generated by an XY series.

This chart is a combination chart that combines a column chart with a scatter chart.

ON THE CD

This example and the example that follows are available in the workbook named `vertical line in column chart.xlsx`, on the companion CD-ROM.

To create this chart, use the following steps:

1. Create a standard column chart using the data in range A2:B8.
2. Select the range D2:E4 and press Ctrl+C to copy the data.

Part II

3. Select the chart and choose Home⇨Clipboard⇨Paste⇨Paste Special. In the Paste Special dialog box, select New Series, Values (Y) in Columns, Series Names in First Row, and Category (X Labels) in First Column.

3. Select the new series (a column series), and change the chart type for the series to XY (Scatter). Use the Scatter with Straight Lines subtype. Excel displays two secondary value axes in the chart (at the top and right).

4. For each of the two new value axes, access the Format Axis dialog box, click the Axis Options tab, and change the Minimum value to 0 and the Maximum value to 100.

5. Add a title, remove the legend, and apply other cosmetic formatting as desired.

NOTE

The XY series uses an arbitrary scale of 0–100 for both axes. This scale could be anything because the scale values are not shown. Using 0–100 enables you to specify the line location in terms of a percentage. In this case, the value 67 (in D3:D4) specifies a line that begins at 67% of the length of the category axis.

Normally, you'll want to hide the secondary axes at the top and on the right. To do so, use the Format Axis dialog box and set the Axis Labels setting to None, and specify None for the Major Tick Mark Type. Note that you don't want to remove the axes by using the Chart Tools⇨Layout⇨Axes⇨Axes control.

You can use a similar procedure to create a horizontal line in a chart. Although the process described in the previous section is simpler, it may not be suitable for a column chart or a line chart because the horizontal line does not extend all the way to the vertical borders of the plot area.

Using Background Columns to Represent a Vertical Line

The example in this section uses the same data as the previous example, but the approach to generating the vertical line is different. In this combination chart, the vertical line is created by using an additional column chart series, plotted on a secondary vertical axis. The line is formed because the plot area is visible for data points with a zero value (see Figure 8-3). The advantage in using this method is that you can provide a different color background for the pre- and post-merger periods.

NOTE

Even though both series use columns, a secondary axis is necessary to control the gap width of the series independently. Technically, this is still classified as a combination chart: a column- column combination chart.

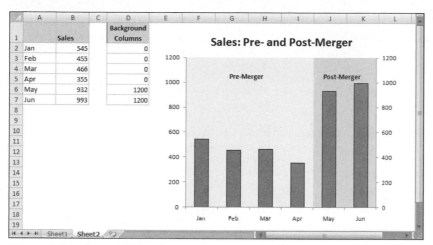

Figure 8-3: The vertical line is generated by colored columns.

Part II

Creating this chart involved the following steps:

1. Create a standard column chart using the data in range A2:B7. Delete the legend and the horizontal gridlines.

2. Select D2:D7 and press Ctrl+C to copy the data.

3. Select the chart and choose Home⇨Clipboard⇨Paste⇨Paste Special. In the Paste Special dialog box, select New Series and Values (Y) in Columns. Excel adds a new column series to the chart.

4. Click the original series (not the newly added series) and access the Series Options tab of the Format Data Series dialog box. Select the Secondary Axis option.

5. Click the newly added series and access the Format Data Series dialog box. Click the Series Options tab and set the Gap Width to 0. Click the Fill tab and specify a fill color (a light color is a good choice). The columns will appear as a single background block.

6. Click the chart's plot area, and apply a fill color.

   This is the background color for the Pre-Merger data.

7. Access the Format Axis dialog box for the left value axis (the axis associated with the background series). Click the Axis Options tab and set the Maximum scale value to 1200 (which is the maximum scale value for the right value axis).

8. Click the secondary value axis and press Delete. Both series will use the primary axis.

9. Add a title and text boxes to indicate the pre-merger and post-merger sections of the chart.

NOTE

If you followed the previous steps, you've realized that the value axis on the left is actually associated with the background column series. This is necessary because a column series plotted on the secondary axis always appears in front of a column series plotted on the primary axis.

This procedure can easily be adapted to other situations — for example, dividing a chart into three vertical sections. Just change the colors of the appropriate background bars. In most cases, you'll want the background series to contain the same number of data points as the actual data series.

Adding Vertical or Horizontal "Bands"

The examples in this section demonstrate a variation on the previous concept. Figure 8-4 shows a chart that displays vertical bands. Again, it's a combination chart — this time an XY scatter series combined with a column chart series.

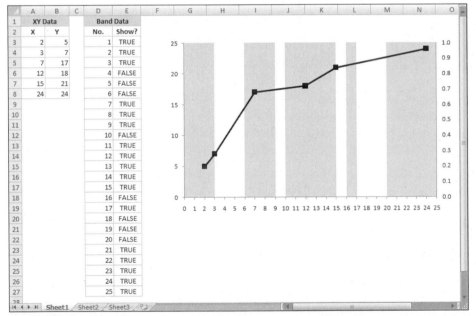

Figure 8-4: The vertical bands are provided by a column series that uses the secondary value axis.

The column chart series, which uses the data in columns D:E, is associated with the secondary value axis and has a scale range from 0 to 1. Normally, you would hide the secondary axis, but it's shown here for clarity. Note that the data consists of TRUE and FALSE values that determine whether the band is visible. In Excel, TRUE has the value of 1 and FALSE has the value of 0. Therefore, these Boolean values map perfectly to the chart's value scale.

ON THE CD

The examples in this section are available on the companion CD-ROM. The filename is `vertical and horizontal bands.xlsx`.

The chart in Figure 8-5 is a line chart that plots 100 data points. The vertical bands in the background display only if the corresponding line series data point is greater than the previous one. Column D contains simple formulas that return TRUE or FALSE, depending on the values in column B.

Figure 8-6 shows another example. In this case, the "band" series consists of 50 horizontal bars rather than columns. The result is a line chart that shows horizontal bars in the background. The visibility of each of the 50 bars is controlled by changing the Boolean values in a range of 50 cells. The axes for the bar series are displayed at the top of the chart in the figure, but you would normally hide these axes.

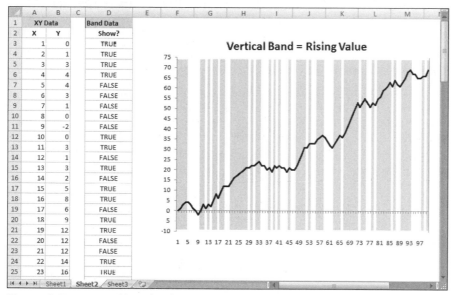
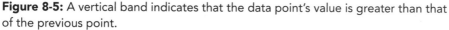

Figure 8-5: A vertical band indicates that the data point's value is greater than that of the previous point.

NOTE

This technique does not work well for a column series. If you start with a bar chart, and then convert the data series to a column chart, the axis labels are messed up (see the left chart in Figure 8-7). If you start with a column chart and convert the band series to a bar chart series, Excel plots the horizontal bars in front of the vertical columns (see the right chart in Figure 8-7). In other words, neither option produces a good result.

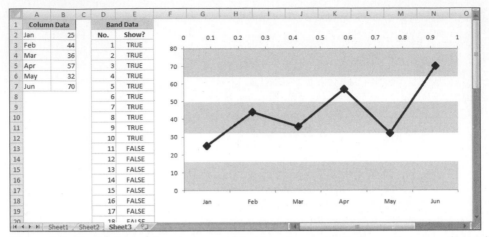

Figure 8-6: The horizontal bands are provided by a bar series that uses the secondary value axis.

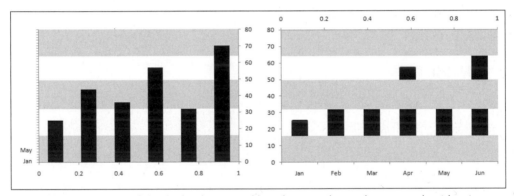

Figure 8-7: Two ways of displaying horizontal bands in a column chart — and neither is satisfactory,

TIP

If you must have a column chart with horizontal bands, add drop lines to the line series and make the drop lines very wide so they look like columns; then hide the line series.

Creating a Scatter Chart with Colored Quadrants

Figure 8-8 shows a scatter chart that plots 10 data points. Notice that the two value axes cross in the center of the chart, forming four equal-size quadrants. Each of these quadrants is a different color — thanks to the assistance of a stacked column chart series.

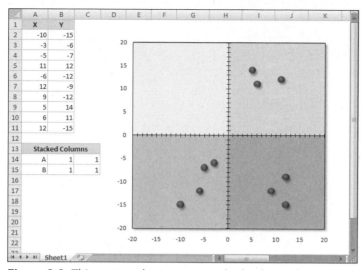

Figure 8-8: This scatter chart uses a stacked column chart to provide four different colors in the background.

 ON THE CD

The example in this section is available on the companion CD-ROM. The filename is `scatter chart with colored quadrants.xlsx`.

Here's how it's done:

1. Create a standard scatter chart using the data in range A2:B11. Delete the legend and gridlines.

2. Select A14:C15 and press Ctrl+C.

3. Select the chart and choose Home⇨Clipboard⇨Paste⇨Paste Special. In the Paste Special dialog box, select New Series, Values (Y) in Columns, and Categories (X Values) in First Column. The chart now has three XY series named Series 1, Series 2, and Series 3.

4. Select Series 2 and access the Format Data Series dialog box. Click the Series Options tab and choose the Secondary Axis option. Repeat these actions for Series 3.

5. Select Series 2 and change it to a 100% stacked column chart. Repeat for Series 3.

6. Use the Chart Tools⇨Layout⇨Axes⇨Axes control and make sure that all four axes are displayed.

7. Select either Series 2 or Series 3 and access the Format Data Series dialog box. Click the Series Options tab and set the Gap Width to 0.

8. Select each of the four individual data points in the column chart and change their color. Remember, the first click selects the series and the second click selects the data point within the series.

9. Select the axis on top, access its Format Axis dialog box, select the Axis Options tab, and set Axis Labels to None. Repeat these actions for the axis on the right.

10. The axis labels for the scatter chart are next to their respective axis. You may prefer to set the Tick Mark Labels option to Low, using the Axis Options tab of the Format Axis dialog box.

TIP

Another way to get a four-color background effect is to create an image file that consists of four colored quadrants. Then you can use the Format Plot Area dialog box to specify this file to be used as the plot area fill.

Charts That Use a Single Data Point

The examples in the following sections demonstrate various ways to display a single value in a chart.

ON THE CD

The examples in the section are available on the companion CD-ROM. The filename is `single data point charts.xlsx`.

Creating a Thermometer Chart

Figure 8-9 shows a minimalist chart, designed to show progress toward a 100% goal. This chart is similar to a thermometer. As the value increases towards 100%, the mercury in the thermometer rises.

Figure 8-9: This minimalist chart is grouped with a text box and a shape.

The chart's title is linked to a cell that contains the percent completed. All other chart elements were removed. The chart is grouped with a text box and a shape to present a concise display.

Figure 8-10 shows a slightly fancier single-point chart. The worksheet is set up to track daily progress toward a goal: 1,000 new customers in a 15-day period. Cell B18 contains the goal value, and cell B19 contains a simple formula that sums the values in column B. Cell B21 contains a formula that calculates the percent of goal.

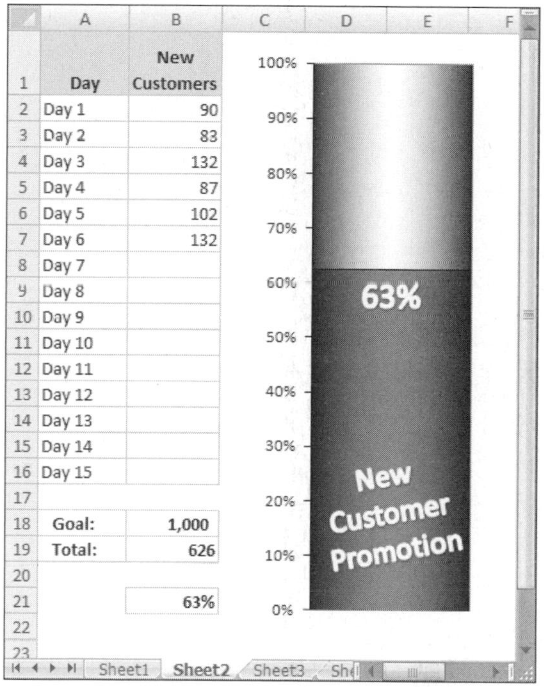

Figure 8-10: This chart displays progress toward a goal.

Following are a few other points about this chart:

- The chart title appears at the bottom of the chart. I used commands in the Chart Tools⇨ Format⇨WordArt Styles group to display the title at an angle.

- A text box (linked to cell B21) displays the percent completed.

- The single-point column series has a gap width of 0 (this makes the column occupy the entire width of the plot area).

- The value scale ranges from 0 to 1. If the goal is exceeded, the column will completely fill the chart.

- The data series uses a gradient fill to give it a rounded appearance.

Figure 8-11 shows a variation on this theme. In this case, the chart is a line chart, with a single data point. I replaced the series marker with a shape in the form of a double-headed arrow. I also added a secondary value axis so that the scale values appear on both sides of the chart.

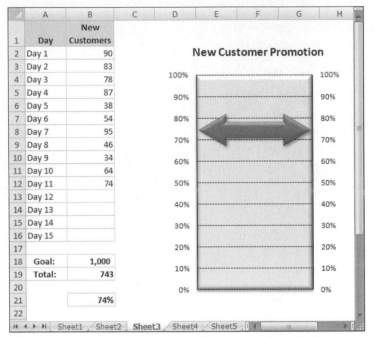

Figure 8-11: This single-value line chart uses a shape for the series marker.

CROSS-REFERENCE

Refer to Chapter 6 for more information about copying shapes and pasting them as series markers.

Creating a Gauge Chart

Figure 8-12 shows a pie chart set up to resemble a gauge. Although this chart displays a single value (entered in cell B1), it actually uses three data points (in A4:A6).

One slice of the pie — the slice at the bottom — always consists of 50%, and that slice is hidden (the slice's fill is None and its border color is No Line). The other two slices are apportioned based on the value in B1. The formula in cell B4 is as follows:

```
=MIN(B1,100%)/2
```

This formula uses the MIN function to display the smaller of two values: the value in cell B1 or 100%. It then divides this value by 2 because you're dealing only with the visible half of the pie chart. Using the MIN function prevents the chart from displaying more than 100%.

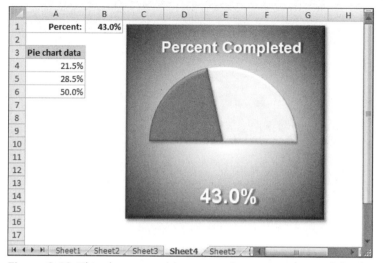

Figure 8-12: This chart resembles a speedometer gauge and displays a value between 0 and 100%.

The formula in A6, which follows, simply calculates the remaining part of the pie — the part to the right of the gauge's "needle."

```
=50%-A5
```

Figure 8-13 shows a variation that uses a doughnut chart with two series. Again, the lower portions of the two series are hidden. The outer series colors (red, yellow, and green) use data labels to indicate the meaning of various ratings.

Figure 8-13: This doughnut chart resembles a tachometer and displays a value between 0 and 100%.

Yet another variation is shown in Figure 8-14. This is a scatter chart with two data points connected by a line. All other parts of the chart are hidden. The semicircle is a shape. Cells A3 and B3 contain 0 and define the bottom point of the needle. Two formulas, which use the value in cell A1, determine the upper data point — and, consequently, the angle:

```
A4: =SIN((30*A1-15)*(2*PI()/60))
A5: =COS((30*A1-15)*(2*PI()/60))
```

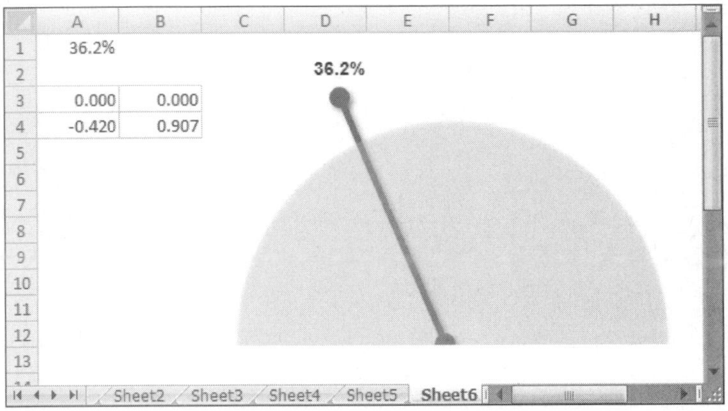

Figure 8-14: A scatter chart creates a gauge that depicts a value between 0% and 100%.

Using a Dummy Axis

The following sections describe a very useful trick that can be applied in a variety of situations. The trick involves using an XY scatter series that simulates a value axis.

ON THE CD

The examples in the section are available on the companion CD-ROM. The filename is `dummy axis examples.xlsx`.

An Introductory Example

A common use for a dummy value axis is to provide descriptive labels. As you probably know, you can't change the text used in the value axis labels — they are always values derived from the numbers in the chart series. You can control the number formatting and font attributes, but the actual contents of these labels are determined by Excel and cannot be changed.

Figure 8-15 shows a chart that seems to defy this rule. This chart displays the results of 10 tests, and the value axis shows letter grades (A–F), not values. Also, notice that the labels appear in between the gridlines.

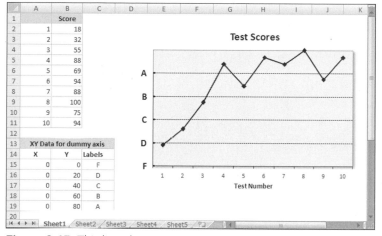

Figure 8-15: This line chart uses an XY series to simulate a value axis.

ABOUT THIS CHART

Following are a few key points regarding this chart:

- The chart is actually a combination chart that combines a standard line chart with a scatter chart.

- The actual value axis is hidden. In its place is an XY series that is formatted to look like an axis.

- The data for the XY series is stored in A15:B19. The Y values represent the scores for each letter grade category. For example, an *F* is 0–19, a *D* is 20–39, and so on.

- The axis labels (the letters A–F) are custom data labels for the XY series.

To better understand how a dummy value axis is set up, refer to Figure 8-16. This is a standard scatter chart, with the data points connected by lines, and series markers set to display a horizontal tick. It uses the five data points specified in A2:B6. Because each X value is the same (1), the series displays as a vertical line. This XY series uses custom data labels to identify each "tick." As you can see, this data series look very much like a vertical axis.

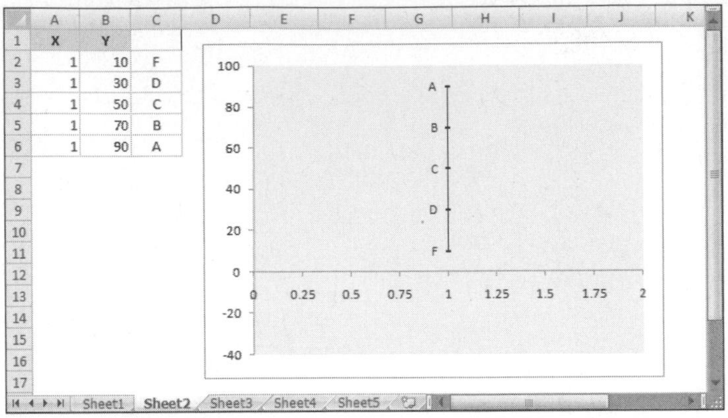

Figure 8-16: This XY series displays as a vertical line with tick marks and uses custom data labels.

CREATING THE CHART

Following are the steps required to create the line chart in Figure 8-15, presented at the beginning of this section.

1. Select the data in A1:B11 and create a standard line chart. Delete the legend.

2. Select A15:B19 and choose Edit⇨Copy.

3. Select the chart and choose Home⇨Clipboard⇨Paste⇨Paste Special. Specify New Series, Values (Y) in Columns, and Category (X Labels) in First Column. Doing so adds a new line series to the chart.

4. Select the new line series and choose Chart Tools⇨Design Type⇨Change Chart Type. Specify an XY (scatter) chart using the subtype that displays straight lines and markers. The XY series will appear on top of the chart's value axis. The X value axis for the new series appears on the top, and its Y value axis appears on the right.

5. Select the XY series and access the Format Data Series dialog box. Make the line color black. Using the Marker Options tab, specify a Built-In horizontal tick as the marker style.

6. Choose Chart Tools⇨Layout⇨Labels⇨Data Labels to add data labels to the series.

7. Select the data labels for the XY series, and access the Format Data Labels dialog box. On the Label Options tab, specify Left for the Label Position. You may need to adjust the size and position of the plot area to accommodate the left-positioned labels.

8. Now it's time to clean up the axes. Select the *real* value axis on the left (this is the axis for the line series). Access the Format Axis dialog box, select the Axis Options tab and set the Minimum to 0, the Maximum to 100, and the Major Unit to 20. These selections create gridlines that divide the chart into five vertical sections to correspond to the five letter grades. Then click the Line Color tab and specify No Line (to hide the axis).

9. Select the X value axis for the XY series (it will be at the top of the chart) and press Delete to remove the axis.

10. Select the Y value axis for the XY series (it will be on the right side of the chart) and press Delete to delete the axis.

11. Finally, select each individual data label for the XY series and change the text to correspond to the letter grade labels in column C. You might prefer to create links to the cells. To create a link, click a data label, click the formula bar, type an equal sign, click the cell to link, and press Enter.

TIP

To apply the data labels automatically, refer to the nearby sidebar, "Applying custom data labels."

Labeling an Axis with Nonequal Intervals

In the previous example, the dummy axis had equal intervals: Each Y value was separated by 20. Figure 8-17 shows another chart that uses a dummy value axis, but this time the scale intervals on the value axis vary in size. Essentially, this chart makes it easy to translate the monthly numeric rating values into descriptive text. As you can see from the chart, June is the only month in which a "Very Good" rating was attained.

Applying custom data labels

Several of the examples in this chapter use custom data labels. You may have discovered that Excel's Data Label feature has a serious limitation: You can't specify a range of cells to be used as data labels for a chart series.

You can, of course, add data labels to a series and then select each data label and edit it manually. A better approach is to use a VBA macro. The author's PUP v7 add-in provides such a macro. (You'll find a trial version of the PUP v7 add-in on the companion CD-ROM.) The accompanying figure shows the dialog box for this utility.

Part II

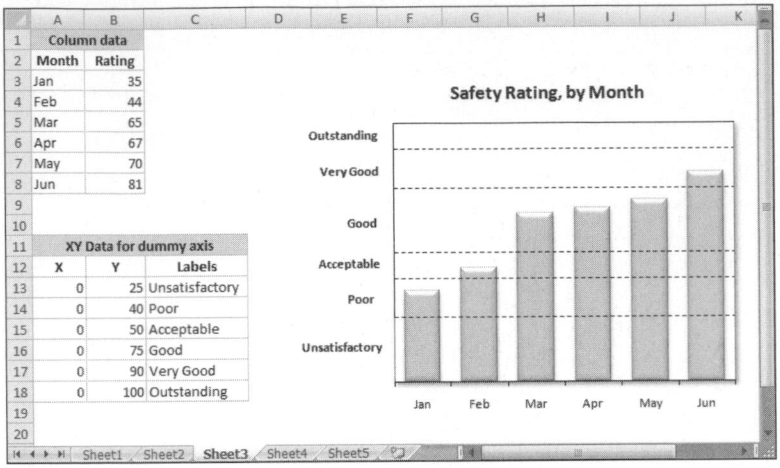

Figure 8-17: This chart uses an XY series to simulate a value axis.

This chart is very similar to the previous example but has one additional twist: It simulates gridlines by using X error bars for the XY series. The normal gridlines for the column chart series are not displayed.

Column and Bar Chart Variations

The following sections contain a number of examples that demonstrate how to create charts that you may have thought were impossible. As you'll see, the key is applying a few charting tricks — and a bit of creativity.

Stacked Column Chart Variations

A stacked column chart enables you to compare relative proportions of individual items across categories. But this type of chart sometimes doesn't quite do the job. Figure 8-18 demonstrates the problem. The goal is to facilitate comparisons by month, across the two years (compare January '06 with January '07, and so on). Because of the data arrangement, this comparison is difficult to do. For example, the January data is separated by five columns.

Figure 8-19 shows an improved version of this chart. Rearranging the data so that the same months are contiguous, as well as inserting blank rows, solves the problem. This chart also has its gap width set to 10%. You may prefer to include an additional blank row at the top and bottom of the series. Doing so would display a gap before the January columns and after the June columns.

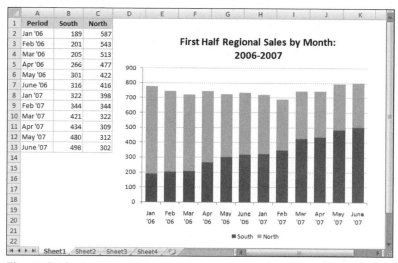

	A	B	C
1	**Period**	**South**	**North**
2	Jan '06	189	587
3	Feb '06	201	543
4	Mar '06	205	513
5	Apr '06	266	477
6	May '06	301	422
7	June '06	316	416
8	Jan '07	322	398
9	Feb '07	344	344
10	Mar '07	421	322
11	Apr '07	434	309
12	May '07	480	312
13	June '07	498	302

Figure 8-18: Comparing data for a specific month is difficult.

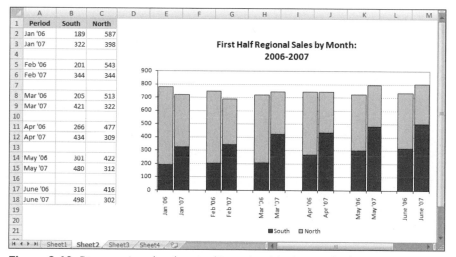

	A	B	C
1	**Period**	**South**	**North**
2	Jan '06	189	587
3	Jan '07	322	398
4			
5	Feb '06	201	543
6	Feb '07	344	344
7			
8	Mar '06	205	513
9	Mar '07	421	322
10			
11	Apr '06	266	477
12	Apr '07	434	309
13			
14	May '06	301	422
15	May '07	480	312
16			
17	June '06	316	416
18	June '07	498	302

Figure 8-19: Rearranging the data and inserting blank rows facilitate comparisons of the same month.

ON THE CD

The examples in this section are available on the companion CD-ROM. The filename is `stacked column chart variations.xlsx`.

In some cases, you may want to compare a single-value column with a stacked column. The chart in Figure 8-20, for example, displays orders for each item, along with a corresponding stacked column that depicts the Inventory amount and the In Production amount.

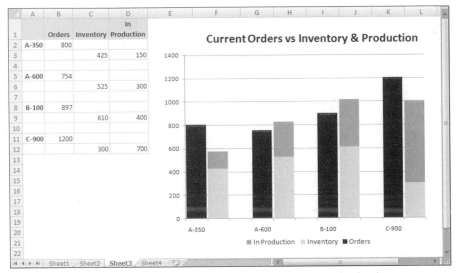

Figure 8-20: This chart displays single columns as well as stacked columns.

Excel doesn't provide a direct way to create a chart with a single column next to a stacked column, but it's fairly easy to do if you arrange your data properly. This is a standard stacked column chart generated from the data in A1:D12. The gap width was set to a small value (10%). The chart actually has 11 categories, although it appears to have only 4.

Figure 8-21 shows a variation on the previous chart. In this case, the data need not be arranged in any special way (as in the previous example). This is actually a combination chart that uses two value axes. The Orders series is assigned to the left value axis, and the other two series are assigned to the right value axis. Normally, the right axis would be removed.

Because the series use different value axes, you can adjust the thickness of the columns independently. In this example, the gap width for the Orders series is 40% and the gap width for the stacked series is 200%.

NOTE

Both value axes must use the same scale. Excel's automatic scaling may cause the two value axes to use different scales. In such a case, you need to adjust one or both of the axis scales manually.

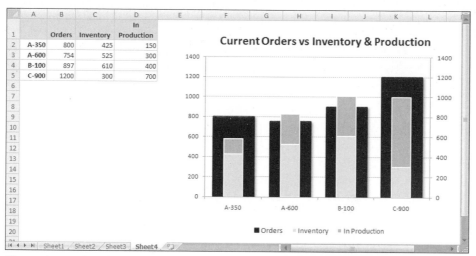

Figure 8-21: This chart displays stacked columns in front of single columns.

Creating a Step Chart

A "step" chart is similar to a hybrid column/line chart. Figure 8-22 shows two charts that use the data in columns A and B. The top chart is a standard line chart, and the bottom chart is a column chart — modified to have a gap width of 0% and no border color. A typical step chart is similar to the column chart, but the columns are not visible. Rather, a step chart depicts a single line with the data points connected at right angles.

ON THE CD

The examples in this section are available on the companion CD-ROM. The filename is `step chart.xlsx`.

Excel does not provide a step chart type, but you can create such a chart by using a scatter chart, along with horizontal and vertical custom error bars. Figure 8-23 shows an example of this type of chart. Columns A and B contain the same data used in the previous charts. In addition, this chart uses the data in columns C and D as the source for the error bars.

CROSS-REFERENCE

Refer to Chapter 5 for more information about using error bars.

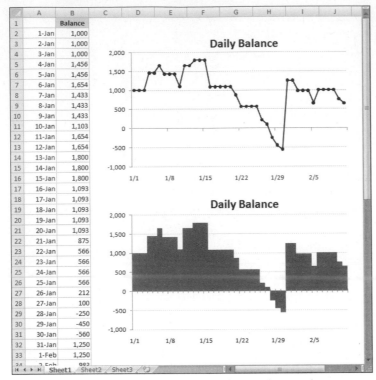

Figure 8-22: A line chart and a column chart — but neither is a true step chart.

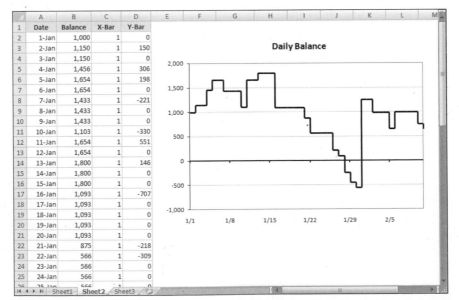

Figure 8-23: This scatter chart, which resembles a step chart, uses the data in columns C and D for horizontal and vertical error bars.

Column C contains simple formulas that calculate the difference between the dates in column A. For example, cell C3 contains this formula:

```
=A3-A2
```

The formulas in column D are similar and calculate the difference between the Balance data in column B. The formula in D3, for example, is as follows:

```
=B3-B2
```

Although the chart is a scatter chart, the series line and series markers are both hidden (formatted as None). Therefore, the chart is composed entirely from the horizontal error bars (column C) and vertical error bars (column D). The error bars are formatted as heavy lines, with no caps at their ends.

Varying Column Widths

The column chart shown in Figure 8-24 is a bit unusual: The width of the columns is not the same. The chart displays the Units Sold data on the value axis, and the width of each column is proportional to the Total Income for the product. In other words, this column chart is conveying more information than a typical column chart.

 ON THE CD

The examples in this section are available on the companion CD-ROM. The filename is `vary column widths.xlsx`.

Although you can control the width of all columns by using the Gap Width setting on the Series Options tab of the Format Data Series dialog box, Excel does not provide an option to vary the width of individual columns. This chart is not actually using the data in A1:D7. Rather, the chart consists of six series, each with 100 data points. A portion of the data is shown in Figure 8-25.

The cells in column J contain formulas that determine the number of columns to show for each of the six series, using the values in column D (Total Income). Remember, this chart contains 100 data points. These data points are allocated among the six series. Formulas in columns K:L determine the starting row and the ending row for the data in each series. For example, Series A will display 12 of the 100 columns. Its 12 data points will be in rows 2–13. Series B will display 5 of the 100 columns, and its 5 data points will be in rows 14–18.

The formulas are relatively complex, but you can easily modify this example to handle other types of data.

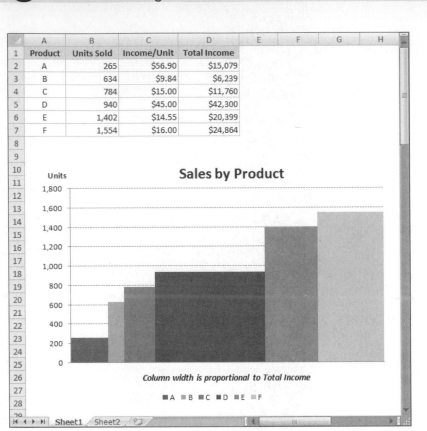

	A	B	C	D	E	F	G	H
1	Product	Units Sold	Income/Unit	Total Income				
2	A	265	$56.90	$15,079				
3	B	634	$9.84	$6,239				
4	C	784	$15.00	$11,760				
5	D	940	$45.00	$42,300				
6	E	1,402	$14.55	$20,399				
7	F	1,554	$16.00	$24,864				

Figure 8-24: Producing a column chart with varying column widths requires a few tricks.

WARNING

This type of chart should be used with care. Although the column width is used to convey information, people may interpret the chart by comparing areas. For example, in Figure 8-24, the Region C bar has a larger area than the Region A bar. But the important value, total income, is smaller for region C.

Conditional Column Colors

You're probably familiar with Excel's conditional formatting feature, which enables you to modify cell formatting based on the value contained in the cell. Unfortunately, Excel does not provide an analogous feature for charts. The Fill tab of the Format Data Series dialog box does have an option labeled Vary Colors By Point, but the colors chosen do not depend on the value of the data point.

	I	J	K	L	M	N	O	P	Q	R	S
1	Series	# Cols	1st Row	Last Row		A	B	C	D	E	F
2	A	12	2	13		265					
3	B	5	14	18		265					
4	C	10	19	28		265					
5	D	35	29	63		265					
6	E	17	64	80		265					
7	F	21	81	101		265					
8						265					
9						265					
10						265					
11						265					
12						265					
13						265					
14							634				
15							634				
16							634				
17							634				
18							634				
19								784			
20								784			
21								784			
22								784			
23								784			
24								784			
25								784			
26								784			
27								784			
28								784			
29									940		
30									940		

Sheet1 / Sheet2

Figure 8-25: Some of the 100 rows of data used to generate the chart in Figure 8-24.

If you would like to display different colors on a chart based on values, you can do so manually. But changing the colors manually is tedious, and it's not *dynamic* (if the values change, you need to re-check the colors). The technique described here takes some set-up work, but the colors change automatically if the data changes. Figure 8-26 shows a column chart that appears to display the data in column B, and the columns are colored based on the values.

ON THE CD

The example in this section is available on the companion CD-ROM. The filename is `conditional column colors.xlsx`.

Actually, this chart consists of four series (each using a different fill color), and it uses the data in columns C:F. The cells in these columns contain formulas that reference the data in column B and use the values in row 1 to determine whether the cell should contain the data value or display an empty string.

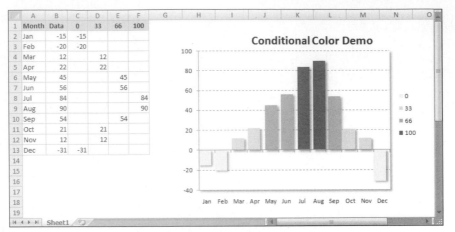

Figure 8-26: The color of each column depends on its value.

The formula in cell C2, for example, is as follows:

```
=IF(B2<=$C$1,B2,"")
```

This formula examines the value in cell B2. If it's less than the value in C1 (0), the value from column B is displayed. Otherwise, the formula returns an empty string.

The formulas in columns D:F are a bit more complex because they need to determine whether the value in column B falls between two values. The formula in D3, for example, is as follows:

```
=IF(AND($B2>C$1,$B2<=D$1),$B2,"")
```

Creating a column chart from the data in columns C:F produces a chart with four data series, and the chart contains gaps for the blank cells. To eliminate the gaps, adjust the Gap Width and Series Overlap settings on the Series Options tab of the Format Data Series dialog box. The chart shown has a Gap Width of 0% and a Series Overlap of 90%.

You can adjust the values in row 1 to create different numeric ranges for the colors. And, of course, you can add more series to display more than four conditional colors.

Creating a Comparative Histogram

A comparative histogram, sometimes known as a population pyramid chart, compares two sets of data using horizontal bars. Figure 8-27 shows an example, which depicts sales by source (online versus offline). Although this type of chart is often used with population data, it can be used in a variety of other situations.

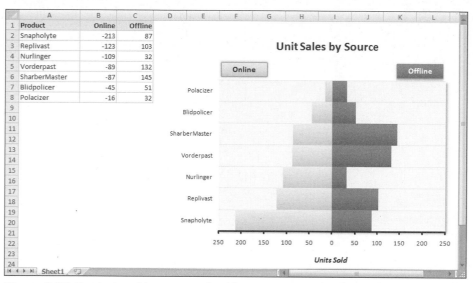

Figure 8-27: Producing this comparative histogram requires a few tricks.

 ON THE CD

The example in this section is available on the companion CD-ROM. The filename is `comparative histogram.xlsx`.

Excel does not provide this type of chart, but you can create such a chart by using the following steps:

1. Enter the data in A1:C8, as shown in Figure 8-27. Notice that the values for the Online series are entered as negative values, which is very important.

2. Select A1:C8 and create a bar chart. Use the subtype labeled Clustered Bar.

3. Select the horizontal axis, and specify the following custom number format on the Number tab of the Format Axis dialog box:

   `0;0;0`

   This custom format eliminates the negative signs in the values.

4. Select the vertical axis and display the Format Axis dialog box. On the Axis Options tab, set all tick marks to None and set the Axis Labels option to Low. This setting keeps the vertical axis in the center of the chart but displays the axis labels at the left side.

5. Select either of the data series and display the Format Data Series dialog box. On the Series Options tab, set the Series Overlap to 100% and the Gap Width to 0%.

6. Delete the legend and add two text boxes to the chart (Online and Offline) to substitute for the legend.

7. Apply other formatting and labels as desired.

Creating Gantt Charts

A Gantt chart is a horizontal bar chart often used in project management applications. Although Excel doesn't support Gantt charts per se, you can fairly easily create a simple Gantt chart. The key is getting your data set up properly.

Figure 8-28 shows a Gantt chart set up to depict the schedule for a project, in range A1:C13. The horizontal axis represents the total time span of the project, and each bar represents a project task. The viewer can quickly see the duration for each task and identify overlapping tasks.

ON THE CD

The example in this section is available on the companion CD-ROM. The filename is `gantt chart.xlsx`.

Column A contains the Task name, column B contains the corresponding Start Date, and column C contains the Duration of the task, in days.

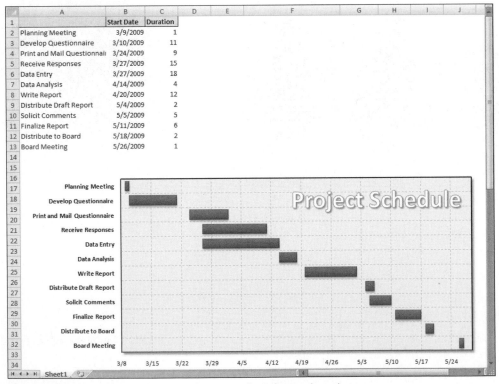

Figure 8-28: You can create a simple Gantt chart from a bar chart.

Follow these steps to create this chart:

1. Select the range A2:C13, and create a stacked bar chart.

2. Delete the legend.

3. Select the category (vertical) axis, and display the Format Axis dialog box. On the Axis Options tab, specify Categories in Reverse Order to display the tasks in order, starting at the top. Choose Horizontal Axis Crosses at Maximum Category to display the dates at the bottom.

4. Select the Start Date data series, and display the Format Data Series dialog box. Click the Fill tab, and specify No Fill. Click the Border Color tab and specify No Line. These steps effectively hide the data series.

5. Select the value (horizontal) axis, and display the Format Axis dialog box. On the Axis Options tab, adjust the Minimum and Maximum settings to accommodate the dates that you want to display on the axis. Unfortunately, you must enter these values as date serial numbers, not actual dates. In this example, the Minimum is 39880 (March 9, 2009) and the Maximum is 39962 (May 29, 2009). Specify **7** for the Major Unit, to display one-week intervals. Use the Number tab to specify a date format for the axis labels.

6. Apply other formatting as desired.

TIP

To determine the serial number for a date, enter the date into a cell and format the cell to use General number formatting.

Identifying the Maximum and Minimum Values in a Series

Figure 8-29 shows a line chart that has its maximum and minimum values identified with a circle and a square, respectively. These identifiers are the result of using two additional series in the chart. You can achieve this effect manually, by adding two shapes, but using the additional series makes it fully automated.

ON THE CD

The example in this section is available on the companion CD-ROM. The filename is `identify max and min data points.xlsx`.

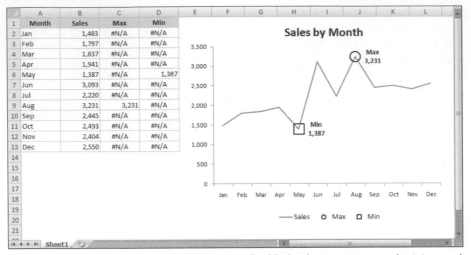

Figure 8-29: This chart uses two XY series to highlight the maximum and minimum data points in the line series.

To create this chart, using the data in range A1:B13, follow these steps:

1. Enter the following formula in cell C2:

   ```
   =IF(B2=MAX($B$2:$B$13),B2,NA())
   ```

2. Enter this formula in cell D2:

   ```
   =IF(B2=MIN($B$2:$B$13),B2,NA())
   ```

3. Copy range C2:D2 down, ending in row 13. These formulas display the maximum and minimum values in column B, and all other cells display #NA.

4. Select C1:D13 and press Ctrl+C.

5. Select the chart and choose Home➪Clipboard➪Paste➪Paste Special. In the Paste Special dialog box, choose New Series, Values (Y) in Columns, and Series Names in First Row. This adds two new series, named Max and Min.

6. Select the Max series and access the Format Data Series dialog box. Specify a circular marker, with no fill, and increase the size of the marker.

7. Repeat Step 6 for the Min series, but use a large, hollow square for the marker.

8. Add data labels to the Max and Min series (the #NA values will not appear).

9. Apply other cosmetic formatting as desired.

NOTE

The formulas entered in Steps 1 and 2 display #NA if the corresponding value in column B is not the maximum or minimum. In a line chart, an #NA value is not plotted — which is exactly what is needed. As a result, only one data point is plotted (or more, if a tie exists for the maximum or minimum). If two or more values are tied for the minimum or maximum, all the tied values will be identified with a square or circle.

Shading between Two Series in a Line Chart

The example in this section describes how to apply shading to the region between two lines in a line chart. Figure 8-30 shows a line chart with two series. The area between the lines is shaded with a fill color.

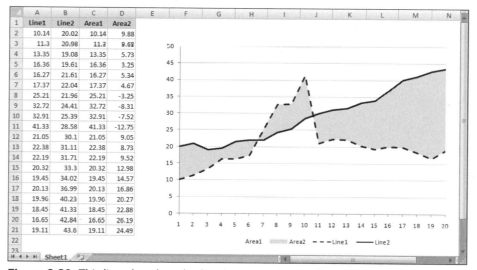

Figure 8-30: This line chart has shading between the two line series.

 ON THE CD

The example in this section is available on the companion CD-ROM. The filename is `shade between lines.xlsx`.

This type of chart requires two additional series, formatted as area chart series. One area chart series uses the data in column C. These values are the same as those in column A. You can, in fact, simply create the area chart series from the data in column A. The second area chart series uses the values in column D. These values are generated with a formula that calculates the difference between the first-line and the second-line data point. For example, the formula in D2 is as follows:

```
=B2-A2
```

After adding these two new area chart series, you need to hide the Area1 series. Do this by accessing the Format Data Series dialog box. On the Fill tab, select the No Fill option. On the Border Color tab, select the No Line option. Also, remove the border from the Area2 series.

Creating a Timeline

Figure 8-31 shows a scatter chart, set up to display a timeline of events. The chart uses the data in columns A and B, and the series uses vertical error bars to connect each marker to the timeline (the horizontal value axis). The text consists of customized data labels. The vertical value axis for the chart is hidden, but it is set to display Values in Reverse Order so that the earliest events display higher in the vertical dimension.

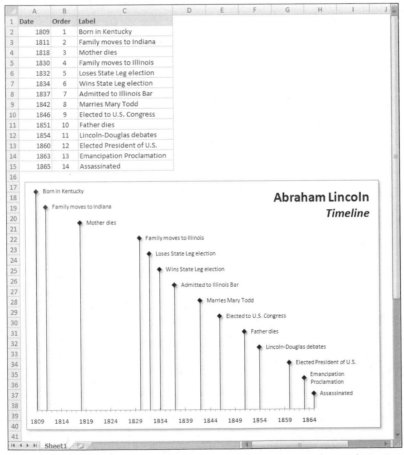

Figure 8-31: This scatter chart uses data labels and vertical error bars to connect its points to the horizontal value axis.

This type of chart is limited to relatively small amounts of text — otherwise, the data labels wrap and the text may be obscured.

ON THE CD

This example is available on the companion CD-ROM. The filename is `scatter chart timeline.xlsx`.

Creating "Impossible" Charts by Stacking and Overlaying

The following sections present a few examples of what might be considered "impossible" charts — charts that were created by combining two or more charts. The examples in this section are not combination charts. Rather, they are two (or more) separate charts that have been combined either by stacking or overlaying.

Stacking Charts

Figure 8-32 shows a simple example of combining charts. I simply stacked these three single-series line charts vertically. I removed the category axis from the top two charts, so they appear to share a single category axis.

ON THE CD

This example is available on the companion CD-ROM. The filename is `stacked and grouped.xlsx`.

TIP

After creating the charts, use the tools in the Chart Tools⇨Format⇨Arrange⇨Align control to assist with positioning the charts. After they have been positioned, you may want to group the charts into a single object. Press Ctrl while you select each chart; then, right-click and choose Group⇨Group from the shortcut menu. After the charts are grouped, you can move and resize them as a single object.

Figure 8-33 shows another example of stacked charts, this time with different chart types. The charts share a common category axis but use different value axes. Each chart has its own title, and I added a text box to provide a descriptive title of the collection. The three charts are stacked on top of a shape, with 3-D formatting, to provide a frame effect.

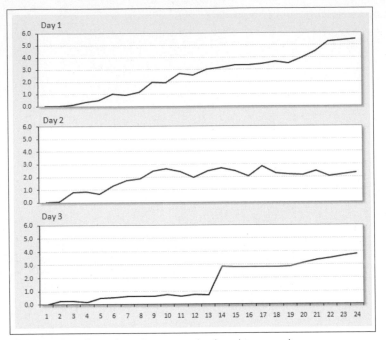

Figure 8-32: Three line charts, stacked and grouped.

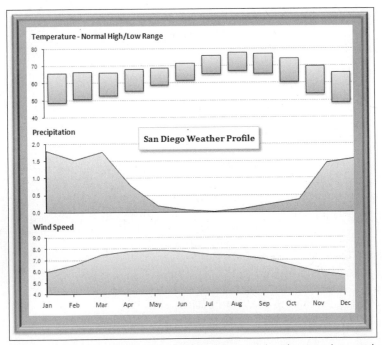

Figure 8-33: Three charts, stacked and grouped with a text box and a background shape.

Overlaying Charts

The examples in this section demonstrate chart overlays — charts that are positioned on top of other charts.

 ## ON THE CD

The examples in this section are available on the companion CD-ROM. The filename is `overlay charts.xlsx`.

COMBINING TWO CHARTS IN ONE FRAME

Figure 8-34 shows an example of two charts combined. The two column charts are displayed on top of a shape (to provide a frame effect). The smaller chart shows the details of the Q4 column. A Bent Arrow shape is used to connect the charts.

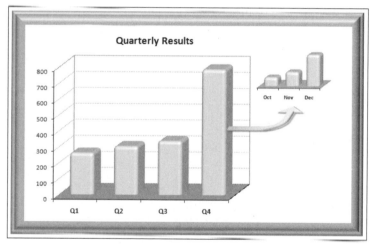

Figure 8-34: Two charts that work together.

Figure 8-35 shows another example: a 3-D pie chart and a 3-D column chart, presented as a single unit. The frame effect results from adding a border around a range of cells. Both charts have a transparent chart area and plot area, and they were positioned over the bordered range. The title is actually text entered into a range of merged cells.

A 2-D CHART COMBINED WITH A 3-D CHART

If you attempt to create a combination chart that uses any of the 3-D chart types, you'll find that Excel does not allow this. If you *must* create such a chart, the only option is to create separate charts and overlay one on top of the other.

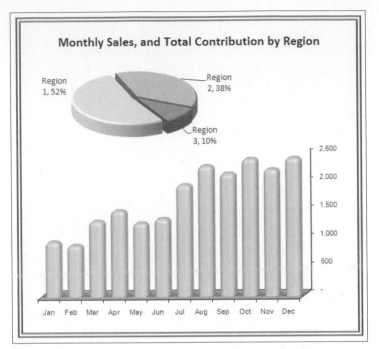

Figure 8-35: These two charts appear to be a single object.

Figure 8-36 shows an example of a 2-D line chart overlaid on a 3-D column chart. I stripped the line chart of all elements (except the line itself) and made the Plot Area and Chart Area transparent. I then carefully sized and positioned the line chart so that it aligned properly with the 3-D chart.

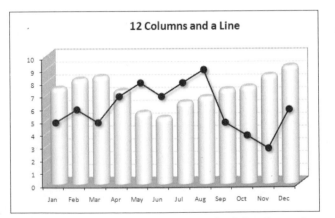

Figure 8-36: A 2-D line chart on top of a 3-D column chart.

NOTE

When overlaying charts, the stack order of the objects is very important. The top chart in the stack must be higher in the stack order. To change the stack order of objects in a worksheet, select the object, right-click, and choose Order Menu from the shortcut menu. When working with charts, you must select the chart object (not the chart). To select the chart object, press Ctrl or Shift while you click the chart.

When overlaying charts, you must keep the value scales identical. In this case, I set the value scale for both charts manually. It was still necessary to adjust the height of the line chart to force the axes to line up. Letting Excel adjust the scaling often results in mismatched scales and an inaccurate chart.

Overlaying charts is a manual task and will almost always require a bit of trial and error to get things looking right.

CREATING A STACKED 3-D COLUMN CHART

You may have discovered a limitation with Excel's 3-D stacked column charts: You can't plot additional series in the depth dimension. In other words, Excel does not provide the option of creating a true 3-D stacked column chart.

As you should know by now, work-arounds are often possible. Figure 8-37 shows three stacked 3-D column charts (one for each year), combined to display a depth dimension. This chart allows comparisons by region, month, and year.

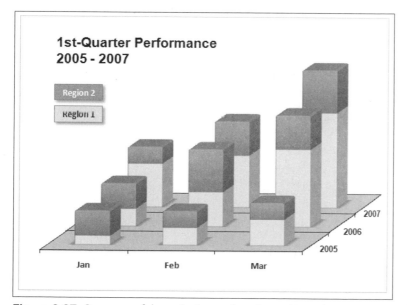

Figure 8-37: Some careful overlaying makes these three charts appear to be a single chart.

I removed the walls from all charts, and only the frontmost chart has a value axis. The title, legend, and year labels are text boxes that I added separately. When you're combining charts like this, the value axes must use identical scaling. Also, any modification to the 3-D view (for example, rotation) must be applied to all the charts.

Simulating a "Broken" Value Axis

The final example in Figure 8-38 shows a standard column chart, along with another chart that simulates a "broken" value axis. This type of chart is often used when a few data points greatly exceed the others. In the example, the value for June is much larger than the other values. When plotted on a standard chart, the other values are dwarfed.

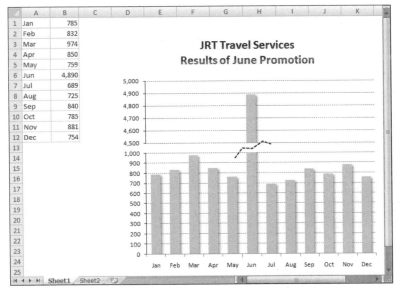

Figure 8-38: Two charts are combined to simulate a broken axis.

ON THE CD

The examples in this section are available on the companion CD-ROM. The filename is `broken axis.xlsx`.

The chart with the broken axis actually consists of two charts, shown in Figure 8-39. Both charts use the same data but have different value axis scaling. The main chart (on the left) contains the title and lots of white space above the plot area. The value axis Maximum is set to 1,000. The secondary chart has a transparent chart area with no border, and its value axis ranges from 4,500 to 5,000. A freeform shape is used to indicate the fact that the column is not continuous.

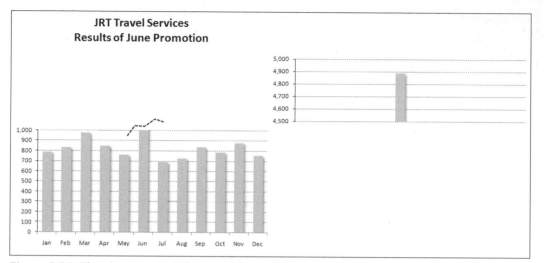

Figure 8-39: The chart on the right is positioned on top of the chart on the left to form the chart shown in Figure 8-38.

Creating this type of chart is a manual process and will likely require a fair amount of tweaking.

Another approach uses a single chart, with the Maximum value for the value axis set manually to accommodate the "normal" data. A shape is placed over the "outlier" column, along with a text box that contains the value for this column (see Figure 8-40).

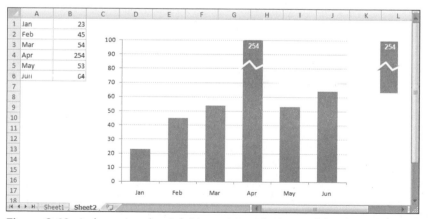
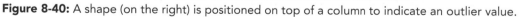

Figure 8-40: A shape (on the right) is positioned on top of a column to indicate an outlier value.

Displaying Multiple Charts on a Chart Sheet

As you know, an Excel chart can reside in either of two locations: embedded in a worksheet or on a separate chart sheet. A worksheet can hold any number of charts, but a chart sheet holds only one chart. Well, that's how it normally works. With a little trickery, you can store multiple charts on a single chart sheet.

Following is the general procedure:

1. Start by creating your charts in a worksheet.

2. Activate an empty cell that is surrounded by empty cells.

3. Press F11 to create a chart sheet that contains an empty chart. The chart on this chart sheet contains a single chart element: the chart area.

4. Activate the worksheet that contains the embedded charts.

5. Click a chart and choose Chart Tools⇨Design⇨Move Chart to display the Move Chart dialog box.

6. In the Move Chart dialog box, select the Object In option, and use the drop-down control to select the chart sheet that you created in Step 3.

7. Click the OK button, and Excel inserts the embedded chart inside the chart area of the empty chart on the chart sheet.

Repeat Steps 4 through 7 for each of the embedded charts. Note that you can move and resize the charts on the chart sheet. One little quirk, however, is that the size of the text does not adjust when you change the chart size. Therefore, you may need to resize the text elements on the charts.

Figure 8-41 shows a chart sheet that contains six charts. I used the controls in the Drawing Tools⇨Format context tab to get the charts aligned and sized identically. To use these controls with charts, you must select the charts as objects. Do this by pressing Ctrl while you click the charts.

ON THE CD

This workbook, named `multiple charts on chart sheet.xlsx`, is available on the companion CD-ROM.

Because these charts are contained in a chart area element, you'll find that you can resize the underlying chart area, and the embedded charts will resize to correspond to the chart area. Figure 8-42 shows the six charts after I change the size of the chart area.

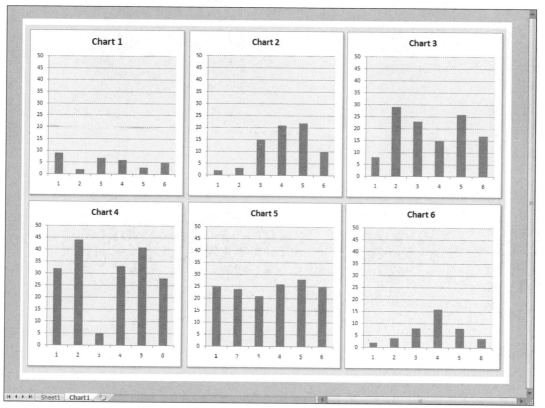

Figure 8-41: A chart sheet that contains six embedded charts.

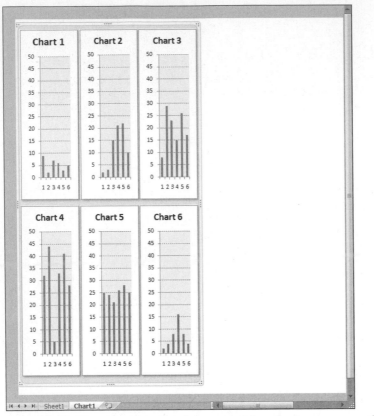

Figure 8-42: Changing the size of the underlying chart area causes the embedded charts to resize accordingly.

Chapter 9

In-Cell Charting Techniques

In This Chapter

◆ Using the new data visualization conditional formatting options

◆ Creating charts by using formulas and text characters

◆ Creating sparklines by using tiny Excel charts

◆ Identifying commercial add-ins for in-cell charting

This chapter describes some charting techniques that you may find useful. You'll find a variety of data visualization examples that go beyond traditional charting.

Visualizing Data with Conditional Formatting

Conditional formatting has improved significantly in Excel 2007, and it's now a useful tool for visualizing numeric data. In some cases, you may be able to use conditional formatting in lieu of a chart.

To apply a conditional formatting rule to a cell or range, select the cells and then use one of the commands on the Home⇨Styles⇨Conditional Formatting drop-down list to specify a rule. This book covers only the following conditional formatting options: data bars, color scales, and icon sets.

NEW

This type of conditional formatting is new to Excel 2007, and it is not compatible with previous versions of Excel.

Figure 9-1 shows a few examples of conditional formatting that are relevant to visualizing data.

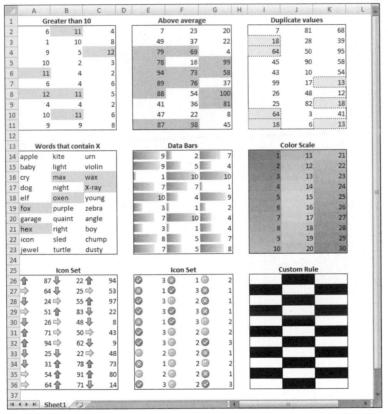

Figure 9-1: An overview of conditional formatting types useful for data visualization.

Data Bars

The data bars conditional format displays horizontal bars directly in a range of cells. By default, the length of the bar is based on the value in the cell relative to the other values in the range. Data bars are easy to apply and allow you to quickly see outliers, spot trends, and compare values.

Figure 9-2 shows a range with student names and test scores. Data bars are applied to the second column.

ON THE CD

The examples in this section are available on the companion CD-ROM. The filename is `data bars examples.xlsx`.

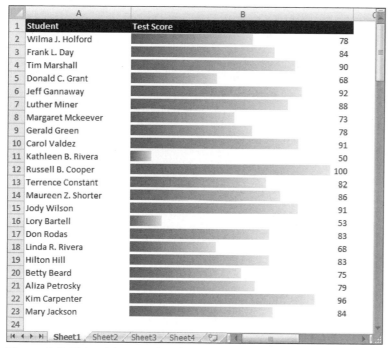

Figure 9-2: This table uses data bars conditional formatting.

 WARNING

Using data bars can be a bit deceptive because Excel does not use a zero base. For example, in Figure 9-2 compare the length of the bars in rows 11 and 12. Most people would expect that a data bar for the value 100 (row 12) would be twice as long as the data bar for a value of 50 (row 11). Clearly that is not the case. The result is similar to creating a bar chart that doesn't use zero as its minimum scale value.

Adding data bars to a range is simple. Follow these steps:

1. Select the range of values (in this example, B2:B23).

2. Choose Home⇨Styles⇨Conditional Formatting⇨Data Bars, and select one of the six data bar colors.

For more control over the data bars, choose Home⟹Styles⟹Conditional Formatting⟹ Data Bars⟹More Rules, which displays the New Formatting Rule dialog box shown in Figure 9-3.

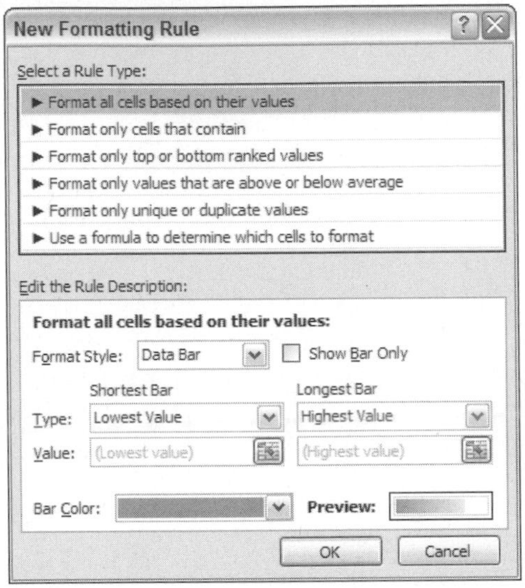

Figure 9-3: Use the New Formatting Rule dialog box to specify a few parameters for data bars.

To display the data bars only (no values), select the Show Bar Only check box. You can also specify how the bars are generated by using the Type drop-down lists. By default, the shortest bar represents the lowest value in the range, and the longest bar represents the highest value. Other options are as follows:

- **Number:** Enter a value. For the shortest bar option, if a number is lower than the specified value, Excel displays the shortest bar. For the longest bar option, if a number is greater than the specified value, Excel displays the longest bar.

- **Percent:** Enter a percentage value between 0 and 100. Bar length is based on the numeric range of the data. For example, if your data ranges from 1 to 5,000 and you specify 20% as the shortest bar, cells that have a value less than 1,000 (that is, 20% of 5,000) display the shortest bar.

- **Formula:** Enter a formula that evaluates to a value. The formula must use absolute cell references.

- **Percentile:** Enter a percent value between 0 and 100. Unlike the Percent option, the Percentile option rank-orders the data and bases the bar length on the ordinal position. This option is useful if you'd like to identify values that appear in a particular percentile — use the longest bar for all values above the 80th percentile.

The New Formatting Rule dialog box also lets you specify the color of the data bars. Also, keep in mind that you can apply a fill color to a range that uses data bars. In other words, you can display colored bars on top of a colored range.

WARNING

If you need to modify the conditional formatting for a range, choose Home⇨ Styles⇨Conditional Formatting⇨Manage Rules and then click the Edit Rule button in the Conditional Formatting Rules Manager dialog box. If you choose Home⇨Styles⇨ Conditional Formatting⇨Data Bars⇨More Rules, you will add a new conditional formatting rule to the range.

Using the data bars conditional formatting can sometimes serve as a quick alternative to creating a chart. Figure 9-4 shows a range of data with data bars (range (D4:D15) and a bar chart created from the same data. The bar chart might take a bit more time to create, but it's a lot more flexible. But for a quick-and-dirty chart, data bars are a good option — especially when you need to create several such charts.

Note, however, that the data bar display looks quite a bit different than the bar chart. That's because the data bars don't use zero as the base. In this case, the minimum scale value is approximately 2,400. Unfortunately, Excel does not provide a way to specify the scaling for data bars.

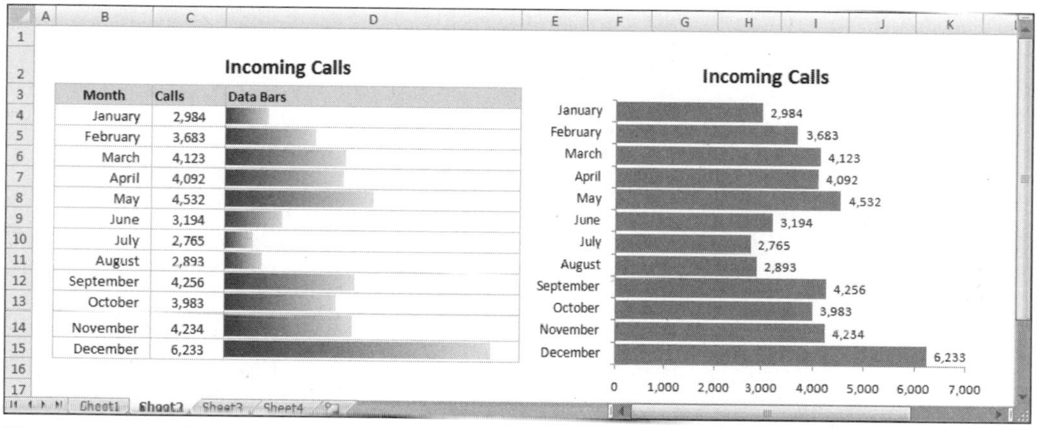

Figure 9-4: Data bars conditional formatting compared with a bar chart.

Figure 9-5 shows a worksheet that uses data bars to display the results of a dozen survey items. Applying conditional formatting was much faster than creating 12 separate charts.

 NOTE

In this example, all the data bar cells are part of the same conditional formatting range. Each survey item is not a separate conditional formatting range. As a result, each item uses the same scale, and it's easy to compare the items. To select a noncontiguous range of cells prior to applying conditional formatting, press Ctrl while you select the ranges with the mouse.

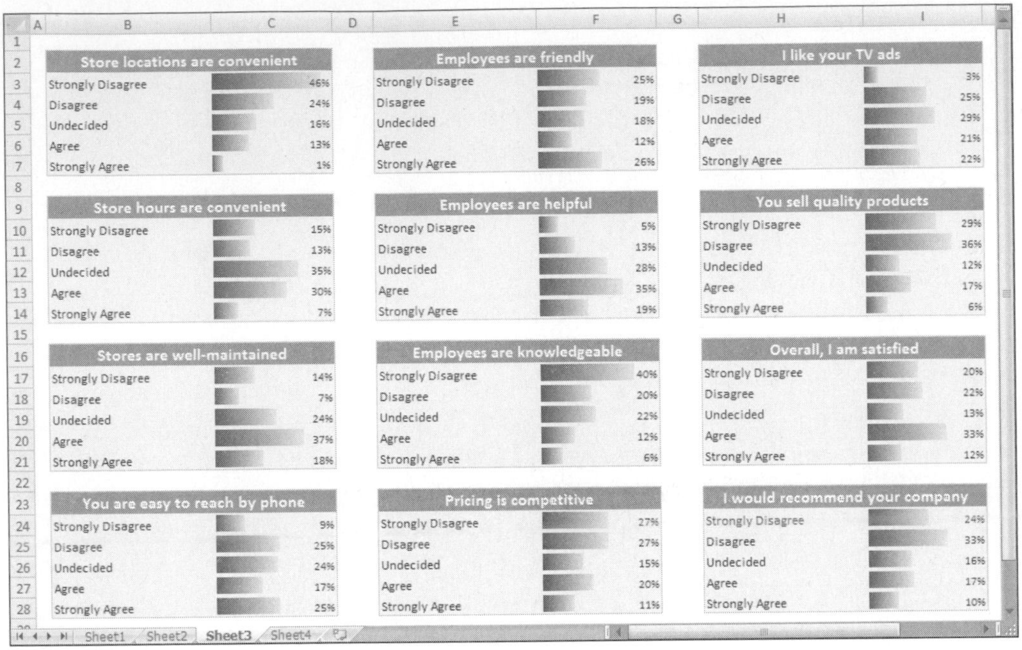

Store locations are convenient

Strongly Disagree	46%
Disagree	24%
Undecided	16%
Agree	13%
Strongly Agree	1%

Employees are friendly

Strongly Disagree	25%
Disagree	19%
Undecided	18%
Agree	12%
Strongly Agree	26%

I like your TV ads

Strongly Disagree	3%
Disagree	25%
Undecided	29%
Agree	21%
Strongly Agree	22%

Store hours are convenient

Strongly Disagree	15%
Disagree	13%
Undecided	35%
Agree	30%
Strongly Agree	7%

Employees are helpful

Strongly Disagree	5%
Disagree	13%
Undecided	28%
Agree	35%
Strongly Agree	19%

You sell quality products

Strongly Disagree	29%
Disagree	36%
Undecided	12%
Agree	17%
Strongly Agree	6%

Stores are well-maintained

Strongly Disagree	14%
Disagree	7%
Undecided	24%
Agree	37%
Strongly Agree	18%

Employees are knowledgeable

Strongly Disagree	40%
Disagree	20%
Undecided	22%
Agree	12%
Strongly Agree	6%

Overall, I am satisfied

Strongly Disagree	20%
Disagree	22%
Undecided	13%
Agree	33%
Strongly Agree	12%

You are easy to reach by phone

Strongly Disagree	9%
Disagree	25%
Undecided	24%
Agree	17%
Strongly Agree	25%

Pricing is competitive

Strongly Disagree	27%
Disagree	27%
Undecided	15%
Agree	20%
Strongly Agree	11%

I would recommend your company

Strongly Disagree	24%
Disagree	33%
Undecided	16%
Agree	17%
Strongly Agree	10%

Figure 9-5: Using data bars as a substitute for charts.

Conditional formatting data bars are useful, but they do have some limitations:

- Data bars always display as a dark-to-light gradient, and you can't specify a solid color or a different gradient.

- Data bars don't handle negative numbers the way you might like. People are accustomed to viewing a negative value in a bar chart to extend in the opposite direction. This is not the case with data bars.

- In some cases, you might prefer that the data bar is hidden for a zero value. Every cell in a range that's formatted with data bars will display a bar — even zero values.

- Data bars are not accurate, and they can even be deceiving. Figure 9-6, for example, shows a set of data bars in a range. A viewer might expect that each data bar would be 10 times longer than the data bar in the cell above. Clearly, that's not the case.

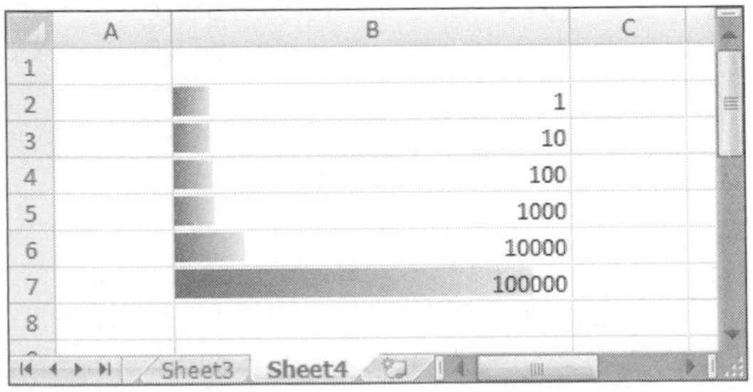

A	B	C
	1	
	10	
	100	
	1000	
	10000	
	100000	

Figure 9-6: Data bars do not always depict data accurately.

Color Scales

The color scale conditional formatting option varies the background color of a cell based on the cell's value, relative to other cells in the range. Figure 9-7 shows a range of cells that use color scale conditional formatting. It uses a two-color scale (black to white) and is set up such that higher scores have a lighter color.

	A	B	C
1	**Student**	**Test Score**	
2	Wilma J. Holford	78	
3	Frank L. Day	84	
4	Tim Marshall	90	
5	Donald C. Grant	68	
6	Jeff Gannaway	92	
7	Luther Miner	88	
8	Margaret Mckeever	73	
9	Gerald Green	78	
10	Carol Valdez	91	
11	Kathleen B. Rivera	53	
12	Russell B. Cooper	69	
13	Terrence Constant	82	
14	Maureen Z. Shorter	86	
15	Jody Wilson	91	
16	Lory Bartell	100	
17	Don Rodas	83	
18	Linda R. Rivera	68	
19	Hilton Hill	83	
20	Betty Beard	75	
21	Aliza Petrosky	79	
22	Kim Carpenter		
23	Mary Jackson	84	
24			

Sheet1 / Sheet2 / Sheet

Figure 9-7: A range that uses color scale conditional formatting.

 ON THE CD

The examples in this section are available on the companion CD-ROM. The filename is `color scale examples.xlsx`.

Applying a color scale is as easy as applying data bars. Follow these steps:

1. Select the range of values (in this example, B2:B23).

2. Choose Home⟹Styles⟹Conditional Formatting⟹Color Scales, and select one of the eight color scale choices.

Excel provides four 2-color scale presets and four 3-color scales presets. For more control over the colors, choose Home⟹Styles⟹Conditional Formatting⟹Color Scales⟹More Rules, which displays the New Formatting Rule dialog box. This dialog box lets you specify the format style (2-Color Scale or 3-Color Scale), the type, and the colors. The Type options are the same as for data bars (described earlier in this chapter).

Figure 9-8 shows another color scale example. The worksheet depicts the number of employees on each day of the year. This is a 3-color scale that uses red for the lowest value, yellow for the midpoint, and green for the highest value. Values in between are displayed using a color within the gradient. The grayscale figure doesn't do this example justice. The effect is much more impressive when you view it in color, and it's very easy to spot staffing trends.

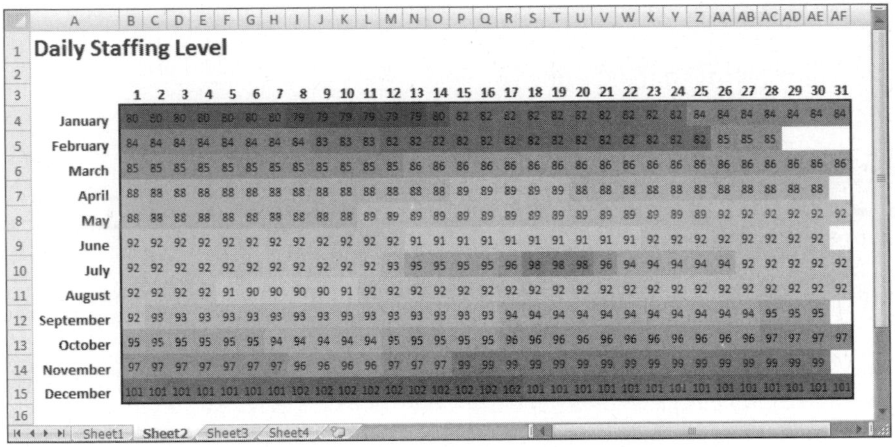

Figure 9-8: Using a 3-color scale to depict daily staffing levels.

It's important to understand that color scale conditional formatting uses a gradient. For example, if you format a range using a 2-color scale, you will get a lot more than two colors. You'll get colors with the gradient between the two specified colors.

Figure 9-9 shows an extreme example that uses color scale conditional formatting on a range of 10,000 cells (100 rows x 100 columns). The column width was adjusted so that each cell is a square. The worksheet is zoomed down to 30% to display a very smooth 3-color gradient. The range contains formulas like this one, in cell C5:

```
=SIN($A2)+COS(B$1)
```

Values in column A and row 1 range from 0 to 4, in increments of 0.04. Change the value in cell A1, and the colors change instantly. This type of gradient contour display can be a good alternative to a surface chart. Figure 9-10 shows the same data, displayed as a surface chart.

The result, when viewed on-screen, is stunning (it loses a lot when converted to grayscale).

Figure 9-9: This worksheet, which uses color scale conditional formatting, is zoomed to 30%.

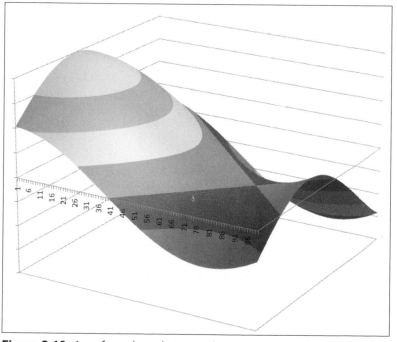

Figure 9-10: A surface chart that uses the same data as depicted in Figure 9-9.

Part II

Icon Sets

The third new conditional formatting option displays an icon in the cell. The icon depends on the value of the cell, relative to other cells in the specified range. Excel provides 17 icon sets to choose from (and you can't create your own set of icons). The number of icons in the sets ranges from 3 to 5.

Figure 9-11 shows an example that uses the icon set named 3 Symbols (Uncircled). The symbols graphically depict the sales volume of each salesperson, relative to the group as a whole.

	A	B	C
1			
2	**Salesperson**	**Sales**	
3	Ann	✖ 509,433	
4	Bob	✖ 594,829	
5	Charley	✖ 559,126	
6	Denise	✖ 586,617	
7	Ellen	✖ 534,771	
8	Frank	✔ 873,323	
9	George	! 647,703	
10	Hilda	✖ 538,399	
11	Inez	✖ 541,815	
12	Jimbob	! 649,849	
13	Kenneth	✖ 535,293	
14	Luann	! 630,072	
15			

Figure 9-11: A range that uses an icon set.

 ON THE CD

The examples in this section are available on the companion CD-ROM. The filename is `icon set examples.xlsx`.

Follow these steps to apply an icon set to a range:

1. Select the range of values (in this example, B3:B14).

2. Choose Home➪Styles➪Conditional Formatting➪Icon Sets, and select one of the 17 sets of icons.

If you would like more control over how the icons are assigned, choose Home➪Styles➪ Conditional Formatting➪Icon Sets➪More Rules to display the New Formatting Rule dialog box. Figure 9-12 shows this dialog box. Notice that you can specify the exact cutoff points for the icons.

If you don't use the New Formatting Rule dialog box, the symbols are assigned using percents. In Figure 9-11, notice that only one value has a check mark. That's because Frank's sales are significantly higher than the others. The algorithm used to convert values into percents is as follows:

```
percent = (value - minimum) / (maximum - minimum)
```

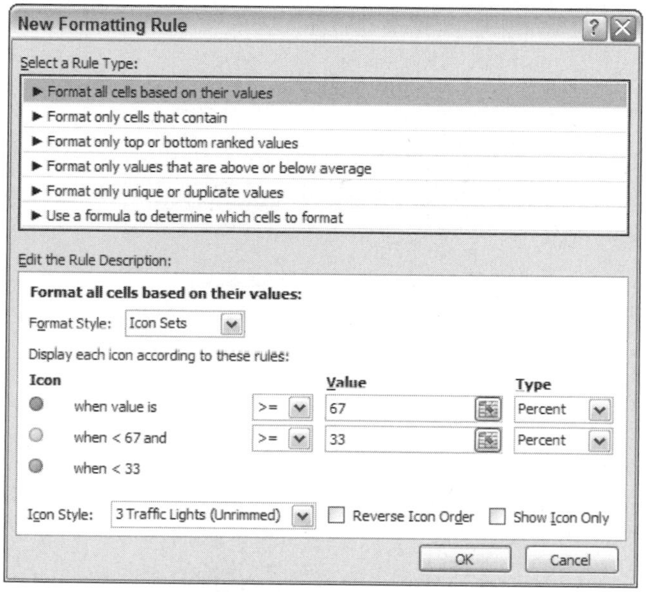

Figure 9-12: Specifying an icon set.

Using this algorithm, Frank's sales is the only value in the range that exceeds 67% (the minimum value for the third icon). If you would like an equal number of symbols, use the Percentile option.

> **TIP**
>
> Unfortunately, the icons always appear on the left side of the cell. If you have multiple columns of data, it's very easy to mistakenly associate an icon with the value in the cell to the left. One solution to this problem is to create a separate column for the icons, to the right of the data. Figure 9-13 shows an example. In the table on the left, the icons seem to be associated with the Day 3 column, rather than with the Total column. Column K contains simple references to the values in Column J.
>
> Also, if an icon occupies a cell in which the value is not displayed, the icon responds to horizontal alignment settings (left, center, or right). If the value is displayed, only the value is aligned.

Figure 9-14 shows another icon set example. The table contains two test scores for each student. The Change column contains a formula that calculates the difference between the two tests. The Trend column uses an icon set to display the trend graphically.

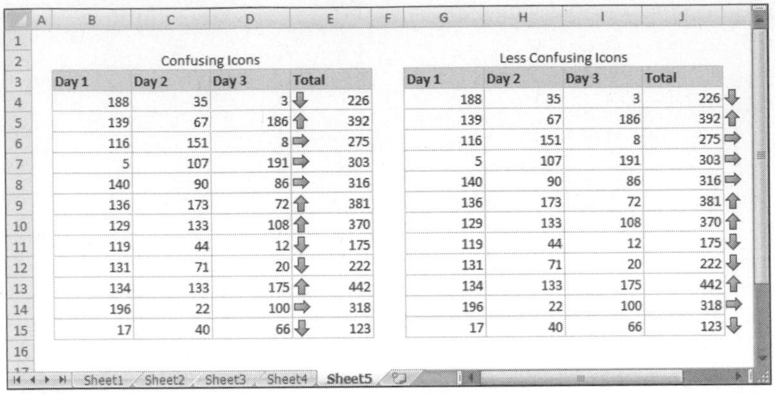

	A	B	C	D	E	F	G	H	I	J
1										
2			Confusing Icons					Less Confusing Icons		
3		Day 1	Day 2	Day 3	Total		Day 1	Day 2	Day 3	Total
4		188	35	3 ⬇	226		188	35	3	226 ⬇
5		139	67	186 ⬆	392		139	67	186	392 ⬆
6		116	151	8 ➡	275		116	151	8	275 ➡
7		5	107	191 ➡	303		5	107	191	303 ➡
8		140	90	86 ➡	316		140	90	86	316 ➡
9		136	173	72 ⬆	381		136	173	72	381 ⬆
10		129	133	108 ⬆	370		129	133	108	370 ⬆
11		119	44	12 ⬇	175		119	44	12	175 ⬇
12		131	71	20 ⬇	222		131	71	20	222 ⬇
13		134	133	175 ⬆	442		134	133	175	442 ⬆
14		196	22	100 ➡	318		196	22	100	318 ➡
15		17	40	66 ⬇	123		17	40	66	123 ⬇
16										

Sheet1 / Sheet2 / Sheet3 / Sheet4 / **Sheet5**

Figure 9-13: One way to avoid associating icons with the wrong data.

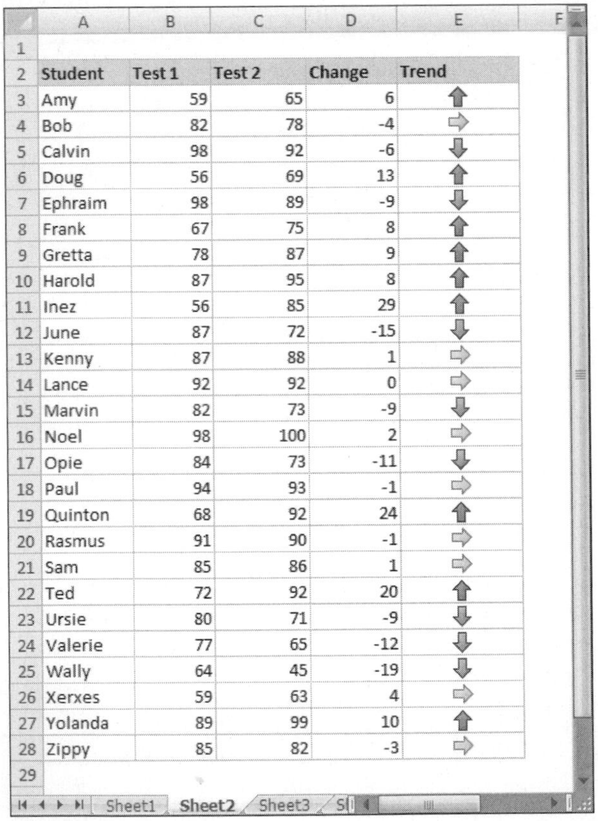

	A	B	C	D	E	F
1						
2	Student	Test 1	Test 2	Change	Trend	
3	Amy	59	65	6	⬆	
4	Bob	82	78	-4	➡	
5	Calvin	98	92	-6	⬇	
6	Doug	56	69	13	⬆	
7	Ephraim	98	89	-9	⬇	
8	Frank	67	75	8	⬆	
9	Gretta	78	87	9	⬆	
10	Harold	87	95	8	⬆	
11	Inez	56	85	29	⬆	
12	June	87	72	-15	⬇	
13	Kenny	87	88	1	➡	
14	Lance	92	92	0	➡	
15	Marvin	82	73	-9	⬇	
16	Noel	98	100	2	➡	
17	Opie	84	73	-11	⬇	
18	Paul	94	93	-1	➡	
19	Quinton	68	92	24	⬆	
20	Rasmus	91	90	-1	➡	
21	Sam	85	86	1	➡	
22	Ted	72	92	20	⬆	
23	Ursie	80	71	-9	⬇	
24	Valerie	77	65	-12	⬇	
25	Wally	64	45	-19	⬇	
26	Xerxes	59	63	4	➡	
27	Yolanda	89	99	10	⬆	
28	Zippy	85	82	-3	➡	
29						

Sheet1 / **Sheet2** / Sheet3 / S

Figure 9-14: The arrows depict the trend from Test 1 to Test 2.

This example uses the icon set named 3 Arrows, and I customized the rule as follows:

- **Up arrow:** When the value is >= 5
- **Level arrow:** When the value is < 5 and >= –5
- **Down arrow:** When the value is < –5

In other words, a difference of five points or fewer in either direction is considered an even trend. An improvement of more than five points is considered a positive trend, and a decline of more than five points is considered a negative trend.

NOTE

The Trend column contains a formula that references the Change column. I used the Show Icon Only option in the Trend column.

In some cases, you might want to display only one icon from an icon set. Excel doesn't provide this option directly, but you can display a single icon if you use two rules. Figure 9-15 shows a range of values. Only the values greater than or equal to 80 display an icon.

	A	B	C	D	E
1	Showing only one icon for values >=80				
2					
3		● 84	● 98	26	17
4		● 89	22	73	53
5		39	● 94	58	6
6		8	2	19	19
7		15	● 93	56	43
8		1	50	● 91	5
9		43	12	● 83	19
10		68	29	53	69
11		72	28	● 98	● 91
12		28	41	66	46
13		58	56	55	39
14		● 94	36	● 90	37
15		● 91	59	1	14
16					

Sheet1 / Sheet2 / **Sheet3** / Sheet4

Figure 9-15: Displaying only one icon from an icon set.

Here's how to set up an icon set such that only values greater than or equal to 80 display an icon:

1. Select the cells, choose Home⇨Styles⇨Conditional Formatting⇨Icon Sets, and select any icon set. Keep in mind that only the last icon of the set will be used.

2. With the range selected, choose Home⇨Styles⇨Conditional Formatting⇨Manage Rules. Excel displays its Conditional Formatting Rules Manager dialog box.

3. Click the Edit Rule button to display the Edit Formatting Rule dialog box.

4. Change the first icon setting to When Value Is >= 80 and specify Number as the type. Leave the other icon settings as they are, and click the OK button to return to the Conditional Formatting Rules Manager dialog box.

5. Click the New Rule button, and then choose this rule type: Format Only Cells That Contain.

6. In the bottom section of the dialog box, specify Cell Value Less Than 80 and click the OK button to return to the Conditional Formatting Rules Manager dialog box. The range now has two rules.

7. For the first rule, select the Stop If True check box. Figure 9-16 shows the completed dialog box.

8. Click the OK button.

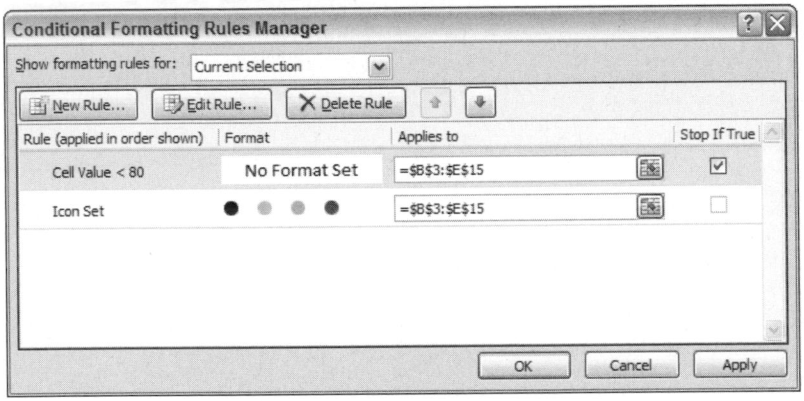

Figure 9-16: Setting up an icon set so that it shows only one icon.

The first rule checks whether the value is less than 80. If so, rule checking stops, and no conditional formatting is applied. If the value is greater than or equal to 80, the second rule kicks in. This rule indicates that values greater than or equal to 80 are displayed with an icon.

Figure 9-17 shows one more icon set example. Sales data is entered into a calendar display at the top, and an icon set indicates the relative sales on a daily basis. Each cell in the lower calendar contains a formula that references the corresponding cell in the upper calendar. The icon set uses the Show Icon Only option.

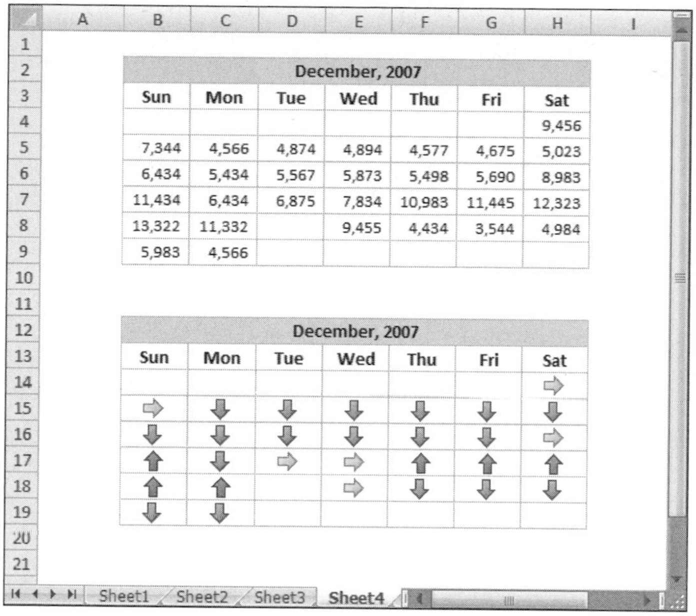

December, 2007						
Sun	Mon	Tue	Wed	Thu	Fri	Sat
						9,456
7,344	4,566	4,874	4,894	4,577	4,675	5,023
6,434	5,434	5,567	5,873	5,498	5,690	8,983
11,434	6,434	6,875	7,834	10,983	11,445	12,323
13,322	11,332		9,455	4,434	3,544	4,984
5,983	4,566					

Figure 9-17: Using an icon set in a calendar display.

Plotting Data without a Chart

This section presents two methods of creating charts directly in a range. The examples use formulas and text characters to display data visually. As you'll discover, this technique does not offer the level of precision available in a "real" chart, but it does have several advantages over the data bars discussed earlier in this chapter.

Figure 9-18 shows a simple example. Column D contains formulas that convert the value in column C to a series of "pipe" characters (that is, the vertical-line character usually located on the backslash key). The formula in cell D3 is as follows:

```
=REPT("|",C3/10000)
```

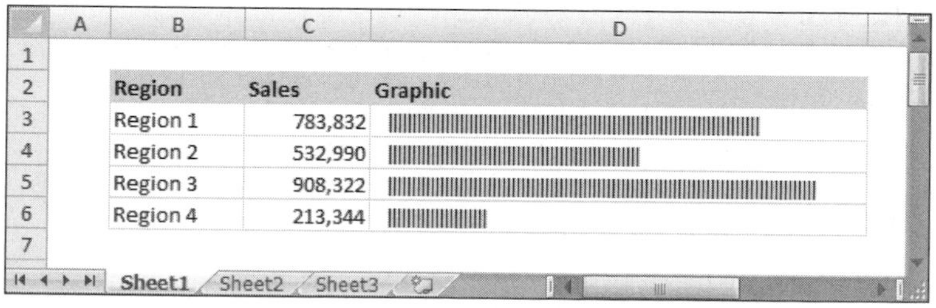

Region	Sales	Graphic
Region 1	783,832	
Region 2	532,990	
Region 3	908,322	
Region 4	213,344	

Figure 9-18: This chart is made up of text characters displayed in cells.

ON THE CD

The examples in this section are available on the companion CD-ROM. The filename is `text character charts.xlsx`.

The key to this technique is the use of the REPT function, which displays a character (specified in the function's first argument) the number of times specified in the function's second argument. Notice that the formula "scales" the value by dividing it by 10,000. Without this scaling, the formula would attempt to display 783,832 characters. The scaling factor you use will depend on the magnitude of the data. But, in all cases, the scaling factor should be the same for all values that make up the chart.

Figure 9-19 shows another example. This chart uses a character from the Wingdings 2 font. The scaling factor is 400 (each character represents 400 units of sales). As you can see, this type of chart has limited precision. For example, Fanny and Georgette both have the same number of characters, even though their sales amounts differed by 399 units. In many situations, absolute accuracy isn't critical.

Sales Rep	Sales	Graphic
Anne	8,806	■■■■■■■■■■■■■■■■■■■■■■
Betsy	7,599	■■■■■■■■■■■■■■■■■■■
Celia	3,211	■■■■■■■■
Duane	7,883	■■■■■■■■■■■■■■■■■■■■
Edward	2,873	■■■■■■■
Fanny	4,000	■■■■■■■■■■
Georgette	4,399	■■■■■■■■■■

Figure 9-19: Another example of a chart created by formulas.

Figure 9-20 shows another in-cell chart that displays percent values in a crude "dot chart." In this case, the scaling is done by multiplying the value. For example, the formula in cell I3 is as follows:

```
=REPT(" ",H3*600)&"O"
```

The REPT function generates a series of space characters, and an uppercase letter *O* is appended to the string. Figure 9-20 also shows a variation that substitutes a hyphen character for the space character.

As you may have figured out, the possibilities for in-cell charting are virtually limitless. Experiment with different characters, scaling factors, and font sizes. You can even toss in some conditional formatting to vary the colors based on the values.

The example in Figure 9-21 uses formulas that are slightly more complex. Columns F and H contain formulas that graphically depict monthly budget variances by displaying a series of characters in the Wingdings font.

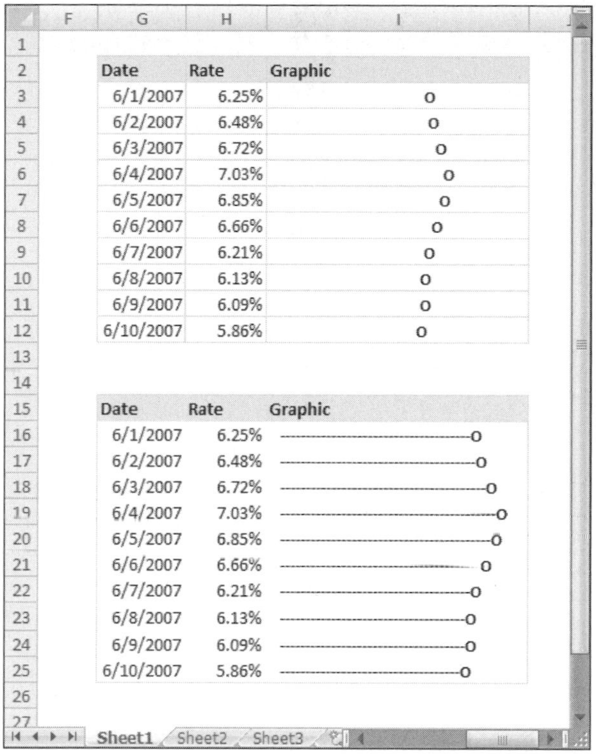

Date	Rate	Graphic
6/1/2007	6.25%	o
6/2/2007	6.48%	o
6/3/2007	6.72%	o
6/4/2007	7.03%	o
6/5/2007	6.85%	o
6/6/2007	6.66%	o
6/7/2007	6.21%	o
6/8/2007	6.13%	o
6/9/2007	6.09%	o
6/10/2007	5.86%	o

Date	Rate	Graphic
6/1/2007	6.25%	------o
6/2/2007	6.48%	------o
6/3/2007	6.72%	------o
6/4/2007	7.03%	------o
6/5/2007	6.85%	------o
6/6/2007	6.66%	------o
6/7/2007	6.21%	------o
6/8/2007	6.13%	------o
6/9/2007	6.09%	------o
6/10/2007	5.86%	------o

Figure 9-20: Two ways to create a dot chart directly in a range.

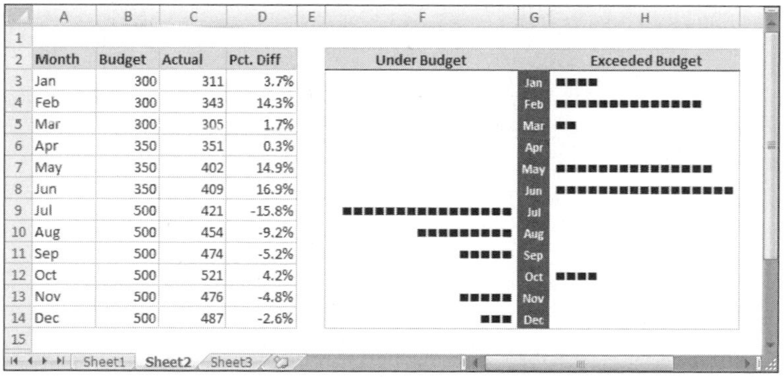

Month	Budget	Actual	Pct. Diff
Jan	300	311	3.7%
Feb	300	343	14.3%
Mar	300	305	1.7%
Apr	350	351	0.3%
May	350	402	14.9%
Jun	350	409	16.9%
Jul	500	421	-15.8%
Aug	500	454	-9.2%
Sep	500	474	-5.2%
Oct	500	521	4.2%
Nov	500	476	-4.8%
Dec	500	487	-2.6%

Figure 9-21: This chart is made up of text characters displayed in cells.

The data used in this chart is in columns A:C. Formulas in column D calculate the percent difference between the Budget and Actual amounts. Columns F and H contain formulas that use the value in column D. The formulas for columns F and H follow. I copied these formulas down to accommodate the 12 rows of data:

```
E2: =IF(D2<0,REPT("n",-ROUND(D2*100,0)),"")
G2: =IF(D2>0,REPT("n",-ROUND(D2*-100,0)),"")
```

The cells that display the bars use the Wingdings font — the letter *n* in this font produces a rectangular block. In column F, the text is aligned to the right. In column H, the text is aligned to the left.

The final example in this section is shown in Figure 9-22. It's a Gantt chart that displays a project schedule graphically in a range by using formulas. Column B contains the Start Date for each task, and column C contains the duration of the task. Formulas in column D calculate the End Date for each task. Formulas, beginning in column F, display a character that represents a day in the task.

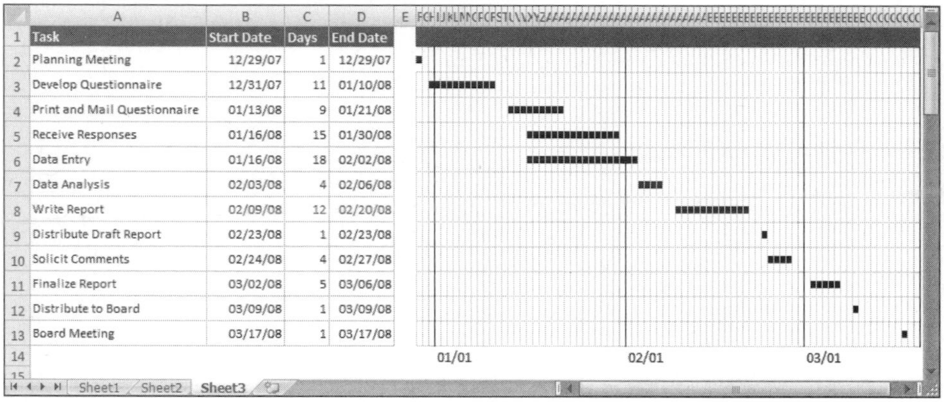

Figure 9-22: A Gantt chart created by using formulas.

The formula in cell F2, which is copied to all other cells in the chart range, is as follows:

```
=IF(AND(F$1>=$B2,F$1<=$D2),"n","")
```

Row 1, above the chart, contains consecutive dates that begin with the earliest project date and end with the latest date. Note that the columns are so narrow, these dates aren't even visible. The formula uses an IF function to determine whether the date value for the column is between the Start Date and the End Date. If so, the cells display the character. The cells are formatted using the Wingdings font, so the *n* character displays as a small rectangle.

CROSS-REFERENCE

Refer to Chapter 8 for instructions on creating a Gantt chart from a bar chart.

Creating Sparkline Charts

Edward Tufte coined the term *sparkline* to refer to a minimalist chart that appears in line with text. A sparkline can be described as a tiny graphic that reveals a general trend. Often, several sparklines are displayed together, and this type of chart is often used in dashboard applications.

Excel doesn't officially support sparkline charts, but you can create such charts by using text, or with an actual (very small) chart. The sections that follow describe both techniques.

Sparkline Charts from Text

Figure 9-23 shows three examples of sparkline charts that depict the sequence of games won and lost by four teams. These charts use identical formulas. The only difference is the characters used to represent games won and games lost.

		1	2	3	4	5	6	7	8	9	10	Team
Example 1												
		W	L	L	I	W	L	L	W	W	W	Tigers
		L	L	W	L	W	L	L	L	L	L	Sox
		W	W	W	W	L	L	L	L	W	L	Wranglers
		W	L	L	W	W	L	W	L	L	L	Coyotes
Example 2		1	2	3	4	5	6	7	8	9	10	Team
		W	L	L	L	W	L	L	W	W	W	Tigers
		L	L	W	L	W	L	L	L	L	L	Sox
		W	W	W	W	L	L	L	L	W	L	Wranglers
		W	L	L	W	W	L	W	L	L	L	Coyotes
Example 3		1	2	3	4	5	6	7	8	9	10	Team
		W	L	L	L	W	L	L	W	W	W	Tigers
		L	L	W	L	W	L	L	L	L	L	Sox
		W	W	W	W	L	L	L	L	W	L	Wranglers
		W	L	L	W	W	L	W	L	L	L	Coyotes

Figure 9-23: Three sparkline charts created from characters.

ON THE CD

The examples in this section are available on the companion CD-ROM. The filename is `sparkline text charts.xlsx`.

NOTE

The graphic characters used in these charts are from the Arial Unicode MS font. I used the Symbol dialog box (choose Insert⟳Text⟳Symbol) to locate these characters (see Figure 9-24). This font is unusual because the correct character displays regardless of the font used for the formula cell.

The formula in cell B3 is as follows:

```
=SUBSTITUTE(SUBSTITUTE(C3&D3&E3&F3&G3&H3&I3&J3&K3&L3,
"W","_"),"L","_")
```

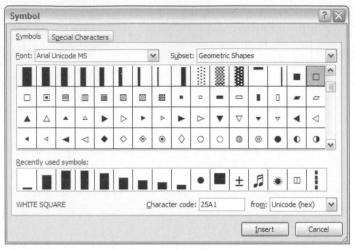

Figure 9-24: Using the Symbol dialog box to locate graphic characters in the Arial Unicode MS font

This formula concatenates the *W* and *L* characters in columns C through L, and then substitutes a character for the *W* and a different character for the *L*. The characters used in the formulas are as follows:

- **Example 1:** Character code 2534 and character code 252C, from the Box Drawing subset of the Arial Unicode MS font

- **Example 2:** Character code 25A0 and character code 25A1, from the Geometric Shapes subset of the Arial Unicode MS font

- **Example 3:** Character code 2584 and character code 2580, from the Block Elements subset of the Arial Unicode MS font

Using characters to display a sparkline chart is appropriate when the data values take on only a very limited number of values. The Arial Unicode MS font contains characters that display columns of various heights (character codes 2581 through 2588). If you don't mind complicated formulas, you can use these characters to create sparkline charts.

Figure 9-25 shows some sparkline charts that use eight characters to display columns. The formula bar displays the formula in cell B27. As you can see, the formula is lengthy and rather complicated. However, it accurately depicts the data, which ranges from 1 to 8.

Sparkline Charts from a Chart

If you like the idea of sparkline charts, but require more flexibility than the text-based sparklines described in the previous section, the solution is to use a real Excel chart. Figure 9-26 shows a few examples of charts as sparklines: column charts, column charts with no gap, line charts, area charts, pie charts, and 100% stacked bar charts.

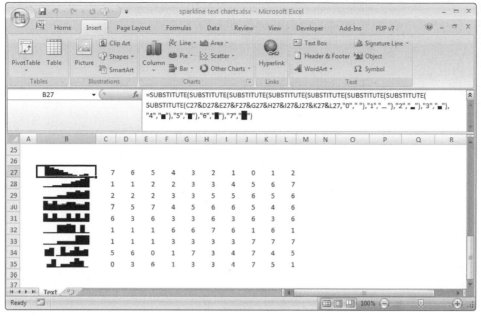

Figure 9-25: Sparkline charts that use eight characters.

 ON THE CD

The examples in this section are available on the companion CD-ROM. The filename is `sparkline chart examples.xlsm`. This workbook contains the PositionAndSizeChartsByName macro, described later in this chapter.

To create a cell-sized chart, follow these steps:

1. Create a normal-sized chart as usual. For best results use only one data series.

2. Delete all chart elements from the chart, except the series itself.

3. Make the chart area and plot area transparent (no fill).

4. Remove the border from the chart area.

5. Make the chart's plot area as large as possible so that it fills the entire chart area.

6. Adjust the colors and series formatting.

7. If you will be displaying multiple sparkline charts that will be compared with one another, you might want to make the value scale use fixed values rather than automatic values.

8. Drag a corner of the chart and reduce its size until it's the size of a cell.

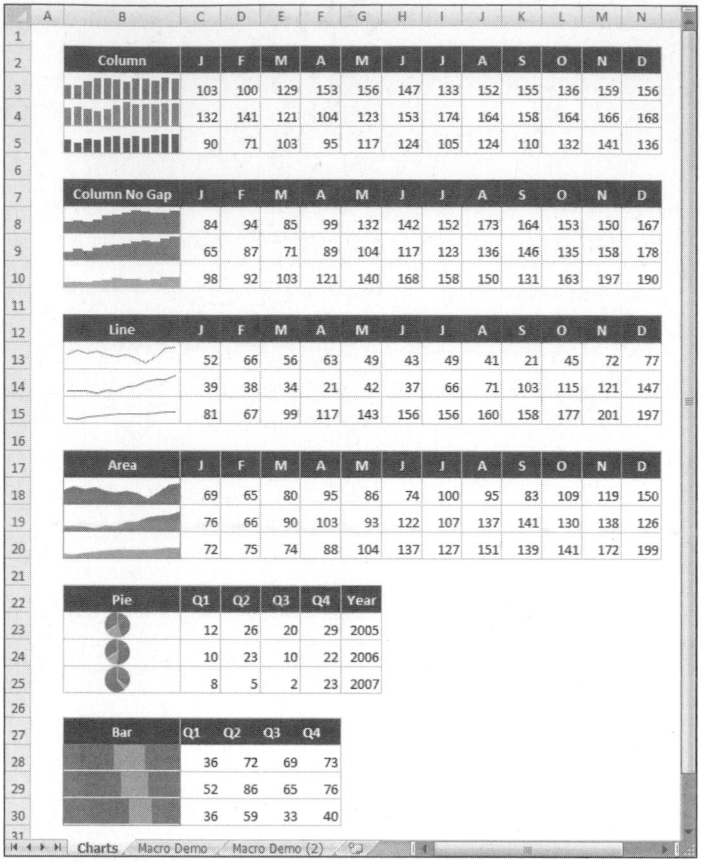

Figure 9-26: Miniature charts as sparklines.

SPARKLINE TIPS

Following are some general tips for creating tiny sparkline charts:

- After you've reduced the size of the chart, you'll find that it's much easier to position the chart (and modify its formatting) if you increase the zoom level of the worksheet. Use the Zoom controls on the right side of the status bar. Also, press Alt while moving the chart to enable "snap to grid."

- If you need to create multiple charts, create the first and then make a copy of the chart for each additional range. After you've made the copy, change its data range by selecting the series and dragging the outline that appears around the range.

- By default, charts change their size if you change the column width or row height. In addition, if you copy or move the underlying cell, the chart is also copied or moved. If, for some reason, you don't want a chart to move and size with cells, you can change this setting on the Properties tab of the Size and Properties dialog box. To display this dialog box, activate the chart and then click the dialog box launcher in the Chart Tools⇨Format⇨Size group. The dialog box launcher is the small icon to the right of the word *Size*.

CHART-POSITIONING AND -SIZING MACRO

Sizing and positioning a tiny sparkline chart can be very frustrating. I created a VBA macro to help.

Following is a macro that can size and position all charts in the active worksheet. Before you use this macro, you must rename your charts so that each name corresponds to the cell over which it will be placed. For example, if you'd like a chart to be positioned above cell F32 and be exactly the same size as cell F32, name the chart **CellF32**.

NOTE

To change the name of a chart, select the chart and use the Chart Name control in the Chart Tools⇨Layout⇨Properties group.

If a chart's name doesn't adhere to the naming convention I described, its size and position are not changed by the macro.

```
Sub PositionAndSizeChartsByName()
  Dim ChtObj As ChartObject
  Dim ULC As Range
  For Each ChtObj In ActiveSheet.ChartObjects
    On Error Resume Next
    If UCase(Left(ChtObj.Name, 4)) = "CELL" Then
      Set ULC = Range(Right(ChtObj.Name, Len(ChtObj.Name) - 4))
      If Err.Number = 0 Then
        ChtObj.Left = ULC.Left
        ChtObj.Top = ULC.Top
        ChtObj.Width = ULC.Width
        ChtObj.Height = ULC.Height
      End If
    End If
  Next ChtObj
End Sub
```

Figure 9-27 shows seven charts of various sizes. These charts use the data in the preceding rows (one chart per row of data). The charts are named to correspond to their target cell. The names are CellB3, CellB4, CellB5, and so on.

Charts	J	F	M	A	M	J	J	A	S	O	N	D
	103	112	135	144	134	164	197	210	226	261	266	293
	132	160	178	184	191	200	218	207	199	184	208	218
	43	52	65	96	127	143	151	175	196	229	215	247
	83	101	81	98	80	72	80	61	67	62	43	37
	102	132	128	117	112	139	121	116	98	105	113	129
	61	67	64	82	113	133	140	124	118	130	137	139
	45	29	60	83	86	121	122	105	124	116	110	119

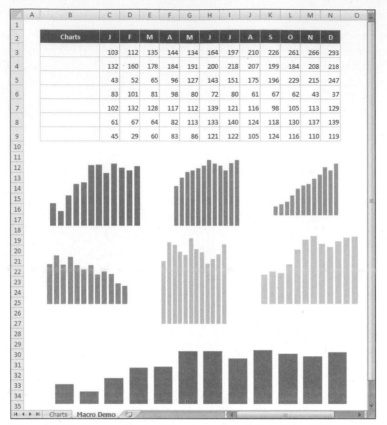

Figure 9-27: These charts will be moved and sized by a VBA macro.

Figure 9-28 shows the worksheet after executing the PositionAndSizeChartsByName macro.

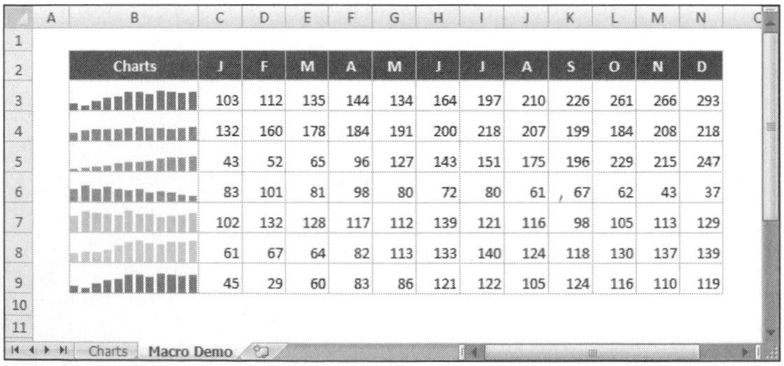

Charts	J	F	M	A	M	J	J	A	S	O	N	D
	103	112	135	144	134	164	197	210	226	261	266	293
	132	160	178	184	191	200	218	207	199	184	208	218
	43	52	65	96	127	143	151	175	196	229	215	247
	83	101	81	98	80	72	80	61	67	62	43	37
	102	132	128	117	112	139	121	116	98	105	113	129
	61	67	64	82	113	133	140	124	118	130	137	139
	45	29	60	83	86	121	122	105	124	116	110	119

Figure 9-28: After running the macro, the charts are moved and sized.

A SPARKLINE ADD-IN

I created a simple Excel 2007 add-in that can facilitate creating sparkline charts. Figure 9-29 shows the dialog box for this add-in. You specify the range of cells that will contain the charts and the range of data for the charts. In addition, you can specify fixed minimum and maximum values for the chart. The chart types are limited to the most commonly used: column charts (including an option with no gaps), line charts, and area charts.

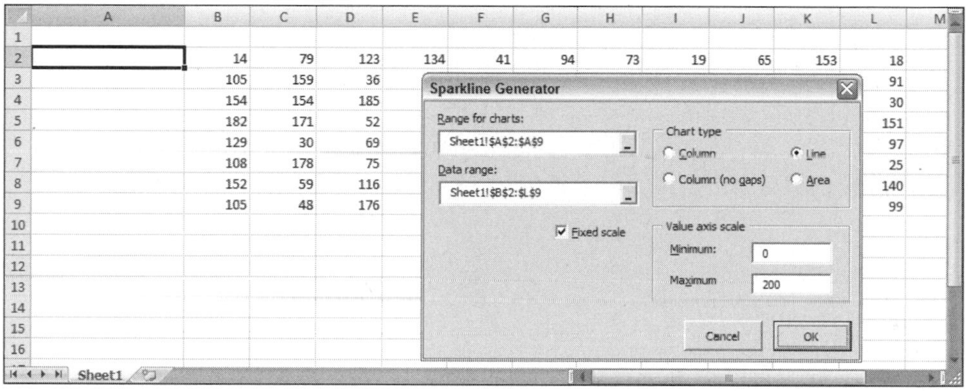

Figure 9-29: Preparing to create sparkline charts with the author's add-in.

ON THE CD

A copy of the Sparkline Generator add-in is available on the companion CD-ROM. The file is named `sparkline generator.xlam`. To install the add-in, copy it to your hard drive. Then press Alt+TI to display the Add-Ins dialog box. Click the Browse button and locate the `sparkline generator.xlam` file. When the add-in is installed, you will see a new Ribbon command: Insert⇨Sparklines⇨Generate Sparklines.

Figure 9-30 shows a worksheet that contains several sparkline charts created by the add-in.

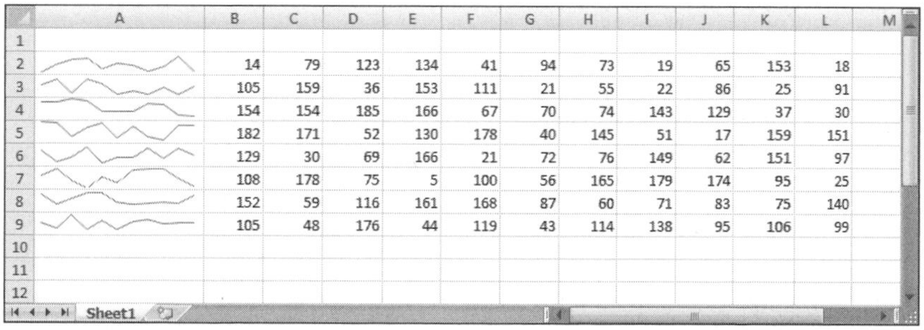

Figure 9-30: These sparkline charts were created by the author's add-in.

Commercial Sparkline Add-Ins

I'm aware of two Excel add-ins that add support for sparklines:

- MicroCharts, from Bonavista Systems (www.bonavistasystems.com)
- SparkMaker, from Bissantz & Company (www.bissantz.com)

Both products provide a wide variety of in-cell charting possibilities, and neither of them uses "real" Excel charts. Both have a trial version that you can download for free.

Figure 9-31 shows some in-cell charts created by MicroCharts.

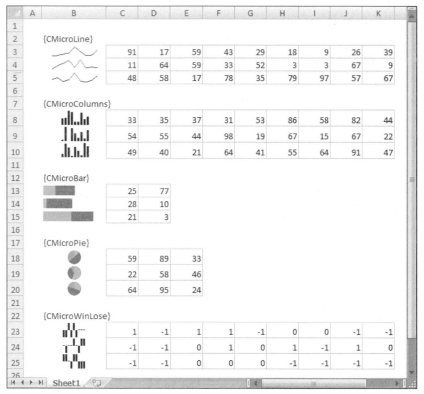

Figure 9-31: Charts created by MicroCharts, an Excel add-in.

Chapter 10

Mathematical and Statistical Charting Techniques

In This Chapter

- ◆ Drawing circles with a scatter chart
- ◆ Connecting data points to the chart axes or the origin
- ◆ Creating frequency distributions and histograms
- ◆ Plotting a normal curve
- ◆ Calculating the area under a curve
- ◆ Creating a box plot
- ◆ Plotting 1- and 2-variable mathematical functions
- ◆ Simulating a 3-D scatter plot

This chapter describes some charting techniques that may be useful for those who are mathematically or statistically inclined. The charts in this chapter use techniques that might not be obvious.

Drawing a Circle with an XY Series

This section describes how to create a scatter chart that displays a perfect circle. To do so, you need two ranges, one for the *x* values and another for the *y* values. The number of data points in the series determines the smoothness of the circle.

The example in Figure 10-1 uses 13 points to create a circle with an origin of 0,0 and a radius of 1. This series uses the Smoothed Line option (on the Marker Line Style tab of the Format Data Series dialog box). When this option is not set, the circle is not very smooth, and its component lines are clearly visible.

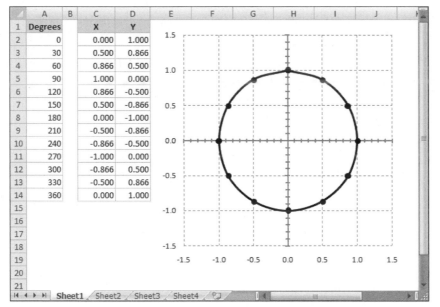

Figure 10-1: This scatter chart uses 13 data points to define a circle.

 ## ON THE CD

The examples in this section (plus a few additional examples) are available on the companion CD-ROM. The filename is `scatter chart circles.xlsx`.

To draw a circle on a chart, generate a series of values such as the ones shown in column A. The numeric series starts with 0 and has 30-degree increments. The ranges that are used in the chart are in columns C and D. The formula in C2 is as follows:

```
=COS(RADIANS(A2))
```

The formula in D2 is as follows:

```
=SIN(RADIANS(A2))
```

The formulas in C2 and D2 are copied down to subsequent rows.

NOTE

To plot a circle with more data points, you need to adjust the increment value in column A (the final value should always be 360). The increment is 360 divided by the number of data points minus 1. The more data points used, the smoother the circle.

TIP

The circle won't look accurate unless the plot area is adjusted so that a vertical unit is exactly the same length as a horizontal unit. The examples in this section all use the same major unit for both axes.

The next example, which builds on the previous example, demonstrates how to use a scatter chart series to draw circles around data points in a chart. Figure 10-2 shows a scatter chart that contains four series: The first series (range A2:B4) plots the three data points (as markers only, no line). Three additional series (ranges B9:C21, D9:E21, and F9:G21) plot a circle around each point (as lines, not markers).

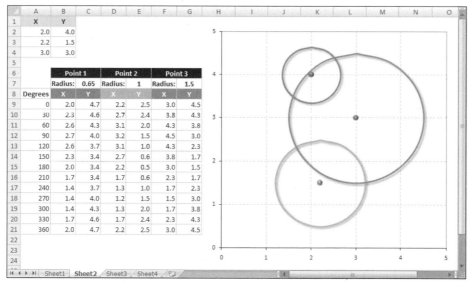

Figure 10-2: Using XY series to draw circles around data points.

The three circle series use formulas similar to those described in the previous section, but these formulas allow a specific origin and radius. The radius of each circle is defined by the entries in row 7.

Connecting Scatter Chart Data Points to the Axes with Error Bars

The example in Figure 10-3 shows a scatter chart in which each data point is projected to the x-and y-axis. These lines are created with error bars. After you create the basic scatter chart using the data in A2:B9, choose Chart Tools➪Analysis➪Layout➪Error Bars➪Error Bars More Options. This command adds default horizontal and vertical error bars to the chart, and also displays the Format Error Bars dialog box.

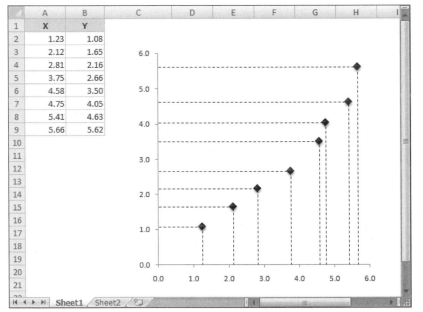

Figure 10-3: Using error bars to project each data point to the axes.

You need to adjust each set of error bars separately. For the vertical error bars, specify the Percentage option and enter 100 Repeat this for the horizontal error bars.

ON THE CD

The examples in this section and the section that follows are available on the companion CD-ROM. The filename is connecting data points.xlsx.

Connecting XY Points to the Origin

Figure 10-4 shows a scatter chart in which each data point is connected to the origin. This type of chart requires an additional series. The chart shown in the figure displays five data points (as markers), and the chart has an additional data series displayed as lines.

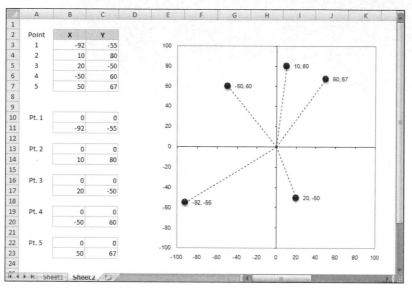

Figure 10-4: Using additional data series to connect each data point with the chart's origin.

The first series uses the data in B3:C7 and is set to display markers (but no line) and data labels. The second series uses the data in B10:C23. This range duplicates the data in B3:C7, but with an additional point at the chart's origin.

After creating the scatter chart using the data in B3:C7, follow these steps to add the additional data series:

1. Select the range B10:C23 and press Ctrl+C.

2. Select the chart and choose Home⇨Clipboard⇨Paste⇨Paste Special.

3. In the Paste Special dialog box, select New Series, Values (Y) in Columns, and Categories (X Values) in First Column. The result will be a new series overlaid on top of the original series.

4. Use the Line Color tab in the Format Data Series dialog box to specify a line for that series. Then format the line any way you like.

Creating Frequency Distributions and Histograms

A *frequency distribution* is a summary table that shows the frequency of each value in a range. For example, an instructor may create a frequency distribution of test scores. The table would show the count of test scores in various numeric ranges. A chart created from a frequency distribution is often referred to as a *histogram*.

Part II

Excel provides a number of ways to create frequency distributions. You can:

- Use the FREQUENCY function
- Use the Analysis ToolPak add-in
- Use a pivot table

CROSS-REFERENCE

The following sections cover the FREQUENCY function and the Analysis ToolPak options. Refer to Chapter 11 for examples of using a pivot table to create a histogram.

ON THE CD

The examples in the following sections are available on the companion CD-ROM. The filename is `frequency distributions.xlsx`.

Using the FREQUENCY Function

Excel's FREQUENCY function provides a relatively easy way to create a frequency distribution. This function always returns an array, so you must use it in an array formula entered into a multicell range.

Figure 10-5 shows a workbook with data in range A2:A1001 (named Data). These values range from 43 to 100. The range C5:C14 contains the *bins* used for the frequency distribution. Each cell in this bin range contains the upper limit for the bin. In this case, the bins consist of <=55, 56–60, 61–65, and so on. See the nearby sidebar, "Creating bins for a frequency distribution," to discover an easy way to create a bin range.

To create the frequency distribution, select a range of cells that correspond to the number of cells in the bin range — in this example, range D5:D14. Then enter the following array formula into the selected range:

```
=FREQUENCY(Data,C5:C14)
```

NOTE

Enter an array formula by pressing Ctrl+Shift+Enter.

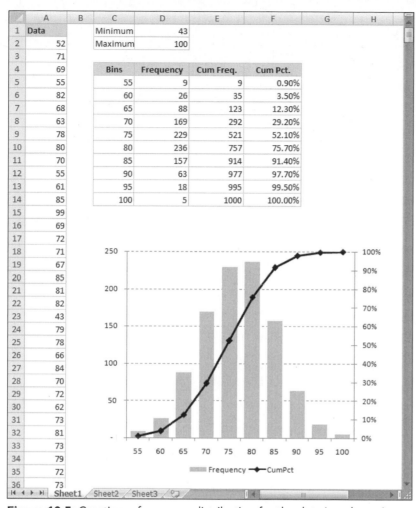

Figure 10-5: Creating a frequency distribution for the data in column A.

The array formula is entered into all the selected cells and returns the count of values in the Data range that fall into each bin. You can then create other formulas that make use of the frequencies. For example, column E displays cumulative frequencies, and column F shows cumulative percent.

The combination chart was created using the frequency data in column D (the column series) and the cumulative percent data in column F (the line series). The histogram suggests that the data approximates a normal distribution.

Creating bins for a frequency distribution

When creating a frequency distribution, you must first enter the values into the bin range. The number of bins determines the number of categories in the distribution. Most of the time, each of these bins represents an equal range of values.

To create 10 evenly spaced bins for values in a range named Data, enter the following array formula into a range of 10 cells in a column:

```
=MIN(Data)+(ROW(INDIRECT("1:10"))*(MAX(Data)-MIN(Data))/10)
```

To enter a multicell array formula, select the range, type the formula, and press Ctrl+Shift+Enter.

This formula creates 10 bins, based on the values in the Data range. The upper bin will always equal the maximum value in the range.

To create more or fewer bins, use a value other than 10 and enter the array formula into a range that contains the same number of cells. For example, to create five bins, enter the following array formula into a five-cell vertical range:

```
=MIN(Data)+(ROW(INDIRECT("1:5"))*(MAX(Data)-MIN(Data))/5)
```

Using the Analysis ToolPak to Create a Frequency Distribution

If you install the Analysis ToolPak add-in, you can use the Histogram option to create a frequency distribution. Select Data⇨Analysis⇨Data Analysis to display the Data Analysis dialog box. Next, select Histogram and click the OK button. You should see the Histogram dialog box shown in Figure 10-6.

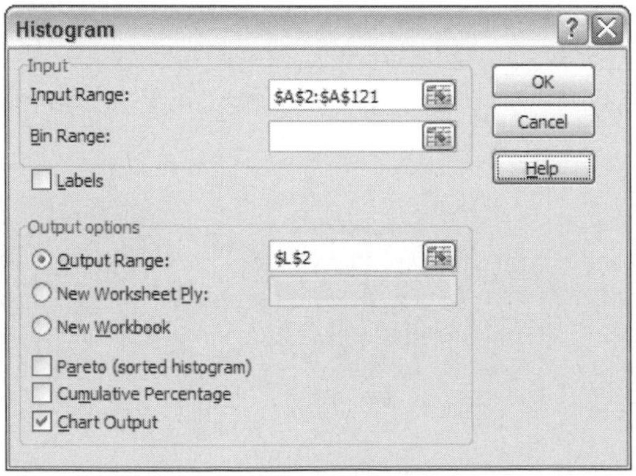

Figure 10-6: The Analysis ToolPak's Histogram dialog box.

NOTE

If the Data⇨Analysis⇨Data Analysis command is not available, you need to install the Analysis ToolPak. Press Alt+TI, and select the Analysis ToolPak check box.

Specify the range for your data (Input Range). If you've created a bin range, specify that range — otherwise, leave it blank and the program will generate bins automatically. Specify the upper-left cell for the results (Output Range) and then select any options. Figure 10-7 shows a frequency distribution (and chart) created with the Histogram option.

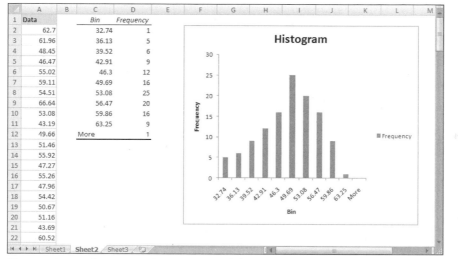

Figure 10-7: A frequency distribution and chart generated by the Analysis ToolPak's Histogram option.

WARNING

A potential problem with using this technique is that the frequency distribution consists of values, not formulas. Therefore, if you make any changes to your input data, you need to rerun the Histogram procedure to update the results.

Using Adjustable Bins to Create a Histogram

Figure 10-8 shows a worksheet with student grades listed in column B (67 students total). Columns D and E contain formulas that calculate the upper and lower limits for bins, based on the entry in cell E1 (named BinSize). For example, if BinSize is 10 (as in the figure), each bin contains 10 scores (1–10, 11–20, and so on).

The chart uses two named formulas. The name Categories is defined as follows:

```
=OFFSET(Sheet3!$E$4,0,0,ROUNDUP(100/BinSize,0))
```

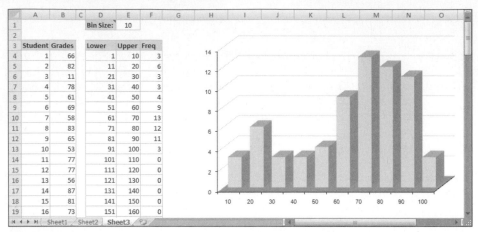

Figure 10-8: The chart displays a histogram; the contents of cell E1 determine the number of categories.

The name Frequencies is defined as follows:

```
=OFFSET(Sheet3!$F$4,0,0,ROUNDUP(100/BinSize,0))
```

The net effect is that the chart adjusts automatically when you change the BinSize cell. Figure 10-9 shows the chart when the bin size is 6.

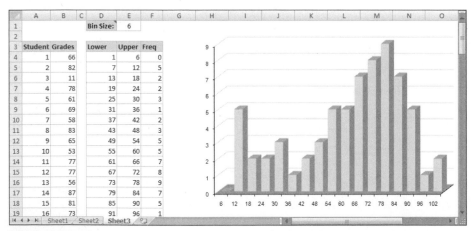

Figure 10-9: The previous chart, after changing the bin size.

CROSS-REFERENCE

See Chapter 7 for more about creating charts that use named formulas in their SERIES formulas.

Plotting a Normal Curve

Figure 10-10 shows two scatter charts that display a normal distribution and the cumulative normal distribution. The top chart uses the data in columns A and B. The bottom chart uses the data in columns A and C. Cell B1, named Mean, controls the mean of the distribution, and cell B2, named SD, controls the standard deviation.

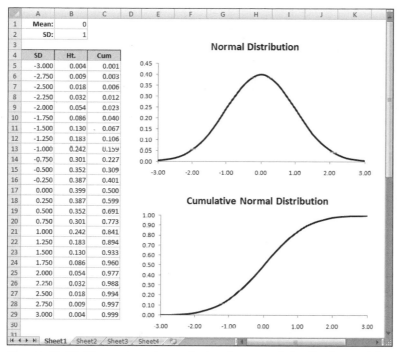

Figure 10-10: The scatter charts display the normal distribution and the cumulative normal distribution.

 ON THE CD

The examples in this section (plus several other examples) are available on the companion CD-ROM. The filename is normal distribution.xlsx.

Column A contains formulas that generate values ranging from –3 SD units to +3 SD units. The formula in cell A5, which was copied to the cells below, is as follows:

```
=(-SD*3)+Mean
```

Column B contains formulas that generate the height of the curve for a given mean and standard deviation. The formula in cell B5 is as follows:

```
=NORMDIST(A5,Mean,SD,FALSE)
```

Part II

The formulas in column C also use the NORMDIST function, but the fourth argument is set to TRUE. The formula in C5 is as follows:

```
=NORMDIST(A5,Mean,SD,TRUE)
```

In some cases, you may want to compare a histogram created from your data with the theoretical normal distribution. Figure 10-11 shows an example of how this can be done. The chart is a combination chart with two value axes. The data consists of 2,600 data points in column A. Simple formulas in column D calculate key statistics for the data.

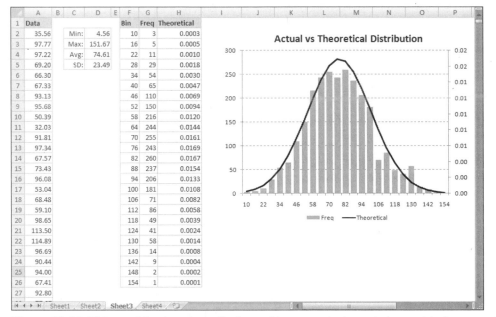

Figure 10-11: This combination chart displays a histogram (columns) along with the normal distribution curve.

The histogram is generated from the data in column G, using the FREQUENCY function (see the section "Using the FREQUENCY Function," earlier in this chapter). The normal distribution curve uses the data in column H. The formula in cell H2, which is copied to the cells below, is as follows:

```
=NORMDIST(F2,$D$4,$D$5,FALSE)
```

The companion CD-ROM contains another example that applies a scaling factor to the theoretical values. The theoretical data is multiplied by the number of data points (2,600) times the bin size (6). After this transformation, both data series can use a single value axis.

Plotting Z-Scores with Standard Deviation Bands

Figure 10-12 shows a scatter chart that plots 500 values. Each data point in column A is converted to a z-score (column B), and these values are used in the chart. A z-score is a way of standardizing data, such that the transformed data has a mean of 0 and a standard deviation of 1. The midpoint on the vertical axis corresponds to the average data value, and the gridlines correspond to standard deviation units.

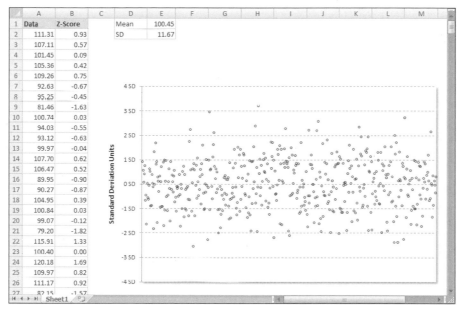

Figure 10-12: This combination chart uses a bar chart series to display horizontal bands that correspond to standard deviation units.

 ON THE CD

This example is available on the companion CD-ROM. The filename is `z-score plot.xlsx`.

Formulas calculate the mean and standard deviation of the data, and these cells are given names (Mean and SD). The z-score calculation is done with simple formulas. Cell B2, for example, contains this formula:

```
=(A2-Mean)/SD
```

Because the chart plots transformed data, the chart can be used for any data set without modification.

Calculating the Area under a Curve

If you use a scatter chart to generate a curve, you may need to calculate the area under the curve. I start with an elementary example, shown in Figure 10-13. The gridlines in this chart are separated by one unit, so calculating the area under this curve can be done manually. It consists of 10.5 square units (nine complete squares plus three half-squares).

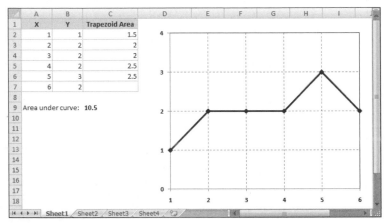

Figure 10-13: Calculating the area under this curve is a no-brainer.

ON THE CD

The examples in this section are available on the companion CD-ROM. The filename is `area under a curve.xlsx`.

If you don't feel like counting squares, you can take a more calculated approach and use formulas to calculate the area under a curve. This is known as the "trapezoid" method. A trapezoid, as you may recall, is a four-sided figure with two parallel sides. This method essentially divides the area under the curve into a series of trapezoids and then calculates the area of each one. The area under the curve is the sum of the trapezoid areas.

To calculate the area of a trapezoid, multiply the "average" height by the base. In the preceding example (Figure 10-13), the left side of the first trapezoid has a height of 1 and the right side has a height of 2. The average height is 1.5. The base is one unit, so the area of the first trapezoid is 1.5. The area of the second trapezoid is 2, and so on.

The formulas in column C calculate the area for each trapezoid. Cell C2, for example, contains the following formula:

```
=((B2+B3)/2)*(A3-A2)
```

This formula is copied down to accommodate the number of data points. Note that the last cell (cell C7) is empty. That's because each formula refers to the subsequent row, and the formula is not valid for the last row of data. The formula in C9 simply adds these segment areas together.

This formula works fine — except when negative values are involved. In such a case, the formula gets much more complex because triangles (as well as trapezoids) enter the picture. The curve shown in Figure 10-14 presents more of a challenge because it has negative values. When using the previous formula to calculate trapezoid areas for this chart, the result is 3.5, which is clearly incorrect.

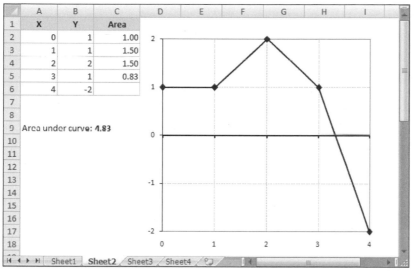

Figure 10-14: Calculating the area under this curve requires complex formulas.

When negative numbers are involved, a more complex formula is required. The following formula (entered in cell C2) is a general-purpose formula that works in all situations:

```
=IF(B2*B3>=0,ABS(((B2+B3)/2)*(A3-A2)),ABS(((B2^2+B3^2)/(B2-B3)/2)*(A3-A2)))
```

The formula uses an IF function that determines whether the calculation returns the area of a trapezoid or the area of two triangles. In this example, the formula is used four times to yield the final result. The first, second, and third calculations compute the area of a trapezoid. The fourth calculation, however, computes the area of the two triangles that result from the line crossing the x-axis. The sum of the areas of these two triangles is 0.83. The total area under the curve is 4.83.

It's important to understand that the area calculation is *approximate.* Generally, the accuracy of the calculation increases with the number of data points that define the curve. Figure 10-15 shows three charts, all of which plot a sine curve. The charts vary, however, in the number of data points used and, subsequently, in the number of area calculations performed. The calculated area under the curve ranges from 220.01 to 229.16, the latter being the most accurate.

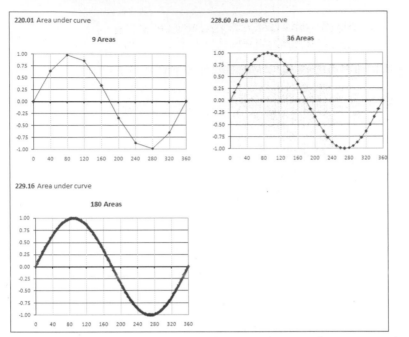

Figure 10-15: Calculating the area under a sine curve, with varying numbers of data points.

Creating a Box Plot

A box plot (sometimes known as a *quartile plot* or a *box and whisker plot*) is often used to summarize data. Figure 10-16 shows a box plot created for four groups of subjects. Each group has a diagram, the height of which represents the numerical range of the data (minimum and maximum values). The "boxes" represent the 25th through the 75th percentile. The horizontal line inside the box is the median value (or 50th percentile). This type of chart enables the viewer to make quick comparisons among groups of data.

 ON THE CD

The example in this section is available on the companion CD-ROM. The CD contains an additional example that creates a box plot using a line chart with high-low lines and up/down bars. The filename is box plot.xlsx.

The raw data appears in columns A:D. The data is summarized in range F1:J7, with simple formulas. The following table lists the formulas for Group 1 (G3:G7). These formulas were copied to the three columns to the right.

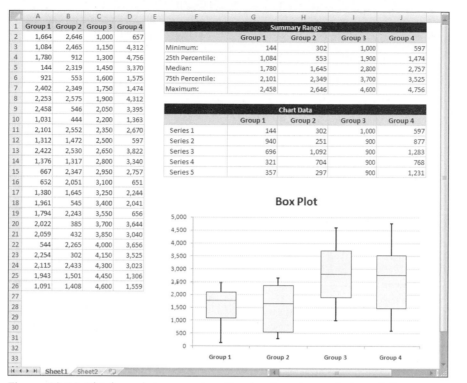

Figure 10-16: This box plot summarizes the data in columns A through D.

Cell	Calculation	Formula
G3	Minimum	`=MIN(A$2:A$26)-`
G4	25th Percentile	`=PERCENTILE(A$2:A$26,0.25)`
G5	Median	`=MEDIAN(A$2:A$26)`
G6	75th Percentile	`=PERCENTILE(A$2:A$26,0.75)`
G7	Maximum	`=MAX(A$2:A$26)`

The summary data must be transformed to create the box plot. This transformation is done in the section labeled Chart Data (F11:J14). This range contains simple formulas that calculate the difference between the row values in the Summary Range section. For example, the formula in cell G12 is as follows:

`=G4-G3`

Follow these steps to create the box plot:

1. Select the range F10:J14 and create a stacked column chart.

   Notice that Series 5 is not included in the range select. However, this range is used in Step 5.

2. Select Series 1 and set the border color to No Line and the fill to No Fill.

3. Select Series 2 and set the border color to No Line and the fill to No Fill.

4. With Series 2 still selected, choose Chart Tools⇨Layout⇨Analysis⇨Error Bars⇨More Error Bars Options. In the Format Error Bars dialog box, specify Minus error bars, with a percentage error amount of 100%.

5. Select Series 4 and choose Chart Tools⇨Layout⇨Analysis⇨Error Bars⇨More Error Bars Options. In the Format Error Bars dialog box, specify Plus error bars. Click the Specify Value button and specify G15:J15 as the custom range (the Series 5 range).

   You'll probably want to delete the legend because it provides no meaningful information.

The only two bars that remain visible are Series 3 and Series 4. Vertical error bars extend to cover the space occupied by the hidden Series 2 and Series 5 (which is not plotted). You can adjust the gap width to adjust the width of the boxes.

You can also create a horizontal box plot by starting with a stacked bar chart and using the same series of steps.

Plotting Mathematical Functions

The examples in the following sections demonstrate how to plot mathematical functions that use one variable (a 2-D line chart) and two variables (a 3-D surface chart).

 NOTE

The examples make use of Excel's Data Table feature, which enables you to evaluate a formula using varying input values. Coverage of this feature is beyond the scope of this book. Excel's Help provides a good overview.

Plotting Functions with One Variable

A scatter chart is useful for plotting various mathematical and trigonometric functions. For example, Figure 10-17 shows a plot of the SIN function. The chart plots y for values of x (expressed in radians) from −5 to +5 in increments of 0.5. Each pair of x and y values appears as a data point in the chart, and the points connect with a line.

ON THE CD

This workbook, named `function plots.xlsx`, is available on the companion CD-ROM.

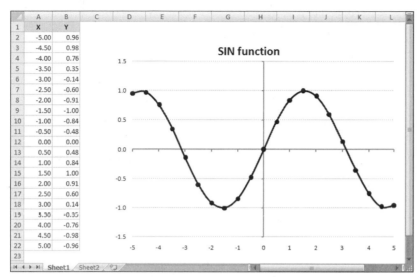

Figure 10-17: This chart plots the SIN(x).

The function is expressed as follows:

```
y = SIN(x)
```

The corresponding formula in cell B2 (which is copied to the cells below) is as follows:

```
=SIN(A2)
```

Figure 10-18 shows a general-purpose, single-variable plotting application. The data for the chart is calculated by a data table in columns I:J and is not shown in the figure.

ON THE CD

This example, named `function plot 2D.xlsx`, is available on the companion CD-ROM.

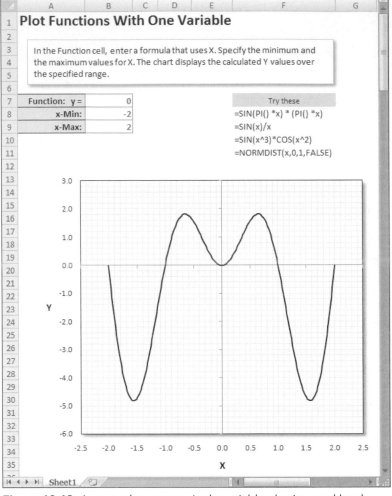

Figure 10-18: A general-purpose, single-variable plotting workbook.

To use this application, follow these steps:

1. Enter a formula in cell B7. The formula should contain at least one *x* variable. In the figure, the formula in cell B3 is as follows:

   ```
   =SIN(PI()*x)*(PI()*x)
   ```

2. Enter the minimum value for *x* in cell B8.

3. Enter the maximum value for *x* in cell B9.

The formula in cell B7 displays the value of *y* for the minimum value of *x*. The data table, however, evaluates the formula for 200 equally spaced values of *x*, and these values appear in the chart. In addition, the chart's title displays the function that's plotted.

Plotting Functions with Two Variables

The preceding section describes how to plot functions that use a single variable (x). You also can plot functions that use two variables. For example, the following function calculates a value of z for various values of two variables (x and y):

```
z = SIN(x)*COS(y)
```

Figure 10-19 shows a surface chart that plots the value of z for 21 x values ranging from 2 to 5 (in 0.15 increments), and for 21 y values ranging from –3 to 0 (also in 0.15 increments).

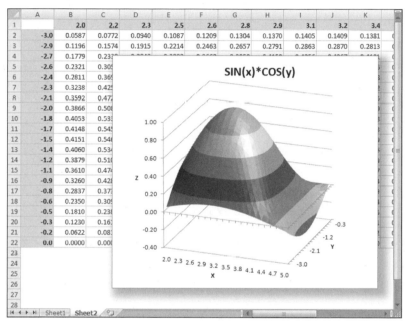

Figure 10-19: Using a surface chart to plot a function with two variables.

Figure 10-20 shows a general-purpose, two-variable plotting application, similar to the 2-D function plot workbook described in the previous section. The data for the chart is a 25 x 25 data table range in columns K:AL (not shown in the figure).

 ON THE CD

This example, named `function plot 3D.xlsm`, is available on the companion CD-ROM. The workbook contains VBA macros to assist in rotating the chart.

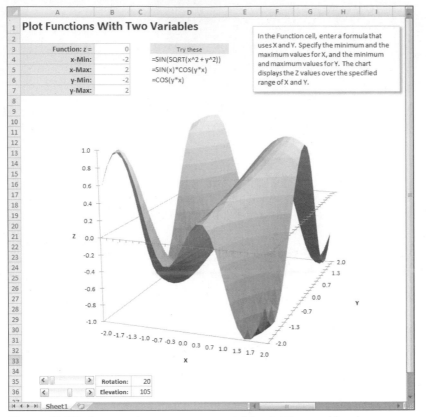

Figure 10-20: A general-purpose, two-variable plotting workbook.

Follow these steps to use this application:

1. Enter a formula in cell B3. The formula should contain at least one *x* variable and at least one *y* variable. In the figure, the formula in cell B3 is as follows:

   ```
   =SIN(x)*COS(y*x)
   ```

2. Enter the minimum *x* value in cell B4 and the maximum *x* value in cell B5.

3. Enter the minimum *y* value in cell B6 and the maximum *y* value in cell B7.

The formula in cell B3 displays the value of *z* for the minimum values of *x* and *y*. The data table evaluates the formula for 25 equally spaced values of *x* and 25 equally spaced values of *y*. These 625 values are plotted in the surface chart.

Creating a 3-D Scatter Plot

One of the most requested chart types for Excel is a 3-D scatter plot. Unfortunately, however, Microsoft has not paid attention to these requests. This type of chart is like an XY scatter chart but with an added "depth" dimension (Z).

Andy Pope, a charting expert from the U.K., sent me an interesting workbook that simulates a 3-D scatter plot. Each data point is entered as three coordinate values (*x*, *y*, and *z*). Formulas then transform the data to make it appear in a 3-D space. The chart includes additional series to display the x-, y-, and z-axes, as well as the cube that encompasses the 3-D space.

I took Andy's idea and spent many hours refining it and (I hope) making it easier to understand. The result, shown in Figure 10-21, has quite a few accoutrements. The three scroll bars control the angle of each of the three axes, and the buttons perform animations.

	A	B	C	D	E	F	G	H	I	J	K
1		Data				Axes Angles					
2	X	Y	Z		X	Y	Z	Rotate X		Show Axes	Data scaling
3	8.00	0.25	-0.04		155	150	80			Show Cube	Single scale for all data
4	8.60	0.17	-0.16					Rotate Y		Show Data	Separate x,y,z scaling
5	9.20	0.05	-0.21								
6	9.80	-0.07	-0.19								
7	10.40	-0.16	-0.11					Rotate Z			
8	11.00	-0.18	0.00								
9	11.60	-0.14	0.10					Rotate All			
10	12.20	-0.06	0.15								
11	12.80	0.04	0.15								
12	13.40	0.11	0.10								
13	14.00	0.14	0.02								
14	14.60	0.12	-0.06								
15	15.20	0.06	-0.11								
16	15.80	-0.01	-0.13								
17	16.40	-0.08	-0.09								
18	17.00	-0.11	-0.03								
19	17.60	-0.11	0.04								
20	18.20	-0.07	0.09								
21	18.80	-0.01	0.11								
22	19.40	0.05	0.09								
23	20.00	0.09	0.04								
24	20.60	0.10	-0.02								
25	21.20	0.07	-0.07								
26	21.80	0.02	-0.09								
27	22.40	-0.04	-0.08								
28	23.00	-0.07	-0.05								
29	23.60	-0.08	0.00								
30	24.20	-0.07	0.05								
31	24.80	-0.03	0.08								
32	25.40	0.02	0.08								

Figure 10-21: A simulated 3-D scatter plot.

 ON THE CD

This example, named `3D scatterplot.xlsm`, is available on the companion CD-ROM. The workbook contains VBA macros to assist in rotating the chart and hiding various elements.

The *x* values range from 8.0 to 43.4. The *y* values are calculated by this formula:

```
=SIN(A3)/(A3*0.5)
```

The *z* values are generated by this formula:

```
=COS(A3)/(A3*0.5)
```

The resulting curve is a spiraling corkscrew.

Chapter **11**

Using Pivot Charts

In This Chapter

- ◆ An introduction to pivot tables
- ◆ How to create a pivot table
- ◆ How to create a pivot chart
- ◆ Differences between pivot charts and standard charts
- ◆ Pivot chart examples

Many people (author included) consider pivot tables to be the most innovative and powerful analytical feature in Excel. A pivot table can instantly convert a mass of data into a nicely summarized table. Pivot tables have been around since Excel 5. Beginning with Excel 2000, this feature was augmented to include charting capabilities. And, in Excel 2007, pivot charts are better than ever.

This chapter starts out with an introductory overview of pivot tables (for the uninitiated) and then moves on to cover pivot charts. If you're already familiar with pivot tables, you can skip the introductory material and jump straight to the section "Working with Pivot Charts," later in this chapter.

What Is a Pivot Table?

A *pivot table* is essentially a dynamic summary report generated from a database. The database can reside in a worksheet (in the form of a table) or in an external data file. A pivot table can help transform endless rows and columns of numbers into a meaningful presentation of the data.

For example, a pivot table can create frequency distributions and cross-tabulations of several different data dimensions. In addition, you can display subtotals and any level of detail that you want. Perhaps the most innovative aspect of a pivot table is its interactivity. After you create a pivot table, you can rearrange the information in almost any way imaginable and even insert special formulas that perform new calculations. You can even create post hoc groupings of summary items (for example, combine Northern Region totals with Western Region totals). And the icing on the cake: With a few mouse clicks, you can apply formatting to a pivot table to convert it into an attractive report.

One minor drawback to using a pivot table is that, unlike a formula-based summary report, a pivot table does not update automatically when you change information in the source data. This drawback doesn't pose a serious problem, however, because a single click of the Refresh button forces a pivot table to update itself with the latest data.

A Pivot Table Example

The best way to understand the concept of a pivot table is to see one. Start with Figure 11-1, which shows a portion of the data used in creating the pivot table in this chapter.

	Date	Amount	AcctType	OpenedBy	Branch	Customer
2	Sep-01	5,000	IRA	New Accts	Central	Existing
3	Sep-01	14,571	CD	Teller	Central	New
4	Sep-01	500	Checking	New Accts	Central	Existing
5	Sep-01	15,000	CD	New Accts	Central	Existing
6	Sep-01	4,623	Savings	New Accts	North County	Existing
7	Sep-01	8,721	Savings	New Accts	Westside	New
8	Sep-01	15,276	Savings	New Accts	North County	Existing
9	Sep-01	5,000	Savings	New Accts	Westside	Existing
10	Sep-01	15,759	CD	Teller	Westside	Existing
11	Sep-01	12,000	CD	New Accts	Westside	Existing
12	Sep-01	7,177	Savings	Teller	North County	Existing
13	Sep-01	6,837	Savings	New Accts	Westside	Existing
14	Sep-01	3,171	Checking	New Accts	Westside	Existing
15	Sep-01	50,000	Savings	New Accts	Central	Existing
16	Sep-01	4,690	Checking	New Accts	North County	New
17	Sep-01	12,438	Checking	New Accts	Central	Existing
18	Sep-01	5,000	Checking	New Accts	North County	Existing
19	Sep-01	7,000	Savings	New Accts	North County	New
20	Sep-01	11,957	Checking	New Accts	Central	Existing
21	Sep-01	13,636	CD	New Accts	North County	Existing
22	Sep-01	16,000	CD	New Accts	Central	New
23	Sep-01	5,879	Checking	New Accts	Central	Existing
24	Sep-01	4,000	Savings	New Accts	Central	Existing
25	Sep-02	10,000	CD	Teller	North County	Existing
26	Sep-02	7,427	Checking	New Accts	North County	Existing
27	Sep-02	4,500	Checking	New Accts	North County	New
28	Sep-02	12,962	Checking	Teller	Central	Existing
29	Sep-02	500	Checking	New Accts	Central	New
30	Sep-02	5,364	Checking	Teller	Central	New
31	Sep-02	45,000	CD	Teller	North County	Existing
32	Sep-02	14,867	Checking	Teller	North County	Existing
33	Sep-02	13,061	Checking	Teller	Central	New
34	Sep-02	11,779	CD	Teller	Central	New
35	Sep-02	4,995	Checking	New Accts	Central	New
36	Sep-02	10,096	Savings	New Accts	Central	New

data / pt1 / pt2 / q1 / q2 / q3 / q4 / q5 / q6

Figure 11-1: This table is used to create a pivot table.

This table consists of a month's worth of new account information for a three-branch bank. The table contains 712 rows, and each row represents a new account. The table has the following columns:

- The date the account was opened

- The opening amount

- The account type (CD, checking, savings, or IRA)

- Who opened the account (a teller or a new-account representative)

- The branch at which it was opened (Central, Westside, or North County)

- The type of customer (an existing customer or a new customer)

 ON THE CD

This workbook, named bank accounts.xlsx, is available on the companion CD-ROM.

The bank accounts table contains quite a bit of information. But in its current form, the data doesn't reveal much. To make the data more useful, you need to summarize it. Summarizing a table is essentially the process of answering questions about the data. Following are a few questions that may be of interest to the bank's management:

- What is the daily total new deposit amount for each branch?

- How many accounts were opened at each branch, broken down by account type?

- What's the dollar distribution of the different account types?

- What types of accounts do tellers open most often?

- How does the Central branch compare to the other two branches?

- In which branch do tellers open the most checking accounts for new customers?

You can, of course, spend time sorting the data and creating formulas to answer these questions. Often, however, using a pivot table is a much better choice. Creating a pivot table takes only a few seconds, doesn't require a single formula, and produces a nice-looking report (with an optional chart). In addition, pivot tables are much less prone to error than creating formulas.

 CROSS-REFERENCE

Later in this chapter, I present pivot tables and pivot charts that answer the preceding questions.

Figure 11-2 shows a pivot table created from the bank data. This pivot table shows the amount of new deposits, broken down by branch and account type. This particular summary is just one of dozens of summaries that you can produce from this data.

	A	B	C	D	E	F	G
1							
2							
3	Sum of Amount	AcctType					
4	Branch	CD	Checking	IRA	Savings	Grand Total	
5	Central	1,359,385	802,403	68,380	885,757	3,115,925	
6	North County	1,137,911	392,516	134,374	467,414	2,132,215	
7	Westside	648,549	292,995	10,000	336,088	1,287,632	
8	Grand Total	3,145,845	1,487,914	212,754	1,689,259	6,535,772	
9							
10							
11							

data / pt1 / pt2 / q1 / q2 / q3 / q4 / q5

Figure 11-2: A simple pivot table.

Figure 11-3 shows another pivot table generated from the bank data. This pivot table uses a drop-down Report Filter for the Customer item (in row 1). In the figure, the pivot table displays the data only for Existing customers. (The user can also select New or All from the drop-down control.) Notice the change in the orientation of the table? For this pivot table, branches appear as column labels, and account types appear as row labels. This change, which took about five seconds to make, is another example of the flexibility of a pivot table.

	A	B	C	D	E	F
1	Customer	Existing				
2						
3	Sum of Amount	Branch				
4	AcctType	Central	North County	Westside	Grand Total	
5	CD	973,112	845,522	356,079	2,174,713	
6	Checking	505,822	208,375	144,391	858,588	
7	IRA	68,380	125,374	10,000	203,754	
8	Savings	548,198	286,891	291,728	1,126,817	
9	Grand Total	2,095,512	1,466,162	802,198	4,363,872	
10						
11						
12						

data / pt1 / pt2 / q1 / q2 / q3 / q4

Figure 11-3: A pivot table that uses a report filter.

Data Appropriate for a Pivot Table

A pivot table requires your data to be in the form of a rectangular database. You can store the database in either a worksheet range (which can be a table or just a normal range) or an external database file. Although Excel can generate a pivot table from any database, not all databases benefit.

Why "pivot"?

Are you curious about the term *pivot*?

Pivot, as a verb, means to rotate or revolve. If you think of your data as a physical object, a pivot table lets you rotate the data summary and look at it from different angles or perspectives. A pivot table allows you to move fields around easily, nest fields within each other, and even create ad hoc groups of items.

If you were handed a strange object and asked to identify it, you'd probably look at it from several different angles in an attempt to figure it out. Working with a pivot table is similar to investigating a strange object. In this case, the object happens to be your data. A pivot table invites experimentation, so feel free to rotate and manipulate the pivot table until you're satisfied. You may be surprised at what you discover.

If you've created a pivot chart from your pivot table, you'll find that the chart changes to reflect changes made in the pivot table.

Generally speaking, fields (or columns) in a database table consist of two types:

- **Data:** Contains a value or data to be summarized. For the bank account example, the Amount field is a data field.

- **Category:** Describes the data. For the bank account data, the Date, AcctType, OpenedBy, Branch, and Customer fields are category fields because they describe the data in the Amount field.

A single database table can have any number of data fields and category fields. When you create a pivot table, you usually want to summarize one or more of the data fields. Conversely, the values in the category fields appear in the pivot table as rows, columns, or filters.

Exceptions exist, however, and you may find Excel's pivot table feature useful even for databases that don't contain actual numerical data fields. For example, it's very easy to create a pivot table that displays the count of various items.

Figure 11-4 shows an example of an Excel range that is *not* appropriate for a pivot table. This range contains descriptive information about each value, but it's not set up as a table. In fact, this range resembles a pivot table summary.

Figure 11-5 shows the same data in a form that *is* appropriate for a pivot table. Notice that every data cell in the original range shown in Figure 11-4 is represented by a separate row.

ON THE CD

The companion CD-ROM contains a workbook with a VBA macro that can convert a summary table into a 3-column table suitable for a pivot table. The filename is `reverse pivot.xlsm`.

	A	B	C	D	E	F
1		North	South	East	West	
2	Jan	132	233	314	441	
3	Feb	143	251	314	447	
4	Mar	172	252	345	450	
5	Apr	184	290	365	452	
6	May	212	299	401	453	
7	Jun	239	317	413	457	
8	Jul	249	350	427	460	
9	Aug	263	354	448	468	
10	Sep	291	373	367	472	
11	Oct	294	401	392	479	
12	Nov	302	437	495	484	
13	Dec	305	466	504	490	
14						

Sheet1

Figure 11-4: This range is not appropriate for a pivot table.

	F	G	H	I	J
1		Month	Region	Sales	
2		Jan	North	132	
3		Jan	South	233	
4		Jan	East	314	
5		Jan	West	441	
6		Feb	North	143	
7		Feb	South	251	
8		Feb	East	314	
9		Feb	West	447	
10		Mar	North	172	
11		Mar	South	252	
12		Mar	East	345	
13		Mar	West	450	
14		Apr	North	184	
15		Apr	South	290	
16		Apr	East	365	
17		Apr	West	452	
18		May	North	212	
19		May	South	299	
20		May	East	401	
21		May	West	453	
22		Jun	North	239	
23		Jun	South	317	
24		Jun	East	413	

Sheet1

Figure 11-5: The data in Figure 11-4, in a form that's appropriate for a pivot table.

Creating a Pivot Table

In the following sections, I describe the basic steps required to create a pivot table, using the bank account data as a model. Creating a pivot table is an interactive process. It's not at all uncommon to experiment with various pivot table layouts until you find one that you're satisfied with.

Specifying the Data

If your data is in a worksheet range, select any cell in that range and then choose Insert⇨ Tables⇨PivotTable, which displays the dialog box shown in Figure 11-6.

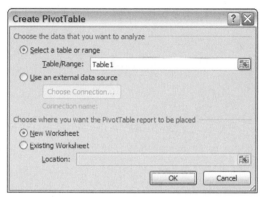

Figure 11-6: In the Create PivotTable dialog box, you tell Excel where the data is and where you want the pivot table.

Excel attempts to guess the range, based on the location of the active cell. If you're creating a pivot table from an external data source, you need to select that option and then click the Choose Connection button to specify the data source. If you're working with an external data source, the location of the active cell is not important.

TIP

If you're creating a pivot table from data in a worksheet, it's a good idea to first create a table for the range (by choosing Insert⇨Tables⇨Table). Then, if you expand the table by adding new rows of data, Excel will refresh the pivot table without the need to manually indicate the new data range.

Specifying the Location for the Pivot Table

Use the bottom section of the Create PivotTable dialog box to indicate the location for your pivot table. The default location is in a new worksheet, but you can specify any range in any worksheet, including the worksheet that contains the data. You can specify a single cell that will be the upper left corner of the pivot table.

Click the OK button, and Excel creates an empty pivot table and displays its PivotTable Field List, as shown in Figure 11-7.

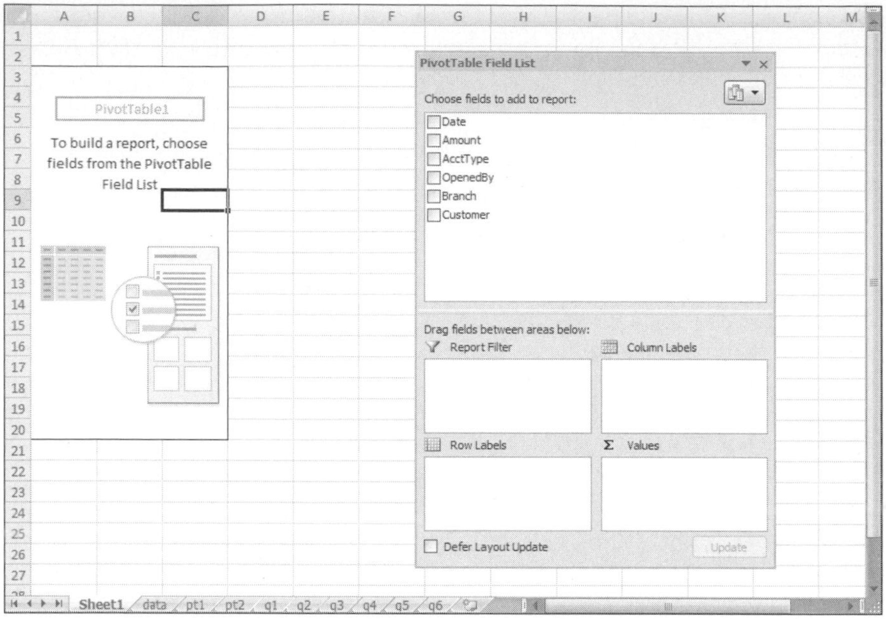

Figure 11-7: Use the PivotTable Field List to build the pivot table.

Tip

The PivotTable Field List is normally docked on the right side of Excel's window. By dragging its title bar, you can move it anywhere you like. Also, if you click a cell outside the pivot table, the PivotTable Field List is hidden.

Laying Out the Pivot Table

Next, set up the actual layout of the pivot table by using the PivotTable Field List. You can do so by using either of these techniques:

- Drag the field names to one of the four boxes on the PivotTable Field List.

- Right-click a field name and choose its location from the shortcut menu.

Note

In previous versions of Excel, you could drag items from the field list directly into the appropriate area of the pivot table. This feature is still available, but it's turned off by default. To enable this feature, choose PivotTable Tools⇨Options⇨PivotTable Options to display the PivotTable Options dialog box. Click the Display tab and select the Classic PivotTable Layout check box.

The following steps create the pivot table presented earlier in this chapter (see the section "A Pivot Table Example"). For this example, I drag the items from the top of the PivotTable Field List to the areas in the bottom of the PivotTable Field List.

1. Drag the Amount field into the Values area. At this point, the pivot table displays the total of all the values in the Amount column.

2. Drag the AcctType field into the Row Labels area. Now the pivot table shows the total amount for each of the account types.

3. Drag the Branch field into the Column Labels area. The pivot table shows the amount for each account type, cross-tabulated by branch (see Figure 11-8).

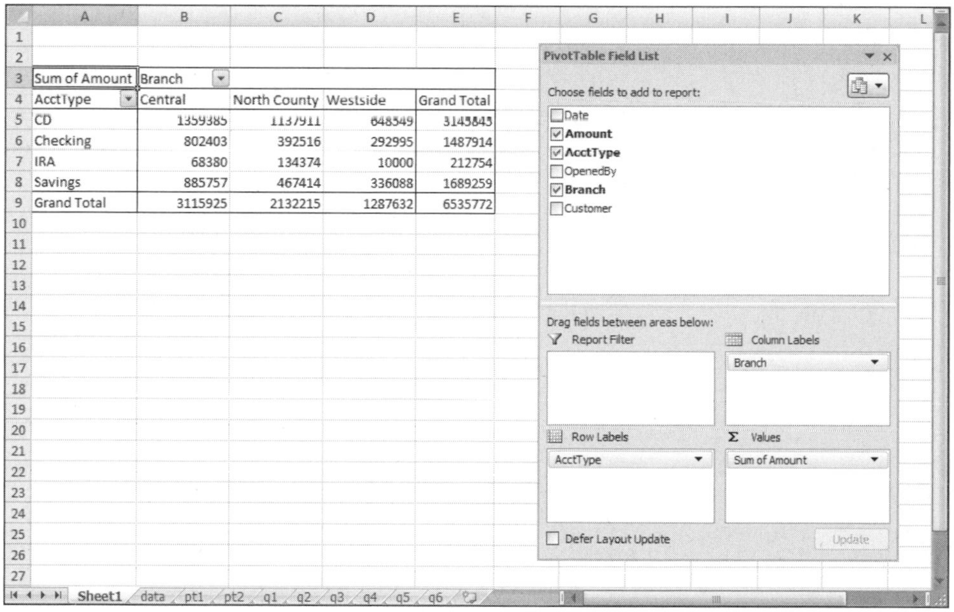

Figure 11-8: After a few simple steps, the pivot table shows a summary of the data.

Formatting the Pivot Table

Notice that the pivot table uses General number formatting. To change the number format used, select any value and choose PivotTable Tools⇨Options⇨Active Field⇨Field Settings to display the Data Field Settings dialog box. Click the Number Format button and change the number format.

You can apply any of several built-in styles to a pivot table. Select any cell in the pivot table and choose PivotTable Tools⇨Design⇨PivotTable Styles to select a style.

You also can use the controls in the PivotTable⇨Design⇨Layout group to control various elements in the pivot table. For example, you can choose to hide the grand totals if you prefer.

The PivotTable Tools⇨Options⇨Show/Hide group contains additional options that affect the appearance of your pivot table. For example, you use the Show Field Headers button to toggle the display of the field headings.

Still more pivot table options are available in the PivotTable Options dialog box, shown in Figure 11-9. To display this dialog box, choose PivotTable Tools⇨Options⇨PivotTable⇨ Options. Or, right-click any cell in the pivot table and choose Table Options from the shortcut menu.

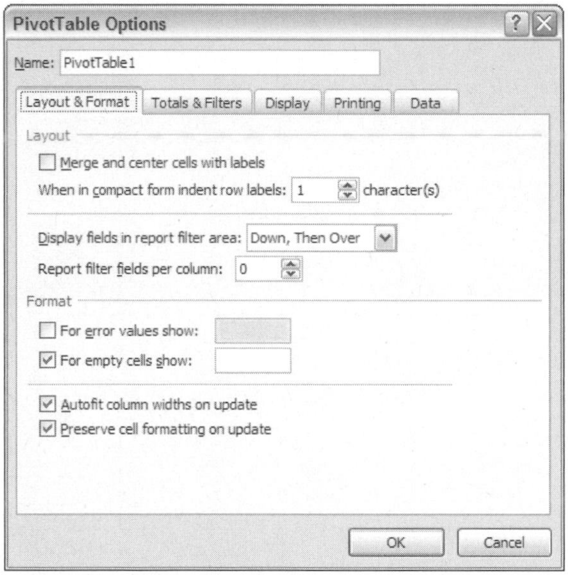

Figure 11-9: The PivotTable Options dialog box.

Pivot table calculations

Pivot table data is most frequently summarized using a sum. However, you can display your data using a number of different summary techniques. Select any cell in the Values area of your pivot table and then choose PivotTable Tools⇨Options⇨Active Field⇨Field Settings to display the Value Field Settings dialog box. This dialog box has two tabs: Summarize By and Show Values As.

Use the Summarize By tab to select a different summary function. Your choices are Sum, Count, Average, Max, Min, Product, Count Numbers, StdDev, StdDevp, Var, and Varp.

To display your values in a different form, use the drop-down control on the Show Values As tab. Then, use the two list boxes (Base Field and Base Item) to refine your choice. Your choices are described in the following table.

Function	Result
Difference From	Displays data as the difference from the value of the Base Item in the Base Field
% Of	Displays data as a percentage of the value of the Base Item in the Base Field
% Difference From	Displays data as the percentage difference from the value of the Base Item in the Base Field
Running Total In	Displays the data for successive items in the Base Field as a running total
% Of Row	Displays the data in each row or category as a percentage of the total for the row or category
% Of Column	Displays all the data in each column or series as a percentage of the total for the column or series
% Of Total	Displays data as a percentage of the grand total of all the data or data points in the report
Index	Calculates data as follows: ((Value in Cell) x (Grand Total of Grand Totals)) / ((Grand Row Total) x (Grand Column Total))

Modifying the Pivot Table

After you've created a pivot table, it's easy to change it. For example, you can add further summary information by using the PivotTable Field List. Figure 11-10 shows the pivot table after I dragged a second field (OpenedBy) to the Row Labels section on the PivotTable Field List. In this example, each account type is broken down by whoever originally opened the account for the client.

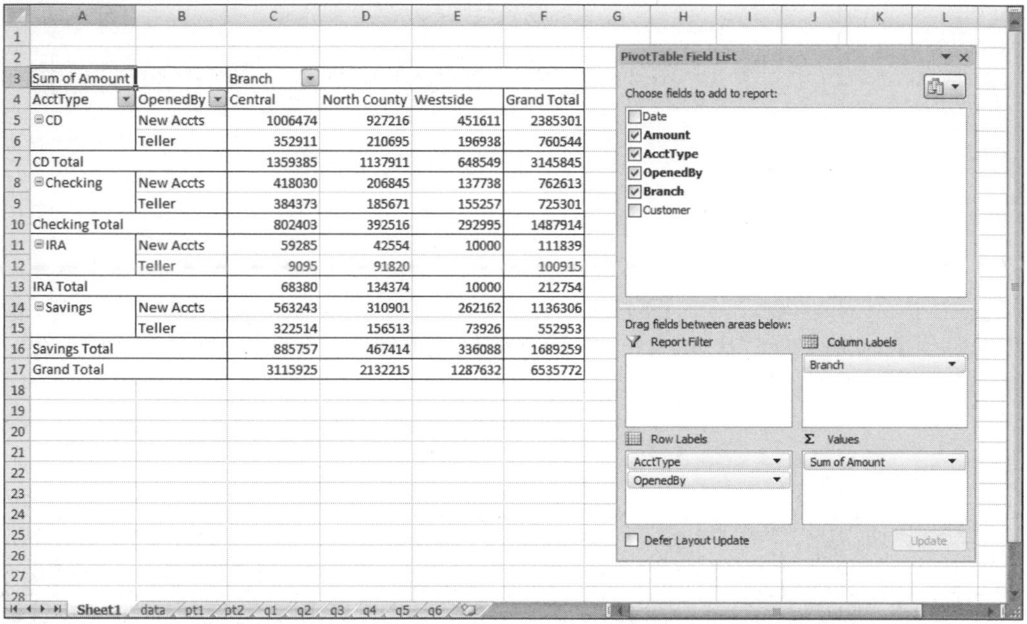

Sum of Amount		Branch			
AcctType	OpenedBy	Central	North County	Westside	Grand Total
CD	New Accts	1006474	927216	451611	2385301
	Teller	352911	210695	196938	760544
CD Total		1359385	1137911	648549	3145845
Checking	New Accts	418030	206845	137738	762613
	Teller	384373	185671	155257	725301
Checking Total		802403	392516	292995	1487914
IRA	New Accts	59285	42554	10000	111839
	Teller	9095	91820		100915
IRA Total		68380	134374	10000	212754
Savings	New Accts	563243	310901	262162	1136306
	Teller	322514	156513	73926	552953
Savings Total		885757	467414	336088	1689259
Grand Total		3115925	2132215	1287632	6535772

Figure 11-10: Two fields are used for row labels.

Following are some tips on other pivot table modifications you can make:

- To remove a field from the pivot, select it in the bottom part of the PivotTable Field List and "drag it away."
- If an area has more than one field, you can change the order in which the fields are listed by dragging the field names. Doing so affects the appearance of the pivot table. You can also change the order of the fields by typing over a field. For example, in cell C4, replace Central by typing **Westside** and the Westside field swaps positions with the Central field.
- To temporarily remove a field from the pivot table, deselect the field name in the top part of the PivotTable Field List. The pivot table is redisplayed without that field. Reselect the field name, and it appears in its previous section.
- If you add a field to the Report Filter section, the field items appear in a drop-down list, which allows you to filter the displayed data by one or more items. Figure 11-11 shows an example. I dragged the Date field to the Report Filter area. The report is now showing the data only for a single day (which I selected from the drop-down list in cell B1).

	A	B	C	D	E	F	G	H	I	J	K	L
1	Date	Sep-04										
2												
3	Sum of Amount		Branch									
4	AcctType	OpenedBy	Central	North County	Westside	Grand Total						
5	⊟CD	New Accts	87067	80228	39824	207119						
6		Teller	9000	14702		23702						
7	CD Total		96067	94930	39824	230821						
8	⊟Checking	New Accts	7480	9000	3075	19555						
9		Teller	500	13465		13965						
10	Checking Total		7980	22465	3075	33520						
11	⊟IRA	New Accts			2000	2000						
12		Teller	9095			9095						
13	IRA Total		9095		2000	11095						
14	⊟Savings	New Accts	6000	2878	65000	73878						
15		Teller	4309	6307		10616						
16	Savings Total		10309	9185	65000	84494						
17	Grand Total		123451	126580	109899	359930						
18												

PivotTable Field List

Choose fields to add to report:
☑ Date
☑ Amount
☑ AcctType
☑ OpenedBy
☑ Branch
☐ Customer

Drag fields between areas below:
▽ Report Filter — Date
Column Labels — Branch
Row Labels — AcctType, OpenedBy
Σ Values — Sum of Amount

☐ Defer Layout Update   Update

Sheet1 / data / pt1 / pt2 / q1 / q2 / q3 / q4 / q5 / q6 /

Figure 11-11: The pivot table is filtered by date.

Copying a pivot table

A pivot table is very flexible, but it does have some limitations. For example, you can't add new rows or columns, change any of the calculated values, or enter formulas within the pivot table. If you want to manipulate a pivot table in ways not normally permitted, make a copy of it.

To copy a pivot table, select the entire table and choose Home⇨Clipboard⇨Copy (or press Ctrl+C). Then select a new worksheet and choose Home⇨Clipboard⇨ Paste⇨Paste Values. The contents of the pivot table are copied to the new location so that you can do whatever you like to them. You also may want to copy the formats from the pivot table. Select the entire pivot table and then choose Home⇨Clipboard⇨ Format Painter. Then click the upper-left corner of the copied range.

Note that the copied information is not a pivot table, and it is no longer linked to the source data. If the source data changes, your copied pivot table does not reflect these changes.

You can also copy the pivot table as a pivot table. Select the pivot table, and press Ctrl+C. Activate a different cell and press Ctrl+V. The result is a new pivot that is linked to the same data as the copied pivot table. You can then manipulate the new pivot table independently of the original pivot table.

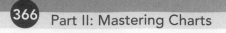

Working with Pivot Charts

The following sections discuss pivot charts and assume that you're familiar with the material already presented in this chapter.

A *pivot chart* is a graphical representation of a data summary displayed in a pivot table. A pivot chart is always based on a pivot table. Although Excel lets you create a pivot table and a pivot chart at the same time, you can't create a pivot chart without a pivot table.

CROSS-REFERENCE

Pivot charts, by their very nature, are interactive charts. Chapter 7 discusses other ways to create interactive charts.

Creating a Pivot Chart

If you're familiar with creating charts in Excel, you'll have no problem creating and customizing pivot charts. Most of Excel's charting features are available in a pivot chart. By the way, if you've used pivot charts in a previous version of Excel — and were frustrated by their limitations — you'll be pleased to know that pivot charts are improved significantly in Excel 2007.

Excel provides three ways to create a pivot chart:

- Select any cell in an existing pivot table and choose PivotTable Tools⇨Options⇨Tools⇨ Pivot Chart.

- Choose Insert⇨Tables⇨Pivot Table⇨Pivot Chart. Excel creates a pivot table and a pivot chart.

- Select any cell in an existing pivot table and select a chart type from the Insert⇨Charts group.

A pivot chart cannot be a scatter chart, a bubble chart, or a stock chart. If you specify any of these chart types, Excel displays an error message.

Which method you choose is up to you. I usually create the pivot table first and then create a pivot chart from the pivot table. If you create the pivot table and pivot chart at the same time, the chart can get in the way.

NOTE

A pivot chart is always based on a pivot table. You can't create a pivot chart without an underlying pivot table. Also, a pivot chart always reflects the layout of the pivot table. If you change the layout of a pivot table, the layout of its corresponding pivot chart also changes.

A Pivot Chart Example

Figure 11-12 shows part of a table that tracks daily sales by region. The Date column contains dates for the entire year (excluding weekends), the Region field contains the region name (Eastern, Southern, or Western), and the Sales field contains the sales amount. The table contains 780 rows. Creating a chart from this table would be very difficult because the data arrangement isn't suitable for a chart.

	A	B	C	D
1	Date	Region	Sales	
2	1/2/2006	Eastern	10,909	
3	1/3/2006	Eastern	11,126	
4	1/4/2006	Eastern	11,224	
5	1/5/2006	Eastern	11,299	
6	1/6/2006	Eastern	11,265	
7	1/9/2006	Eastern	11,328	
8	1/10/2006	Eastern ·	11,494	
9	1/11/2006	Eastern	11,328	
10	1/12/2006	Eastern	11,598	
11	1/13/2006	Eastern	11,868	
12	1/16/2006	Eastern	11,702	
13	1/17/2006	Eastern	11,846	
14	1/18/2006	Eastern	11,898	
15	1/19/2006	Eastern	11,871	
16	1/20/2006	Eastern	12,053	
17	1/23/2006	Eastern	12,073	
18	1/24/2006	Eastern	12,153	
19	1/25/2006	Eastern	12,226	
20	1/26/2006	Eastern	12,413	
21	1/27/2006	Eastern	12,663	
22	1/30/2006	Eastern	12,571	
23	1/31/2006	Eastern	12,508	
24	2/1/2006	Eastern	12,390	
25	2/2/2006	Eastern	12,649	
26	2/3/2006	Eastern	12,697	
27	2/6/2006	Eastern	12,878	
28	2/7/2006	Eastern	13,082	
29	2/8/2006	Eastern	12,903	
30	2/9/2006	Eastern	12,733	

data / Sheet1

Figure 11-12: This data will be used to create a pivot chart.

 ON THE CD

This workbook, named `sales by region.xlsx`, is available on the companion CD-ROM.

The first step is to create a pivot table to summarize the data. Figure 11-13 shows the pivot table. The Date field is in the Row Labels area, and the daily dates have been grouped into months. The Region field is in the Column Labels area. The Sales field is in the Values area (and it's summarized by summing).

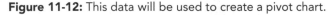

	Eastern	Southern	Western	Grand Total
Sum of Sales	Column Labels			
Row Labels	Eastern	Southern	Western	Grand Total
Jan	259,416	171,897	99,833	531,146
Feb	255,487	135,497	100,333	491,317
Mar	296,958	147,425	107,884	552,267
Apr	248,956	131,401	110,628	490,985
May	293,192	132,165	144,889	570,246
Jun	281,641	122,156	133,153	536,950
Jul	263,899	110,844	147,484	522,227
Aug	283,917	107,935	176,325	568,177
Sep	252,049	101,233	181,518	534,800
Oct	273,592	104,542	212,932	591,066
Nov	292,585	98,041	232,032	622,658
Dec	288,378	95,986	239,514	623,878
Grand Total	3,290,070	1,459,122	1,886,525	6,635,717

PivotTable Field List

Choose fields to add to report:
- ☑ Date
- ☑ Region
- ☑ Sales

Drag fields between areas below:

▼ Report Filter

▦ Column Labels
Region ▼

▦ Row Labels
Date ▼

Σ Values
Sum of Sales ▼

☐ Defer Layout Update   Update

Figure 11-13: This pivot table summarizes sales by region and by month.

TIP

To group dates in a pivot table, right-click a date and choose Group from the shortcut menu. In the Grouping dialog box, indicate the level of grouping. In this example, the dates are grouped by months.

The pivot table is certainly easier to interpret than the raw data, but the trends would be easier to spot on a chart.

To create a pivot chart, select any cell in the pivot table and choose PivotTable Tools⇨ Options⇨Tools⇨Pivot Chart. Excel displays its Create Chart dialog box, from which you can choose a chart type. For this example, select a standard line chart and click the OK button. Excel creates the pivot chart and also displays the PivotChart Filter Pane, shown in Figure 11-14.

The chart makes it easy to see a strong upward sales trend for the Western division, a slight downward trend for the Southern division, and relatively flat sales for the Eastern division.

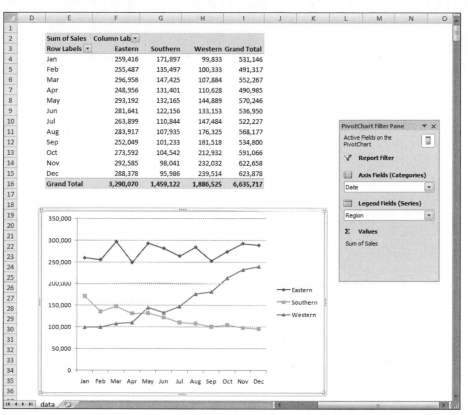

Part II

Figure 11-14: The pivot chart uses the data displayed in the pivot table.

When you select a pivot chart, the Ribbon displays a new context tab: PivotChart Tools. The commands in the Design, Layout, and Format tabs are virtually identical to those for a standard Excel chart, so you're in familiar territory. The commands in the Analyze tab contain a few commands specific to pivot table charts.

If you modify the underlying pivot table, the chart adjusts automatically to display the new summary data. Figure 11-15 shows the pivot chart after I changed the Date grouping to quarters.

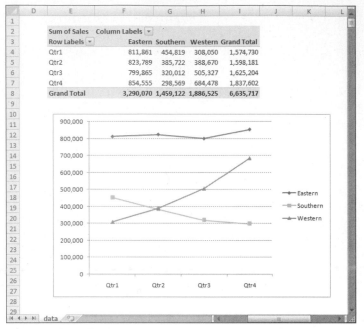

Sum of Sales	Column Labels			
Row Labels	Eastern	Southern	Western	Grand Total
Qtr1	811,861	454,819	308,050	1,574,730
Qtr2	823,789	385,722	388,670	1,598,181
Qtr3	799,865	320,012	505,327	1,625,204
Qtr4	854,555	298,569	684,478	1,837,602
Grand Total	3,290,070	1,459,122	1,886,525	6,635,717

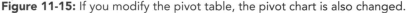

Figure 11-15: If you modify the pivot table, the pivot chart is also changed.

Pivot chart tips

Following are a few points to keep in mind when using pivot charts:

- A pivot table and a pivot chart are joined in a two-way link. If you make structural or filtering changes to one, the other is also changed.

- The PivotChart Filter Pane, which is displayed when you select a pivot chart, contains the same controls as the pivot chart's field headers. These controls allow you to filter the data that's displayed in the pivot table (and pivot chart). If you make changes to the chart using the PivotChart Filter Pane, those changes are also reflected in the pivot table.

- If you find the PivotChart Filter Pane redundant or annoying, just click the X in its title bar to make it go away. To bring it back, choose PivotChart Tools⇨Analyze⇨Show/Hide⇨PivotChart Filter.

- If you have a pivot chart and you delete the underlying pivot table, the pivot chart remains. The chart's SERIES formulas contain the original data, stored in arrays.

- A pivot chart always uses all the data in a pivot table — you can't create a pivot chart from a subset of a pivot table. In addition, you'll notice that all the controls in the Select Data Source dialog box are disabled. You can, however, hide various elements in a pivot table to force a pivot chart to display only part of the data.

- You can't change the orientation of a pivot chart. The Switch Row/Column command is always disabled when a pivot chart is selected. You can, however, change the data orientation in the underlying pivot table. The pivot chart will reflect those changes.

- By default, pivot charts are embedded in the sheet that contains the pivot table. To move the pivot chart to a different worksheet (or to a chart sheet), choose PivotChart⇨Tools⇨Design⇨Location⇨Move Chart.

- You can create multiple pivot charts from a pivot table, and you can manipulate and format the charts separately. However, all the charts display the same data.

- Don't forget about themes. You can choose Page Layout⇨Themes⇨Themes to change the workbook theme, and your pivot table and pivot chart will both reflect the new theme.

Pivot Chart Banking Examples

The following sections contain pivot chart examples that use the banking data presented earlier in this chapter. These examples answer the questions posed earlier (see the section "A Pivot Table Example").

 ON THE CD

The examples in the following sections are available in `bank accounts.xlsx`, available on the companion CD-ROM.

Question 1

What is the daily total new deposit amount for each branch?

Figure 11-16 shows the pivot table and pivot chart that answers this question.

- The Branch field is in the Column Labels section.

- The Date field is in the Row Labels section.

- The Amount field is in the Values section and is summarized by Sum.

The pivot chart is a stacked area chart.

Note that the pivot table can also be sorted by any column. For example, you can sort the Grand Total column in descending order to find out which day of the month had the largest amount of new funds. To sort, just right-click any cell in the column to sort and choose Sort from the shortcut menu. Note that this change to the pivot table will also change the pivot chart.

	Date	Central	North County	Westside	Grand Total
3	Sum of Amount	Branch			
4	Date	Central	North County	Westside	Grand Total
5	Sep-01	135,345	57,402	51,488	244,235
6	Sep-02	79,642	81,794		161,436
7	Sep-03	59,119	65,530	20,117	144,766
8	Sep-04	123,451	126,580	109,899	359,930
9	Sep-05	101,480	50,294	97,415	249,189
10	Sep-06	188,018	91,724	52,738	332,480
11	Sep-07	271,227	196,188	53,525	520,940
12	Sep-08	67,999	24,123	47,329	139,451
13	Sep-09	14,475	41,248	36,172	91,895
14	Sep-10	91,367	24,238	8,512	124,117
15	Sep-11	104,166	32,018	89,258	225,442
16	Sep-12	70,300	43,621	39,797	153,718
17	Sep-13	143,921	176,698	29,075	349,694
18	Sep-14	117,800	114,418	36,064	268,282
19	Sep-15	88,566	41,635	78,481	208,682
20	Sep-16	79,579	21,152	6,534	107,265
21	Sep-17	56,187	29,380	7,037	92,604
22	Sep-18	46,673	42,882	41,300	130,855
23	Sep-19	208,916	213,728	53,721	476,365
24	Sep-20	125,276	140,739	56,444	322,459
25	Sep-21	79,355	35,753	3,419	118,527
26	Sep-22	132,403	149,447	97,210	379,060
27	Sep-23	56,106	15,823		71,929
28	Sep-24	75,606	23,285	28,457	127,348
29	Sep-25	143,283	113,740	57,371	314,394
30	Sep-26	150,139	29,040	94,310	273,489
31	Sep-27	56,379	72,948	43,472	172,799
32	Sep-28	62,192	43,217	12,128	117,537
33	Sep-29	186,955	33,570	36,359	256,884
34	Grand Total	3,115,925	2,132,215	1,287,632	6,535,772

Figure 11-16: This pivot table shows daily totals for each branch.

Question 2

How many accounts were opened at each branch, broken down by account type?

Figure 11-17 shows a pivot table that answers this question.

- The AcctType field is in the Column Labels section.
- The Branch field is in the Row Labels section.
- The Amount field is in the Values section and is summarized by Count.

The most common summary function used in pivot tables is Sum. In this case, I changed the summary function to Count. To change the summary function to Count, right-click any cell in the Value area and choose Summarize Data By⇨Count from the shortcut menu.

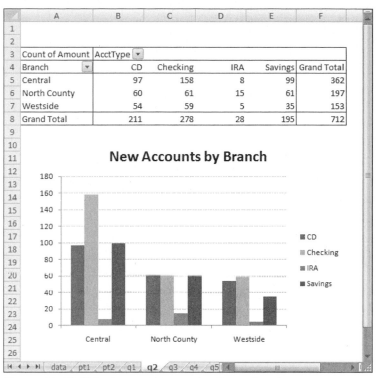

Figure 11-17: This pivot table uses the Count function to summarize the data.

What if you wanted a second chart (a pie chart) to show the data in the Grand Total column? You can't create a pivot chart from only a portion of the pivot table. To create this pie chart, you need to remove the Branch field from the pivot table and move the AcctType field to the Row Labels section. If you would like to show both charts together, you must create a second pivot table (or make a copy of the original one) and generate the pie chart from the second pivot table. Figure 11-18 shows the pivot table and pivot chart that show the number of accounts by account type.

Question 3

What's the dollar distribution of the different account types?

Figure 11-19 shows a pivot table that answers this question. For example, 253 of the new accounts were for an amount of $5,000 or less.

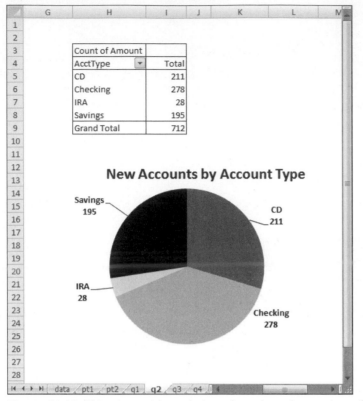

Figure 11-18: This pivot table and pivot chart show the number of new accounts by type, across all branches.

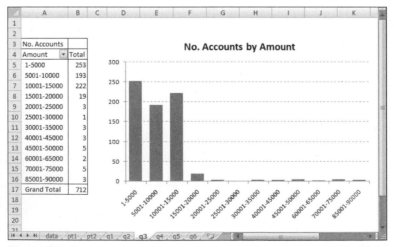

Figure 11-19: This pivot table counts the number of accounts that fall into each value range.

This pivot table uses only one field: Amount.

- The Amount field is in the Row Labels section (grouped).
- The Amount field is also in the Values section and is summarized by Count.

When I initially added the Amount field to the Row Labels section, the pivot table showed a row for each unique dollar amount. I right-clicked one of the row labels and selected Group. Then I used Excel's Grouping dialog box to set up bins of $5,000 increments.

The second instance of the Amount field (in the Values section) is summarized by Count. I right-clicked a value and chose Summarize Data By⇨Count.

Notice that the number of accounts for the larger dollar amounts is small. You may prefer to group these larger bins into a single bin of 20,001 or more. To do so, right-click any cell in the Amount column and choose Group. In the Grouping dialog box, specify 1 for the Start At value, 20,000 for the Ending At value, and 5,000 for the By value. Figure 11-20 shows the result. Notice that Excel incorrectly labels the last column as >20001. Technically, it should be >20000.

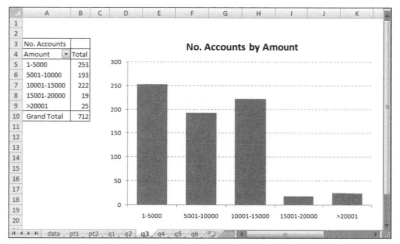

Figure 11-20: The pivot table and pivot chart after changing the grouping parameters.

Question 4

What types of accounts do tellers open most often?

Figure 11-21 shows that the most common account opened by tellers is a checking account.

- The OpenedBy field is in the Report Filters section.
- The AcctType field is in the Row Labels section.

- The Amount field is in the Values section (summarized by Count).

- A second instance of the Amount field is in the Values section (summarized by Percent of Total).

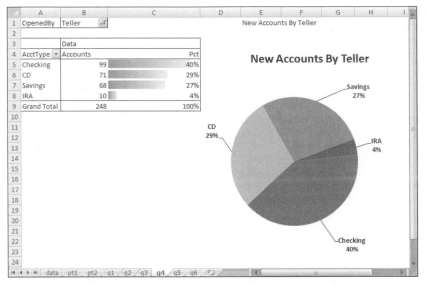

Figure 11-21: This pivot table uses a report filter to show only the teller data.

This pivot table uses the OpenedBy field as a report filter and is showing the data only for tellers. I sorted the pivot table rows so that the largest value is at the top, and I also used conditional formatting to display data bars for the percentages.

 CROSS-REFERENCE

Refer to Chapter 9 for more information about conditional formatting.

Using the data bars in the pivot table is an alternative to a pivot chart. However, a pie chart might be a better choice for this information. Note that the pivot chart's title is linked to cell E1, which contains this formula:

```
="New Accounts By "&B1
```

Using a linked formula enables you to make the chart's title more descriptive. If I select a different value for the Report Filter field, the chart's title updates accordingly. Without the linked formula, the pivot chart's title would always display Accounts.

Question 5

How does the Central branch compare to the other two branches?

Figure 11-22 shows a pivot table that sheds some light on this rather vague question. It simply shows how the Central branch compares to the other two branches combined.

- The AcctType field is in the Row Labels section.

- The Branch field is in the Column Labels section.

- The Amount field is in the Values section (summarized by Sum).

I grouped the North County and Westside branches together and named the group Other Branches. The pivot table (and pivot chart) shows the amount, by account type.

Part II

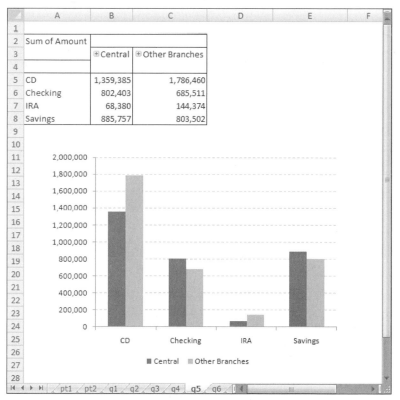

Figure 11-22: This pivot table (and pivot chart) compares the Central branch with the other two branches combined.

Question 6

In which branch do tellers open the most checking accounts for new customers?

Figure 11-23 shows a pivot table that answers this question. At the Central branch, tellers opened 23 checking accounts for new customers.

- The Customer field is in the Report Filters section.

- The OpenedBy field is in the Report Filters section.

- The AcctType field is in the Report Filters section.

- The Branch field is in the Row Labels section.

- The Amount field is in the Values section, summarized by Count.

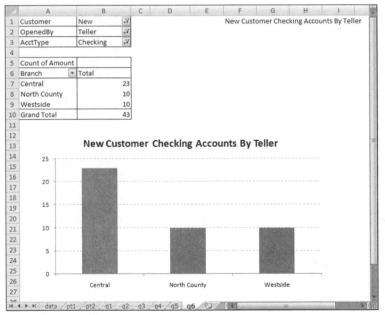

Figure 11-23: This pivot table uses three report filters.

This pivot table uses three report filters. The Customer field is filtered to show only New, the OpenedBy field is filtered to show only Teller, and the AcctType field is filtered to show only Checking.

The pivot table depicts the result graphically. Note that I used a linked formula for the chart's title to make the title more descriptive. The title is linked to cell F1, which contains the following formula that gets information from the three report filters:

```
=B1&" Customer "&B3&" Accounts By "&B2
```

More Pivot Chart Examples

The following sections present three additional examples of pivot tables and pivot charts.

Creating a Quick Frequency Distribution Chart

The example in this section describes how to use a pivot table to create a frequency distribution chart, sometimes known as a histogram. This technique works with values and text.

Figure 11-24 shows a workbook with ratings from a survey item. Column A consists of the respondent number (from 1 to 192), and column B contains the rating. The objective is to create a frequency distribution chart that shows the number of each rating response. Note that column A is not actually required. A frequency distribution can be created from a single column.

ON THE CD

This workbook, named `frequency distribution chart.xlsx`, is available on the companion CD-ROM.

	A	B	C	D
1	Respondent	Rating		
2	1	Good		
3	2	Very Good		
4	3	Very Good		
5	4	Good		
6	5	Good		
7	6	Poor		
8	7	Very Poor		
9	8	Good		
10	9	Excellent		
11	10	Very Good		
12	11	Very Good		
13	12	Good		
14	13	Poor		
15	14	Excellent		
16	15	Good		
17	16	Very Good		
18	17	Excellent		
19	18	Good		
20	19	Good		
21	20	Good		
22	21	Very Poor		
23	22	Excellent		
24	23	Good		
25	24	Good		
26	25	Very Good		
27	26	Good		
28	27	Good		

Sheet1 / Sheet2

Figure 11-24: A pivot chart can display the frequency of each response in column B.

To create the frequency distribution chart, follow these steps:

1. Select any cell in columns A or B.

2. Choose Insert⇨Tables⇨PivotTable to display the Create PivotTable dialog box.

3. In the Create PivotTable dialog box, verify that Excel identified the data range correctly, and specify the location for the pivot table and pivot chart. Click the OK button.

   Excel creates an empty pivot table and displays the PivotTable Field List.

4. On the PivotTable Field List, drag the Rating item to the Row Labels section, and then drag it again to the Values section.

5. Select any cell in the pivot table, and choose PivotTable Tools⇨Options⇨Tools⇨Pivot Chart to display the Insert Chart dialog box.

6. In the Insert Chart dialog box, select a chart type and click the OK button. (A clustered column chart is a good choice.)

Figure 11-25 shows the pivot table and pivot chart. Because the items in the Values section are non-numeric, Excel defaults to the Count summary method — which is exactly what I want.

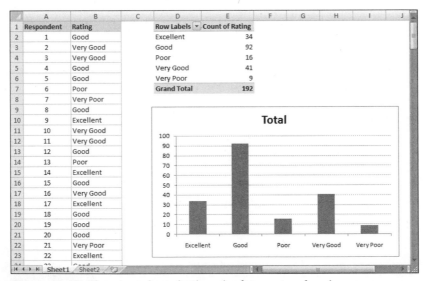

Figure 11-25: The pivot chart displays the frequency of each response.

Notice that the Rating items are listed in alphabetical order in the pivot table, and on the category axis of the pivot chart. To change the order of the items, you can either

- Click and drag the left or right border of an item in the pivot table, and drag it to a new position. The pivot chart will adjust accordingly.

- Just type the name of an item (for example, **Good**) in the cell where you want it, and let Excel rearrange the items.

If the data consists of numerical values, you might want to create groups (or bins). To do so, right-click the field button in the pivot table and choose Group. Then specify the parameters for the grouping. Figure 11-26 shows a frequency distribution for numeric data, with the results grouped. Note that the pivot table displays a count of the values. By default, the pivot table will display the sum. You'll need to change this by right-clicking a value in the pivot table and choosing Summarize Data By⇨Sum.

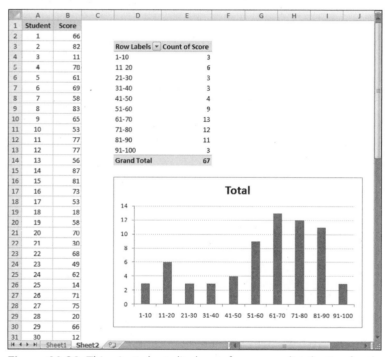

Figure 11-26: This pivot chart displays a frequency distribution for the data in column B, in groups of 10.

Selecting Rows to Plot

This section describes how to enable the user to determine which pivot table rows to display in a pivot chart. In other words, it's an interactive chart. Figure 11-27 shows a range of data — results from a customer survey. Each of the 450 customers responded to 14 survey items. Responses are coded as numbers:

1. Strongly Disagree

2. Disagree

3. Undecided

4. Agree

5. Strongly Agree

	A	B	C
1	Respondent	Item	Rating
2	1	Employees are friendly	5
3	1	Employees are helpful	2
4	1	Employees are knowledgeable	3
5	1	I like your TV ads	4
6	1	I like your web site	1
7	1	I would recommend your company	3
8	1	Overall, I am satisfied	1
9	1	Pricing is competitive	2
10	1	Store hours are convenient	3
11	1	Store locations are convenient	1
12	1	Stores are well-maintained	3
13	1	You are easy to reach by phone	1
14	1	You have a good selection of products	1
15	1	You sell quality products	2
16	2	Employees are friendly	5
17	2	Employees are helpful	3
18	2	Employees are knowledgeable	5
19	2	I like your TV ads	2
20	2	I like your web site	3
21	2	I would recommend your company	5
22	2	Overall, I am satisfied	1
23	2	Pricing is competitive	2
24	2	Store hours are convenient	3
25	2	Store locations are convenient	5
26	2	Stores are well-maintained	5
27	2	You are easy to reach by phone	3
28	2	You have a good selection of products	1

Sheet1 / Sheet2 /

Figure 11-27: This survey data will be converted to a pivot table.

 ON THE CD

The example in this section, named `survey results.xlsx`, is available on the companion CD-ROM.

The goal is to tabulate the survey results and display a chart that depicts the results for one or more of the survey items.

The first step is to create the pivot table. Follow these steps:

1. Select any cell within the data range and choose Insert⇨Tables⇨PivotTable.

2. Respond to the Create PivotTable dialog box, and create an empty pivot table.

3. Using the PivotTable Field List, drag the Item field to the Row Labels section.

4. Drag the Rating field to the Column Labels section.

5. Drag the Respondent field to the Values section.

6. In the pivot table, edit the column labels by replacing the values (1–5) with descriptive text.

7. Format the pivot table values to display as Percent of Row. Right-click any value and choose Summarize Data By⇨More Options. In the Value Field Settings dialog box, click the Show Values As tab, and select the % of Row option on the drop-down list.

Next, create a pivot chart by selecting any cell in the pivot table and choosing PivotTable Tools⇨Options⇨Tools⇨Pivot Chart.

Figure 11-28 shows the pivot table and pivot chart.

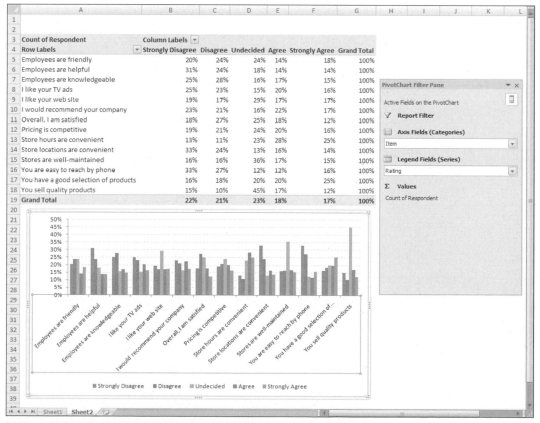

Figure 11-28: This pivot chart displays the results for all survey items.

The pivot chart is not very usable because it shows too much information. To limit the amount of information in the chart, use either of these methods:

- Click the drop-down arrow in the Row Labels header in the pivot table and deselect the Select All check box. Then, select one or more items to display. The change is reflected in the pivot chart.

- Activate the pivot chart, and use the Pivot Chart Filter Pane. Click the drop-down arrow labeled Axis Fields (Category) and deselect the Select All check box. Then, select one or more items to display. The change is reflected in the pivot table.

Using this filtering capability, the user can show the results for any single survey item, and even compare multiple items side by side. Figure 11-29 shows the pivot table and pivot chart after filtering the data to show three survey items.

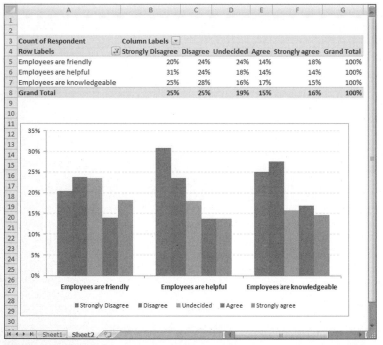

Figure 11-29: The pivot chart shows the results for only three items.

Using Data from Multiple Sheets

In some situations, you might have data in multiple worksheets within a workbook. Figure 11-30, for example, shows a workbook that contains three sheets, named Yr2005, Yr2006, and Yr2007. Each sheet contains data for a year, and each has a similar four-column range of cells. This is a simple example. In actual practice, the sheets would probably contain much more data. Also, keep in mind that the data can come from different workbooks.

	A	B	C	D	E
1	**Month**	**Income**	**Expenses**	**Ratio**	
2	Jan	98,085	42,874	30.42%	
3	Feb	98,698	44,167	30.92%	
4	Mar	102,403	43,349	29.74%	
5	Apr	106,044	43,102	28.90%	
6	May	105,361	45,005	29.93%	
7	Jun	105,729	44,216	29.49%	
8	Jul	105,557	43,835	29.34%	
9	Aug	109,669	41,952	27.67%	
10	Sep	107,233	44,071	29.13%	
11	Oct	105,048	43,185	29.13%	
12	Nov	107,446	44,403	29.24%	
13	Dec	105,001	45,129	30.06%	
14					
15					

Yr2005 Yr2006 Yr2007

Figure 11-30: This workbook contains data in three worksheets.

ON THE CD

This example, named `pivot chart from multiple sheets.xlsx`, is available on the companion CD-ROM.

You can create a pivot table to combine the information from these three sheets, although the procedure is certainly not obvious. This section describes how to create a pivot table and pivot chart to summarize the data in these three sheets.

Before Excel 2007, the PivotTable and PivotChart Wizard was used to created pivot tables. The Excel 2007 Ribbon interface has replaced this wizard. Unfortunately, the only way to create a pivot table from multiple data sources is to use this wizard. Here's how to add the missing PivotTable and PivotChart Wizard command to your Quick Access Toolbar (QAT):

1. Right-click the QAT, and choose Customize Quick Access Toolbar from the shortcut menu. Excel displays the Customize tab of the Excel Options dialog box.

2. In the drop-down control on the left, choose Commands Not in the Ribbon.

3. In the list below, select PivotTable and PivotChart Wizard.

4. Click the Add button to add the command to your QAT.

5. Click the OK button to close the Excel Options dialog box.

Now that you have access to the missing wizard, follow these steps:

1. Activate the Yr2005 worksheet.

2. Start the PivotTable and PivotChart Wizard by clicking its icon in your QAT. Choose the Multiple Consolidation Ranges option as well as the option to create a pivot table and a pivot chart. Click the Next button.

Part II

3. In Step 2 of the wizard, choose the Create a Single Page Field for Me option. Click the Next button.
4. In Step 2b of the wizard, you specify the ranges. Select range A1:D13 in the first worksheet and click the Add button. Repeat this step for the other sheets. The All Ranges box should display three ranges. Click the Next button.
5. In Step 3 of the wizard, specify New Worksheet and click the Finish button. In the pivot table, notice that the Report Filter displays generic item names (Item1, Item2, and Item3).
6. Using the PivotTable Field List, drag the Page1 field to the Row Labels section (above the Row item). Doing so converts the field to a Row field. You can now change the item's names to more meaningful text: 2005, 2006, and 2007.
7. The Grand Total column is not meaningful, so delete it. Choose PivotTable Tools➪Design➪Layout➪Grand Totals➪Off for Rows and Columns.

Figure 11-31 shows the pivot table and pivot chart after making these changes.

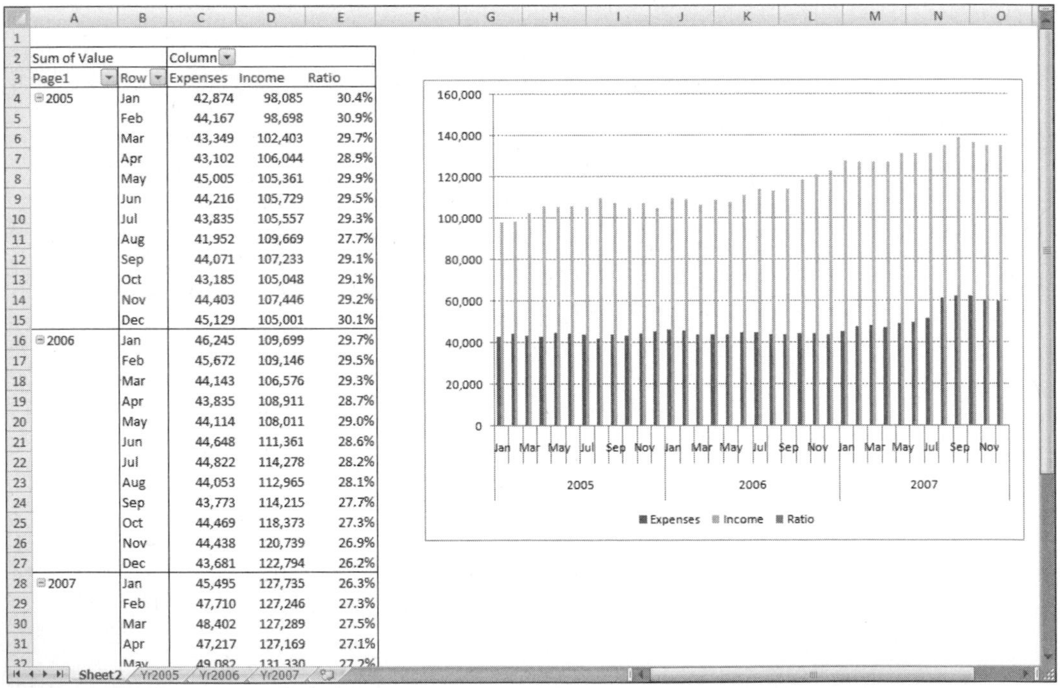

Sum of Value		Column		
Page1	Row	Expenses	Income	Ratio
2005	Jan	42,874	98,085	30.4%
	Feb	44,167	98,698	30.9%
	Mar	43,349	102,403	29.7%
	Apr	43,102	106,044	28.9%
	May	45,005	105,361	29.9%
	Jun	44,216	105,729	29.5%
	Jul	43,835	105,557	29.3%
	Aug	41,952	109,669	27.7%
	Sep	44,071	107,233	29.1%
	Oct	43,185	105,048	29.1%
	Nov	44,403	107,446	29.2%
	Dec	45,129	105,001	30.1%
2006	Jan	46,245	109,699	29.7%
	Feb	45,672	109,146	29.5%
	Mar	44,143	106,576	29.3%
	Apr	43,835	108,911	28.7%
	May	44,114	108,011	29.0%
	Jun	44,648	111,361	28.6%
	Jul	44,822	114,278	28.2%
	Aug	44,053	112,965	28.1%
	Sep	43,773	114,215	27.7%
	Oct	44,469	118,373	27.3%
	Nov	44,438	120,739	26.9%
	Dec	43,681	122,794	26.2%
2007	Jan	45,495	127,735	26.3%
	Feb	47,710	127,246	27.3%
	Mar	48,402	127,289	27.5%
	Apr	47,217	127,169	27.1%
	May	49,082	131,330	27.2%

Figure 11-31: The pivot table and pivot chart that summarizes data on three worksheets.

Excel creates a clustered column chart, which is not appropriate because the data in the Ratio series is much smaller in magnitude (and not even visible in the chart). To fix this pivot chart, follow these steps:

1. Use the PivotChart Filter Pane to display only one year. This makes the chart less cluttered and easier to work with.

2. Access the Format Data Series dialog box for the Ratio series and assign it to the secondary axis.

3. Select the Ratio series and choose PivotChart Tools⇨Design⇨Type⇨Change Chart Type. Change the series to a line series.

Figure 11-32 shows the pivot chart after making these changes.

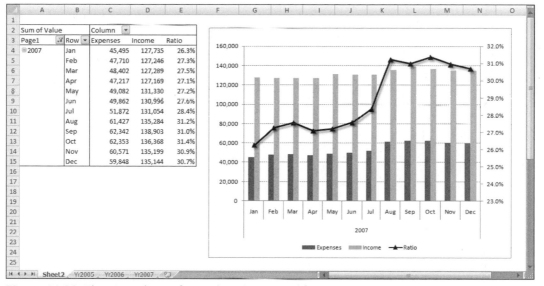

Figure 11-32: The pivot chart, after making some modifications.

Part II

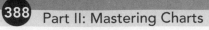

Chapter 12

Avoiding Common Chart-Making Mistakes

In This Chapter

◆ Various ways in which a chart can be inaccurate

◆ Potential problems related to using an inappropriate chart type

◆ Chart complexity

◆ Stylistic and aesthetic considerations

◆ A chart maker's checklist

In a perfect world, every chart you create is a work of art that communicates a message clearly, efficiently, and unambiguously. In the real world, of course, charts are subject to a wide variety of problems.

This chapter discusses some frequent problems related to charts, and it may help you avoid some common pitfalls — and create more effective charts.

Know Your Audience

Every chart has an audience or a potential audience. In some cases, the audience is only yourself. But in the majority of cases, the charts you produce will be viewed by others — in the context of your Excel workbook, or perhaps in the form of a PowerPoint presentation, part of a printed report, or a Web page. The finished product (that is, the chart) should be geared toward its intended audience.

389

Key points to consider include the following:

- **The accuracy of the data:** A chart can present data that is perfectly accurate, yet can be very misleading in a number of different ways.

- **The complexity of the information presented:** A general rule of thumb: Those higher in the corporate pecking order typically desire more simple information. When you're faced with a decision to make a simple chart or a complex chart, a simpler chart is often the better choice. In some cases you can make your point better by using multiple charts rather than a single complicated chart.

- **The appropriateness of the chart type:** Just about everyone can understand a simple column chart, but nontechnical types usually cringe at the sight of more esoteric charts such as a radar chart.

- **The overall "style" of the chart, ranging on a scale from informal to formal:** A chart intended for an employee newsletter will probably look much different than a chart prepared for a board of directors meeting.

- **The choice of colors used in the chart:** A chart that looks great in color may be incomprehensible when printed on a black-and-white printer, photocopied, or faxed.

The sections that follow expand upon these general points.

Chart Accuracy

When people view a chart, they almost always make the implicit assumption that the chart reflects the truth. In fact, an attractive chart may even *create* a sense of accuracy. After all, the chart maker surely wouldn't go through all that work if the numbers weren't accurate!

But, of course, truth is relative. The accuracy of the data that comprises the chart is a key consideration. Inaccurate data comes from measurement error and human error (including incorrect formulas in your worksheet). Only you can determine whether your data (and calculations that use the data) are accurate.

A chart can present a less-than-truthful picture in a number of ways. The sections that follow present examples that demonstrate various ways in which charts can mislead the viewer and possibly lead to incorrect conclusions.

 ON THE CD

The examples that follow are available on the companion CD-ROM. The filename is `misleading charts.xlsx`.

Is a chart really necessary?

Before you create a chart, you might ask yourself a simple question: Is a chart really necessary? The purpose of a chart is to present information. But, depending on your audience, a chart may not always be the *best* way to present your information. Before you assume that a chart is required, consider the alternatives and then make a decision.

For simple data, a nicely formatted text table may be a better option. The data in the accompanying figure, for example, does not reveal any significant changes over time, and it does not benefit by being viewed in the form of a chart.

Also, keep in mind that creating too many charts may simply overwhelm the audience. Viewing an endless series of charts that don't have a compelling message may even disrupt the viewers' attention and cause them to overlook the charts that *do* have a message.

Finally, don't forget about some potential chart alternatives. Chapter 9 covers some of the new conditional formatting options in Excel 2007. In some cases, using data bars, icons sets, or color scales may be better than using a chart.

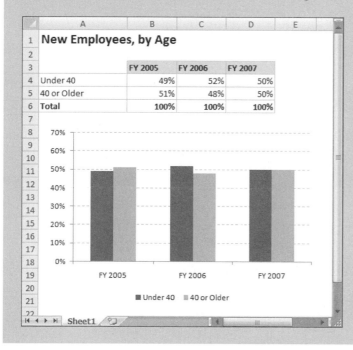

Part II

Plotting Data Out of Context

Typically, data that's presented in a chart should be presented in its proper context. Figure 12-1 shows an example. The top chart displays data for three months and leaves the impression that a downward trend in the numbers exists. But, when viewed in the context of the entire year, the last three data points do not seem at all out of the ordinary.

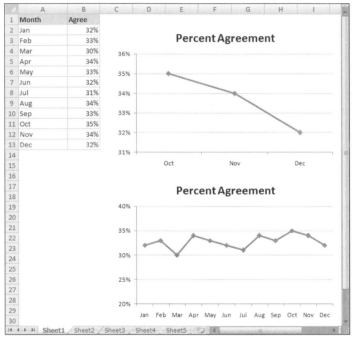

Figure 12-1: Plotting only the last three data points does not tell the entire story.

Exaggerating Differences or Similarities

The scale settings for the value axis of a chart can have a major effect on a chart's overall impact. Figure 12-2 shows two charts. Both charts display the same data, but they present dramatically different messages.

In the top chart, the value axis has a range of 14,000 units. In the bottom chart, the axis has a range of only 2,500 units, which causes the minor deviations in the data to be magnified.

Figure 12-3 shows another example of a misleading value axis scale. The casual viewer might conclude that the median home price had more than doubled in a six-month period. In fact, the July value is only 0.67% higher than the January value.

NOTE
I should point out that the median home price chart uses the default value axis scale. In other words, Excel does nothing to help prevent you from creating misleading charts.

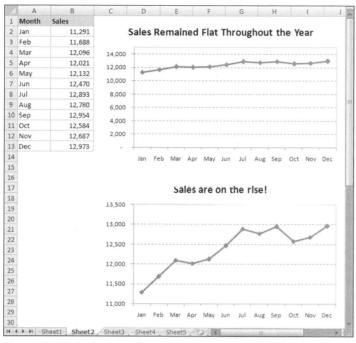

Figure 12-2: A chart's value axis can exaggerate differences in data points.

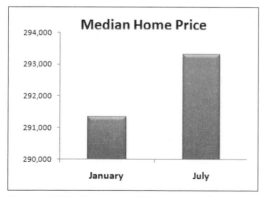

Figure 12-3: Fast-paced housing market, or misleading chart?

A chart's aspect ratio can also affect the chart's overall message. The term *aspect ratio* refers to the chart's width-to-height relationship. A "normal" aspect ratio is 4:3, which means that the chart is four units wide and three units high (this also corresponds to common computer display resolutions and non–widescreen TVs).

Figure 12-4 shows three line charts that display the same data. Even though the value axis scale is identical for the three charts, they present very different impressions of the data.

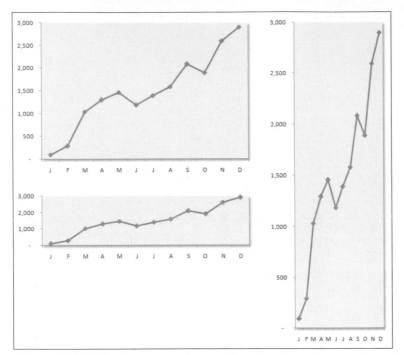

Figure 12-4: A chart's aspect ratio can affect the viewer's perception of the data.

Plotting Percent Change versus Actual Change

Time-based data is often summarized by calculating a percent change from one period to another. These percentage calculations do not take into account the magnitude of the values and can therefore mislead the viewer.

The chart in Figure 12-5 displays the percentage change for three products. Product C, of course, stands out in the chart — even though its values are almost insignificant when compared to the other products. The data is completely accurate, yet the chart is very misleading. Creating a chart from the data in columns B and C would be a much better choice.

Grouping with Unequal Bin Sizes

Figure 12-6 shows another example of a misleading chart. Both charts display a histogram of the same data: the ages of a group of 100 people. The only difference in the charts is the size of the bins. Although both charts are technically accurate, the top chart uses bins of unequal size and conveys the impression that younger people dominate the group. The bottom chart uses equal-size bins and presents a more accurate picture of the age distribution.

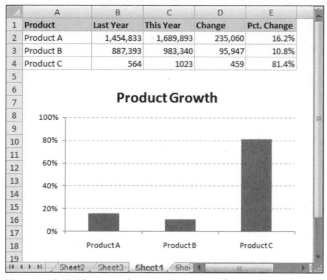

Figure 12-5: Plotting changes in terms of percentage can lead to incorrect conclusions.

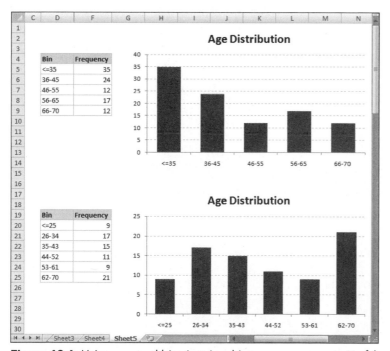

Figure 12-6: Using unequal bin sizes in a histogram can present a false impression of the data.

Problems with Chart Type Selection

As you know, Excel offers a wide variety of chart types. Selecting the most appropriate chart type for a particular set of data is sometimes difficult. The following sections present examples of potential problems that stem from using an incorrect chart type.

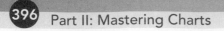

ON THE CD

The examples in this section are available on the companion CD-ROM. The filename is `chart type problems.xlsx`.

Category versus Value Axis

A common problem with charts stems from confusion between a category axis and a value axis. This topic is covered in Chapter 4, but it's worth revisiting.

Common chart types, such as a column chart, line chart, area chart, and bar chart, all use a standard category axis. Usually, a category axis does not convey any numerical information. A scatter chart, on the other hand, uses two value axes, both of which convey numerical information. In addition, a line chart can use a date-based scale which, in effect, gives the chart two value axes.

Figure 12-7 shows a worksheet with a company's net income data for seven periods of time, along with a line chart that plots the numbers. Note that the year increments are not equal. The chart is misleading because the last three data points use a different time interval, and the chart gives the false impression that net income growth has slowed considerably. The use of a line chart usually implies a continuous stream of data — which is not the case with this chart.

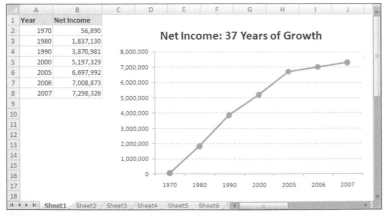

Figure 12-7: Using a line chart for this data presents an incorrect picture of the growth.

Figure 12-8 presents a more accurate picture of the growth. The chart in this figure is a line chart, but I specified that the horizontal axis is a date axis. Therefore, Excel treats the horizontal scale as numeric. To change the horizontal axis type of a line chart, select the axis and press Ctrl+1 to display the Format Axis dialog box. Click the Axis Options tab, and make the change in the Axis Type section.

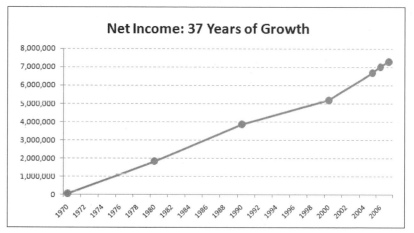

Figure 12-8: Using a date axis for the line chart treats the years as values.

Because the years aren't entered as dates, Excel treats these year values as days. In actual practice, it makes no difference. The key point is that the values are treated as numbers rather than arbitrary text.

 NOTE
Another way to correct the chart is to use a scatter chart instead of a line chart.

Problems with Pie Charts

Pie charts are one of the most commonly used chart types. A single pie chart is often appropriate, as long as the number of categories is kept to a reasonable number. Often, however, people present multiple pie charts to make a comparison.

Figure 12-9 shows an example. This group of charts suffers from several problems. The charts essentially look identical. With no numerical labels, the viewer cannot draw any conclusions. But more important, the charts provide no clue as to the total "value" of each pie.

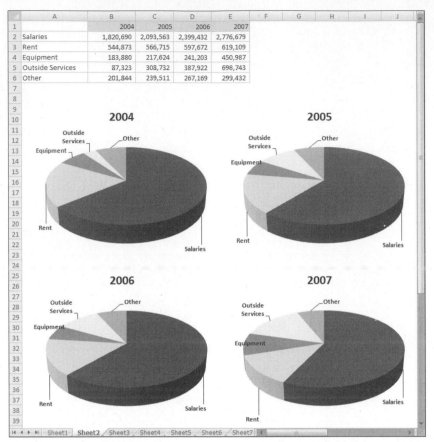

	A	B	C	D	E	F	G	H	I	J
1		2004	2005	2006	2007					
2	Salaries	1,820,690	2,093,563	2,399,432	2,776,679					
3	Rent	544,873	566,715	597,672	619,109					
4	Equipment	183,880	217,624	241,203	450,987					
5	Outside Services	87,323	308,732	387,922	698,743					
6	Other	201,844	239,511	267,169	299,432					

Figure 12-9: It's virtually impossible to make comparisons by using multiple pie charts.

Three alternatives are shown in Figure 12-10. Any of these charts is superior to the four pie charts. The stacked column chart (lower left) provides all the information in the pie charts; it also allows the viewer to make overall comparisons by year. The two clustered column charts also present all of the data. One is useful for comparing expenses across years; the other is useful for comparing expenses within each year.

A common problem is that pie charts often have too many slices. Figure 12-11 shows a pie chart that was published on the Web by a federal government agency.

NOTE

The chart in the figure is my reproduction of the chart. It's not identical to the original chart (which was created in Excel), but it's very close.

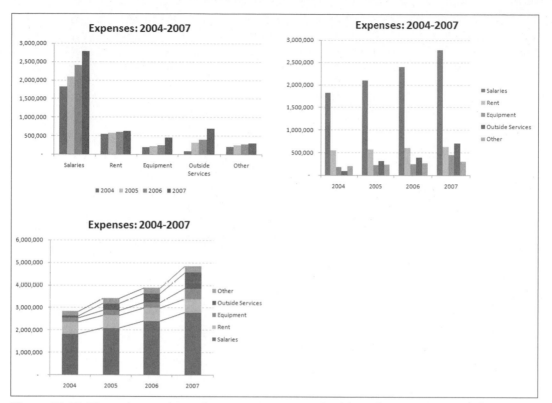

Figure 12-10: These three-column chart variations are preferable to four pie charts.

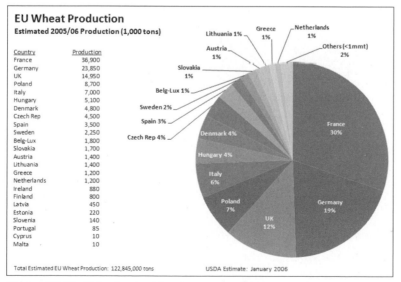

Figure 12-11: This pie chart has too many slices.

Part II

This chart certainly conveys the information, but most would agree that 17 slices in a pie chart is excessive. Figure 12-12 shows a possible makeover that retains all the original information, yet doesn't appear as cluttered. The pie chart displays a slice only if the country has a production of 5,000 or more. The other countries are grouped together. I inserted a shape (named Right Brace 3) to the right of the table of data so that the reader can easily see the countries that make up the Others group. That table of data, by the way, is a range that was copied and then pasted as a picture (using Home⇨Clipboard⇨Paste⇨As Picture⇨ Paste as Picture).

Figure 12-13 show another alternative to the cluttered pie chart: A bar chart. This chart shows all the numerical information from the original chart and is very uncluttered. In fact, the large area of white space is a perfect spot for the chart title and note. The vertical axis labels (country name and production amount) consist of a range that was copied and pasted as a picture. Excel cannot handle multicolumn vertical axis labels very well, but creating pseudo axis labels with a picture of range worked well in this case.

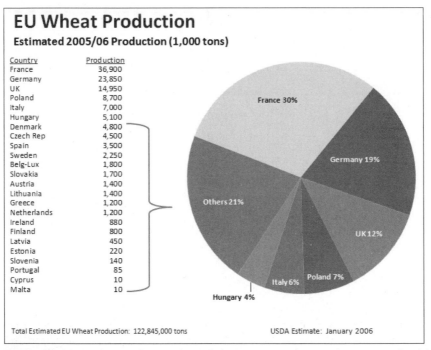

Figure 12-12: Reducing the number of slices in a pie chart makes it more legible.

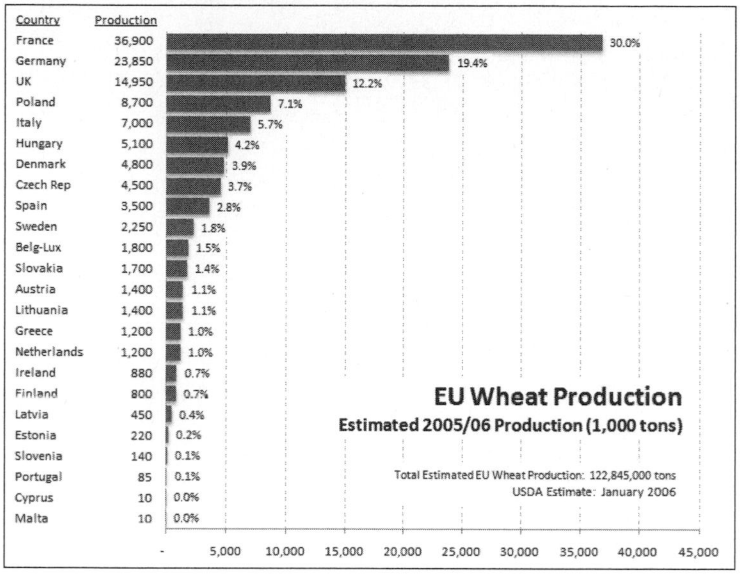

Country	Production		
France	36,900		30.0%
Germany	23,850		19.4%
UK	14,950		12.2%
Poland	8,700		7.1%
Italy	7,000		5.7%
Hungary	5,100		4.2%
Denmark	4,800		3.9%
Czech Rep	4,500		3.7%
Spain	3,500		2.8%
Sweden	2,250		1.8%
Belg-Lux	1,800		1.5%
Slovakia	1,700		1.4%
Austria	1,400		1.1%
Lithuania	1,400		1.1%
Greece	1,200		1.0%
Netherlands	1,200		1.0%
Ireland	880		0.7%
Finland	800		0.7%
Latvia	450		0.4%
Estonia	220		0.2%
Slovenia	140		0.1%
Portugal	85		0.1%
Cyprus	10		0.0%
Malta	10		0.0%

EU Wheat Production
Estimated 2005/06 Production (1,000 tons)

Total Estimated EU Wheat Production: 122,845,000 tons
USDA Estimate: January 2006

- 5,000 10,000 15,000 20,000 25,000 30,000 35,000 40,000 45,000

Figure 12-13: Using a bar chart instead of a pie chart.

Consider Alternative Chart Types

Whenever you create a pie chart, ask yourself a question: *Is a pie chart really necessary?* Figure 12-14 shows a handsome pie chart, complete with a "plastic" 3-D look. It looks great (especially in color), and certainly attracts attention. Rather than focus on the data, perhaps the first question viewers will have is, *How did you make that chart?*

The figure also shows the source data for the pie chart — including conditional formatting data bars. The small range of data actually conveys more information than the fancy pie chart.

Problems with Negative Values

Some chart types don't handle negative numbers as you might expect. For example, a pie chart (or a doughnut chart) simply converts all negative values to positive values. This, of course, is rarely what you want. Figure 12-15 shows a pie chart that presents an incorrect view of the data. The only way the reader would know that Net Domestic Migration is negative is by making note of the negative sign in the data label.

Part II

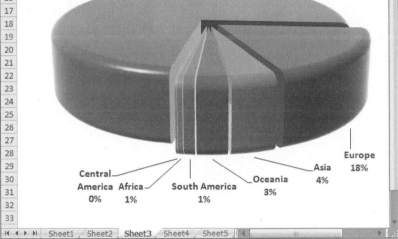

Figure 12-14: A pie chart with lots of eye appeal.

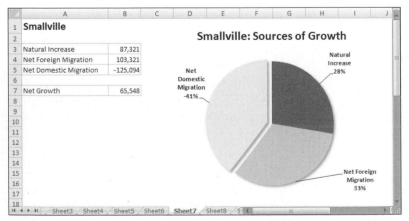

Figure 12-15: The pie chart converts negative values to positive values.

Figure 12-16 shows the same data presented in a column chart and in a stacked column chart. Although the stacked column chart does put the negative value below the category axis scale, the chart is still somewhat misleading because the stacked columns imply that the total is just under 200,000. The clustered column chart clearly presents the most accurate picture of this data. However, it requires a text box to indicate the net growth amount.

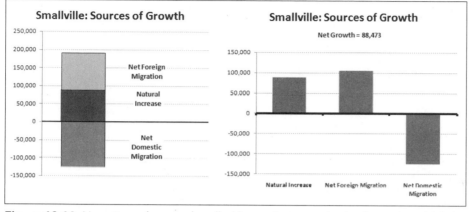

Figure 12-16: Negative values are handled better by a standard column chart (right).

Scatter Charts with the Smoothed Line Option

When you create a scatter chart, you have an option to connect the points with a straight line. Another option is to create a "smoothed line." When the Smoothed Line option is in effect, the data markers are connected with a line that contains curves.

Figure 12-17 shows two scatter charts that plot the same data. One uses straight lines and the other uses the Smoothed Lines option. Note that the chart on the bottom is deceiving. The chart shows the data extending below zero, even though none of the Y data values is less than zero. In addition, the line extends above the 1.5 value, even though the largest value is 1.5.

Don't Be Tempted by 3-D Charts

Excel's 3-D charts have a special appeal because they often seem more artistic and add a bit of pizzazz to an otherwise boring presentation. But, when all is said and done, 3-D charts offer few real advantages — and lead to quite a few potential problems. I won't say that you should *never* use 3-D charts, but you should understand their weaknesses.

Three-dimensional charts are often acceptable if your goal is to show general relationships and complete accuracy is not required. But for technical charts in which the viewer may want to make detailed comparisons, a 2-D chart is always preferable. Figure 12-18 shows a 3-D line chart with three data series. What's the value of the Qtr-3 data point for the WA series? Which series has the highest value in Qtr-2? These questions cannot be answered by looking at the chart.

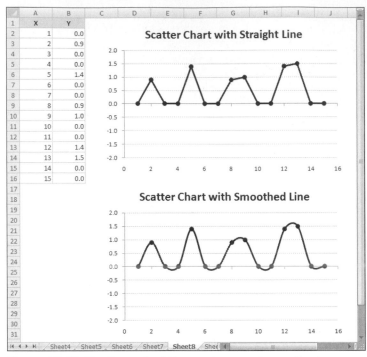

Figure 12-17: The Smoothed Line option can distort the data.

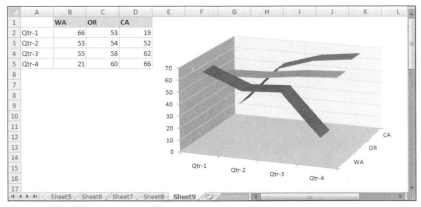

Figure 12-18: A 3-D chart can depict general relationships — sometimes.

With 3-D charts, you always have the possibility of hidden data (see Figure 12-19). Can you determine the Qtr-1 value for CA? You can rotate the chart or change the order of the series, but changing the chart type is probably the best solution — unless, of course, your goal is to keep the data hidden!

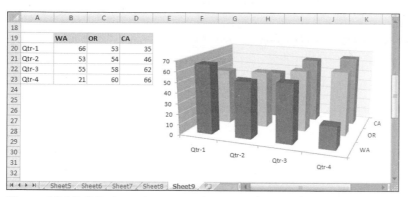

Figure 12-19: 3-D charts have a tendency to obscure data.

And for those who really want to obscure their data, Excel enables you to add perspective distortion, as shown in Figure 12-20. This setting, in effect, displays the chart as if viewed through a very wide-angle lens.

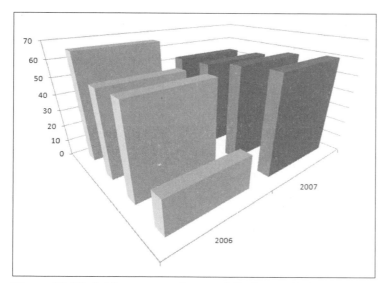

Figure 12-20: Adding perspective to a 3-D chart makes it even more difficult to understand.

Chart Complexity

The KISS principle (*Keep It Simple, Stupid*) is particularly applicable to charts. The main purpose of a chart, after all, is to present information in a manner that makes the information easy to understand. A chart that is unnecessarily complex defeats the purpose.

ON THE CD

The examples in this section are available on the companion CD-ROM. The filename is `chart complexity.xlsx`.

Just Plain Bad

We've all seen charts like the one in Figure 12-21. This chart is so bad that it doesn't even deserve further discussion.

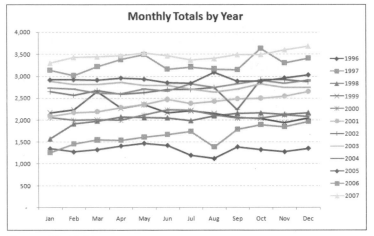

Figure 12-21: No comment.

Maximizing "Data Ink"

Edward R. Tufte, author of several books that deal with the visual presentation of data, refers to the principle of *data ink maximization*. Simply put, this principle states that the most effective charts use their "ink" to display data — not chart accoutrements such as grid lines and labels. Consequently, nonessential chart elements can often be deleted with little or no adverse affect on the readability of the chart.

Figure 12-22 shows a typical column chart, and a "minimalist" version of the chart below it. There's certainly nothing wrong with the original version of this chart. The chart on the right, however, removes all nonessential elements — and the basic message remains. The chart on the right underwent the following modifications:

- The plot area fill color was removed.

- The gridlines were removed.

- The category axis was hidden.

- The axis labels were removed

- Data labels were added to the bottom of the columns.

- The value axis number format was simplified, and minor unit tick marks were displayed.

- The chart's title was changed to reflect the scale units and eliminate the superfluous reference to the years.

- The chart's title was moved into the plot area, where it also serves as the axis title.

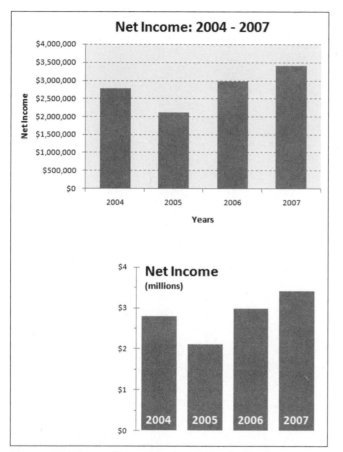

Figure 12-22: A column chart before and after removing all nonessential elements.

Another chart makeover is shown in Figure 12-23. This chart started as an area chart, and the modified version is a line chart. Adding color to the area below each line really adds nothing to the chart. Other modifications are as follows:

- The plot area fill color was removed.

- The vertical gridlines were removed.

- The horizontal gridlines use a lighter color and display dashes.

- The value axis was moved to the right side of the chart, closer to the line segments that represent the more recent (and more relevant) data.

- The value axis number format was simplified.

- The legend was replaced with text boxes that identify each line.

- The category axis was simplified to display fewer labels.

- The title was simplified to eliminate the superfluous reference to the years and moved inside the plot area.

- The "Adjusted for inflation" note was moved to the bottom of the plot area and reduced in size.

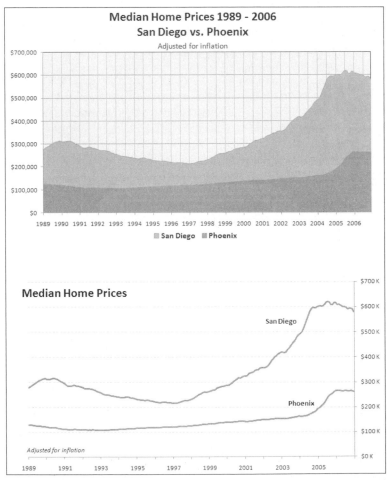

Figure 12-23: An area chart before and after removing all nonessential elements.

The modified chart conveys all the information of the original chart in an (arguably) more efficient manner.

Chart Style

When someone views a chart, he or she often has an immediate reaction to it, and that reaction is due in large part to the overall style or appearance of the chart. Does it look inviting, or is it a jumbled mess?

To paraphrase Plato, beauty is in the eye of the beholder. A chart that looks terrible to me may look great to you. That said, following are some general aesthetic guidelines to keep in mind when creating charts:

- Don't let design elements detract from the chart. For example, if you use a clip art image in a chart's plot area, make sure that the image is relevant to the chart's subject matter and is not overpowering.

- For time-based data, the standard arrangement (at least for most Western cultures) is left to right. If you must use a bar chart with a vertical category axis, arrange the time-based categories from top to bottom.

- In general, avoid using colors that aren't part of the document theme. The theme colors were selected because they look good together. And if the user switches to a different theme, non–theme colors aren't changed — which means that the color combination will probably be less than satisfactory.

- If possible, avoid using vertically oriented text.

- If you display gridlines, make sure that they don't overpower the chart. Often, using a gray dashed line is sufficient.

- If you're using multiple charts, it is critical that they all have the same "look." This includes elements such as color, font, number formatting, sizing, and so on.

Text and Font Mistakes

Quite a few chart elements can contain text: titles, axis labels, legends, data labels, and so on. Perhaps the most common problem is too much text on a chart. A chart should stand on its own, and lengthy explanatory text should not be necessary (see Figure 12-24).

ON THE CD

The examples in this section are available on the companion CD-ROM. The filename is `text problems.xlsx`.

A very common problem with Excel charts is displaying text correctly on the category axis. The problem is that lengthy text often doesn't fit, and Excel automatically rotates the text.

Figure 12-25 shows an example of a chart in which the category axis text has been rotated. The main problem is that the text takes up an inordinate amount of space in the chart, at the expense of the plot area.

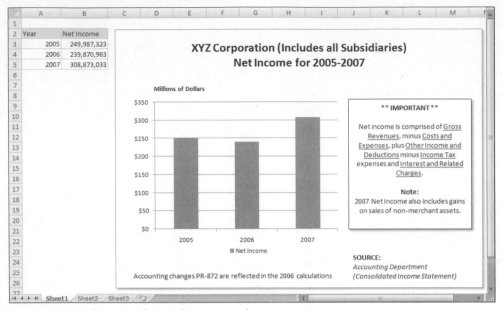

Figure 12-24: There's a chart in here somewhere.

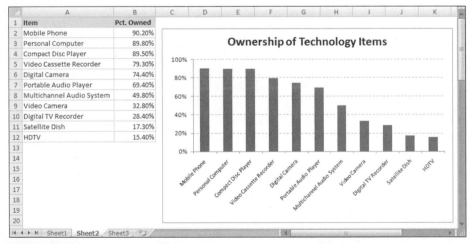

Figure 12-25: A common problem is text in category axis labels.

Excel adjusts the orientation automatically, based on its algorithms. For more control over the axis text, access the Format Axis dialog box and click the Alignment tab. You can then force the text alignment to be a specific angle (0 degrees results in normal horizontally oriented text).

After making this change, you might find that Excel skips some of the axis labels. You can force all axis labels to be displayed by using the Axis Option tab of the Format Axis dialog box. Specify a value of 1 for the Interval Between Labels setting. Then, you can adjust the font size, plot area width, and chart width to ensure that all category axis labels are displayed properly and not at an angle (see Figure 12-26). Note that I had to make the chart much wider. Excel does not wrap the text in the category labels unless the chart is wide enough to accommodate the labels. Otherwise, the text is displayed at an angle.

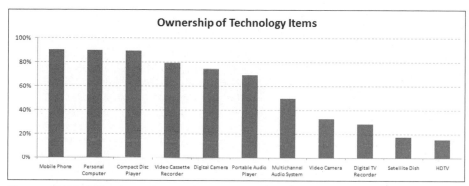

Figure 12-26: Adjusting a few settings ensures that the text is displayed horizontally.

NOTE

Another option, of course, is to use a bar chart instead of a column chart. Figure 12-27 shows the column chart after converting it to a bar chart.

Font mistakes generally fall into one or more of the following categories:

- **Too many different font faces:** One font per chart almost always works.

- **Poor choice of fonts:** When in doubt, use the default font for the active document theme.

- **Poor choice of font sizes:** All text should be large enough to be legible. Use bold or italic to draw attention to a particular element.

- **All uppercase or all lowercase text:** Text in a chart should generally be "proper" case, like the title of a book.

The chart in Figure 12-28 demonstrates all these problems.

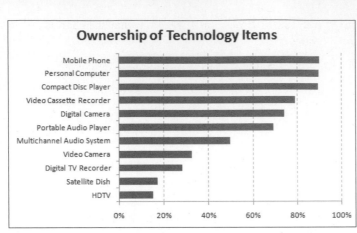

Figure 12-27: A bar chart is a better choice if you have lengthy category labels.

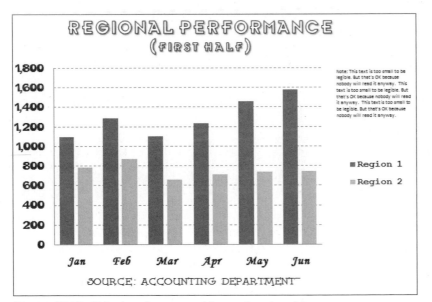

Figure 12-28: This chart has several font-related problems.

A Chart Maker's Checklist

You collected the data, sliced it and diced it, and summarized it in the form of several charts. Before you unleash your creation on the world (or your boss), take a minute to review the following items:

- Does the chart actually convey a message? If your boss asks you what the chart is telling him, will you have an answer?

- On the "formality" scale, is the overall look and tone of the chart appropriate for its intended audience?

- Is the data accurate? Have you double-checked your formulas?

- Is the chart type the most appropriate chart type for the data? Have you even considered using another type?

- If it's a pie chart, have you considered any alternatives?

- If it's a 3-D chart, can the viewer actually derive the values for each data point?

- Could anything about the chart possibly be misleading? Confusing? Not clear?

- Are your axes correct? If you use numerical values for a category axis, are the categories at equal intervals?

- Does the value axis scale for a bar or column chart start at zero?

- Is anything in the chart not necessary?

- Is the chart legible when printed on a non–color printer? When photocopied? When faxed?

- Is the numeric scale of the value axis identified (for example, thousands or millions)?

- Is the measurement unit specified?

- If your chart uses two value axes, can the viewer easily identify the appropriate axis for each series?

- If you're creating multiple charts, do they all have a similar look? Do they use the same color scheme? Same fonts and text sizes?

- Does the chart still look presentable if the user applies a new document theme? To change the document theme, choose Page Layout➪Themes➪Theme.

- Is all the text readable?

- Is all the text necessary? Can it be shortened?

- Does the text use more than one type font? If so, consider using a single font from the current document theme.

- Does the text use all uppercase or all lowercase letters?

- Are the words spelled correctly?

Chapter 13

Just for Fun

In This Chapter

- ◆ Some amusing and recreational aspects of charting
- ◆ Animated charts using VBA

Although Excel is used primarily for serious applications, many users discover that this product has a lighter side. This is especially apparent in the area of charts and graphics. Although the topics discussed here deal with nonserious applications of graphics in Excel, you'll quite possibly discover some techniques that you can apply to your more serious charting efforts.

 NOTE
All of the examples in this chapter are on the companion CD-ROM, and many of these examples use macros. I don't discuss the programming aspects in this chapter, but the VBA projects are all unprotected, so a password is not needed if you'd like to view and experiment with the code. Depending on your settings, you may receive a security warning when the workbook is opened. Be assured that these files are virus-free.

Animating Stuff

When people think of animation software, Excel certainly isn't the first application that comes to mind. But, with the aid of some relatively simple macros, you can coax some crude animations out of Excel.

415

NOTE

If you're a VBA programmer, be aware that the "secret" to producing animations in Excel is to use the following VBA statement within a loop:

```
DoEvents
```

This statement causes a refresh of the screen. Without this statement, the results of your animation code are not displayed until the macro ends — which pretty much defeats the purpose of animation! Also, I've found that animations that work fine in previous versions of Excel often require an additional `DoEvents` statement in Excel 2007.

Animated Shapes

Chapter 6 covers the wonderful world of shapes. If you've played around with shapes, you may enjoy seeing them in action. Create an AutoShape, add a touch of 3-D formatting, and toss in a VBA macro. You have a recipe for a simple animation.

The practical applications are limited or maybe even nonexistent. But most people are amazed to discover that you can do this sort of thing in Excel, and it's a good way to take a break from number crunching.

ON THE CD

The examples in this section are available on the companion CD-ROM. The filenames are `bouncing shapes.xlsm` and `rotating shape.xlsm`.

Figure 13-1 shows three shapes that bounce around inside of a cell. The code is written such that you can add more shapes. The speed of the bouncing depends on your processor speed and the complexity of the shapes. For example, if you use a gradient fill, 3-D formatting, or a shadow, the action takes place at a much slower speed because Excel must do additional calculations before rendering the shapes.

The shape in the worksheet in Figure 13-2 rotates. You select which axes to rotate by using the check boxes. Notice that the text rotates along with the shape, and the text has depth. As the shape rotates, the depth of the text becomes apparent.

Animated Charts

When you get tired of watching the animated shapes, turn your attention to animated charts. A relatively simple macro can convert a chart into an action-packed piece of entertainment. The macros in these examples increment the value in a cell. This cell is then used in formulas that are displayed in the chart.

Figure 13-3 shows an example of an animated chart. This is a 3-D line chart. When animated, the effect is reminiscent of bird wings in flight.

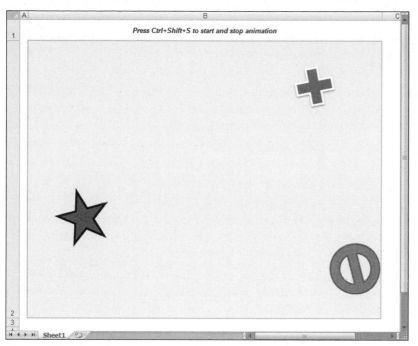

Figure 13-1: The shapes rotate and bounce around inside the box.

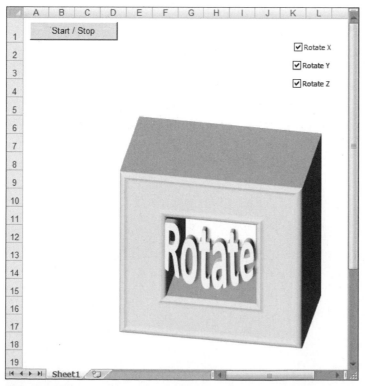

Figure 13-2: This shape rotates along any of three axes.

ON THE CD

The companion CD-ROM includes this animated chart, plus several other examples. The filename is `animated charts.xlsm`.

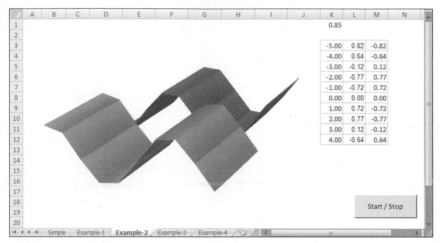

Figure 13-3: These two 3-D line chart series get animated with the help of a VBA macro.

Doughnut Chart Wheel of Fortune

Round and round it goes. Where it stops, nobody knows.

Figure 13-4 shows a doughnut chart with 12 data points, set up like a carnival wheel of fortune. The numbers are data labels, and the slices were formatted individually to get the alternating color effect.

Click the button to kick off a macro that systematically changes the angle of the first slice, which results in a rotating chart. The difficult part was programming the macro so that the spinning gradually slows before the wheel comes to a stop.

ON THE CD

This example, named `doughnut chart spinner.xlsm`, is available on the companion CD-ROM.

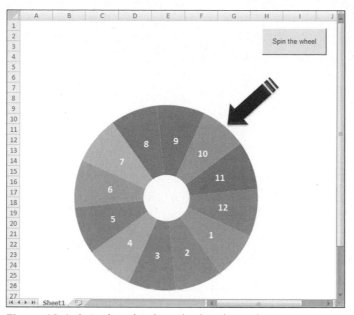

Figure 13-4: Spin the wheel — uh, doughnut chart.

Fun with Trigonometry

Charts that plot data generated by trigonometric functions can be stunning. Even if you don't know the difference between a SIN function and a stop sign, you can still create some incredible designs.

A Simple Sine-versus-Cosine Plot

I start with a simple example. The scatter chart in Figure 13-5 plots the data in column B against the data in column C (the chart axes are hidden). Column A contains formulas that generate a sequence of numbers, using the increment value in cell A1.

 ON THE CD

This example, named `plot sin and cosine.xlsx`, is available on the companion CD-ROM.

The formula in B3, which is copied to 99 cells below it, is as follows:

```
=SIN(A3)
```

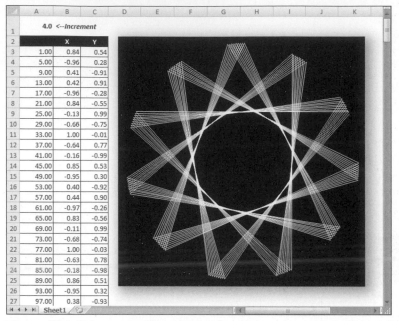

	A	B	C	D	E	F	G	H	I	J	K
1	4.0 <--Increment										
2		X	Y								
3	1.00	0.84	0.54								
4	5.00	-0.96	0.28								
5	9.00	0.41	-0.91								
6	13.00	0.42	0.91								
7	17.00	-0.96	-0.28								
8	21.00	0.84	-0.55								
9	25.00	-0.13	0.99								
10	29.00	-0.66	-0.75								
11	33.00	1.00	-0.01								
12	37.00	-0.64	0.77								
13	41.00	-0.16	-0.99								
14	45.00	0.85	0.53								
15	49.00	-0.95	0.30								
16	53.00	0.40	-0.92								
17	57.00	0.44	0.90								
18	61.00	-0.97	-0.26								
19	65.00	0.83	-0.56								
20	69.00	-0.11	0.99								
21	73.00	-0.68	-0.74								
22	77.00	1.00	-0.03								
23	81.00	-0.63	0.78								
24	85.00	-0.18	-0.98								
25	89.00	0.86	0.51								
26	93.00	-0.95	0.32								
27	97.00	0.38	-0.93								

Figure 13-5: This scatter chart plots various values generated with the SIN and COS functions.

The formula in C3, which is also copied to the cells below, is as follows:

```
=COS(A3)
```

The chart looks dramatically different with various increment values in cell A1. Figure 13-6 shows the chart when cell A1 contains 4.2. To display various geometric shapes, use a formula in the form of the following, varying the value of *n*. For example, when *n* is 4, the chart displays an octagon.

```
=PI()/n
```

Hypocycloid Charts

Figure 13-7 shows a scatter chart that displays "hypocycloid" curves. A hypocycloid curve is defined as follows:

> *The curve produced by fixed point P on the circumference of a small circle of radius b rolling around the inside of a large circle of radius a > b*

In other words, this type of curve is the same as that generated by Hasbro's popular Spirograph toy, which you may remember from your childhood.

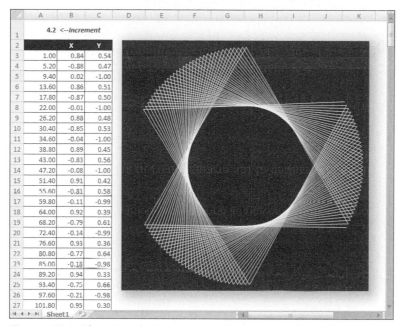

Figure 13-6: Changing the increment value causes a dramatic change in the chart.

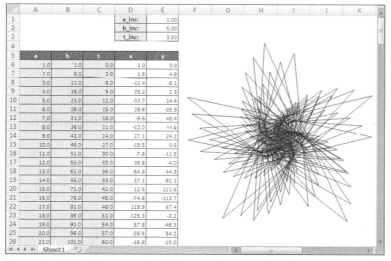

Figure 13-7: This hypocycloid chart is driven by the three parameters in column E.

The formulas that generate the data used in the series are rather complex, but they use three parameters, stored in E1:E3. Change any of these parameters, and you get a completely different design. I guarantee that you will be amazed by the variety of charts that you can generate — some of them are simply stunning. Figure 13-8 shows a few more examples.

Part II

ON THE CD
The companion CD-ROM contains two versions of this file. The first, named
`hypocycloid chart.xlsx`, enables you to change the parameters manually.
A more sophisticated version (`hypocycloid chart - animated.xlsm`) uses
macros to randomly generate parameter values and even has an animation option.

Figure 13-8: Four examples of hypocycloid charts.

Radar Chart Designs

The chart in Figure 13-9 is a radar chart with three series. The chart has 360 axes, which represent the degrees in a circle. The axes are hidden. If they were visible, they would completely overwhelm the chart.

Data for the three series is generated by formulas in columns B:D. These formulas use trigonometric functions and depend on the values in column A and the three adjustment parameters in B1:B3. These cells are linked to Scroll Bar controls. Manipulating the scroll bars results in many variations on the design.

Part II

ON THE CD

This workbook, named `radar chart designs.xlsx`, is available on the companion CD-ROM.

	A	B	C	D	E	F	G	H	I	J	K
1	Adjust1	49									
2	Adjust2	47									
3	Adjust3	48									
4											
5		Series1	Series2	Series3							
6	0	1.00	4.70	3.42							
7	49	0.66	5.45	3.07							
8	98	-0.14	5.69	2.84							
9	147	-0.84	5.24	2.93							
10	196	-0.96	4.42	3.90							
11	245	-0.42	3.79	4.66							
12	294	0.41	3.79	4.74							
13	343	0.96	4.41	3.21							
14	392	0.85	5.23	3.56							
15	441	0.16	5.69	3.81							
16	490	-0.64	5.47	2.77							
17	539	-1.00	4.72	1.52							
18	588	-0.67	3.96	2.80							
19	637	0.12	3.71	3.24							
20	686	0.83	4.14	2.62							
21	735	0.97	4.96	1.63							
22	784	0.44	5.60	1.69							
23	833	-0.39	5.62	2.33							
24	882	-0.95	5.01	0.19							
25	931	-0.86	4.18	0.36							
26	980	-0.17	3.72	1.67							

Figure 13-9: Creating designs with a radar chart.

Chart Art

Sometimes a chart can resemble a picture. This section presents two examples of chart art (and I use the term *art* loosely).

A Mountain Range Chart

One day I was working with an area chart, and it occurred to me that the chart resembled a mountain range. I quickly abandoned my original task and set out to create the ultimate mountain range chart. The result is shown in Figure 13-10 (it looks better in color). Okay, I cheated. The moon and stars are actually shapes.

ON THE CD

This workbook, named `mountain ranges.xlsx`, is available on the companion CD-ROM.

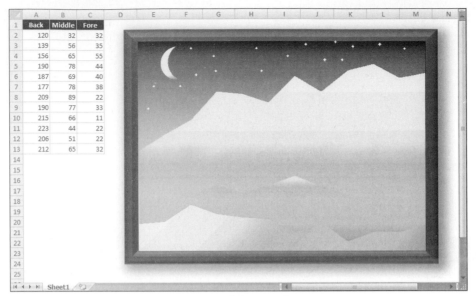

Figure 13-10: Creating a mountain out of an area chart.

A Bubble Chart Mouse Head

Work with bubble charts long enough and you may start seeing faces take shape. Figure 13-11 shows a cartoon-like mouse face made up of a data series with nine data points. The data in columns B and C position the data points, and the values in column D control the size of the bubbles. Each bubble was formatted separately to control the color and gradient effects.

The folks at Pixar Animation Studios have nothing to worry about.

ON THE CD

This workbook, named `bubble chart mouse.xlsx`, is available on the companion CD-ROM.

A Smile Chart

The chart shown in Figure 13-12 displays a frown or a smile (and expressions in between) based on the value in cell D1. A value of −1 results in an unhappy face, and a value of +1 displays a very happy face. A value of 0 shows a neutral face.

Actually, only the mouth is a chart (an XY chart). The other facial parts are shapes. The mouth shape is determined by 24 formulas that use the SIN function.

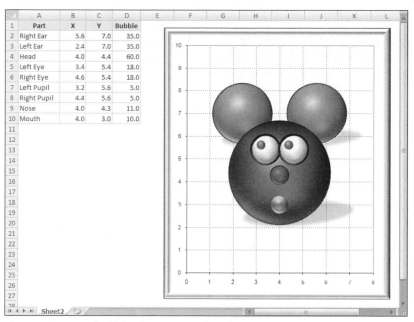

Figure 13-11: A bubble chart mouse head.

Part II

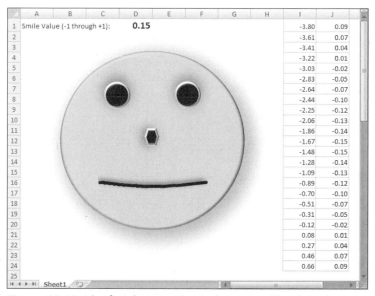

Figure 13-12: The facial expression is determined by the value in cell D1.

ON THE CD

This workbook, named `smile chart.xlsx`, is available on the companion CD-ROM.

Scatter Chart Drawings

Because a scatter chart can connect dots displayed at any XY coordinate, this type of chart has lots of fun potential. Figure 13-13 shows a simple example: an arrow drawn with eight connected data points.

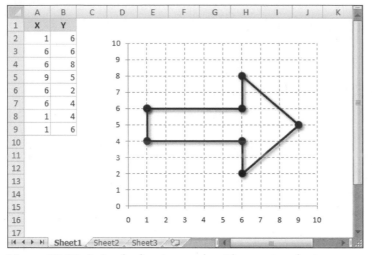

Figure 13-13: A simple drawing made with a scatter chart.

 ON THE CD

The examples in this section are available on the companion CD-ROM. The filename is `scatter chart drawings.xlsx`.

 NOTE

Previous versions of Excel allowed you to click a data point on a chart and drag it to a new location. This action also modified the underlying data for the chart. That feature, which made it very easy to create scatter chart drawings, was removed from Excel 2007.

Figure 13-14 shows a scatter chart that displays a geometric design generated by two columns of formulas. Figure 13-15 shows the same chart after applying some randomness, glow, shadow, and a smoothed line.

 NOTE

In the previous edition of this book, I included a few examples of maps created with a scatter chart. For example, I created a detailed outline map of California that uses more than 3,000 data points. Unfortunately, Excel 2007 cannot handle such complex charts. Performance slows to an unacceptable level — or else Excel simply stops responding.

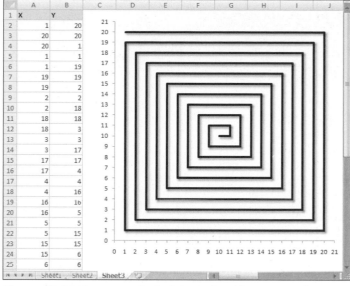

Figure 13-14: A geometric design made with a scatter chart.

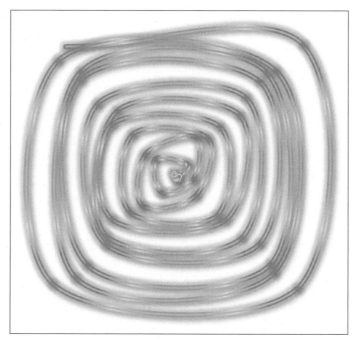

Figure 13-15: A more interesting variation of the scatter chart geometric design.

An Analog Clock Chart

Figure 13-16 shows a scatter chart formatted to look like a clock. It not only *looks* like a clock but also functions like one. There is really no reason that anyone would need to display a clock such as this on a worksheet, but creating the workbook was challenging, and you may find it instructive.

The chart uses three data series for the clock hands: one for the hour hand, one for the minute hand, and one for the second hand. These series contain formulas that use Excel's NOW function (which returns the current time). The formulas use trigonometric functions to determine the angle of the hands for the time of day. A simple macro is executed at one-second intervals. This macro simply calculates the sheet, which updates the formulas and the clock.

The chart uses another series to display the numbers. This data series draws a circle with 12 data points. The numbers consist of manually entered data labels.

Deselect the Analog Clock check box to reveal a hidden digital clock (see Figure 13-17). This clock consists of 28 merged cells that contain a simple formula:

```
=NOW()
```

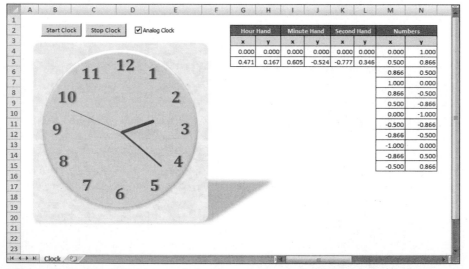

Figure 13-16: This fully functional clock is actually a scatter chart in disguise.

ON THE CD

The example in this section, named `analog clock chart.xlsx`, is available on the companion CD-ROM.

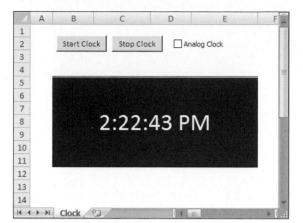

Figure 13-17: The digital clock is much easier to create.

Roll the Dice

The workbook shown in Figure 13-18 simulates rolling two dice. The outcome of each roll is stored in a range, which is displayed in a chart. The chart shows the actual distribution of the dice rolls, as well as the theoretical distribution of throwing two dice. This workbook may be useful for teaching elementary probability theory.

 ON THE CD

This example, named `dice roller.xlsm`, is available on the companion CD-ROM.

Following are a few points to keep in mind while you examine this workbook:

- A simple VBA macro, triggered by the Roll 'em button, is used to store the history of the dice rolls in columns A:D. Another macro, which deletes the history, is attached to the Clear History button.

- The dice picture uses no graphics. The graphics are generated by IF functions that determine whether a particular dot should be visible, based on the randomly generated dice value. The dot is actually a Wingdings font character.

- The chart series that displays the theoretical distribution uses an array, not a range. Because the series never changes, you don't need to store the values in a range.

- A text box in the chart displays the number of dice rolls. This text box is linked to a cell that determines the number of items in the History area of the worksheet.

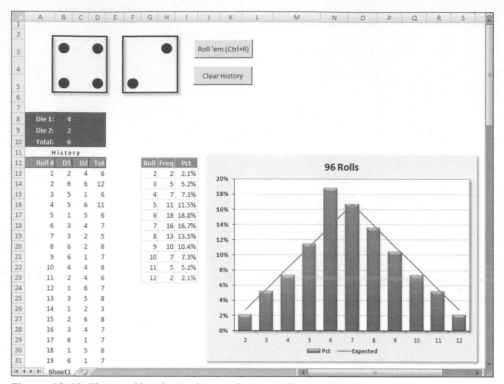

Figure 13-18: This workbook simulates rolling two dice.

Horse Race Chart

Nothing's more exciting than a horse race at the office. Figure 13-19 show a scatter chart that contains four data points. Each data point was replaced by a clip art image of a horse. Click the Run button, and a random horse moves forward. Just keep clicking until a horse wins. Come to think of it, changing the toner cartridge in the printer might be more fun than this.

Figure 13-19: Horse Number 3 takes the lead.

ON THE CD

This example, named `horse race.xlsm`, is available on the companion CD-ROM.

Using Clip Art

Microsoft Office 2007 includes tons of clip art that many people never bother to use. Figure 13-20 shows two examples of using clip art to augment a chart. Your boss might not appreciate the humor.

Part II

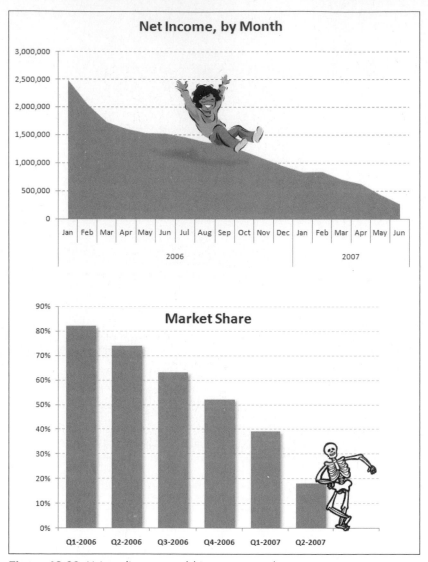

Figure 13-20: Using clip art to add interest to a chart.

 ON THE CD

The examples in this section are available on the companion CD-ROM. The filename is `clip art with charts.xlsx`.

Figure 13-21 shows a few other examples of combining clip art with a chart.

Figure 13-21: More examples of using clip art with charts.

Part III

Mastering Charts

Chapter 14

VBA Overview and Basic Examples

In This Chapter

◆ An overview of using Visual Basic for Applications (VBA) to manipulate charts

◆ Macros to activate and deactivate charts

◆ Macros to determine whether a chart is selected

◆ Macros to count and loop through all charts

◆ Macros to delete charts and print charts

This is the first of three chapters that deal with Visual Basic for Applications (VBA). VBA is Excel's programming language, and it is used to automate various aspects of Excel — including charts.

VBA in a Nutshell

VBA is Microsoft's common application scripting language. VBA is included with all Office 2007 applications, and it's also available in applications from other vendors. You use VBA to write procedures, frequently known as macros.

NOTE

This chapter assumes a basic familiarity with VBA. You should know how to use the VB Editor, enter code, execute procedures, and so on. If you have no experience using VBA, the material in this and the next two chapters will not make much sense. The remainder of this section presents a quick overview of VBA — useful as a refresher for those who haven't used VBA in a while. It's also useful to help novices decide whether learning VBA would be helpful.

Ready for the nutshell version of VBA? Here goes:

- **You perform actions in VBA by executing VBA code.**

- **You write (or record) VBA code, which is stored in a VBA module.**

- **VBA modules are stored in an Excel workbook, but you view or edit a module using the Visual Basic Editor.**

- **A VBA module consists of procedures.**

  A procedure is basically a unit of computer code that performs some action. Here's an example of a simple Sub procedure called Test. This procedure calculates a simple sum and then displays the result in a message box:

  ```
  Sub Test()
      Sum = 1 + 1
      MsgBox "The answer is " & Sum
  End Sub
  ```

- **In addition to Sub procedures, a VBA module can have Function procedures.**

  A Function procedure returns a single value. A function can be called from another VBA procedure, or used in a worksheet formula. This book does not cover Function procedures.

- **VBA manipulates objects contained in its host application (in this case, Excel is the host application).**

  Excel provides you with more than 100 classes of objects to manipulate. Examples of objects include a workbook, a worksheet, a range in a worksheet, a chart, and a shape. Many more objects are at your disposal, and you can manipulate them using VBA code.

- **Object classes are arranged in a hierarchy.**

  Objects can act as containers for other objects. For example, Excel is an object called Application, and it contains other objects, such as Workbook and Add-In objects. The Workbook object can contain other objects, such as Worksheet objects and Chart objects. A Worksheet object can contain objects such as Range objects, PivotTable objects, embedded chart objects (called ChartObjects), and so on. The arrangement of these objects is referred to as Excel's object model.

- **Like objects form a collection.**

  For example, the `Worksheets` collection consists of all the worksheets in a particular workbook. The `Charts` collection consists of all `Chart` sheet objects. The `ChartObjects` collection consists of all charts embedded in a single worksheet. Collections are objects in themselves.

- **When you refer to a contained or member object, you specify its position in the object hierarchy using a period (also known as a "dot") as a separator between the container and the member.**

  For example, you can refer to a workbook named `Book1.xlsx` as follows:

  ```
  Application.Workbooks("Book1.xlsx")
  ```

  This refers to the `Book1.xlsx` workbook in the `Workbooks` collection. The `Workbooks` collection is contained in the `Excel Application` object. Extending this to another level, you can refer to Sheet1 in Book1 as follows:

  ```
  Application.Workbooks("Book1.xlsx").Worksheets("Sheet1")
  ```

  You can take it to still another level and refer to a specific cell as follows:

  ```
  Application.Workbooks("Book1.xlsx").Worksheets("Sheet1").Range("A1")
  ```

  If you omit a specific reference to an object, Excel uses the active objects.

  If Book1 is the active workbook, the preceding reference can be simplified as follows:

  ```
  Worksheets("Sheet1").Range("A1")
  ```

  If you're certain that Sheet1 is the active sheet, you can simplify the reference even more:

  ```
  Range("A1")
  ```

- **Objects have *properties*.**

  A property can be thought of as a setting for an object. For example, a `Range` object has properties such as `Value` and `Name`. A `Chart` object has properties such as `HasTitle` and `ChartType`. You can use VBA to determine object properties and also to change them.

- **You refer to properties by combining the object with the property, separated by a period.**

  For example, you can refer to the value in cell A1 on Sheet1 as follows:

  ```
  Worksheets("Sheet1").Range("A1").Value
  ```

- **You can assign values to VBA variables.**

  Think of a variable as a name that you can use to store a particular value.

  To assign the value in cell A1 on Sheet1 to a variable called `Interest`, use the following VBA statement:

  ```
  Interest = Worksheets("Sheet1").Range("A1").Value
  ```

- **You can also assign a variable's value to a cell.**

  To assign a variable called `Interest` to cell A1 on Sheet1, use the following VBA statement:

  ```
  Worksheets("Sheet1").Range("A1").Value = Interest
  ```

- **Objects have *methods*.**

  A method is an action that is performed with the object. For example, one of the methods for a `Range` object is `ClearContents`. This method clears the contents of the range.

- **You specify methods by combining the object with the method, separated by a period.**

  For example, to clear the contents of cell A1 on the active worksheet, use this statement:

  ```
  Range("A1").ClearContents
  ```

- **VBA also includes all the constructs of modern programming languages, including arrays, looping, and so on.**

Believe it or not, this summary pretty much describes VBA. Now it's just a matter of learning some details.

The Macro Recorder and Charts

I often recommend using the macro recorder to learn about objects, properties, and methods. Unfortunately, Microsoft took a major step backward in Excel 2007 when it comes to recording chart actions. Although you can record a macro while you create and customize a chart, the recorded macro might not produce the same result when you execute it. Even worse, some actions are simply ignored.

Following is a macro that I recorded while I created a column chart, deleted the legend, and then added a shadow effect to the column series:

```
Sub RecordedMacro()
    ActiveSheet.Shapes.AddChart.Select
    ActiveChart.SetSourceData Source:=Range("Sheet1!$A$2:$B$4")
    ActiveChart.ChartType = xlColumnClustered
    ActiveChart.Legend.Select
    Selection.Delete
    ActiveSheet.ChartObjects("Chart 1").Activate
    ActiveChart.SeriesCollection(1).Select
End Sub
```

The chart is shown in Figure 14-1.

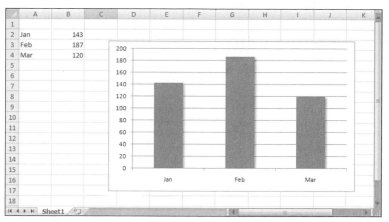

Figure 14-1: The macro recorder was turned on while this chart was created and customized.

Notice the following points:

- Even though I selected the range before I turned on the macro recorder, the source data range is hard-coded in the macro. In other words, the recorded macro does not use the `Selection` object, which is typical of other recorded macros. Therefore, you can't record a macro that creates a chart from the selected range. You can, however, create such a macro manually.

- The macro also hard-codes the chart's name. When this macro is played back, it's unlikely that the newly created chart will be named Chart 1, so the macro will either select the wrong chart or end with an error if a chart with that name does not exist.

- Although selecting the data series was recorded, the formatting command was not. So, if you would like to find out which objects and properties are used to format a data series, the macro recorder is of no help.

Bottom line? In Excel 2007, Microsoft downgraded macro recording for charts to the point where it's almost useless in some situations. I don't know why this happened, but it's likely that the programmers just didn't have the time, and meeting the product ship date was deemed a higher priority.

Despite the flaws, recording a chart-related macro can still be of *some* assistance. For example, you can use a recorded macro to figure out how to insert a chart, change the chart type, add a series, and so on. But when it comes to learning about formatting, you're on your own.

CROSS-REFERENCE
See Chapter 15 for sample macros that create charts.

The Chart Object Model

When you use VBA to work with charts, you'll quickly discover that the `Chart` object model is very complex. First, keep in mind that a `Chart` object can have either one of two different parent objects. The parent object of a chart on a chart sheet is the `Workbook` object that contains the chart sheet. The object hierarchy is as follows:

```
Workbook
   Chart
```

The parent object of an embedded chart is a `ChartObject` object. The parent of a `ChartObject` object is a `Worksheet` object. The object hierarchy for an embedded chart is as follows:

```
Workbook
   Worksheet
      ChartObject
         Chart
```

A `Chart` object contains, of course, other objects. Following is a *partial* object hierarchy for a `Chart` object:

```
Chart
   ChartArea
   PlotArea
   ChartTitle
   Legend
   DataTable
   Axes (Collection)
   SeriesCollection (Collection)
```

These objects, in turn, can contain other objects. Consider the `SeriesCollection`, which is a collection of all `Series` objects in the chart. A `Series` object contains the following objects:

```
Series
   Border
   Points (Collection)
   Interior
```

Now consider the `Points` collection. Each `Point` object contains the following objects:

```
Point
  Border
  DataLabel
  Interior
```

And it doesn't stop here. The `DataLabel` object contains an additional object: `Font`.

Assume that you want to change the font size of a single data label. Furthermore, assume that this data label belongs to the first point of the first series of the first chart in the first worksheet of the active workbook. Your VBA statement, as follows, needs to traverse this object hierarchy to get to the `Size` property of the `Font` object:

```
Workbook
  Worksheet
    ChartObject
      Chart
        Series
          Point
            DataLabel
              Font
```

Here's a VBA statement that does the job (this is a single statement that spans two lines):

```
ActiveWorkbook.Worksheets(1).ChartObjects(1).Chart.SeriesCollection(1) _
  .Points(1).DataLabel.Font.Size - 24
```

If you also wanted to make that data label bold, you need an additional statement:

```
ActiveWorkbook.Worksheets(1).ChartObjects(1).Chart.SeriesCollection(1) _
  .Points(1).DataLabel.Font.Bold = True
```

About collection names

As you know, a collection is an object that contains similar objects. Normally, the name of the collection consists of the plural form of the object. For example, the `Workbooks` collection contains all open `Workbook` objects, and the `ChartObjects` collection consists of all `ChartObject` objects in a worksheet. But what about the collection of `Series` objects? Because the singular and plural forms of the word *Series* are identical, the designers deviated from this naming convention. Therefore, the collection of all `Series` objects is known as a `SeriesCollection` object (not a `Series` collection object).

Part III

> **NOTE**
>
> Actually, it's even a bit more complex. Setting the `Size` or `Bold` property for a `Font` object will generate an error if the data point doesn't have a data label (that is, if the `HasDataLabel` property of the `Point` object is `False` (its default setting).

Using Object Variables

The deeply nested objects in the `Chart` object model can be confusing, and result in very long VBA statements. One way to make your code more efficient is to use object variables. For example, refer to the object hierarchy for changing the font of a single data label. Here's a VBA procedure that creates an object variable (`MyFont`) that represents the `Font` object:

```
Sub DeclareObjectVariable()
    Dim MyFont As Font
    Set MyFont = ActiveSheet.ChartObjects(1).Chart. _
        SeriesCollection(1).Points(1).DataLabel.Font
    MyFont.Size = 24
    MyFont.Bold = True
End Sub
```

The `Dim` statement declares the variable as a specific object type (in this case, a `Font` object). The `Set` statement creates the variable. After the `MyFont` variable is declared and created, you can use the `MyFont` object variable instead of the lengthy reference. In general, object variables are most useful when your code needs to refer to an object in several different places.

Following is a VBA procedure that declares object variables for each object in the hierarchy (six of them). This isn't really a practical example. It's more useful as a way to help understand the object hierarchy and object variables.

```
Sub ObjectVariableDemo()
    Dim MyChartObject As ChartObject
    Dim MyChart As Chart
    Dim MySeries As Series
    Dim MyPoint As Point
    Dim MyDataLabel As DataLabel
    Dim MyFont As Font


    Set MyChartObject = ActiveSheet.ChartObjects(1)
    Set MyChart = MyChartObject.Chart
    Set MySeries = MyChart.SeriesCollection(1)
    Set MyPoint = MySeries.Points(1)
    Set MyDataLabel = MyPoint.DataLabel
```

```
    Set MyFont = MyDataLabel.Font
    MyFont.Size = 24
    MyFont.Bold = True
End Sub
```

Using the With-End With construct

Another way to deal with lengthy object references is to use a With-End With structure, as follows:

```
Sub With_Demo()
    With ActiveSheet.ChartObjects(1).Chart. _
      SeriesCollection(1).Points(1).DataLabel.Font
        .Size = 24
        .Bold = True
    End With
End Sub
```

The two statements between the With and the End With statements are property settings for the Font objects.

This technique also works with object variables. In the procedure that follows, an object variable is declared and created, and this object variable is used in the With-End With structure:

```
Sub With_Demo2()
    Dim MyFont As Font
    Set MyFont = ActiveSheet.ChartObjects(1).Chart. _
      SeriesCollection(1).Points(1).DataLabel.Font


    With MyFont
        .Size = 24
        .Bold = True
    End With
End Sub
```

Finding Out More about the Chart Object Model

Covering the Chart object model in a comprehensive manner would require a complete book. And it would be a very boring book. The best way to become familiar with the Chart object model is to find out about the pieces as you need them. The sections that follow describe some ways to help you determine which objects, methods, and properties are required to perform a particular VBA task.

USING THE HELP SYSTEM

Many people complain about the Help system for Microsoft Office. It's certainly not perfect, but it can be very helpful for understanding objects, methods, and properties. When you're working in the VB Editor, you can type a search term in the Type a Question for Help box. Or just move the cursor over any keyword in your code and press F1. Figure 14-2 shows the Help window that displays when I pressed F1 when the cursor is located within the word *Series*.

Notice that, when a Help topic is displayed, its location within the Table of Contents is highlighted. Using the Table of Contents can often help you located related information. Also, you can click a link at the bottom (Series Object Members) to view the methods and properties of this object.

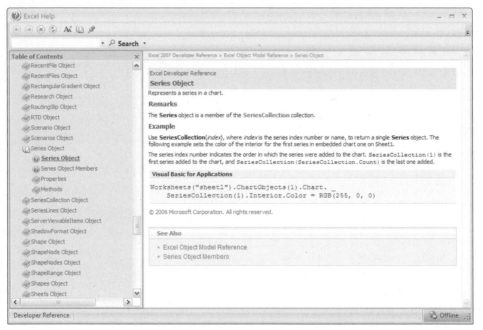

Figure 14-2: The Help topic for Series.

DECLARING OBJECT VARIABLES AND USING INTELLISENSE

The section "Using Object Variables," earlier in this chapter, describes how to declare and create object variables. One significant advantage to creating object variables is that you can use IntelliSense when writing your VBA code. When you're typing code, Excel continually monitors what you type. If it knows exactly which object you're working with, it offers assistance in the form of a drop-down list.

Figure 14-3 shows an example. Here, `MyChart` is an object variable that represents a `Chart` object. When I type the dot after the variable name, Excel displays a list of properties and methods for the object. If you continue typing, the IntelliSense feature scrolls the list to show items that begin with the characters you typed. Select an item from the list and press Tab, and Excel adds it to your code.

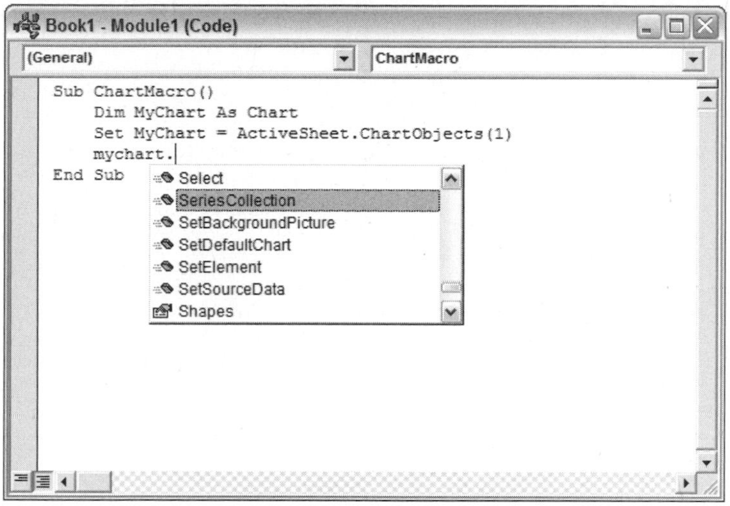

Figure 14-3: When you create an object variable, the Autocomplete feature can help you identify properties and methods.

USING THE MACRO RECORDER
As I noted earlier, the macro recorder in Excel 2007 leaves much to be desired when it comes to recording chart-related macros. However, the macro recorder is not *completely* useless.

You can find out quite a bit by turning on the macro recorder while you create and modify charts. The code itself won't win any awards (assuming that it even works), but you'll often gain some insights regarding objects, properties, and methods. Then you can use the Help system to understand the details.

SEARCHING THE INTERNET
In a typical week, I may get 20–30 unsolicited questions via e-mail. I don't have the time to answer individual questions, but I have noticed that approximately 95% of these questions can be answered simply by searching the Internet.

The Web contains a massive amount of information about Excel — including lots of VBA coding examples. Even if the code you find isn't exactly what you need, it can often lead you in the right direction.

✖ CROSS-REFERENCE
See Appendix B for more information about searching the Web for Excel chart-related information.

Simple Chart Macros

The sections that follow present simple VBA code examples that work with charts.

 CROSS-REFERENCE
Additional examples are presented in Chapter 15.

Activating and Deactivating a Chart

Clicking an embedded chart activates the chart. Your VBA code can activate an embedded chart using the `Activate` method. Here's an example that activates the first embedded chart on the active sheet:

```
ActiveSheet.ChartObjects(1).Activate
```

Note that the `Activate` method applies to the `ChartObject` object — not the `Chart` object contained in the `ChartObject`.

The following statement, for example, generates an error:

```
ActiveSheet.ChartObjects(1).Chart.Activate
```

When a chart is on a chart sheet, however, the `Activate` method does apply to the `Chart` object. To activate the chart on the first chart sheet in the active workbook, use a statement like this:

```
ActiveWorkbook.Charts(1).Activate
```

When a chart is activated, you can refer to it in your code with the `ActiveChart` property, which returns a `Chart` object. For example, the following statement displays the name of the active chart. If no existing chart is active, the statement generates an error.

```
MsgBox ActiveChart.Name
```

If you use the macro recorder to create chart-related macros, you'll find that the recorded code always activates the chart and then selects the objects that are manipulated. To modify a chart with VBA, you don't have to activate it or make any selections. In fact, it's usually more efficient if your code does *not* activate charts and select elements.

The following two procedures have exactly the same effect. (They change the embedded chart named Chart 1 to an area chart.) The first procedure activates the chart before performing the manipulations; the second one doesn't.

```
Sub ModifyChart1()
    ActiveSheet.ChartObjects("Chart 1").Activate
    ActiveChart.Type = xlArea
End Sub
```

```
Sub ModifyChart2()
    ActiveSheet.ChartObjects("Chart 1").Chart.Type = xlArea
End Sub
```

Following is another variation that creates an object variable for the chart. Again, the chart is not activated.

```
Sub ModifyChart3()
    Dim MyChart As Chart
    Set MyChart = ActiveSheet.ChartObjects("Chart 1").Chart
    MyChart.Type = xlArea
End Sub
```

You can use the `Activate` method to activate a chart, but how do you deactivate (that is, deselect) a chart? According to the Help system, you can use the `Deselect` method, as follows, to deactivate a chart:

```
ActiveChart.Deselect
```

However, this statement simply doesn't work — at least in the initial release of Excel 2007.

As far as I can tell, the only way to deactivate a chart by using VBA is to select something other than the chart. For an embedded chart, you can use the `RangeSelection` property of the `ActiveWindow` object to deactivate the chart and select the range that was selected before the chart was activated:

```
ActiveWindow.RangeSelection.Select
```

The following statement also deselects an embedded chart and selects the active cell (not the previously selected range):

```
ActiveCell.Select
```

Determining whether a Chart Is Activated

A common type of macro performs some manipulations on the active chart — the chart selected by a user. For example, a macro might change the chart's type, apply a style, or export the chart to a graphics file.

The simple macro that follows adds a title to the active chart. If a chart is not active when this macro is executed, the macro fails and you'll see the rather cryptic error message shown in Figure 14-4.

```
Sub AddTitle()
    With ActiveChart
        .SetElement msoElementChartTitleAboveChart
        .ChartTitle.Text = "Budget Projections"
    End With
End Sub
```

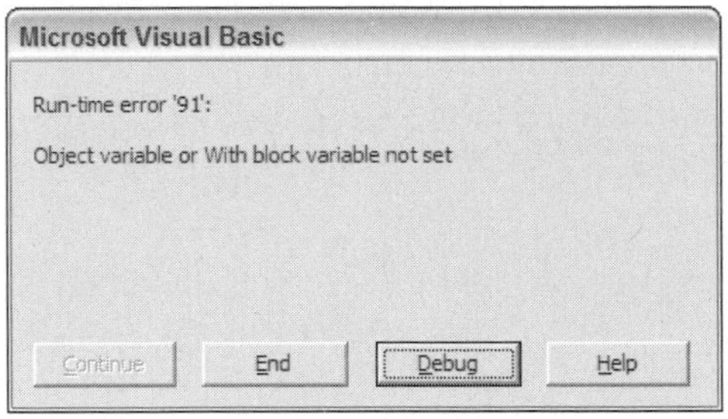

Figure 14-4: This error message appears if a chart is not active.

Your VBA code can determine whether the user has actually selected a chart by checking whether ActiveChart is Nothing. If so, a chart is not active. The AddTitle macro follows, showing the modification that checks for an active chart. If a chart is not selected, the user sees a message (see Figure 14-5) and the procedure ends with no further action.

```
Sub AddTitle()
    If ActiveChart Is Nothing Then
        MsgBox "Select a chart before running this macro.", vbInformation
        Exit Sub
    End If
```

```
    With ActiveChart
        .SetElement msoElementChartTitleAboveChart
        .ChartTitle.Text = "Budget Projections"
    End With
End Sub
```

This code will run without error if an embedded chart is active or if a chart sheet is selected.

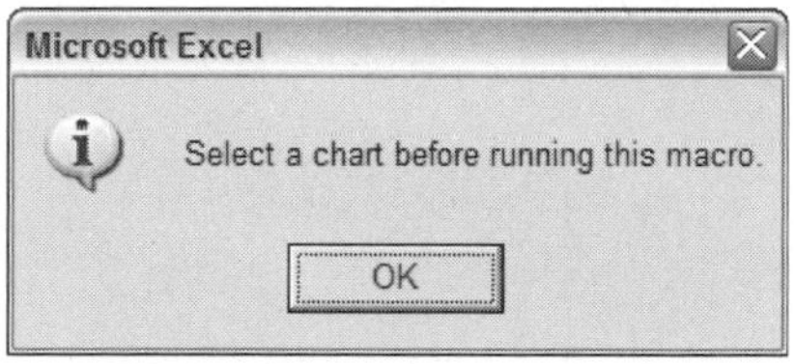

Figure 14-5: Using a message box to inform the user that a chart must be selected before executing the macro.

Determining whether the Active Chart Is Embedded

As you know, a chart can be either one of two types: an embedded chart or a chart on a chart sheet. In some cases, your macro may need to make this determination. The `TypeOfSelection` macro, which follows, displays one of three messages:

```
Sub TypeOfSelection()
    If ActiveChart Is Nothing Then
        MsgBox "No Chart"
        Exit Sub
    End If
    If TypeName(ActiveChart.Parent) = "Workbook" Then
        MsgBox "Chart Sheet"
        Exit Sub
    End If
    If TypeName(ActiveChart.Parent) = "ChartObject" Then
        MsgBox "Embedded Chart"
    End If
End Sub
```

The `TypeOfSelection` macro first checks for whether a chart is active. If not, it displays `No Chart` and the macro ends. The next two `If` statements use VBA's `TypeName` function to determine the object type of the active chart's "parent" object. (An object's parent is the object that contains it.) The `Chart` object in an embedded chart is contained in a `ChartObject` object. The `ChartObject`'s parent is the worksheet in which it is embedded. The parent of a chart sheet is the `Workbook` object that contains it.

Deleting from the ChartObjects or Charts Collection

To delete a chart in a worksheet, your VBA code must know the name or index of the ChartObject. The following statement deletes the ChartObject named Chart 1 in the active worksheet:

```
ActiveSheet.ChartObjects("Chart 1").Delete
```

To delete all ChartObject objects in a worksheet, use the Delete method of the ChartObjects collection, as follows:

```
ActiveSheet.ChartObjects.Delete
```

In Excel 2007, you can also delete embedded charts by accessing the Shapes collection. The following statement deletes Chart 1 in the active worksheet:

```
ActiveSheet.Shapes("Chart 1").Delete
```

To delete a single chart sheet, you must know the chart sheet's name or index. The following statement deletes the chart sheet named Chart1:

```
Charts("Chart1").Delete
```

Alternatively, you can use the following statement:

```
Sheets("Chart1").Delete
```

To delete all chart sheets in the active workbook, use the following statement:

```
ActiveWorkbook.Charts.Delete
```

Deleting sheets causes Excel to display a warning like the one shown in Figure 14-6. The user must reply to this prompt for the macro to continue. If you are deleting a sheet with a macro, you probably won't want this warning prompt to appear. To eliminate the prompt, use the following series of statements:

```
Application.DisplayAlerts = False
ActiveWorkbook.Charts.Delete
Application.DisplayAlerts = True
```

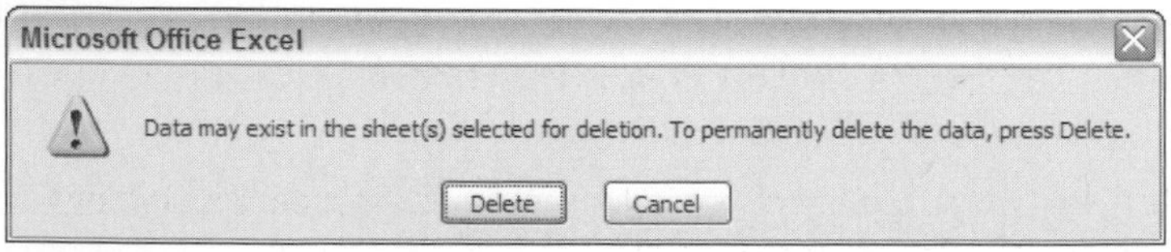

Microsoft Office Excel

⚠ Data may exist in the sheet(s) selected for deletion. To permanently delete the data, press Delete.

[Delete]   [Cancel]

Figure 14-6: Attempting to delete one or more chart sheets results in this message.

Counting and Looping through Charts

The examples in the following sections deal with various aspects of counting charts and looping through all charts in a worksheet or workbook.

Counting Chart Sheets

To determine how many chart sheets are in the active workbook, access the `Count` property of the `Charts` collection. For example, the following statement displays the number of chart sheets in the active workbook:

```
MsgBox Activeworkbook.Charts.Count
```

Counting Embedded Charts

To count the number of embedded charts in a particular worksheet, access the `Count` property of the `ChartObjects` collection. The following statement, for example, displays the number of embedded charts on Sheet1 of the active workbook:

```
MsgBox ActiveWorkbook.Worksheets("Sheet1").ChartObjects.Count
```

Looping through All Charts

A common task is to perform an operation on all existing charts. For example, you may want to write a macro to resize all embedded charts, or add the current date to each chart's title. The following macro loops through all embedded charts in the active worksheet and displays a list of their names in a message box:

```
Sub LoopThruChartObjects()
    Dim ChtObj As ChartObject
    Dim Msg As String
    Msg = ""
    For Each ChtObj In ActiveSheet.ChartObjects
        Msg = Msg & ChtObj.Name & vbNewLine
    Next ChtObj
    MsgBox Msg
End Sub
```

The `LoopThruChartObjects` macro uses a variable named `Msg` to store the names of the charts and then displays the list in a message box. `vbNewLine` is a built-in constant that adds a line break to the `Msg` variable.

The previous examples looped through embedded charts. The following procedure is similar, but it loops through all chart sheets in the active workbook:

```
Sub LoopThruChartSheets()
    Dim Cht As Chart
    Dim Msg As String
    Msg = ""
    For Each Cht In ActiveWorkbook.Charts
        Msg = Msg & Cht.Name & vbNewLine
    Next Cht
    MsgBox Msg
End Sub
```

The listing that follows combines the two previous macros and uses two loops: One loop cycles through all worksheets, and another loop cycles through all embedded charts. The result is a listing of all embedded charts in all worksheets. The result of running this macro is shown in Figure 14-7. This workbook contains six embedded charts in three worksheets.

```
Sub LoopThruChartObjects2()
    Dim Wks As Worksheet
    Dim ChtObj As ChartObject
    Dim Msg As String
    Msg = ""
    For Each Wks In ActiveWorkbook.Worksheets
        For Each ChtObj In Wks.ChartObjects
            Msg = Msg & Wks.Name & " - " & ChtObj.Name & vbNewLine
        Next ChtObj
    Msg = Msg & vbNewLine
    Next Wks
    MsgBox Msg
End Sub
```

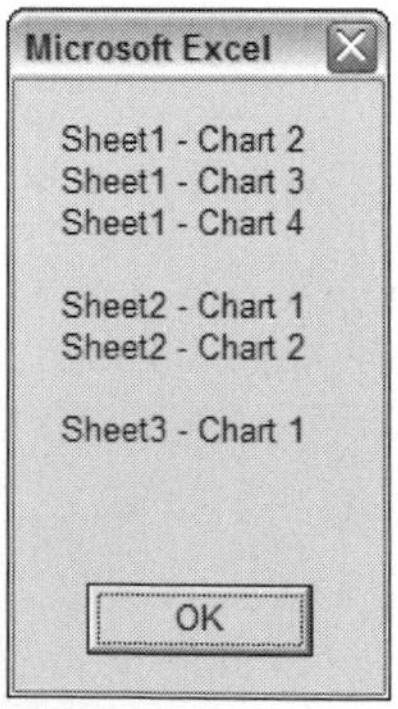

Figure 14-7: Displaying the names of all embedded charts in all worksheets.

Changing the Location of All Charts

The Location method of a Chart object moves a chart. You can use this method to convert embedded charts to chart sheets (and vice versa).

The following macro loops through all embedded charts on the active sheet and moves each chart to a chart sheet:

```
Sub ConvertToChartSheets()
    Dim ChtObj As ChartObject
    For Each ChtObj In ActiveSheet.ChartObjects
        ChtObj.Chart.Location Where:=xlLocationAsNewSheet
    Next ChtObj
End Sub
```

The macro that follows performs the opposite task: It loops through all chart sheets and converts each chart to an embedded chart on the active sheet.

```
Sub ConvertToEmbeddedCharts()
    Dim Cht As Chart
    For Each Cht In ActiveWorkbook.Charts
        Cht.Location Where:=xlLocationAsObject, Name:=ActiveSheet.Name
    Next Cht
End Sub
```

NOTE

After running the ConvertToEmbeddedCharts macro, all the embedded charts are stacked on top of each other. You may want to modify this macro such that the embedded charts are better positioned. For more information, see the section "Sizing and Aligning Charts," later in this chapter.

Printing All Embedded Charts

As you know, printing a worksheet also prints the embedded charts in that worksheet. In some cases, you may prefer that each chart be printed on a separate page. The example in this section prints all embedded charts on the active sheet:

```
Sub PrintAllCharts()
    Dim ChtObj As ChartObject
    For Each ChtObj In ActiveSheet.ChartObjects
        ChtObj.Chart.PrintOut
    Next ChtObj
End Sub
```

This procedure loops through all `ChartObject` objects and uses the `PrintOut` method of the `Chart` object. If you just want to preview the charts, use the `PrintPreview` method instead of the `PrintOut` method.

Setting Axis Values

Figure 14-8 shows a worksheet with a line chart that uses the data in column A. In addition, the sheet has three named cells: AxisMin (D2), AxisMax (D3), and MajorUnit (D4). Clicking the button executes the following macro, which retrieves the data in the named cells and uses the values as property settings for the `Axis` object:

```
Sub SetAxisValues()
    With ActiveSheet.ChartObjects(1).Chart.Axes(xlValue)
        .MinimumScale = Range("AxisMin")
        .MaximumScale = Range("AxisMax")
        .MajorUnit = Range("MajorUnit")
    End With
End Sub
```

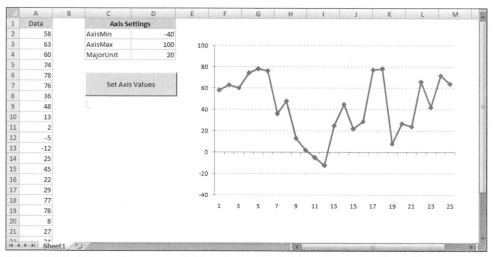

Figure 14-8: Using a macro to modify axis settings using values stored in cells.

ON THE CD

This example, named `axis settings.xlsm`, is available on the companion CD-ROM.

This macro accesses the `Axes` collection of the `Chart` object. Using the `xlValue` argument causes it to use the value axis. As you know, a chart can have additional axes. The following table shows how to access each of the possible `Axis` objects on a chart. Note that specifying `xlPrimary` as the second argument is optional (if omitted, `xlPrimary` is assumed).

Axis Type	How to Reference It
Primary category (X) axis	`Axes(xlCategory, xlPrimary)`
Primary value (Y) axis	`Axes(xlValue, xlPrimary)`
Secondary category (X) axis	`Axes(xlCategory, xlSecondary)`
Secondary value (Y) axis	`Axes(xlValue, xlSecondary)`
Series axis	`Axes(xlSeriesAxis)`

Assigning a macro to a ChartObject

You can assign a macro to an embedded chart. To do so, Ctrl+click the chart (to select the `Chart` object's container — a `ChartObject` object); then, right-click and choose Assign Macro from the shortcut menu. This displays the Assign Macro dialog box, in which you can select the macro to be executed.

After assigning the macro, clicking the embedded chart executes the macro. If you assign the macro that follows, for example, clicking the chart displays a message box that contains the chart's name (the `Caller` property returns the name of the object that called the procedure):

```
Sub Chart_Click()
    Dim ChtName As String
    ChtName = Application.Caller
    MsgBox "You clicked " & ChtName
End Sub
```

Also, be aware that this macro makes it difficult to edit the chart because the chart isn't activated when it is clicked. To edit the chart, right-click and press Esc to hide the shortcut menu.

Part III

Keep in mind that the properties for an `Axis` object vary, depending on the type. For example, a category axis does not have the properties used in the preceding macro — unless it's specified as a date category axis. To make a category axis a date category axis, use a statement like this:

```
ActiveChart.Axes(xlCategory).CategoryType = xlTimeScale
```

Other `CategoryType` settings are `xlCategoryScale` and `xlAutomatic`. These correspond to the options available on the Axis Options tab of the Format Axis dialog box.

CROSS-REFERENCE

See Chapter 15 for an example that uses an event procedure to perform this task automatically when you change a value.

Sizing and Aligning Charts

When you work with several embedded charts, you may prefer that the charts are all the same size and aligned. The following macro does the job:

```
Sub SizeAndAlignCharts()
    Dim ChtWidth As Long, ChtHeight As Long
    Dim TopPosition As Long, LeftPosition As Long
    Dim ChtObj As ChartObject
    If ActiveChart Is Nothing Then
        MsgBox "Select a chart"
        Exit Sub
    End If

    'Get size of active chart
    ChtWidth = ActiveChart.Parent.Width
    ChtHeight = ActiveChart.Parent.Height
    TopPosition = ActiveChart.Parent.Top
    LeftPosition = ActiveChart.Parent.Left

    'Loop through all Chart Objects
    For Each ChtObj In ActiveSheet.ChartObjects
        ChtObj.Width = ChtWidth
        ChtObj.Height = ChtHeight
        ChtObj.Top = TopPosition
        ChtObj.Left = LeftPosition
        TopPosition = TopPosition + ChtObj.Height
    Next ChtObj
End Sub
```

The SizeAndAlignCharts macro requires that a chart is active and uses this chart as a "base." The procedure resizes all other charts on the sheet such that they are the same size as the active chart. In addition, the charts are repositioned so that they are all aligned vertically.

The TopPosition variable stores the vertical position of the chart and is modified each time through the loop. The new vertical position is the previous vertical position plus the height of the ChartObject object. The result is a stack of charts, neatly aligned with no space in between each.

ON THE CD

This example, named size and align charts.xlsm, is available on the companion CD-ROM.

Part III

Chapter **15**

Advanced VBA Examples

In This Chapter

◆ Macros to create and format

◆ Macros to apply data labels to a series

◆ Macros to export charts as GIF files

◆ Macros to identify and modify ranges used by a chart

◆ A macro to create a word cloud in a shape

◆ Macros that are triggered by events

This chapter presents a wide variety of macros that manipulate charts in various ways. These examples are intended to demonstrate how to work with the objects that comprise a chart. You may be able to use some of these as written, but others may require some modification to make them more useful to you.

Compatibility note

The VBA code in this book uses many new chart-related properties and methods that were introduced in Excel 2007. As a result, some of the code presented here will not work with previous versions of Excel.

Creating Charts with VBA

The following sections describe how to use VBA to create an embedded chart and a chart on a chart sheet.

Creating an Embedded Chart

In Excel 2007, a `ChartObject` is a special type of `Shape` object. Therefore, it's a member of the `Shapes` collection. To create a new chart, use the `AddChart` method of the `Shapes` collection. The following statement creates an empty embedded chart:

```
ActiveSheet.Shapes.AddChart
```

The `AddChart` method can use five arguments (all are optional):

- **Type:** The type of chart. If omitted, the default chart type is used. Constants for all the chart types are provided (for example, `xlArea`, `xlColumnClustered`, and so on).

- **Left:** The left position of the chart, in points. If omitted, Excel centers the chart horizontally.

- **Top:** The top position of the chart, in points. If omitted, Excel centers the chart vertically.

- **Width:** The width of the chart, in points. If omitted, Excel uses 354.

- **Height:** The height of the chart, in points. If omitted, Excel uses 210.

In many cases, you may find it more efficient to create an object variable when the chart is created. The following procedure creates a line chart that can be referenced in code by using the `MyChart` object variable:

```
Sub CreateChart()
    Dim MyChart As Chart
    Set MyChart = ActiveSheet.Shapes.AddChart(xlLineMarkers).Chart
End Sub
```

A chart without data is not very useful, so you'll want to use the `SetSourceData` method to add data to a newly created chart. The procedure that follows demonstrates the `SetSourceData` method. This procedure creates the chart shown in Figure 15-1.

```
Sub CreateChart()
    Dim MyChart As Chart
    Dim DataRange As Range
    Set DataRange = ActiveSheet.Range("A1:C7")
    Set MyChart = ActiveSheet.Shapes.AddChart.Chart
    MyChart.SetSourceData Source:=DataRange
End Sub
```

ON THE CD

The examples in this section are available on the companion CD-ROM. The filename is create a chart.xlsm.

Creating a chart the old way

Using the `AddChart` method of the `Shapes` collection is the "new" way of creating charts, introduced in Excel 2007. For compatibility purposes, you can still use the `Add` method of the `ChartObjects` collection. This method, unlike the `AddChart` method of the `Shapes` collection, does not allow you to specify the chart type as an argument, so you need to use the `ChartType` property if you want to use anything except the default chart type. In addition, the `Left`, `Top`, `Width`, and `Height` arguments are required.

The procedure that follows uses the `Add` method of the `ChartObjects` collection to create an embedded chart:

```
Sub CreateChart2()
    Dim MyChart As Chart
    Dim DataRange As Range
    Set DataRange = ActiveSheet.Range("A1:C7")
    Set MyChart = ActiveSheet.ChartObjects.Add(10, 10, 354, 210).Chart
    MyChart.SetSourceData Source:=DataRange
    MyChart.ChartType = xlColumnClustered
End Sub
```

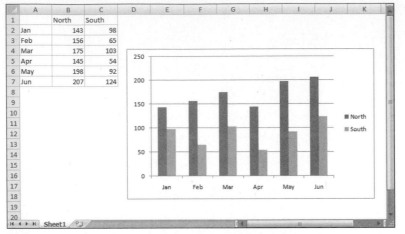

Figure 15-1: A few lines of VBA code created this chart.

Creating a Chart on a Chart Sheet

The preceding section describes the basic procedures for creating an embedded chart. To create a chart on a chart sheet, use the Add method of the Charts collection. The Add method of the Charts collection uses several optional arguments, but these arguments specify the position of the chart sheet — not chart-related information.

The example that follows creates a chart on a chart sheet and specifies the data range and chart type:

```
Sub CreateChartSheet()
    Dim MyChart As Chart
    Dim DataRange As Range
    Set DataRange = ActiveSheet.Range("A1:C7")
    Set MyChart = Charts.Add
    MyChart.SetSourceData Source:=DataRange
    ActiveChart.ChartType = xlColumnClustered
End Sub
```

Using VBA to Apply Chart Formatting

A common type of chart macro applies formatting to one or more charts. For example, you may create a macro that applies consistent formatting to all charts in a worksheet. If you experiment with the macro recorder, you'll find that commands in the following Ribbon groups are recorded:

- Chart Tools⇨Design⇨Chart Layouts
- Chart Tools⇨Design⇨Chart Styles
- Chart Tools⇨Layout⇨Labels
- Chart Tools⇨Layout⇨Axes
- Chart Tools⇨Layout⇨Background

Unfortunately, formatting any individual chart element (for example, changing the color of a chart series) is *not* recorded by the macro recorder. Therefore, you'll need to figure out the objects and properties on your own. The sections that follow provide lots of pointers.

Formatting a Chart

I used output from the macro recorder as the basis for the `FormatChart` procedure shown here, which converts the active chart to a clustered column chart (using Chart Tools⇨Design⇨Type⇨Change Chart Type), applies a particular layout (using Chart Tools⇨Design⇨Chart Layouts), applies a chart style (using Chart Tools⇨Design⇨Chart Styles), and removes the gridlines (using Chart Tools⇨Layout⇨Axes⇨Gridlines):

```
Sub FormatChart()
    If ActiveChart Is Nothing Then Exit Sub
    With ActiveChart
        .ChartType = xlColumnClustered
        .ApplyLayout 3
        .ChartStyle = 28
        .SetElement msoElementPrimaryValueGridLinesNone
        .ClearToMatchStyle
    End With
End Sub
```

ON THE CD

This example, named `format a chart.xlsm`, is available on the companion CD-ROM. The CD also contains an example (`format all charts.xlsm`) that applies formatting to several charts.

Figure 15-2 shows a chart before and after executing the `FormatChart` macro.

NOTE

After executing this macro, the actual appearance of the chart depends on the document theme that's in effect.

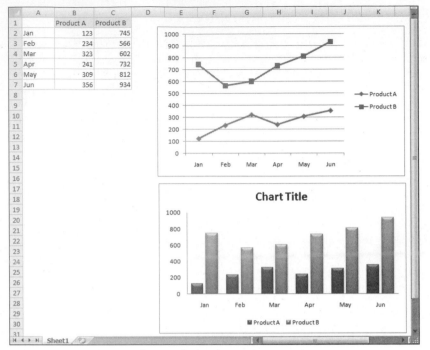

Figure 15-2: A chart, before and after being formatted.

Note the following points about the `FormatChart` procedure:

- VBA provides constants for the various chart types, and you can assign these constants to the `ChartType` property.

- The `ApplyLayout` method uses a number to represent the layout, and the numbers vary with the chart type. These numbers appear as ToolTips when you hover the mouse pointer over an icon in the Chart Tools⇨Design⇨Chart Layouts gallery. The `ApplyLayout` method can also specify a chart type as its second argument. Therefore, I could have eliminated the statement that changes the `ChartType` property and used this statement:

  ```
  .ApplyLayout 3, xlColumnClustered
  ```

- The `ChartStyle` property also uses a nondescriptive number (from 1 to 48) for its argument. These numbers appear as ToolTips when you hover the mouse pointer over an icon in the Chart Tools⇨Design⇨Chart Styles gallery.

- The `SetElement` method controls the visibility of just about every aspect of the chart. It accepts more than 120 descriptive constants. For example, the constant `msoElementChartTitleNone` hides the chart's title.

- The `ClearToMatchStyle` method clears all user-applied formatting on the chart. This method is typically used in conjunction with the `ChartStyle` property to ensure that the applied style does not contain any formatting that's not part of the style.

More Chart Formatting Examples

As I've noted, the macro recorder in Excel 2007 ignores many formatting commands when working with a chart. This deficiency is especially irksome if you're trying to figure out how to apply some of the new formatting options such as shadows, beveling, and gradient fills.

In this section, I provide some examples of chart formatting. I certainly don't cover all the options, but it should be sufficient to help you get started so that you can explore these features on your own. These examples assume an object variable named MyChart, created as follows:

```
Dim MyChart As Chart
Set MyChart = ActiveSheet.ChartObjects(1).Chart
```

If you apply these examples to your own charts, you need to make the necessary modifications so that MyChart points to the correct Chart object.

 TIP

To delete all user-applied (or VBA-applied) formatting from a chart, use the ClearToMatchStyle method of the Chart object. For example:

```
MyChart.ClearToMatchStyle
```

ADDING A SHADOW

One of the most interesting formatting effects in Excel 2007 is shadows. A shadow can give a chart a three-dimensional look and make it appear as if it's floating above your worksheet.

The following statement adds a default shadow to the chart area of the chart:

```
MyChart.ChartArea.Format.Shadow.Visible = msoTrue
```

In this statement, the Format property returns a ChartFormat object, and the Shadow property returns a ShadowFormat object. Therefore, this statement sets the Visible property of the ShadowFormat object, which is contained in the ChartFormat object, which is contained in the ChartArea object, which is contained in the Chart object.

Not surprisingly, the ShadowFormat object has some properties that determine the appearance of the shadow. Here's an example of setting five properties of the ShadowFormat object, contained in a ChartArea object, and Figure 15-3 shows the effect:

```
With MyChart.ChartArea.Format.Shadow
    .Visible = msoTrue
    .Blur = 10
    .Transparency = 0.4
    .OffsetX = 6
    .OffsetY = 6
End With
```

Figure 15-3: Applying a shadow to a chart.

The example that follows adds a subtle shadow to the plot area of the chart:

```
With MyChart.PlotArea.Format.Shadow
    .Visible = msoTrue
    .Blur = 3
    .Transparency = 0.6
    .OffsetX = 1
    .OffsetY = 1
End With
```

If an object has no fill, applying a shadow to the object has no visible effect. For example, a chart's title usually has a transparent background (no fill color). To apply a shadow to an object that has no fill, you must first add a fill color. This example applies a white fill to the chart's title and then adds a shadow:

```
MyChart.ChartTitle.Format.Fill.BackColor.RGB = RGB(255, 255, 255)
With MyChart.ChartTitle.Format.Shadow
    .Visible = msoTrue
    .Blur = 3
    .Transparency = 0.3
    .OffsetX = 2
    .OffsetY = 2
End With
```

ADDING A BEVEL

Adding a bevel to a chart can provide an interesting 3-D effect. Figure 15-4 shows a chart with a beveled chart area. To add the bevel, I used the ThreeD property to access the ThreeDFormat object. The code that added the bevel effect is as follows:

```
With MyChart.ChartArea.Format.ThreeD
    .Visible = msoTrue
    .BevelTopType = msoBevelDivot
    .BevelTopDepth = 12
    .BevelTopInset = 32
End With
```

CROSS-REFERENCE

Chapter 16 contains some additional charting examples that deal with color.

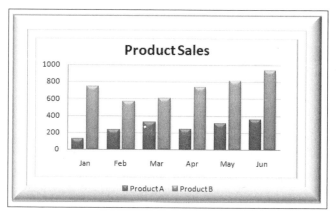

Figure 15-4: This chart has a bevel effect.

Applying Data Labels

As you may know, applying data labels to a chart series has a serious limitation: Excel does not allow you to specify an arbitrary range for the data label text. With a fairly simple macro, however, you can overcome this limitation and apply data labels from any range.

A Basic Data Label Macro

Figure 15-5 shows an XY chart. The goal is to label each point with the corresponding name in column A. The following macro accomplishes this goal:

```
Sub ApplyDataLabels()
    Dim Ser As Series, Pt As Point
    Dim Counter As Long
    Set Ser = ActiveSheet.ChartObjects(1).Chart.SeriesCollection(1)
```

```
      Ser.HasDataLabels = True
      Counter = 1
      For Each Pt In Ser.Points
          Pt.DataLabel.Text = Range("A1").Offset(Counter, 0)
          Counter = Counter + 1
      Next Pt
End Sub
```

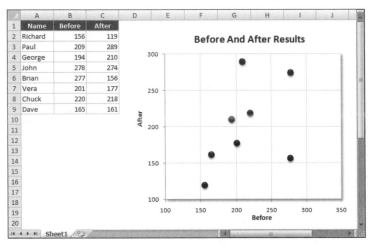

Figure 15-5: Excel does not provide a direct way to use the text in column A as data labels in the chart.

The `ApplyDataLabels` macro creates an object variable (`Ser`) that represents the chart's data series. It then sets the `HasDataLabels` property to `True`. (Without this statement, the macro would end with an error.) The next statement initializes a variable (`Counter`) to 1. The next four statements comprise a `For Each-Next` loop, which loops through each `Point` object in the series. The code sets the `Text` property of the `Point` object's `DataLabel` object equal to a cell that is offset from cell A1. The offset row is specified by the `Counter` variable, which is incremented each time through the loop.

Figure 15-6 shows the chart after executing the `ApplyDataLabels` macro.

Applying Linked Data Labels

A data label can contain a simple formula that refers to a cell. In such a case, the data label is linked to that cell — if the cell changes, so does the corresponding data label. It's a simple matter to modify the `ApplyDataLabels` macro from the previous section so that it creates links to the cells. Only one statement needs to be changed:

```
Pt.DataLabel.Text = "=" & Range("A1").Offset(Counter, 0) _
   .Address(True, True, xlR1C1, True)
```

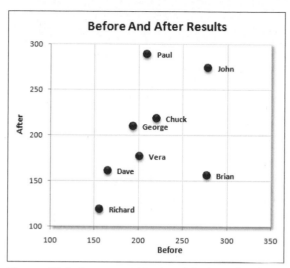

Figure 15-6: A macro adds data labels to the chart.

This statement inserts an equal sign (to indicate a formula), followed by the Address property of the cell. The Address property takes four arguments. After executing the modified macro, the first data label in the series contains this formula:

```
=Sheet1!$A$2
```

NOTE

The arguments for the Address property specify that the cell address be represented as an absolute reference (arguments 1 and 2), in R1C1 reference style (argument 3) and in "external" format (argument 4). Using the external format ensures that the sheet name is appended to the cell reference. The requirement to use an R1C1 reference style is an unusual quirk that's not documented.

Prompting for a Range

The preceding macros hard-code the data label range, so they are not general-purpose macros. A better approach is to specify the range interactively. The following macro uses the InputBox method to display a simple dialog box in which the user can specify a range by clicking a cell (see Figure 15-7).

Figure 15-7: The InputBox method prompts the user for a range.

ON THE CD

This example, named `data labels.xlsm`, is available on the companion CD-ROM. In addition, the author's PUP v7 add-in includes a utility to apply data labels to charts. A 30-day trial version is available on the companion CD-ROM.

The `DataLabelsWithPrompt` macro, which follows, is similar to the preceding macros but contains additional code to display the dialog box. The cell specified by the user is assigned to a `Range` object variable (`RngLabels`). Notice that a statement checks to see whether `RngLabels` is `Nothing`. That will be the case if the user clicks the Cancel button. If so, the macro ends with no action. The `On Error Resume Next` statement is present because clicking Cancel causes an error. That statement simply ignores the error. Also, notice the second `Set` statement that uses the `RngLabels` object. This statement ensures that if the user selects a multicell range, only the first cell in the selected range is assigned to `RngLabels`.

```
Sub DataLabelsWithPrompt()
    Dim RngLabels As Range
    Dim Ser As Series
    Dim Counter As Long
    On Error Resume Next


    If ActiveChart Is Nothing Then
        MsgBox "Select a chart."
        Exit Sub
    End If


    Set RngLabels = Application.InputBox _
        (prompt:="Range for data labels?", Type:=8)
    If RngLabels Is Nothing Then Exit Sub 'Canceled


    On Error GoTo 0
    If RngLabels.Rows.Count > 1 And RngLabels.Columns.Count > 1 Then
        MsgBox "Select a single row or column for labels."
        Exit Sub
    End If


    Set Ser = ActiveChart.SeriesCollection(1)
    Ser.HasDataLabels = True
    For Counter = 1 To Ser.Points.Count
        Ser.Points(Counter).DataLabel.Text = _
            RngLabels.Cells(Counter)
    Next Counter
End Sub
```

The DataLabelsWithPrompt procedure always works with the first series in the chart. A more general macro would prompt the user for the series if the chart has more than one series.

Exporting Charts as GIF Files

Saving a chart as a GIF file is very easy: Just use the Export method of the Chart object. Here's a simple macro that saves the active chart as a GIF file named mychart.gif:

```
Sub ExportToGIF()
    If ActiveChart Is Nothing Then
        MsgBox "Select a chart."
    Else
        ActiveChart.Export "mychart.gif", "GIF"
    End If
End Sub
```

The macro first checks to ensure that a chart is active. If so, it saves the chart to the current directory.

If you prefer to be prompted for a filename and location, use the macro that follows. This macro uses the GetSaveAsFilename function to display a dialog box with a default filename (the chart's name) and directory. The user can then accept these defaults or select a different directory or filename. Figure 15-8 shows the dialog box that's displayed when this macro is executed. If the Cancel button is clicked, the function returns False. In such a case, the macro ends with no action.

```
Sub SaveAsGIF()
    Dim FileName As Variant
    If ActiveChart Is Nothing Then
        MsgBox "Select a chart."
        Exit Sub
    End If
'   Get the filename
    FileName = Application.GetSaveAsFilename( _
        InitialFileName:=ActiveChart.Name & ".gif", _
        FileFilter:="GIF Files (*.gif), *.gif", _
        Title:="Save chart as GIF file")
    If FileName <> False Then
        ActiveChart.Export FileName, "GIF"
    End If
End Sub
```

ON THE CD

This example, named `save as gif.xlsm`, is available on the companion CD-ROM. In addition, the author's PUP v7 add-in includes a utility to export charts as GIF files. A 30-day trial version is available on the companion CD-ROM.

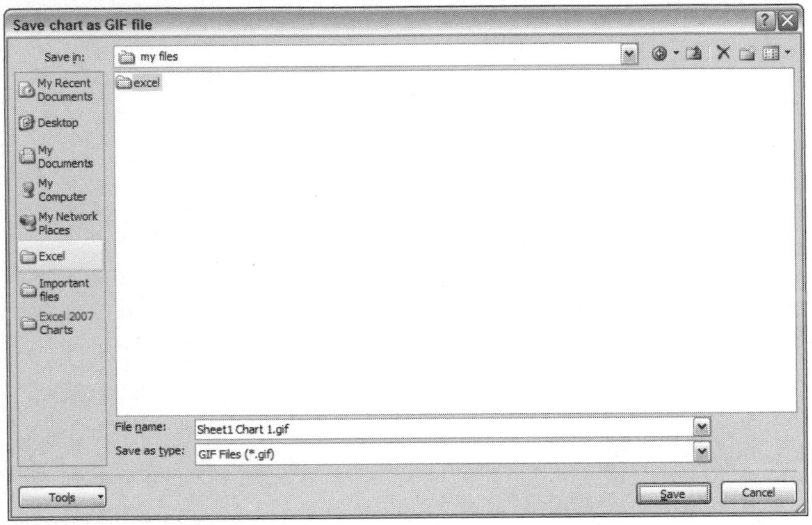

Figure 15-8: Using the `GetSaveAsFilename` function to prompt for a filename and directory.

Creating a Scrolling Chart

Figure 15-9 shows a chart with 5,218 data points in each series. The workbook contains these six names:

- StartDay: A name for cell F1

- NumDays: A name for cell F2

- Increment: A name for cell F3 (used for automatic scrolling)

- Date: A named formula:

  `=OFFSET(Sheet1!$A$1,StartDay,0,NumDays,1)`

- ProdA: A named formula:

  `=OFFSET(Sheet1!$B$1,StartDay,0,NumDays,1)`

- ProdB: A named formula:

  `=OFFSET(Sheet1!$C$1,StartDay,0,NumDays,1)`

Each of the SERIES formulas on the chart uses names for the category values and the data. The SERIES formula for the Product A series is as follows:

```
=SERIES(Sheet1!$B$1, Sheet1!Date, Sheet1!ProdA,1)
```

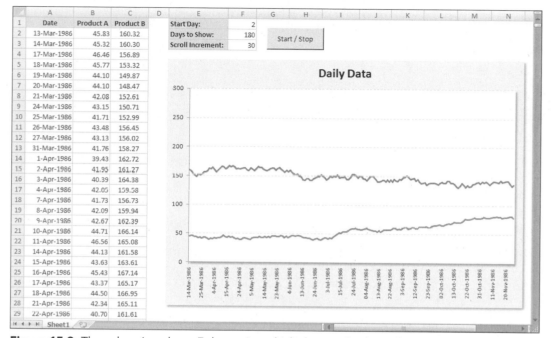

Figure 15-9: The values in column F determine which data to display in the chart.

The SERIES formula for the Product B series is as follows:

```
=SERIES(Sheet1!$C$1, Sheet1!Date, Sheet1!ProdB,2)
```

Using these names enables the user to specify a value for StartDay and NumDays, and the chart will display a subset of the data.

 ON THE CD

The companion CD-ROM contains a workbook that includes this animated chart. The file-name is `scrolling chart.xlsm`.

A relatively simply macro makes the chart scroll. The button in the worksheet executes the following macro that scrolls (or stops scrolling) the chart:

```
Public AnimationInProgress As Boolean

Sub AnimateChart()
    Dim StartVal As Long, r As Long
```

```
    If AnimationInProgress Then
        AnimationInProgress = False
        End
    End If
    AnimationInProgress = True
    StartVal = Range("StartDay")
    For r = StartVal To 5219 - Range("NumDays") _
        Step Range("Increment")
        Range("StartDay") = r
        DoEvents
    Next r
    AnimationInProgress = False
End Sub
```

The `AnimateChart` procedure uses a public variable (`AnimationInProgress`) to keep track of the animation status. The animation results from a loop that changes the value in the StartDay cell. Because the two chart series use this value, the chart is continually updated with a new starting value. The Scroll Increment setting determines how quickly the chart scrolls.

To stop the animation, I use an `End` statement rather than an `Exit Sub` statement. For some reason, `Exit Sub` doesn't work reliably and may even crash Excel.

Creating a Word Cloud

The example in this section doesn't use a chart. Rather, it uses a shape object to display words that vary in font size. (The font size is proportional to a value associated with each word.) Such a display is often seen on Web sites, and is referred to as a *word cloud*.

Figure 15-10 shows a word cloud that depicts the population of each of the 50 states in the United States.

ON THE CD

The macro that creates the word cloud shape is rather lengthy, so I don't show the code here. The example, named `word cloud.xlsm`, is available on the companion CD-ROM.

This macro can be used with any two-column list of data in which the first column is text and the second column contains values. Adjust the following statements in the WordCloud macro:

```
'Two column range that contains the data
Set DataRange = Range("A1:B50")

'Minimum and maximum font size
FontMin = 8
FontMax = 80
```

	A	B
1	Alabama	4,599,030
2	Alaska	670,053
3	Arizona	6,166,318
4	Arkansas	2,810,872
5	California	36,457,549
6	Colorado	4,753,377
7	Connecticut	3,504,809
8	Delaware	853,476
9	Florida	18,089,888
10	Georgia	9,363,941
11	Hawaii	1,285,498
12	Idaho	1,466,465
13	Illinois	12,831,970
14	Indiana	6,313,520
15	Iowa	2,982,085
16	Kansas	2,764,075
17	Kentucky	4,206,074
18	Louisiana	4,287,768
19	Maine	1,321,574
20	Maryland	5,615,727
21	Massachusetts	6,437,193
22	Michigan	10,095,643
23	Minnesota	5,167,101
24	Mississippi	2,910,540
25	Missouri	5,842,713
26	Montana	944,632
27	Nebraska	1,768,331
28	Nevada	2,495,529
29	New Hampshire	1,314,895
30	New Jersey	8,724,560
31	New Mexico	1,954,599

Figure 15-10: The text size of each state name is proportional to the state's population.

Determining the Ranges Used by a Chart

You might need a VBA macro that, as part of its job, must first determine the ranges used by each series in chart. For example, you may want to increase the size of each series by adding a new cell. Following is a description of three properties that seem relevant to this task:

- **Formula property:** Returns or sets the SERIES formula for the series. When you select a series on a chart, its SERIES formula is displayed in the formula bar. The `Formula` property returns this formula as a string.

- **Values property:** Returns or sets a collection of all the values in the series. This can be a range in a worksheet or an array of constant values, but not a combination of both.

- **XValues property:** Returns or sets an array of x values for a chart series. The `XValues` property can be set to a range in a worksheet or to an array of values — but it can't be a combination of both. The `XValues` property can also be empty.

Part III

If you create a VBA macro that needs to determine the data range used by a particular chart series, you may think that the Values property of the Series object is just the ticket. Similarly, the XValues property seems to be the way to get the range that contains the *x* values (or category labels). In theory, that certainly *seems* correct. But in practice, it doesn't work. When you set the Values property for a Series object, you can specify a Range object or an array. But when you read this property, it is always an array. Unfortunately, the object model provides no way to get a Range object used by a Series object.

One possible solution is to write code to parse the SERIES formula and extract the range addresses. This sounds simple, but it's actually a difficult task because a SERIES formula can be very complex. Following are a few examples of valid SERIES formulas.

```
=SERIES(Sheet1!$B$1,Sheet1!$A$2:$A$4,Sheet1!$B$2:$B$4,1)
=SERIES(,,Sheet1!$B$2:$B$4,1)
=SERIES(,Sheet1!$A$2:$A$4,Sheet1!$B$2:$B$4,1)
=SERIES("Sales Summary",,Sheet1!$B$2:$B$4,1)
=SERIES(,{"Jan","Feb","Mar"},Sheet1!$B$2:$B$4,1)
=SERIES(,(Sheet1!$A$2,Sheet1!$A$4),(Sheet1!$B$2,Sheet1!$B$4),1)
=SERIES(Sheet1!$B$1,Sheet1!$A$2:$A$4,Sheet1!$B$2:$B$4,1,Sheet1!$C$2:$C$4)
```

As you can see, a SERIES formula can have missing arguments, use arrays, and even use noncontiguous range addresses. And to confuse the issue even more, a bubble chart has an additional argument (for example, the last SERIES formula in the preceding list). Attempting to parse out the arguments is certainly not a trivial programming task.

I worked on this problem for several years, and I eventually arrived at a solution. The trick involves evaluating the SERIES formula by using a dummy function. This function accepts the arguments in a SERIES formula and returns a 2 x 5 element array that contains all the information in the SERIES formula.

I simplified the solution by creating four custom VBA functions, each of which accepts one argument (a reference to a Series object) and returns a two-element array. These functions are the following:

- **SERIESNAME_FROM_SERIES:** The first array element contains a string that describes the data type of the first SERIES argument (Range, Empty, or String). The second array element contains a range address, an empty string, or a string.

- **XVALUES_FROM_SERIES:** The first array element contains a string that describes the data type of the second SERIES argument (Range, Array, Empty, or String). The second array element contains a range address, an array, an empty string, or a string.

- **VALUES_FROM_SERIES:** The first array element contains a string that describes the data type of the third SERIES argument (Range or Array). The second array element contains a range address or an array.

- **BUBBLESIZE_FROM_SERIES:** The first array element contains a string that describes the data type of the fifth SERIES argument (Range, Array, or Empty). The second array element contains a range address, an array, or an empty string. This function is relevant only for bubble charts.

Note that a function to get the fourth SERIES argument (plot order) is not needed. This argument can be obtained directly by using the PlotOrder property of the Series object.

The following example demonstrates how to determine the address of the values range for the first series in the active chart.

```
Sub ShowValueRange()
    Dim Ser As Series
    Dim x As Variant
    Set Ser = ActiveChart.SeriesCollection(1)
    x = VALUES_FROM_SERIES(Ser)
    If x(1) - "Range" Then
        MsgBox Range(x(2)).Address
    End If
End Sub
```

The variable x is defined as a variant and will hold the two-element array that's returned by the VALUES_FROM_SERIES function. The first element of the x array contains a string that describes the data type. If the string is Range, the message box displays the address of the range contained in the second element of the x array.

 ON THE CD

The VBA code for these functions is too lengthy to be presented here, but it's available on the companion CD-ROM. It's documented such that it can be easily adapted to other situations. The filename is get series ranges.xlsm.

Event Procedure Examples

The following sections present examples of VBA event procedures. An event procedure is a macro that responds to certain events. For example, opening a workbook is an event, and you can write a macro that is executed when that particular event occurs. Excel supports many other events; several of them are described in the sections that follow.

Worksheet_Change Event Procedures

The examples in this section deal with the Worksheet_Change event, which is one of many events available at the worksheet level. This event is triggered whenever a cell is changed in a worksheet. As you'll see, these types of macros can be very useful when you want to update charts automatically.

NOTE

The event macros in this section must be located in the code module for the worksheet (for example, the module named `Sheet1`). They do not work if they are contained in a standard VBA module.

TIP

When you activate a code module for a chart, sheet, or workbook, you can use the drop-down lists at the top to select an object and event. Figure 15-11 shows a code module for a worksheet. The object (`Worksheet`) is selected in the left drop-down list, and the right drop-down list displays all the events that can be monitored for the object. When you choose an item from the list, the procedure "shell" (consisting of the first and last statements) is inserted for you.

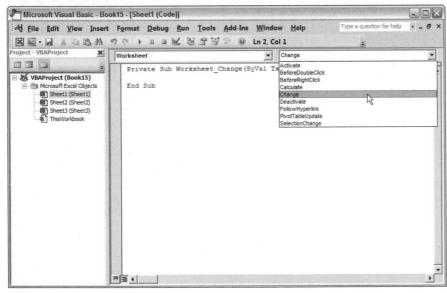

Figure 15-11: Using the drop-down lists in a code module to select an event.

HIDING AND DISPLAYING CHARTS

The worksheet shown in Figure 15-12 contains five embedded charts, four of which are hidden. Cell B2 controls which of the five charts is visible. This cell uses data validation to display a list of values from 1 through 5, plus an additional entry: (none).

ON THE CD

This example, named `hide charts - event macro.xlsm`, is available on the companion CD-ROM.

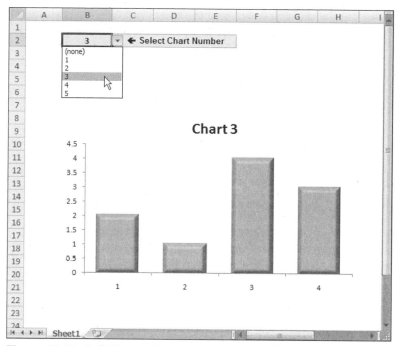

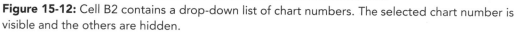

Figure 15-12: Cell B2 contains a drop-down list of chart numbers. The selected chart number is visible and the others are hidden.

The worksheet uses a `Worksheet_Change` event procedure, which follows. The macro is executed whenever a cell is changed on the sheet. Notice that this procedure has an argument: `Target`. This argument is a variable that represents the cell or range that is changed. If the address of `Target` is $B$2, the macro performs two operations: It hides all members of the `ChartObjects` collection and then unhides the chart that corresponds to the value in cell B2. The `On Error` statement ignores the error that occurs if an invalid `ChartObject` number is referenced, or when the user selects (none).

```
Private Sub Worksheet_Change(ByVal Target As Range)
    If Target.Address = "$B$2" Then
        ActiveSheet.ChartObjects.Visible = False
        On Error Resume Next
        ChartObjects(Target.Value).Visible = True
    End If
End Sub
```

The five embedded charts are stacked on top of each other, so they all appear in the same position on-screen.

ADJUSTING AXIS SCALING

The example in this section further uses an event macro to adjust a chart's value axis. Figure 15-13 shows the worksheet. The Axis property values are entered in the cells in column D. These cells are named AxisMin, AxisMax, and MajorUnit.

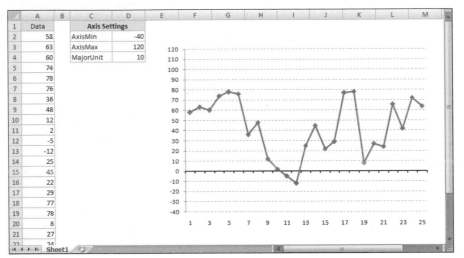

Figure 15-13: An event macro, executed when any cell on the sheet is changed, modifies properties for the chart's value axis.

The Worksheet_Change procedure that follows is executed whenever any cell in the sheet is changed. The first statement of the macro checks the Column property of the Target variable, which represents the cell that was changed. If the changed cell is in column D, the property values are retrieved from the sheet and applied to the chart. Otherwise, nothing happens.

```
Private Sub Worksheet_Change(ByVal Target As Range)
    If Target.Column = 4 Then
        On Error Resume Next
        With ActiveSheet.ChartObjects(1).Chart.Axes(xlValue)
.MinimumScale = Range("AxisMin")
            .MaximumScale = Range("AxisMax")
            .MajorUnit = Range("MajorUnit")
        End With
    End If
End Sub
```

This procedure doesn't do any error handling. Rather, it uses an On Error Resume Next statement to ignore any errors that occur. For example, if the user types a non-numeric entry for the AxisMax setting, no error is generated.

ON THE CD

This example, named `axis settings – event macro.xlsm`, is available on the companion CD-ROM.

Selection_Change Event Procedures

A `Selection_Change` event occurs whenever the user selects a different cell or range. You can use this event to create interactive charts.

CHANGING THE BEGINNING POINT OF A SERIES

Figure 15-14 shows an example. The data displayed on the chart depends on the active cell. The chart displays 12 data points, beginning with the data in the row of the active cell.

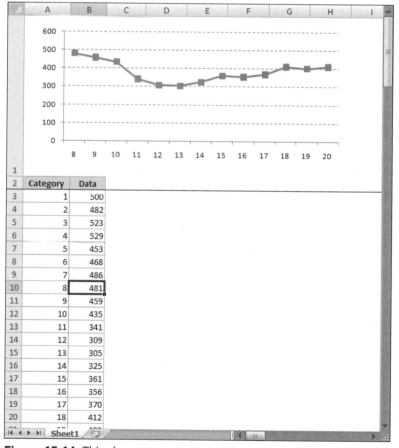

Figure 15-14: This chart uses a `Selection_Change` event procedure to display 12 data points beginning in the row of the active cell.

ON THE CD

This example, named `series based on active cell - event macro.xlsm`, is available on the companion CD-ROM.

The event macro, located in the code module for Sheet1, is as follows:

```
Private Sub Worksheet_SelectionChange(ByVal Target As Range)
    Dim Ser As Series
    If ActiveCell.Column > 2 Or ActiveCell.Row < 3 Then Exit Sub


    Set Ser = ActiveSheet.ChartObjects("Chart 1").Chart.SeriesCollection(1)
'   Specify values
    Ser.Values = Range(Cells(ActiveCell.Row, 2), _
      Cells(ActiveCell.Row + 12, 2))
'   Specify category
    Ser.XValues = Range(Cells(ActiveCell.Row, 1), _
      Cells(ActiveCell.Row + 12, 1))
End Sub
```

Whenever the user makes a new cell or range selection, the Worksheet_SelectionChange macro is executed. This macro first checks the active cell. If the active cell is not within the two-column data range, the macro ends. Otherwise, it creates an object variable (`Ser`), which represents the chart's data series. It then sets the `Values` property and the `XValues` property of the `Series` object, based on the active cell.

PLOTTING DATA IN THE ACTIVE ROW

The example in this section is similar to the previous examples. It uses the `Selection_Change` event to display data that's determined by the active cell. Figure 15-15 shows a chart that displays the responses to a survey question. The data displayed in the chart depends on the position of the active cell.

ON THE CD

This example, named `plot data in active row- event macro.xlsm`, is available on the companion CD-ROM.

The event procedure is as follows:

```
Private Sub Worksheet_SelectionChange(ByVal Target As Range)
    Dim Ser As Series
    If ActiveCell.Row > 2 And ActiveCell.Row < 17 Then
        ActiveSheet.ChartObjects("Chart 1").Visible = True
        Set Ser = ActiveSheet.ChartObjects("Chart 1"). _
          Chart.SeriesCollection(1)
'       Specify values
```

```
        Ser.Values = Range(Cells(ActiveCell.Row, 2), _
        Cells(ActiveCell.Row, 6))
        Specify title
        ActiveSheet.ChartObjects("Chart 1").Chart.ChartTitle.Text = _
            Cells(ActiveCell.Row, 1)
    Else
        ActiveSheet.ChartObjects("Chart 1").Visible = False
    End If
End Sub
```

This procedure uses an `If-Then-Else` construct. If the active cell is in a row that contains data, the code modifies the `Values` property of the `Series` object and also specifies the title. If the active cell is in any other row, the chart is hidden.

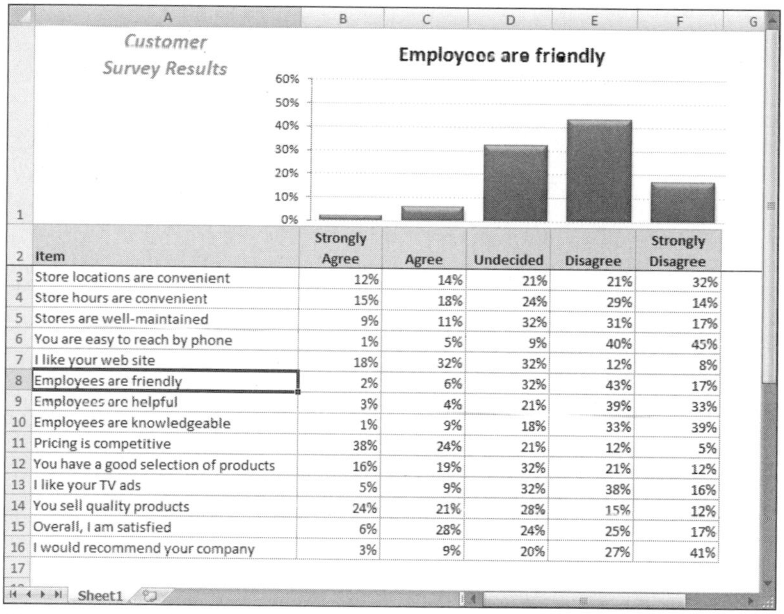

Figure 15-15: The chart displays the data in the row of the active cell.

Chapter 16

Working with Colors

In This Chapter

- ◆ Specifying colors in VBA code
- ◆ VBA conversion functions for various color models
- ◆ Converting colors to grayscale
- ◆ Working with Excel 2007 document themes
- ◆ Modifying colors in Shape objects and charts

One of the most significant changes in Excel 2007 is the abandonment of the old 56-color workbook palette. This chapter describes how color is used in Excel 2007, including the new "themes." I include many examples that should help you understand how these changes affect your workbooks and charts. The chapter also contains VBA code that deals with colors.

About Excel 2007 Colors

Dealing with color in Excel 2007 is no trivial matter. I'm the first to admit that it can be complicated. And often, recording a macro while you change the color of a cell or object only adds to the confusion. In this chapter, I attempt to pull it all together.

Back in the pre–Excel 2007 days, a workbook stored a palette of 56 colors. These colors were the only ones available for cell backgrounds, cell text, and charts. Sure, you could modify any or all of those colors, but you couldn't exceed the 56-color limit for a workbook.

But things have changed. You now have access to a virtually unlimited number of colors in a workbook — actually, the limit is 16,777,216 colors, but that certainly qualifies as "virtually" unlimited as far as I'm concerned.

Specifying Colors

Using VBA, you specify a color as a numeric color value, which is a number between 0 and 16,777,215. For example, the VBA statement that follows changes the background color of the active cell to a dark maroon:

```
ActiveCell.Interior.Color = 5911168
```

In addition, VBA has some predefined constants for some common colors. For example, vbRed has a value of 255 (the value for pure red) and vbGreen has a value of 65,280.

No one, of course, can keep track of nearly 17 million colors, and the predefined constants are limited. A better way to change a color is to specify the color in terms of its red, green, and blue components — the RGB color system.

The RGB Color System

The RGB color system combines various levels of three colors: red, green, and blue. Each of these component colors can range from 0 through 255. Therefore, the total number of possible colors is 256 x 256 x 256 = 16,777,216. When all three color components are 0, the color is pure black. When all three components are 255, the color is pure white. When all three are 128 (the half-way point), the color is medium gray. The remaining 16,777,213 possible combinations of these three values represent other colors.

To specify a color using the RGB system in VBA, use the RGB function. This function accepts three arguments that represent the red, green, and blue components of a color. The function returns a decimal color value.

 NOTE

The numeric color values I've referred to aren't really a different color system. A decimal color value is simply the base 10 equivalent of an RGB color. For the color white, the RGB values of 255, 255, 255 are written as FF, FF, FF in base 16 (hexadecimal). The values are concatenated to get the base 16 color value FFFFFF, which in base 10, is written 16,777,215. For lack of a better term, I refer to these base 10 color value as *decimal color values.*

The statement that follows uses the RGB function to assign a color that's exactly the same as the one assigned in the preceding section (that dark maroon, 5911168):

```
ActiveCell.Interior.Color = RGB(128, 50, 90)
```

Table 16-1 shows the RGB components and the decimal color code of some common colors.

TABLE 16-1 COLOR EXAMPLES

Name	Red Component	Green Component	Blue Component	Color Value
Black	0	0	0	0
White	255	255	255	16777215
Red	255	0	0	255
Green	0	255	0	65280
Blue	0	0	255	16711680
Yellow	255	255	0	65535
Pink	255	0	255	16711935
Turquoise	0	255	255	16776960
Brown	153	51	0	13209
Indigo	51	51	153	10040115
80% Gray	51	51	51	3355443

The HSL Color System

If you select the More Colors option when choosing a color in Excel, you'll see the Colors dialog box. Click the Custom tab, and you can choose from two color models to specify your color: RGB and HSL. Figure 16-1 shows the Colors dialog box with the HSL color model selected.

In the HSL color system, colors are specified using three parameters: hue, saturation, and luminance. As with RGB colors, each of these parameters can range from 0 to 255. Each RGB color has an equivalent HSL color, and each HSL color has an equivalent RGB color value. In other words, any of the 16,777,216 colors can be specified by using either the HSL or RGB color system.

NOTE

Although the Colors dialog box lets you specify a color using the HSL color model, this is actually the only area in which Excel supports the HSL color model. For example, when you specify a color using VBA, it must be an RGB color value. You can either use the RGB function, or enter a decimal color value directly. However, VBA does not have a corresponding HSL function.

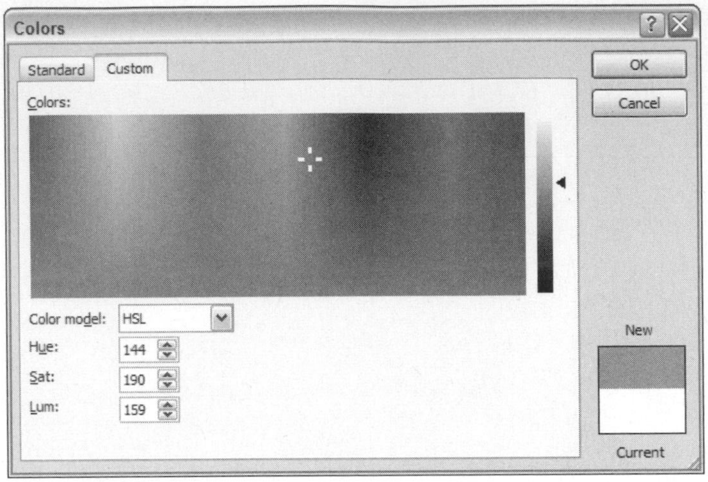

Figure 16-1: Choosing a color using the HSL color system.

Converting Colors

If you know the three color component values, converting an RGB color to a decimal color value is easy. Just use VBA's RGB function. Assume three variables (r, g, and b), each of which represents a color component value between 0 and 255. To calculate the equivalent decimal color value, use a statement like this:

```
DecimalColor = RGB(r, g, b)
```

To perform this conversion in a worksheet formula, create this simple VBA function in a VBA module:

```
Function RGB2DECIMAL(R, G, B)
'    Converts from RGB to decimal color
     RGB2DECIMAL = RGB(R, G, B)
End Function
```

The following example worksheet formula assumes that the three color values are in A1:C1:

```
=RGB2DECIMAL(A1,B1,C1)
```

Converting a decimal color to its red, green, and blue components is not so simple. Here's a function that returns a three-element array:

```
Function DECIMAL2RGB(ColorVal) As Variant
'    Converts a color value to an RGB triplet
'    Returns a 3-element variant array
     DECIMAL2RGB = Array(ColorVal \ 256 ^ 0 And 255, _
```

```
        ColorVal \ 256 ^ 1 And 255, ColorVal \ 256 ^ 2 And 255)
End Function
```

To use the DECIMAL2RGB function in a worksheet formula, the formula must be entered as a three-cell array formula. For example, assume that cell A1 contains a decimal color value. To convert that color value to its RGB components, select a three-cell horizontal range and then enter the following formula. Press Ctrl+Shift+Enter to make it an array formula, and don't enter the braces.

```
{=DECIMAL2RGB(A1)}
```

If the three-cell range is vertical, you need to transpose the array, as follows:

```
{=TRANSPOSE(DECIMAL2RGB(A1))}
```

Figure 16-2 shows the DECIMAL2RGB function in use in a worksheet.

	A	B	C	D	E	F
1	**Decimal**		**Decimal-To-RGB**			
2	Color Value		R	G	B	
3	0		0	0	0	
4	167,772		92	143	2	
5	335,544		184	30	5	
6	503,316		20	174	7	
7	671,088		112	61	10	
8	838,860		204	204	12	
9	1,006,632		40	92	15	
10	1,174,404		132	235	17	
11	1,342,176		224	122	20	
12	1,509,948		60	10	23	
13	1,677,720		152	153	25	
14	1,845,492		244	40	28	
15	2,013,264		80	184	30	
16	2,181,036		172	71	33	
17	2,348,808		8	215	35	
18	2,516,580		100	102	38	
19	2,684,352		192	245	40	
20	2,852,124		28	133	43	
21	3,019,896		120	20	46	
22	3,187,668		212	163	48	

Sheet1

Figure 16-2: The DECIMAL2RGB function converts a decimal color value to its red, green, and blue components.

ON THE CD

The companion CD-ROM contains a workbook with the following color conversion functions: DECIMAL2RGB, DECIMAL2HSL, HSL2RGB, RGB2DECIMAL, RGB2HSL, and HSL2DECIMAL. The file is named color conversion functions.xlsm.

Understanding Grayscale

When you create worksheets and charts, it's important to remember that not everyone has a color printer. And even if your chart is printed on a color printer, it might be photocopied or faxed.

When content is printed on a noncolor device, colors are converted to grayscale. Sometimes you'll be lucky and your colors will display nicely when converted to grayscale. Other times, you won't be so lucky. For example, the columns in a chart may be indistinguishable when the colors are converted.

Every grayscale color has an equal component of red, green, and blue. Pure black is `RGB(0, 0, 0)`. Pure white is `RGB(255, 255, 255)`. Neutral gray is `RGB(128, 128, 128)`. Using this color system produces 256 shades of gray.

To create a 256-color grayscale gradient in a range of cells, execute the procedure that follows. It colors the background of cells in the range A1:A256, starting with black and ending with white. You might want to zoom out in the worksheet to see the entire range.

```
Sub GenerateGrayScale()
    Dim r As Long
    For r = 0 To 255
        Cells(r + 1, 1).Interior.Color = RGB(r, r, r)
    Next r
End Sub
```

Converting Colors to Gray

One approach to grayscale conversion is to simply average the red, green, and blue components of a color and use that single value for the red, green, and blue components of its grayscale equivalent. That approach, however, does not take into account the fact that different colors are perceived as varying levels of brightness. For example, green is perceived to be brighter than red, and red is perceived to be brighter than blue.

Perceptual experiments have arrived at the following "recipe" to convert an RGB color value to a grayscale value:

- 28.7% of the red component
- 58.9% of the green component
- 11.4% of the blue component

For example, consider color value 16751001, a shade of violet that corresponds to `RGB(153, 153, 255)`. Applying the factors listed above, the RGB values are as follows

- Red: 28.7% × 153 = 44
- Green: 58.9% × 153 = 90
- Blue: 11.4% × 255 = 29

The sum of these values is 163. Therefore, the corresponding grayscale RGB value for color value 16751001 is `RGB(163, 163, 163)`.

Following is a VBA function that accepts a decimal color value as its argument, and returns the corresponding grayscale decimal value:

```
Function Grayscale(color)
    Dim r As Long, g As Long, b As Long
    r = (color \ 256 ^ 0 And 255) * 0.287
    g = (color \ 256 ^ 1 And 255) * 0.589
    b = (color \ 256 ^ 2 And 255) * 0.114
    Grayscale = RGB(r + g + b, r + g + b, r + g + b)
End Function
```

Viewing Charts as Grayscale

Here's a technique that can let you see how an embedded chart looks when converted to grayscale:

1. Select the chart.

2. Press Ctrl+C to copy the chart to the Clipboard.

3. Click a cell and choose Home⇨Clipboard⇨Paste⇨As Picture⇨Paste As Picture.

4. Select the picture and choose Picture Tools⇨Format⇨Adjust⇨Recolor and then choose the Grayscale color mode from the drop-down gallery.

These steps are automated in the macro that follows. The `ShowChartAsGrayScale` procedure copies the active chart as a picture and converts the picture to grayscale. After you've determined whether the colors are satisfactory, you can delete the picture.

```
Sub ShowChartAsGrayScale()
'   Copies the active chart as a grayscale picture
'   Embedded charts only
    If ActiveChart Is Nothing Then
        MsgBox "Select a chart."
        Exit Sub
    End If
    ActiveChart.Parent.CopyPicture
```

Part III

```
ActiveChart.Parent.TopLeftCell.Select
ActiveSheet.Pictures.Paste
ActiveSheet.Pictures(ActiveSheet.Pictures.Count). _
    ShapeRange.PictureFormat.ColorType = msoPictureGrayscale
End Sub
```

ON THE CD

A workbook with this example is available on the companion CD-ROM. The filename is `chart to grayscale picture.xlsm`.

Experimenting with Colors

Figure 16-3 shows a workbook that I created that deals with colors. If you're at all confused about how the RGB color model works, spending some time with this color demo workbook can probably make it all very clear.

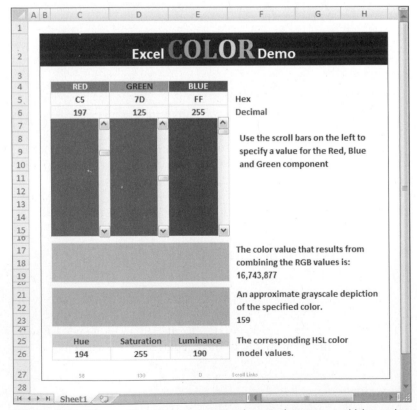

Figure 16-3: This workbook demonstrates how red, green, and blue colors combine.

ON THE CD

This workbook, named `RGB color demo.xlsm`, is available on the companion CD-ROM.

This workbook contains three vertical scroll bars, each of which controls the background color of a range. Use these scroll bars to specify the red, green, and blue component for a color to values between 0 and 255. Moving the scroll bars changes several areas of the worksheet:

- The cells above the scroll bars display the color components in hexadecimal (00–FF) format and in decimal (0–255) format. Hexadecimal RGB color values are often used in specifying colors for HTML documents.

- The ranges next to each scroll bar change intensity, corresponding to the scroll bar's position (that is, the value of the color component).

- A range below the scroll bars depicts the combined color, determined by the RGB values you specify.

- A cell displays the decimal color value.

- Another range depicts the color's approximate appearance when it is converted to grayscale.

- A range of cells shows the corresponding HSL color values.

Understanding Document Themes

A significant new feature in Excel 2007 is document themes. With a single mouse click, the user can change the entire look of a document. A document theme consists of three components: colors, fonts, and effects (for graphic objects). The rationale for using themes is that they may help users produce better-looking and more consistent documents. A theme applies to the entire workbook, not just the active worksheet. In addition, the same themes are available in Word and PowerPoint, making it easy to create complimentary spreadsheets, documents, and presentations.

About Document Themes

Microsoft Office 2007 ships with 20 document themes, and additional themes can be added. The user interface Ribbon includes several style galleries (for example, the Chart Styles gallery). The styles available in these galleries vary depending on which theme is assigned to the document. And, if you apply a different theme to the document, the document changes to reflect the new theme's colors, fonts, and effects.

ON THE CD

If you haven't explored document themes, open the workbook named document theme demo.xlsx found on the companion CD-ROM. This workbook contains a range that shows each theme color, two shapes, text (using the headings and body fonts), and a chart. Choose Page Layout⇨Themes⇨Themes Gallery to see how the worksheet changes with each theme.

You can also mix and match theme elements. For example, you can use the colors from one theme, the fonts from another theme, and the effects from yet a different theme. In addition, the user can create a new color set or a new font set. These customized themes can be saved and then applied to other workbooks.

NOTE

The concept of document themes is based on the notion that users will apply little, if any, "nontheme" formatting to the document. If the user applies colors or fonts that aren't part of the current theme, this formatting will not be modified if a new theme is applied to the document. Therefore, it's still very easy to create an ugly document with mismatched colors and too many different fonts.

Understanding Document Theme Colors

When you apply a color to a cell or object, the color is selected from a control like the one shown in Figure 16-4. The control displays the 60 theme colors (10 columns by 6 rows) plus 10 additional "standard" colors. Clicking the More Colors option displays the Color dialog box, in which the user can specify any of the 16,777,216 available colors.

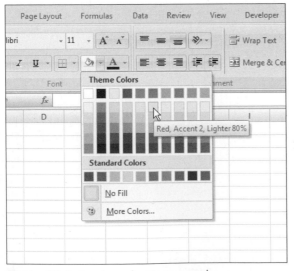

Figure 16-4: A color-selection control.

The 60 theme colors are identified by pop-up ToolTips. For example, using the default Office theme, the color in the second row of the sixth column is known as Red, Accent 2, Lighter 80%. If you're using a different theme, the "Red" part of the ToolTip is replaced by the actual color for that theme.

Table 16-2 shows all 60 theme colors. The first row shows the color name, and the other rows show the light/dark variation of that color. Examine the table, and you won't see much of a pattern — although the accent colors are consistent in terms of the dark/light variations.

Keep in mind that these color names remain the same, even if a different document theme is applied. The document theme colors actually consist of the 10 colors displayed in the top row, and each of these 10 colors has five dark/light variations.

NOTE

If you select Page Layout⇨Themes⇨Colors⇨Create New Theme Colors, you'll see that a theme has two additional colors: Hyperlink and Followed Hyperlink. These are the colors applied when a hyperlink is created, and they are not shown in the color selector control.

You may find it enlightening to record a macro while you change the fill color and text color of a range. Unfortunately, recording your actions while you change the color of a chart element does not generate any code.

Following is a macro that I recorded when a range was selected. For the fill color, I chose "Background 2, Darker 50%," and for the text color, I chose "Text 2, Lighter 80%."

```
Sub Macro1()
    Range("A1:D13").Select
    With Selection.Interior
        .Pattern = xlSolid
        .PatternColorIndex = xlAutomatic
        .ThemeColor = xlThemeColorDark2
        .TintAndShade = -0.499984740745262
        .PatternTintAndShade = 0
    End With
    With Selection.Font
        .ThemeColor = xlThemeColorLight2
        .TintAndShade = 0.799981688894314
    End With
End Sub
```

TABLE 16-2 THEME COLOR NAMES

Row/Column	1	2	3	4	5	6	7	8	9	10
1	Background 1	Text 1	Background 2	Text 2	Accent 1	Accent 2	Accent 3	Accent 4	Accent 5	Accent 6
2	Darker 5%	Lighter 50%	Darker 10%	Lighter 80%	Lighter 80%	Lighter 80%	Lighter 80%	Lighter 80%	Lighter 80%	Lighter 80%
3	Darker 15%	Lighter 35%	Darker 25%	Lighter 60%	Lighter 60%	Lighter 60%	Lighter 60%	Lighter 60%	Lighter 60%	Lighter 60%
4	Darker 25%	Lighter 25%	Darker 50%	Lighter 40%	Lighter 40%	Lighter 40%	Lighter 40%	Lighter 40%	Lighter 40%	Lighter 40%
5	Darker 35%	Lighter 15%	Darker 75%	Darker 25%	Darker 25%	Darker 25%	Darker 25%	Darker 25%	Darker 25%	Darker 25%
6	Darker 50%	Lighter 5%	Darker 90%	Darker 50%	Darker 50%	Darker 50%	Darker 50%	Darker 50%	Darker 50%	Darker 50%

First of all, you can safely ignore the three pattern-related properties (`Pattern`, `PatternColorIndex`, and `PatternTintAndShade`) in the recorded macro. These properties refer to the ugly, old-fashioned (but still supported) cell patterns, which you can specify on the Fill tab of the Format Cells dialog box. These properties simply maintain any existing pattern that may exist in the range.

The recorded macro, after I delete the three pattern-related properties, is as follows:

```
Sub Macro1()
    Range("A1:D13").Select
    With Selection.Interior
        .ThemeColor = xlThemeColorDark2
        .TintAndShade = -0.499984740745262
    End With
    With Selection.Font
        .ThemeColor = xlThemeColorLight2
        .TintAndShade = 0.799981688894314
    End With
End Sub
```

As you can see, each color is specified in terms of a `ThemeColor` property and a `TintAndShade` property. The `ThemeColor` property uses built-in constants. The value for these constants is simply the column number of the 10-x-6 theme color table. For example, `xlThemeColorDark2` has a value of 3 because that color is in the third column of the theme color table. But what about the `TintAndShade` property?

The `TintAndShade` property can have a value between −1 and +1. A value of −1 results in black, and a value of +1 results in white. A `TintAndShade` property value of 0 gives the "pure" color. In other words, as the `TintAndShade` value goes negative, the color gets increasingly darker until it's pure black. As the `TintAndShade` value goes positive, the color gets increasingly lighter until it's pure white. Notice that the TintAndShade values in the recorded macro include many extra decimal places. The TintAndShade value of −0.499984740745262, for example, is equivalent to "Darker 50%."

To arrive at the `TintAndShade` property value that corresponds to a particular theme color variation, look back at Table 16-2.

ON THE CD

For a demonstration of how the `TintAndShade` property changes a color, open the `tintandshade demo.xlsm` workbook on the companion CD-ROM (see Figure 16-5). Specify a starting color, and the macro displays that color with 50 levels of the `TintAndShade` property values, ranging from −1 to +1. It also displays the decimal color value and the red, green, and blue components of the color (which are displayed in a chart).

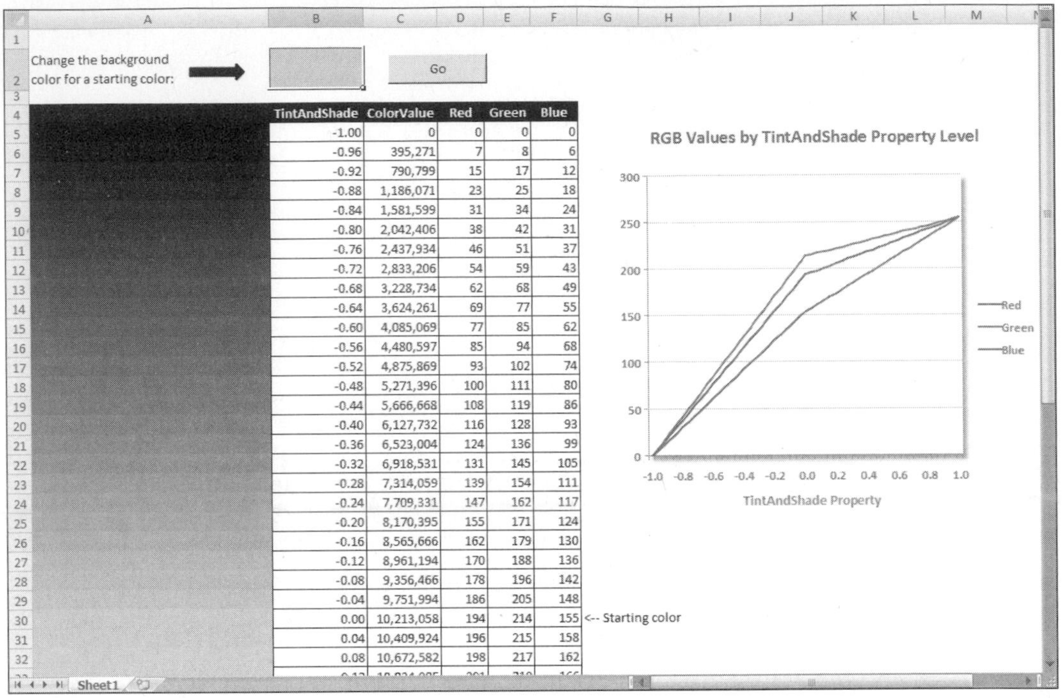

TintAndShade	ColorValue	Red	Green	Blue
-1.00	0	0	0	0
-0.96	395,271	7	8	6
-0.92	790,799	15	17	12
-0.88	1,186,071	23	25	18
-0.84	1,581,599	31	34	24
-0.80	2,042,406	38	42	31
-0.76	2,437,934	46	51	37
-0.72	2,833,206	54	59	43
-0.68	3,228,734	62	68	49
-0.64	3,624,261	69	77	55
-0.60	4,085,069	77	85	62
-0.56	4,480,597	85	94	68
-0.52	4,875,869	93	102	74
-0.48	5,271,396	100	111	80
-0.44	5,666,668	108	119	86
-0.40	6,127,732	116	128	93
-0.36	6,523,004	124	136	99
-0.32	6,918,531	131	145	105
-0.28	7,314,059	139	154	111
-0.24	7,709,331	147	162	117
-0.20	8,170,395	155	171	124
-0.16	8,565,666	162	179	130
-0.12	8,961,194	170	188	136
-0.08	9,356,466	178	196	142
-0.04	9,751,994	186	205	148
0.00	10,213,058	194	214	155
0.04	10,409,924	196	215	158
0.08	10,672,582	198	217	162

Figure 16-5: This workbook demonstrates how the `TintAndShade` property affects a color.

Displaying All Theme Colors

Using the information in Table 16-2, I wrote the following macro, which displays all 60 theme color variations in a range of cells:

```
Sub ShowThemeColors()
  Dim r As Long, c As Long
  For r = 1 To 6
    For c = 1 To 10
        With Cells(r, c).Interior
        .ThemeColor = c
        Select Case c
            Case 1 'Background 1
            Select Case r
                Case 1: .TintAndShade = 0
                Case 2: .TintAndShade = -0.05
                Case 3: .TintAndShade = -0.15
                Case 4: .TintAndShade = -0.25
                Case 5: .TintAndShade = -0.35
                Case 6: .TintAndShade = -0.5
```

```
                End Select
            Case 2 'Text 1
                Select Case r
                    Case 1: .TintAndShade = 0
                    Case 2: .TintAndShade = 0.5
                    Case 3: .TintAndShade = 0.35
                    Case 4: .TintAndShade = 0.25
                    Case 5: .TintAndShade = 0.15
                    Case 6: .TintAndShade = 0.05
                End Select
            Case 3 'Background 2
                Select Case r
                    Case 1: .TintAndShade = 0
                    Case 2: .TintAndShade = -0.1
                    Case 3: .TintAndShade = -0.25
                    Case 4: .TintAndShade = -0.5
                    Case 5: .TintAndShade = -0.75
                    Case 6: .TintAndShade = -0.9
                End Select
            Case Else  'Text 2, and Accent 1-6
                Select Case r
                    Case 1: .TintAndShade = 0
                    Case 2: .TintAndShade = 0.8
                    Case 3: .TintAndShade = 0.6
                    Case 4: .TintAndShade = 0.4
                    Case 5: .TintAndShade = -0.25
                    Case 6: .TintAndShade = -0.5
                End Select
            End Select
            Cells(r, c) = .TintAndShade
            End With
        Next c
    Next r
End Sub
```

Figure 16-6 shows the result of executing the ShowThemeColors procedure. (It looks better in color.) If you change to a different document theme, the colors will be updated to reflect those in the new theme.

ON THE CD

This example, named generate theme colors.xlsm, is available on the companion CD-ROM.

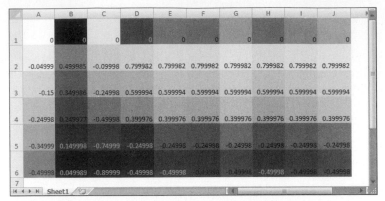

Figure 16-6: A VBA macro generated these theme colors.

So far in this chapter, I've described how to change the fill color of a range by setting the Color property of the Interior object. As I noted, using the VBA RGB function makes this easier. These two statements demonstrate how to change the fill color of a range (they both have the same result):

```
Range("A1:F24").Interior.Color = 5913728
Range("A1:F24").Interior.Color = RGB(128, 60, 90)
```

What if you'd like your code to change the background color of a range to a specific theme color, such as the color in the third row of the sixth column (the color identified as Accent 2, Lighter 60%)?

The Excel 2007 designers seemed to have forgotten to include a direct way to specify a theme color using this type of indexing. You might think that the ColorIndex property would do the job, but it doesn't. The ColorIndex property refers to colors in the (pre–Excel 2007) 56-color palette.

In actual practice, this omission is not a serious problem. When setting a color, the important property is the ThemeColor property, which ranges from 1 to 10. Your code can assign a value to the TintAndShade property to vary that color (a negative value for a darker variation and a positive value for a lighter variation). If the user applies a different document theme, the color will still change in a relative manner.

NOTE

If you modify the Interior.Color property of a cell to a color that corresponds to a theme color, the cell's color is not determined by the current theme. In other words, if you apply a new theme, the cell's color will not change. To change the color of a cell such that it varies with the theme, you must set the Interior.ThemeColor property.

Working with Shape Objects

This chapter has focused exclusively on modifying the color of a range. The following sections provide examples of changing colors in Shape objects. In Excel, use the Insert⇨ Illustrations⇨Shapes group to add a shape to a worksheet.

Figure 16-7 shows a Shape object inserted in a worksheet. This object's default name is Right Arrow 1. The number in the name varies, depending on how many shapes you have inserted. For example, if you had previously inserted two other shapes (of any style), the name would be Right Arrow 3.

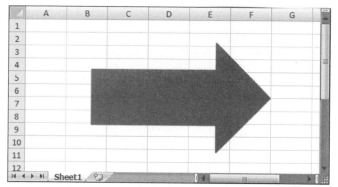

Figure 16-7: A Shape object in a worksheet.

A Shape's Background Color

The background color of a Shape object is determined by the RGB property. So, to get the decimal color value of this shape, use a statement like this:

```
MsgBox ActiveSheet.Shapes("Right Arrow 1").Fill.ForeColor.RGB
```

This statement may be a bit confusing, so I'll break it down. The Fill property of the Shape object returns a FillFormat object. The ForeColor property of the FillFormat object returns a ColorFormat object. So the RGB property actually applies to the ColorFormat object, and this property contains the decimal color value.

NOTE

If you're confused about the use of the ForeColor property in this example, you're not alone. Most people, myself included, would expect to use the BackColor property of the FillFormat object to change the background color of an object. As it turns out, the BackColor property is used for the second color if the object is shaded or filled with a pattern. For an unfilled shape with no pattern, the ForeColor property controls the background color.

When working with Shape objects, you almost always want your code to perform multiple actions. Therefore, it's efficient to create an object variable. The code that follows creates an object variable named Shp:

```
Dim Shp As Shape
Set Shp = ActiveSheet.Shapes("Right Arrow 1")
MsgBox Shp.Fill.ForeColor.RGB
```

TIP

An additional advantage to creating an object variable is that you can take advantage of the VBE's Auto List Members feature, which displays the possible properties and objects as you type (see Figure 16-8). This is particularly helpful in the case of Shape objects because actions you take with shapes are not recorded by Excel's macro recorder.

```
Book3 - Module1 (Code)

(General)                          ModifyShape

Sub ModifyShape()
    Dim Shp As Shape
    Set Shp = ActiveSheet.Shapes("Right Arrow 1")
    Shp.Fill.|
                  Application
End Sub            BackColor
                  Creator
                  ForeColor
                  GradientColorType
                  GradientDegree
                  GradientStops
```

Figure 16-8: Typing a statement with the assistance of the Auto List Members feature.

If you'll be working only with the shape's colors, you can create an object variable for the shape's ColorFormat object, like this:

```
Dim ShpCF As ColorFormat
Set ShpCF = ActiveSheet.Shapes("Right Arrow 1").Fill.ForeColor
MsgBox ShpCF.RGB
```

The RGB property of the ColorFormat object controls the color of the shape. Following are some additional properties. If you're not familiar with document theme colors, see the "Understanding Document Themes" section, earlier in this chapter.

- ObjectThemeColor: A number between 1 and 10 that represents the theme color (that is, a color in the first row of the 10-x-6 theme color grid).

- SchemeColor: A number that ranges from 0 to 80 that represents the color as an index in the current color scheme. These are colors from the old 56-color palette, and I don't see any need to ever use the SchemeColor property.

- TintAndShade: A number between –1 and +1 that represents the lightness or darkness of the theme color.

- Type: A number that represents the ColorFormat object type. As far as I can tell, this read-only property is always 1, which represents the RGB color system.

To set the color of a shape to a theme color, use code like the following:

```
Dim Shp As Shape
Set Shp = ActiveSheet.Shapes("Right Arrow 1")
Shp.Fill.ForeColor.ObjectThemeColor = 3
Shp.Fill.ForeColor.TintAndShade = .25
```

Changing the fill color of a shape does not affect the shape's outline color. To modify the color of a shape's outline, access the ColorFormat object of the shape's LineFormat object. The following statements set a shape's fill color and outline to red:

```
Dim Shp As Shape
Set Shp = ActiveSheet.Shapes("Right Arrow 1")
Shp.Fill.ForeColor.RGB = RGB(255, 0, 0)
Shp.Line.ForeColor.RGB = RGB(255, 0, 0)
```

Here's an alternate way to accomplish the same effect, using object variables:

```
Dim Shp As Shape
Dim FillCF As ColorFormat
Dim LineCF As ColorFormat
Set Shp = ActiveSheet.Shapes("Right Arrow 1")
Set FillCF = Shp.Fill.ForeColor
Set LineCF = Shp.Line.ForeColor
FillCF.RGB = RGB(255, 0, 0)
LineCF.RGB = RGB(255, 0, 0)
```

Using Other Fill Types with a Shape

Shapes can also display other types of fills, such as gradients, pictures, and textures. The examples in this section demonstrate how to apply these other types of fills to a Shape object.

 ON THE CD

All the examples in this section are available on the companion CD-ROM. The filename is shape object colors.xlsm.

Part III

The following code creates a rectangle, hides its border, and applies a two-color gradient. One of the colors is set specifically; the other color is one of the document theme colors. Figure 16-9 shows the result of running this macro.

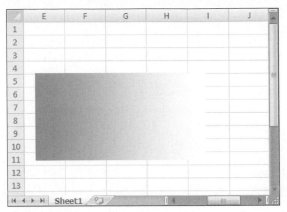

Figure 16-9: A Shape object with a two-color gradient fill.

```
Sub MakeShapeWithGradient()
    Dim Shp As Shape

'   Create the shape
    Set Shp = ActiveSheet.Shapes.AddShape( _
        Type:=msoShapeRectangle, _
        Left:=100, _
        Top:=10, _
        Width:=200, _
        Height:=100)

'   Hide the border
    Shp.Line.Visible = False

'   Add 2-color gradient
    With Shp.Fill
        .TwoColorGradient _
            Style:=msoGradientVertical, Variant:=2
        .ForeColor.RGB = RGB(255, 255, 255) 'white
        .BackColor.ObjectThemeColor = msoThemeColorAccent4
    End With
End Sub
```

The example on the CD-ROM includes additional code that creates the shapes shown in Figure 16-10: a shape with a pattern, a shape with a picture background (and a reflection), a shape with texture (and 3-D effects), and a shape that contains text.

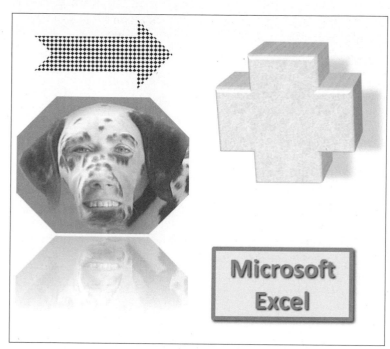

Figure 16-10: These shapes were created with VBA macros.

Finding Out More about Shapes

The information in this section barely scratches the surface when it comes to working with Shape objects. Programming shapes with VBA could easily serve as the subject matter for a complete book.

To find out more about Shape objects, use the Object Browser (press F2 in the VBE), the Help system, the macro recorder (which is of limited value), and the Internet. And don't forget the best tool of them all: experimentation.

Modifying Chart Colors

This section describes how to change colors in a chart. The most important point is to identify the specific chart element that you want to modify. In other words, you need to identify the object and then set the appropriate properties.

Figure 16-11 shows a simple column chart named Chart 1. This chart has two data series, a legend, and a chart title.

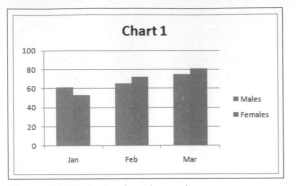

Figure 16-11: A simple column chart.

Following is a VBA statement that changes the color of the first data series to red:

```
ActiveSheet.ChartObjects("Chart 1").Chart. _
    SeriesCollection(1).Format.Fill.ForeColor.RGB = vbRed
```

The object hierarchy is as follows:

The active sheet contains a ChartObjects collection. One object in that collection is the ChartObject named Chart 1. The Chart property of the ChartObject object returns a Chart object. The Chart object has a SeriesCollection collection, and the first Series object in the collection has an index number of 1. The Format property of the Series object returns a ChartFormat object. The Fill property of the ChartFormat object returns a FillFormat object. The ForeColor property of the FillFormat object returns a ColorFormat object. The RGB property of the ColorFormat object is set to red.

Following is another way of writing the preceding statement, using object variables to clarify and identify the object hierarchy:

```
Sub ChangeSeries1Color
    Dim MyChartObject As ChartObject
    Dim MyChart As Chart
    Dim MySeries As Series
    Dim MyChartFormat As ChartFormat
    Dim MyFillFormat As FillFormat
    Dim MyColorFormat As ColorFormat

'   Create the objects
    Set MyChartObject = ActiveSheet.ChartObjects("Chart 1")
    Set MyChart = MyChartObject.Chart
    Set MySeries = MyChart.SeriesCollection(1)
    Set MyChartFormat = MySeries.Format
    Set MyFillFormat = MyChartFormat.Fill
    Set MyColorFormat = MyFillFormat.ForeColor

'   Change the color
```

```
        MyColorFormat.RGB = vbRed
End Sub
```

The RGB property accepts a decimal color value, which I specified using a built-in VBA constant. Alternatively, the color red can be expressed using this RGB function:

```
RGB(255, 0, 0)
```

If you prefer to set the color using a document theme color, two other color-related properties of the ColorFormat object are relevant:

- ObjectThemeColor: A number between 0 and 16 that represents the theme color. VBA provides constants for these values. For example, msoThemeColorAccent3 contains the value 7.

- TintAndShade: A number between –1 and +1 that represents the tint or shade of the theme color.

 ON THE CD

The examples in this section are available on the companion CD-ROM. The filename is chart colors.xlsm.

You can also specify color gradients. Here's an example that applies a preset gradient to the second data series on a chart. Notice that the gradient is set using the FillFormat object:

```
Sub AddPresetGradient()
    Dim MyChart As Chart
    Set MyChart = ActiveSheet.ChartObjects("Chart 1").Chart
    With MyChart.SeriesCollection(1).Format.Fill
        .PresetGradient _
            Style:=msoGradientHorizontal, _
            Variant:=1, _
            PresetGradientType:=msoGradientFire
    End With
End Sub
```

Working with other chart elements is similar. The procedure that follows changes the colors of the chart's chart area and plot area, using colors from the current document theme:

```
Sub RecolorChartAndPlotArea()
    Dim MyChart As Chart
    Set MyChart = ActiveSheet.ChartObjects("Chart 1").Chart
    With MyChart
        .ChartArea.Format.Fill.ForeColor.ObjectThemeColor = _
            msoThemeColorAccent6
```

```
        .ChartArea.Format.Fill.ForeColor.TintAndShade = 0.9
        .PlotArea.Format.Fill.ForeColor.ObjectThemeColor = _
            msoThemeColorAccent6
        .PlotArea.Format.Fill.ForeColor.TintAndShade = 0.5
    End With
End Sub
```

The final example in this section applies a random color to each chart element. Using this macro virtually guarantees an ugly chart. However, this code demonstrates how to change the color for other chart elements. The UseRandomColors procedure uses a simple function, RandomColor, to determine the color used.

```
Sub UseRandomColors()
    Dim MyChart As Chart
    Set MyChart = ActiveSheet.ChartObjects("Chart 1").Chart
    With MyChart
        .ChartArea.Format.Fill.ForeColor.RGB = RandomColor
        .PlotArea.Format.Fill.ForeColor.RGB = RandomColor
        .SeriesCollection(1).Format.Fill.ForeColor.RGB = RandomColor
        .SeriesCollection(2).Format.Fill.ForeColor.RGB = RandomColor
        .Legend.Font.Color = RandomColor
        .ChartTitle.Font.Color = RandomColor
        .Axes(xlValue).MajorGridlines.Border.Color = RandomColor
        .Axes(xlValue).TickLabels.Font.Color = RandomColor
        .Axes(xlValue).Border.Color = RandomColor
        .Axes(xlCategory).TickLabels.Font.Color = RandomColor
        .Axes(xlCategory).Border.Color = RandomColor
    End With
End Sub


Function RandomColor()
    RandomColor = Application.RandBetween(0, RGB(255, 255, 255))
End Function
```

The companion CD-ROM contains another example that applies random theme colors to the chart elements. If you run this procedure, you'll see that some chart objects cannot be colored with a theme color. Specifically, I was not able to find a way to change the color of the legend text or the axis labels. This appears to be a bug in the initial release of Excel 2007.

Part IV

Appendixes

Appendix

What's on the CD-ROM?

This appendix provides you with information on the contents of the CD that accompanies this book. For the latest and greatest information, please refer to the ReadMe file located at the root directory of the CD. Here is what you will find:

- System Requirements
- Using the CD with Windows
- What's on the CD
- Troubleshooting

System Requirements

Make sure that your computer meets the requirements listed in this section. Your PC must have the following:

- Excel 2007 for Windows
- A CD-ROM drive

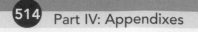

Using the CD

To install the items from the CD to your hard drive, follow these steps:

1. Insert the CD into your computer's CD-ROM drive. The license agreement appears.

   The interface won't launch if you have autorun disabled. In that case, choose Start ⇨ Run. (For Windows Vista, choose Start ⇨ All Programs ⇨ Accessories ⇨ Run.) In the dialog box that appears, type **D:\Start.exe**. (Replace D with the proper letter if your CD drive uses a different letter. If you don't know the letter, see how your CD drive is listed under My Computer.) Click the OK button.

2. Read through the license agreement, and then click the Accept button if you want to use the CD.

   The CD interface appears. The interface allows you to install the programs and run the demos with just a click of a button (or two).

What's on the CD

The following sections provide a summary of the software and other materials you'll find on the CD.

Sample Files for *Excel 2007 Charts*

The files discussed in the book are organized by chapter. The files are all Excel 2007 files that have the following extensions:

- XLSX: An Excel workbook file
- XLSM: An Excel workbook file that contains VBA macros
- XLAM: An Excel add-in file that contains VBA macros

When you open an XLSM file, Excel may display a Security Warning and tell you that macros have been disabled. To enable macros, click the Options button in the Security Warning panel and then select the Enable This Content option.

Because the files on this CD are from a trusted source, you may want to copy the files to your hard drive and then designate the folder as a trusted location. To do so, follow these steps:

1. Open an Explorer window, and select the CD-ROM drive that contains the companion CD-ROM.

2. Right-click the folder that corresponds to the root folder for the samples files, and select Copy from the shortcut menu.

3. Activate the folder on your hard drive where you'd like to copy the files. Right-click the directory, and choose Paste from the shortcut menu.

The CD-ROM files will be copied to a subfolder in the folder you specified in Step 3. To designate this new folder as a trusted location, follow these steps:

1. Start Excel and choose Office ➪ Excel Options to display the Excel Options dialog box.

2. In the Excel Options dialog box, click the Trust Center tab.

3. Click the Trust Center Settings button.

4. In the Trust Center dialog box, click the Trusted Locations tab.

5. Click the Add New Location button to display the Microsoft Office Trusted Location dialog box.

6. In the Microsoft Office Trusted Location dialog box, click the Browse button, and locate the folder that contains the files copied from the CD-ROM.

7. Make sure that you select the Subfolders of This Location Are Also Trusted option.

After performing these steps, when you open XLSM files from this location, the macros are enabled and you don't see the Security Warning.

Following is a list of the sample files, along with a brief description.

NOTE

Some chapters don't use any sample files.

Chapter 01

- `introductory examples.xlsx`: A workbook that contains the examples pictured in Chapter 1

Chapter 02

- `3-d charts.xlsx`: A workbook that contains examples of 3-D charts

- `area charts.xlsx`: A workbook that contains examples of area charts

- `bar charts.xlsx`: A workbook that contains examples of bar charts

- `bubble charts.xlsx`: A workbook that contains examples of bubble charts

- `column charts.xlsx`: A workbook that contains examples of column charts

- `combination charts.xlsx`: A workbook that contains examples of combination charts

- `doughnut charts.xlsx`: A workbook that contains examples of doughnut charts
- `line charts.xlsx`: A workbook that contains examples of line charts
- `pie charts.xlsx`: A workbook that contains examples of pie charts
- `radar charts.xlsx`: A workbook that contains examples of radar charts
- `scatter charts.xlsx`: A workbook that contains examples of scatter charts
- `six chart types.xlsx`: A workbook that shows the same data plotted as six different chart types
- `stock charts.xlsx`: A workbook that contains examples of stock charts
- `surface charts.xlsx`: A workbook that contains examples of surface charts

Chapter 04

- `3-d charts.xlsx`: A workbook that contains examples of formatting 3-D charts
- `axes.xlsx`: A workbook that contains examples of axis formatting
- `data labels.xlsx`: A workbook that contains examples of data labels
- `data table.xlsx`: A workbook that contains a data table example
- `series.xlsx`: A workbook that contains examples of chart series formatting
- `titles.xlsx`: A workbook that contains examples of chart title formatting

Chapter 05

- `error bars.xlsx`: A workbook that contains examples of chart error bars
- `linear trendlines.xlsx`: A workbook that contains examples of linear trendlines
- `moving average.xlsx`: A workbook that contains moving average examples
- `nonlinear trendlines.xlsx`: A workbook that contains examples of nonlinear trendlines
- `other series enhancements.xlsx`: A workbook that contains examples of other chart enhancements (series lines, high-low lines, up/down bars, and varied colors)

Chapter 06

- `annotating charts.xlsx`: A workbook that demonstrates the use of shapes to annotate a chart

- `chart backgrounds.xlsx`: A workbook that demonstrates the use of clip art in a chart background

- `image in plot or chart area.xlsx`: A workbook that demonstrates the use of an image in a chart's plot area or chart area

- `images in a chart series.xlsx`: A workbook that demonstrates the use of images in a chart series

Chapter 07

- `chart with scrollbar.xlsx`: A workbook that demonstrates how to control the data shown in a chart by using a scroll bar

- `climate data chart.xlsx`: A workbook that contains an interactive chart that displays climate information for two selected cities

- `daily.xlsx`: A workbook that demonstrates a self-expanding chart

- `first and last point in series.xlsx`: A workbook that demonstrates how to specify the first and last data points in a chart series

- `first point and number of points.xlsx`: A workbook that demonstrates how to specify the first data point and the number of data points to be displayed in a chart series

- `plot every nth value.xlsx`: A workbook that demonstrates how to plot every nth value in a series

- `plot last n data points.xlsx`: A workbook that demonstrates how to display only the last n data points in a series

- `select series with checkboxes.xlsx`: A workbook that demonstrates how to use check boxes to control which series are displayed in a chart

Chapter 08

- `broken axis.xlsx`: A workbook that demonstrates how to simulate a broken vertical axis in a chart

- `comparative histogram.xlsx`: A workbook that demonstrates how to create a comparative histogram

- `conditional column colors.xlsx`: A workbook that demonstrates how to create a column chart that displays different colors, depending on the value

- `dummy axis examples.xlsx`: A workbook that contains examples of charts that use a dummy axis

- `gantt chart.xlsx`: A workbook that demonstrates how to create a simple Gantt chart

- `horizontal reference line.xlsx`: A workbook that demonstrates how to insert a horizontal reference line into a chart

- `identify max and min data points.xlsx`: A workbook that demonstrates a way to display the maximum and minimum data point values in a chart

- `multiple charts on chart sheet.xlsx`: A workbook that demonstrates how to put multiple charts on a single chart sheet

- `overlay charts.xlsx`: A workbook that demonstrates various ways to combine charts

- `scatter chart with colored quadrants.xlsx`: A workbook that demonstrates how to apply a different color to each quadrant in a scatter chart

- `scatter charts timeline.xlsx`: A workbook that demonstrates how to create a text-based timeline using a scatter chart

- `shade between lines.xlsx`: A workbook that demonstrates how to apply shading between two lines in a chart

- `single data point charts.xlsx`: A workbook that contains several charts that display a single data point

- `stacked and grouped.xlsx`: A workbook that demonstrates various ways to combine charts

- `stacked column chart variations.xlsx`: A workbook that contains several examples of stacked column charts

- `step chart.xlsx`: A workbook that demonstrates how to create a step chart

- `vary column width.xlsx`: A workbook that demonstrates how to create a column chart with varying column widths

- `vertical and horizontal bands.xlsx`: A workbook that demonstrates how to create vertical and horizontal bands in a chart

- `vertical line in column chart.xlsx`: A workbook that demonstrates how to insert a vertical line in a column chart

Chapter 09

- `color scale examples.xlsx`: A workbook that demonstrates conditional formatting color scales

- `data bars examples.xlsx`: A workbook that demonstrates conditional formatting data bars

- `icon set examples.xlsx`: A workbook that demonstrates conditional formatting icon sets

- `sparkline chart examples.xlsm`: A workbook that contains examples of small sparkline charts, plus a macro to position and size sparkline charts

- `sparkline generator.xlam`: An Excel 2007 add-in that creates a series of sparkline charts

- `sparkline text charts.xlsx`: A workbook that demonstrates how to create sparkline charts using text characters

- `text character charts.xlsx`: A workbook that demonstrates how to create simple charts directly in a range

Chapter 10

- `3d scatterplot.xlsm`: A workbook that simulates a 3-D scatter plot, with macros to rotate the chart

- `area under a curve.xlsx`: A workbook that demonstrates how to calculate the area under a curve

- `box plot.xlsx`: A workbook that demonstrates how to create a box plot

- `connecting data points.xlsx`: A workbook that demonstrates how to connect scatter chart data points to the axes

- `frequency distributions.xlsx`: A workbook that demonstrates several ways to create a frequency distribution

- `function plot 2D.xlsx`: A workbook that makes it easy to plot a function with one variable

- `function plot 3D.xlsm`: A workbook that makes it easy to plot a function with two variables

- `function plots.xlsx`: A workbook that demonstrates how to plot a function

- `normal distribution.xlsx`: A workbook that demonstrates how to plot a normal curve

- `scatter chart circles.xlsx`: A workbook that demonstrates how to create a circle on a scatter chart

- `z-score plot.xlsx`: A workbook that demonstrates how to plot z-scores with standard deviation bands

Chapter 11

- `bank accounts.xlsx`: A workbook that contains data suitable for a pivot table

- `frequency distribution chart.xlsx`: A workbook that demonstrates how to create a pivot chart that displays a frequency distribution

- `pivot chart from multiple sheets.xlsx`: A workbook that demonstrates how to create a pivot chart from data in multiple worksheets

- `reverse pivot.xlsm`: A workbook that contains a macro that converts a summary table into a three-column table suitable for a pivot table

- `sales by region.xlsx`: A workbook that contains data suitable for a pivot table

- `survey results.xlsx`: A workbook that contains survey data suitable for a pivot chart

Chapter 12

- `chart complexity.xlsx`: A workbook that demonstrates how to reduce chart complexity

- `chart type problems.xlsx`: A workbook that contains examples of problems resulting from using the wrong chart type

- `misleading charts.xlsx`: A workbook that contains various examples of misleading charts

- `text problems.xlsx`: A workbook that demonstrates text-related problems on charts

Chapter 13

- `analog clock chart.xlsm`: A workbook that displays a clock in a chart

- `animated charts.xlsm`: A workbook that contains examples of animated charts

- `bouncing shapes.xlsm`: A workbook that contains macros that animate shapes

- `bubble chart mouse.xlsx`: A workbook that contains a bubble chart that resembles a cartoon mouse

- `clip art with charts.xlsx`: A workbook that contains examples of using clip art in a chart

- `dice roller.xlsm`: A workbook that simulates tossing two dice and plots the results in a chart

- `doughnut chart spinner.xlsm`: A workbook that uses a macro to convert a doughnut chart into a spinning wheel

- `horse race.xlsm`: A chart that simulates a horse race

- `hypocycloid chart.xlsx`: A workbook that plots a hypocycloid curve

- `hypocycloid chart - animated.xlsm`: A workbook that plots a hypocycloid curve, with a macro to animate the chart

- `mountain ranges.xlsx`: A workbook that simulates mountain ranges using an area chart

- `plot sin and cosine.xlsx`: A workbook that generates a design by plotting SIN and COSINE functions
- `radar chart designs.xlsx`: A workbook that creates designs using a radar chart
- `rotating shape.xlsm`: A workbook that contains macros that animate shapes
- `scatter chart drawings.xlsx`: A workbook that contains examples of drawings created with a scatter chart
- `smile chart.xlsx`: A workbook that contains a chart that displays a smile, based on the value in a cell

Chapter 14

- `axis settings.xlsm`: A workbook that contains a macro that modifies a chart's axis scale values
- `size and align charts.xlsm`: A workbook that contains a macro that sizes and aligns charts in a worksheet

Chapter 15

- `axis scaling - calculate event .xlsm`: A workbook that contains an event procedure that changes axis scaling when the worksheet is calculated
- `axis settings - event macro.xlsm`: A workbook that contains an event procedure that changes axis scaling when a new value is entered into a cell
- `create a chart.xlsm`: A workbook that contains example macros that create a chart
- `data labels.xlsm`: A workbook that contains a macro that adds data labels to a chart series
- `format a chart.xlsm`: A workbook that contains example macros to apply formatting to a chart
- `format all charts.xlsm`: A workbook that contains a macro that applies formatting to all charts in a worksheet
- `get series ranges.xlsm`: A workbook that contains VBA functions that retrieve ranges used by a chart series
- `hide charts - event macro.xlsm`: A workbook that contains an event macro that hides all charts except the chart selected from a drop-down list
- `plot data in active row - event macro.xlsm`: A workbook that contains an event macro that displays a chart series based on the location of the active cell
- `save as gif.xlsm`: A workbook that contains a macro that saves a chart as a GIF file

- `scrolling chart.xlsm`: A workbook that contains a macro to scroll the series in a chart

- `series based on active cell - event macro.xlsm`: A workbook that contains an event macro that displays data on a chart based on the location of the active cell

- `word cloud.xlsm`: A workbook that contains a macro that creates a word cloud in a shape

Chapter 16

- `chart colors.xlsm`: A workbook that contains macros which change colors in charts

- `chart to grayscale picture.xlsm`: A workbook that contains a macro that converts a chart to a grayscale image

- `color conversion functions.xlsm`: A workbook that contains color conversion functions

- `document theme demo.xlsx`: A workbook that demonstrates the effect of applying different document themes

- `generate theme colors.xlsm`: A workbook that contains a macro that generates theme colors in a range of cells

- `rgb color demo.xlsm`: An interactive workbook that demonstrates the RGB color system

- `shape object colors.xlsm`: A workbook that contains macros which apply formatting to shapes

- `tintandshade demo.xlsm`: A workbook that demonstrates the `TintAndShade` property of a theme color

- `weirddog.jpg`: A graphics file used by the `shape object colors.xlsm` example

eBook version of *Excel 2007 Charts*

The complete text of this book is on the CD in Adobe's Portable Document Format (PDF). You can read and search through the file with the Adobe Acrobat Reader (also included on the CD).

Applications

The following applications are on the CD:

- Power Utility Pak v7 (30-Day Trial Version)

Shareware programs are fully functional, trial versions of copyrighted programs. If you like particular programs, register with their authors for a nominal fee and receive licenses, enhanced versions, and technical support.

Freeware programs are copyrighted games, applications, and utilities that are free for personal use. Unlike shareware, these programs do not require a fee or provide technical support.

GNU software is governed by its own license, which is included inside the folder of the GNU product. See the GNU license for more details.

Trial, demo, or evaluation versions are usually limited either by time or functionality (such as being unable to save projects). Some trial versions are very sensitive to system date changes. If you alter your computer's date, the programs will "time out" and will no longer be functional.

Troubleshooting

If you have difficulty installing or using any of the materials on the companion CD, try the following solutions:

- **Turn off any antivirus software that you may have running.** Installers sometimes mimic virus activity and can make your computer incorrectly believe that it is being infected by a virus. (Be sure to turn the antivirus software back on later.)

- **Close all running programs.** The more programs you're running, the less memory is available to other programs. Installers also typically update files and programs; if you keep other programs running, installation may not work properly.

- **Reference the ReadMe file.** Please refer to the ReadMe file located at the root directory of the CD-ROM for the latest product information at the time of publication.

Customer Care

If you have trouble with the CD-ROM, please call Wiley Product Technical Support at (800) 762-2974. Outside the United States, call (317) 572-3994. You can also contact Wiley Product Technical Support at `http://support.wiley.com`. John Wiley & Sons can provide technical support only for installation and other general quality control items. For technical support on the applications themselves, consult the program's vendor or author.

To place additional orders or to request information about other Wiley products, please call (877) 762-2974.

Part IV

Appendix  B

Other Charting Resources

If I've done my job, the information provided in this book can be very useful to you. The book, however, cannot cover every conceivable topic related to Excel charts. Therefore, I've compiled a list of additional resources that you may find helpful. I classify these resources into five categories:

- Excel's Help system
- Microsoft technical support
- Internet newsgroups
- Internet Web sites
- Excel charting add-ins

 NOTE
As you know, the Internet is a dynamic entity that changes rapidly. Web sites are often reorganized, so a particular URL listed in this appendix may not be available when you try to access it.

Excel's Help System

Many users forget about an excellent source of information: the Excel Help system. This Help information is available by clicking the question mark icon in the upper-right corner of Excel's window or just by pressing F1. Either of these methods displays Excel Help in a new window. Then, type your search query and click the Search button.

The Help system certainly isn't perfect — you'll find that it often provides only superficial help, ignores some topics altogether, and also contains lots of errors. But, if you're stuck, it's worth a try.

Microsoft Technical Support

Technical support is the common term for assistance provided by a software vendor. In this case, I'm talking about assistance that comes directly from Microsoft. Microsoft's technical support is available in several different forms.

Support Options

Microsoft's support options are constantly changing. To find out what options are available (both free and fee-based), go to the following Web site:

```
http://support.microsoft.com
```

Microsoft Knowledge Base

Perhaps your best bet for solving a problem may be the Microsoft Knowledge Base, which is the primary Microsoft product information source. It's an extensive, searchable database that consists of tens of thousands of detailed articles containing technical information, bug lists, fix lists, and more.

You have free and unlimited access to the Knowledge Base via the Internet. To access the Knowledge Base, go to the following URL, enter some search terms, and click the Search button:

```
http://support.microsoft.com/search
```

Microsoft Excel Home Page

The official home page of Excel is as follows:

```
www.microsoft.com/office/excel
```

This site contains a variety of material, such as tips, templates, answers to questions, training materials, and links to companion products.

Microsoft Office Home Page

For information about Office 2007 (including Excel), try this site:

```
http://office.microsoft.com
```

You'll find product updates, add-ins, examples, and lots of other useful information.

Internet Newsgroups

Usenet is an Internet service that provides access to several thousand special-interest groups and enables you to communicate with people who share common interests. A newsgroup works like a public bulletin board. You can post a message or questions, and (usually) others reply to your message.

Thousands of newsgroups cover virtually every topic you can think of (and many that you haven't thought of). Typically, questions posed on a newsgroup are answered within 24 hours — assuming, of course, that you ask the questions in a manner that makes others want to reply.

The newsgroup that's most appropriate for chart-related questions is `microsoft.public.excel.charting`.

Accessing Newsgroups by Using a Newsreader

You can use newsreader software to access the Usenet newsgroups. Many such programs are available, but you probably already have one installed: Microsoft Outlook Express, which is installed with Internet Explorer.

Microsoft maintains an extensive list of newsgroups, including quite a few devoted to Excel. If your Internet service provider doesn't carry the Microsoft newsgroups, you can access them directly from Microsoft's news server. (In fact, that's the preferred method.) You need to configure your newsreader software (not your Web browser) to access Microsoft's news server at this address:

```
msnews.microsoft.com
```

Accessing Newsgroups by Using a Web Browser

As an alternative to using newsreader software, you can read and post to the Microsoft newsgroups directly from your Web browser. This option is often significantly slower than using standard newsgroup software and is best suited for situations in which newsgroup access is prohibited by network policies.

- Access thousands of newsgroups at Google Groups:

    ```
    http://groups.google.com
    ```

- Access the Microsoft newsgroups (including Excel newsgroups) from this URL:

  `www.microsoft.com/communities/newsgroups/default.mspx`

Searching Newsgroups

The fastest way to find a quick answer to a question is to search past newsgroup postings. Often, searching past newsgroup postings is an excellent alternative to posting a question to the newsgroup because you can get the answer immediately. Unless your question is very obscure, there's an excellent chance that your question has already been asked and answered. The best source for searching newsgroup postings is Google Groups:

`http://groups.google.com`

Tips for posting to a newsgroup

If you're new to online newsgroups, here are some pointers:

1. Conduct a search first to make sure that your question has not already been answered.

2. Make the subject line descriptive. Postings with a subject line like "Help me!" and "Another Question" are less likely to be answered than postings with a more specific subject, such as "Sizing a Chart's Plot Area."

3. Specify the Excel version that you use. In many cases, the answer to your question depends on your version of Excel.

4. For best results, ask only one question per message.

5. Make your question as specific as possible.

6. Keep your question brief and to the point, but provide enough information so that someone can answer it adequately.

7. Indicate what you've done to try to answer your own question.

8. Post in the appropriate newsgroup, and don't cross-post to other groups unless the question applies to multiple groups.

9. Don't type in all uppercase or all lowercase; check your grammar and spelling.

10. Don't include a file attachment.

11. Avoid posting in HTML format. Plain text is the preferred format.

12. If you request an e-mail reply in addition to a newsgroup reply, don't use an "anti-spam" e-mail address that requires the responder to modify your address. Why cause extra work for someone doing you a favor?

How does searching work? Suppose that you have a problem creating a trendline in a chart. You can perform a search using the following keywords: Excel, Chart, and Trendline. The Google search engine will probably find dozens of newsgroup postings that deal with these topics.

If the number of results is too large, refine your search by adding search terms. Sifting through the messages may take a while, but you have an excellent chance of finding an answer to your question. In fact, I estimate that at least 90 percent of the questions posted in the Excel newsgroups can be answered by searching Google.

Internet Web Sites

The World Wide Web has dozens of excellent sites devoted to Excel and charting. I list a few of my favorites here.

The Spreadsheet Page

www.j-walk.com/ss

This is my own Web site, which contains files to download, developer tips, instructions for accessing Excel Easter eggs, spreadsheet jokes, an extensive list of links to other Excel sites, and information about my books.

Daily Dose of Excel

http://DailyDoseOfExcel.com

This is a frequently updated Web log created by Dick Kusleika, with about a dozen contributors (including me). It covers a variety of topics, and readers can leave comments.

Jon Peltier's Excel Page

http://peltiertech.com/Excel

Those who frequent the `microsoft.public.excel.charting` newsgroup are familiar with Jon Peltier. Jon has an uncanny ability to solve practically any chart-related problem. His Web site contains many Excel tips and an extensive collection of charting examples.

Excel User

www.exceluser.com

This site, by Charley Kyd, is packed with Excel information — with an emphasis on charting.

Tushar Mehta Consulting

www.tushar-mehta.com

Tushar Mehta is a consultant, with an extensive Web site that contains many examples — including lots of useful chart examples.

Pearson Software Consulting

www.cpearson.com/excel.htm

This site, maintained by Chip Pearson, contains dozens of useful examples of VBA and clever formula techniques.

Stephen Bullen's Excel Page

www.bmsltd.co.uk/excel

Stephen's Web site contains some fascinating examples of Excel code, including a section titled "They Said It Couldn't Be Done."

David McRitchie's Excel Pages

www.mvps.org/dmcritchie/excel/excel.htm

David's site is jam-packed with useful Excel information and is updated frequently.

Mr. Excel

www.MrExcel.com

Mr. Excel, also known as Bill Jelen, maintains an extensive site devoted to Excel. The site also features a message board.

Junk Charts

This is an interesting blog that deals with charting and data visualization. The URL is as follows:

http://junkcharts.typepad.com

Excel Charting Add-Ins and Enhancements

This section describes some commercial add-ins and related software that augment Excel's built-in charting capability. The list is by no means comprehensive.

NOTE

The products are listed in alphabetical order. I have not tried all of these products, and listing them here does not imply an endorsement. You'll need to evaluate the products and make the final decision as to their value. Many of these products are available in a demo or trial version.

The Chart Assistant

The Chart Assistant, from Macro Systems, is an Excel add-in that makes it easy to generate a large number of charts automatically and arrange them to your liking. For more information, visit Macro Systems' Web site:

www.add-ins.com/

Crystal Xcelsius

This product, from Business Objects, creates dashboards from a variety of data sources, including Excel. The URL is as follows:

www.xcelsius.com

Grab-It

Grab-It, from DataTrends Software, is an Excel add-in that enables you to digitize data contained in a picture of a chart. After the data is generated, you can use it for further analysis or create your own chart. For more information, or to download a free demo, visit the DataTrends Web site:

www.datatrendsoftware.com

MicroCharts

From BonaVista Systems, this add-in creates small sparkline charts. The Web site is as follows:

www.bonavistasystems.com

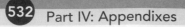

Power Utility Pak

This add-in, written by the author of this book, contains a variety of tools for working with charts. A 30-day trial version is on the companion CD-ROM, and you'll find a coupon in the back of this book to order a licensed version at a discount. For more information, visit this Web site:

```
www.j-walk.com/ss
```

SparkMaker

From Bissantz, this add-in creates sparkline charts in Excel. The URL is as follows:

```
www.bissantz.com/sparkmaker
```

Speedometer Chart Creator

This add-in creates "dial" charts that resemble a speedometer. It's available from Mr. Excel Consulting:

```
www.mrexcel.com/speedometer.html
```

XY Chart Labeler

The XY Chart Labeler add-in was developed by Rob Bovey. It makes adding data text labels to a chart very easy, and the labels can be stored in any range. The add-in is available at no charge from the AppsPro Web site:

```
www.appspro.com
```

Index

Symbols & Numerics

continued

continued

continued

Wiley Publishing, Inc.
End-User License Agreement

READ THIS. You should carefully read these terms and conditions before opening the software packet(s) included with this book "Book". This is a license agreement "Agreement" between you and Wiley Publishing, Inc. "WPI". By opening the accompanying software packet(s), you acknowledge that you have read and accept the following terms and conditions. If you do not agree and do not want to be bound by such terms and conditions, promptly return the Book and the unopened software packet(s) to the place you obtained them for a full refund.

1. **License Grant.** WPI grants to you (either an individual or entity) a nonexclusive license to use one copy of the enclosed software program(s) (collectively, the "Software") solely for your own personal or business purposes on a single computer (whether a standard computer or a workstation component of a multi-user network). The Software is in use on a computer when it is loaded into temporary memory (RAM) or installed into permanent memory (hard disk, CD-ROM, or other storage device). WPI reserves all rights not expressly granted herein.

2. **Ownership.** WPI is the owner of all right, title, and interest, including copyright, in and to the compilation of the Software recorded on the physical packet included with this Book "Software Media". Copyright to the individual programs recorded on the Software Media is owned by the author or other authorized copyright owner of each program. Ownership of the Software and all proprietary rights relating thereto remain with WPI and its licensers.

3. **Restrictions on Use and Transfer.**

   (a) You may only (i) make one copy of the Software for backup or archival purposes, or (ii) transfer the Software to a single hard disk, provided that you keep the original for backup or archival purposes. You may not (i) rent or lease the Software, (ii) copy or reproduce the Software through a LAN or other network system or through any computer subscriber system or bulletin-board system, or (iii) modify, adapt, or create derivative works based on the Software.

   (b) You may not reverse engineer, decompile, or disassemble the Software. You may transfer the Software and user documentation on a permanent basis, provided that the transferee agrees to accept the terms and conditions of this Agreement and you retain no copies. If the Software is an update or has been updated, any transfer must include the most recent update and all prior versions.

4. **Restrictions on Use of Individual Programs.** You must follow the individual requirements and restrictions detailed for each individual program in the "About the CD" appendix of this Book or on the Software Media. These limitations are also contained in the individual license agreements recorded on the Software Media. These limitations may include a requirement that after using the program for a specified period of time, the user must pay a registration fee or discontinue use. By opening the Software packet(s), you agree to abide by the licenses and restrictions for these individual programs that are detailed in the "About the CD" appendix and/or on the Software Media. None of the material on this Software Media or listed in this Book may ever be redistributed, in original or modified form, for commercial purposes.

5. Limited Warranty.

(a) WPI warrants that the Software and Software Media are free from defects in materials and workmanship under normal use for a period of sixty (60) days from the date of purchase of this Book. If WPI receives notification within the warranty period of defects in materials or workmanship, WPI will replace the defective Software Media.

(b) WPI AND THE AUTHOR(S) OF THE BOOK DISCLAIM ALL OTHER WARRANTIES, EXPRESS OR IMPLIED, INCLUDING WITHOUT LIMITATION IMPLIED WARRANTIES OF MERCHANTABILITY AND FITNESS FOR A PARTICULAR PURPOSE, WITH RESPECT TO THE SOFTWARE, THE PROGRAMS, THE SOURCE CODE CONTAINED THEREIN, AND/OR THE TECHNIQUES DESCRIBED IN THIS BOOK. WPI DOES NOT WARRANT THAT THE FUNCTIONS CONTAINED IN THE SOFTWARE WILL MEET YOUR REQUIREMENTS OR THAT THE OPERATION OF THE SOFTWARE WILL BE ERROR FREE.

(c) This limited warranty gives you specific legal rights, and you may have other rights that vary from jurisdiction to jurisdiction.

6. Remedies.

(a) WPI's entire liability and your exclusive remedy for defects in materials and workmanship shall be limited to replacement of the Software Media, which may be returned to WPI with a copy of your receipt at the following address: Software Media Fulfillment Department, Attn.: *Excel® 2007 Charts*, Wiley Publishing, Inc., 10475 Crosspoint Blvd., Indianapolis, IN 46256, or call 1-800-762-2974. Please allow four to six weeks for delivery. This Limited Warranty is void if failure of the Software Media has resulted from accident, abuse, or misapplication. Any replacement Software Media will be warranted for the remainder of the original warranty period or thirty (30) days, whichever is longer.

(b) In no event shall WPI or the author be liable for any damages whatsoever (including without limitation damages for loss of business profits, business interruption, loss of business information, or any other pecuniary loss) arising from the use of or inability to use the Book or the Software, even if WPI has been advised of the possibility of such damages.

(c) Because some jurisdictions do not allow the exclusion or limitation of liability for consequential or incidental damages, the above limitation or exclusion may not apply to you.

7. U.S. Government Restricted Rights.
Use, duplication, or disclosure of the Software for or on behalf of the United States of America, its agencies and/or instrumentalities "U.S. Government" is subject to restrictions as stated in paragraph (c)(1)(ii) of the Rights in Technical Data and Computer Software clause of DFARS 252.227-7013, or subparagraphs (c) (1) and (2) of the Commercial Computer Software - Restricted Rights clause at FAR 52.227-19, and in similar clauses in the NASA FAR supplement, as applicable.

8. General.
This Agreement constitutes the entire understanding of the parties and revokes and supersedes all prior agreements, oral or written, between them and may not be modified or amended except in a writing signed by both parties hereto that specifically refers to this Agreement. This Agreement shall take precedence over any other documents that may be in conflict herewith. If any one or more provisions contained in this Agreement are held by any court or tribunal to be invalid, illegal, or otherwise unenforceable, each and every other provision shall remain in full force and effect.